Sociology

Looking through the Window of the World

SIXTH EDITION

ADRIAN M. RAPP

LYNDA I. DODGEN

LONE STAR COLLEGE—NORTH HARRIS

KENDALL/HUNT PUBLISHING COMPANY

4050 Westmark Drive   Dubuque, Iowa 52002

Copyright © 1994 by Kendall/Hunt Publishing Company
Copyright © 1993, 1996, 1999, 2002, 2006, 2008 by Lynda I. Dodgen and Adrian M. Rapp

ISBN: 978-0-7575-5139-0

Printed in the United States of America
10   9

THIS BOOK IS DEDICATED IN MEMORY OF PAULINE MURPHY

THE TIME IS NOW

IF YOU ARE EVER GOING TO LOVE ME,
LOVE ME NOW, WHILE I CAN KNOW
THE SWEET AND TENDER FEELINGS
WHICH FROM TRUE AFFECTION FLOW.
LOVE ME NOW
WHILE I AM LIVING,
DO NOT WAIT UNTIL I'M GONE
AND THEN HAVE IT CHISELED IN MARBLE,
SWEET WORDS ON ICE COLD STONE.
IF YOU HAVE TENDER THOUGHTS OF ME
PLEASE TELL ME NOW.
IF YOU WAIT UNTIL I AM SLEEPING
NEVER TO AWAKEN,
THERE WILL BE DEATH BETWEEN US
AND I WON'T HEAR YOU THEN.
SO, IF YOU LOVE ME, EVEN A LITTLE BIT,
LET ME KNOW IT WHILE I AM LIVING
SO I CAN TREASURE IT.

UNKNOWN

CONTENTS IN BRIEF

Preface xi

THE FRAMEWORK

Chapter 1   *Peeking at Sociology*   1
Chapter 2   *Looking at Sociological Research* 23
Chapter 3   *Gazing at Culture* 45
Chapter 4   *Seeking the Self* 65
Chapter 5   *Focusing on the Group* 89

THE CURTAINS AND THE VALANCES

Chapter 6   *Checking Out Collective Behavior* 109
Chapter 7   *Analyzing Deviance* 129
Chapter 8   *Deliberating Social Stratification* 147
Chapter 9   *Examining Minorities* 167
Chapter 10 *Peering at Population and Ecology* 187

THE VIEW VIA THE INSTITUTIONS

Chapter 11 *Grilling the Government* 209
Chapter 12 *Examining the Economy* 229
Chapter 13 *Perusing Religion* 249
Chapter 14 *Investigating Education* 269
Chapter 15 *Beholding the Family* 289

Index 311

CONTENTS

Preface xi

▼ THE FRAMEWORK

1   Peeking at Sociology   1

What Is Sociology?   3
What Is the Sociological Perspective?   4
What Triggered the Birth of Sociology?   6
Who Were the Founding Fathers of Sociology?   7
How Did Sociology Mature in the United States?   11
What Are the Three Basic Sociological Theories?   12

CHAPTER READING: "Sociology as an Individual Pastime" by Peter Berger   18

2   Looking at Sociological Research   23

What Is Science?   25
What Is the Scientific Method?   26
What Is Involved in Identifying the Problem?   26
What Is Involved in Surveying the Literature?   27
How Do We Formulate Hypotheses?   27
What Are the Research Designs?   28
What Are the Time Frames Used for Sociological Research?   33
How Do We Collect Data?   33
How Do We Analyze Data?   34
Why Make Conclusions, Formulate Theories and Write Reports?   35
What Are the Difficulties in Conducting Sociological Research?   36
What Are the Ethics in Conducting Sociological Research?   37

CHAPTER READING: "Not So SILI: Sociology Information Literacy Infusion as the Focus of Faculty and Librarian Collaboration" by Lynda Dodgen, Sarah Naper, Olia Palmer and Adrian Rapp   39

3   Gazing at Culture   45

What Is Society?   47
Why Is Society Important?   47
What Are the Characteristics of a Society?   47
What Is Culture?   49
What Are the Characteristics of a Culture?   49
What Are the Components of Culture?   51
What Is the Difference between Ideal and Real Culture?   56
What Are Subcultures and Countercultures?   57
How Does a Culture Change?   58

CHAPTER READING: Excerpt from *Cows, Pigs, Wars, and Witches* by Marvin Harris   62

4   Seeking the Self   65

What Is Socialization?   67
What Are the Functions of Socialization?   67
What Are the Socialization Processes?   68
What Is the Nature versus Nurture Debate?   69
What Impact Does Biological Inheritance Have on Socialization?   70
What Are the Social Factors in the Socialization Process?   70
What Is Self-Concept?   73
What Is the Sociological Perspective of the Self or Me?   73
What Is Anticipatory Socialization?   76
What Is Adult Socialization?   76
What Are the Differences between Adult and Childhood Socialization?   77
What Is Resocialization?   79
What Are the Agencies of Socialization?   79

CHAPTER READING: "Coping with Losses" by Lynda Dodgen and Adrian Rapp   83

5   Focusing on the Group   89

What Is a Group?   91
What Do We Call Different Sized Groups?   92
What Are the Differences between Primary Group and Secondary Group?   92

What Are the Differences between In-Group and Out-Group? 95

What Are the Differences between Gemeinschaft and Gesellschaft? 96

What Is a Formal Organization? 96

What Is a Reference Group? 99

What Is a Social Process? 100

What Is a Status? 102

What Is a Role? 103

What Are Role Strain and Role Conflict? 104

CHAPTER READING: Excerpt from *Social Theory and Social Structure* by Robert Merton 107

▼ THE CURTAINS AND THE VALANCES

6   **Checking Out Collective Behavior** 109

What Is Collective Behavior? 111

What Are the Forms of Collective Behavior? 112

What Is a Social Movement? 117

How Do Social Movements Start and What Are the Stages of a Social Movement? 118

What Are the Types of Social Movements? 119

How Do Sociologists Explain Collective Behavior? 120

What Does the Future Hold? 123

CHAPTER READING: "A Typology of Collectors and Collecting Behavior" by Adrian Rapp and Lynda Dodgen 125

7   **Analyzing Deviance** 129

What Is Deviance? 131

What Is Considered Deviant? 133

What Is Criminal Behavior? 133

How Does the Structural Functional Theory Explain Deviance? 134

How Does the Conflict Theory Explain Deviance? 137

How Does the Symbolic Interactionist Theory Explain Deviance? 138

What Is Social Control? 141

What Is a Social Problem? 142

CHAPTER READING: Excerpt from *The Rich Get Richer and the Poor Get Prison! Ideology, Class and Criminal Justice* by Jeffrey Reiman 144

8   **Deliberating Social Stratification** 147

What Is Stratification? 149

What Are the Two Basic Types of Social Stratification Systems? 149

What Is the Basis of Social Inequality? 150

Why Is the Sociologist Interested in Social Stratification? 154

How Does the Conflict Theory Explain Social Stratification? 154

How Does the Structural Functional Theory Explain Social Stratification? 155

How Is Social Class Measured in the United States? 156

How Many Social Classes Exist in the United States? 158

What Is Social Mobility? 159

What Are the Factors That Affect Mobility Rates? 160

How Can the Individual Experience Upward Social Mobility? 161

CHAPTER READING: "Work-and-Spend Is a Middle-Class Affliction" by Juliet B. Schor from *The Overworked American* 164

9   **Examining Minorities** 167

What Is a Minority Group? 169

What Are the Types of Minority Groups? 169

What Is the Difference between Prejudice and Discrimination? 171

What Are Racism, Sexism and Ageism? 174

How Do Minority Groups Emerge? 176

How Does the Majority Treat the Minority? 177

How Does the Minority React to the Majority? 180

How Do the Theoretical Perspectives Address Minority Groups? 181

CHAPTER READING: "Introduction: Blame It On Feminism" from *Backlash* by Susan Faludi 184

10   **Peering at Population and Ecology** 187

What Is Demography? 189

What Did Thomas Malthus Say about Population Growth? 189

What Do the Neo-Malthusians Believe? 189

What Are Pronatalist and Antinatalist Policies? 190

What Is the Theory of Demographic Transition? 191

What Are the Consequences of Rapid Population Growth and Overpopulation? 194

What Are the Solutions to the Population Problem? 195

What Factors Do Demographers Study? 196

What Is a City and an Urban Environment? 199

What Are the Theories of Urban Growth? 200

What Is the Urban Way of Life? 201

What Are the Suburbs? 201

What Are the Major Urban Ecological Processes? 202

CHAPTER READING: "The Nations of the Western Community" by Ben Wattenberg and Karl Zinsmeister 205

▼ THE VIEW VIA THE INSTITUTIONS

11 **Grilling the Government** 209

What Is Government? 211

What Is Power? 211

What Are Types of Authority? 212

What Are the Forms of Government? 213

What Are the Functions of Government? 216

What Are the Trends in the Government of the United States? 217

What Are the Models of Power Structure in the United States? 219

What Influences Voter Participation in the United States? 221

How Do the Theories Differ in Assessing the Government? 222

CHAPTER READING: "At Home in the Parliament of Whores" by P. J. O'Rourke 225

12 **Examining the Economy** 229

What Is the Economy? 231

What Are the Different Types of Production? 231

What Are the Economic Systems in Preindustrial Societies? 232

What Are the Economic Systems in Industrial Societies? 232

What Is the Economic System in Postindustrial Societies? 234

What Are the Manifest Functions of the Economic Institution? 235

What Are Some of the Latent Functions of the Economic Institution? 236

What Are the Trends in the Economic Institution in the United States? 239

How Do the Different Theoretical Perspectives Explain the Economic Institution? 242

CHAPTER READING: "What to Do about Choice" by Barry Schwartz 244

13 **Perusing Religion** 249

What Is Religion? 251

What Are the Manifest Functions of Religion? 252

What Are the Elements of Religious Behavior? 253

What Is a Secular Religion or Civil Religion? 258

What Are the Trends in Religion in the United States? 259

How Do the Three Major Theories View Religion? 261

CHAPTER READING: "I Lost My Daughters to a 'Cult'" by Kaylan Pickford as told to Claire Safran 265

14 **Investigating Education** 269

What Is Education? 271

What Are the Structures within the Educational System? 271

What Are the Manifest Functions of Education? 273

What Are the Latent Functions of Education? 275

What Changes Can Be Made in the Educational System? 277

What Are the Trends in Education in the United States? 278

How Do the Three Major Theories View the Educational System? 281

CHAPTER READING: Excerpt from *What Your 1st Grader Needs to Know* by E.D. Hirsch, Jr. 286

15 **Beholding the Family** 289

What Is the Family? 291

What Are the Types of Families? 291

What Is Marriage? 292

What Determines Whom We Marry? 293

What Authority Structures Exist within Families? 295

How Is Family Residence Determined? 295

How Are Kinship Patterns Determined? 295

What Are the Functions of the Family? 295
*What Are the Trends of the Family in the
    United States?* 298
How Do the Theories Look at the Family? 303

CHAPTER READING: A Living History: The
    Old Order Amish by Adrian Rapp and
    Lynda Dodgen 306

Index 311

PREFACE

This sixth edition of *Sociology: Looking through the Window of the World* has had years of forethought. For many years we have worked on professional articles and papers together. We have also team taught large sections of principles of sociology. Throughout these years we have talked about sitting down and combining knowledge and ideas for a principles of sociology textbook. We have finally taken that step from thought to action and opened the door to writing this book in order to bring together what we, personally, would like to see in a student-oriented textbook.

This textbook is student-oriented because through the years we have actively asked students what they like and dislike in a textbook and what they read and do not read. Through listening to students, we have written what we hope is a student-friendly book. In a later section of this preface we will discuss what we have included in this textbook. For just a few lines, let us discuss what students do not like or want in textbooks. Students, on the whole, do not read introductory material such as personal experience or cross-cultural references. Nor do students tend to read long-winded statistics or passages discussing current and past research. According to students, they also tend to skip over "boxes" and "inserts" when these aids are frequent or long. For this reason, we have avoided these types of material. Students also prefer shorter chapters. One way that we have been able to have chapters approximately fifteen pages is to eliminate what students do not read anyway. This textbook focuses on what students say that they read.

The theme of our book, *Sociology: Looking through the Window of the World*, is based on the theme that we have used for many years to both advertise sociology courses and to decorate our sociology syllabi. For this reason, we have used a similar theme for the cover of this textbook.

We use the symbolism of the open window because we believe that a course in sociology generates for the student a new way of thinking about and understanding the world around them. We assert that sociology has much to offer the student in interpreting their own behavior and in helping them in whatever roles they may be playing in their lives. Not only is sociology important for the student's daily life but, in the shrinking world that we live in, it is essential that students also have empathy, if not knowledge, of other cultures. Sociology is exciting because it is the field that provides the knowledge and framework for the human condition.

Purpose

The purpose of this book is to bring to the student forty years of student-oriented, interactive teaching experience. Sociology is a field about and for people; therefore, it makes good sense to bring the student actively into the learning process. We want to impart to the student the basic knowledge of sociology in a useful, fun and informative manner.

The joy of this text is that it is not just a textbook but a game plan for a course.

Tools for this textbook include a study guide, student workbook and readings. Each chapter includes exercises to add information, clarify material in the text and stimulate class discussion. These exercises include sociological experiments, critical thinking exercises and application projects. A reading from either a well-known professional or from the popular literature is provided for each chapter to increase student information and promote class discussion. For each chapter a thought question is provided in the form of a journal. With the tools close at hand for reading, delving and interacting with the material, it is our hope that students leave the course with a knowledge and enjoyment of sociology that they can apply to their current and future lives.

In this text, we leave behind all the ruffles and extra topics that have crept into the introductory sociology books through the years and return to the basic topics of sociology. There are fifteen chapters in this text. There are no added institutions of military or health and medicine, just the original basic five of family, government, economic, religion and education. We leave behind the chapters on "everyday living." Since the text covers the basic material of sociology, the instructor is free to move on into discussion and supporting topics of sociological interest. The book builds the house; the instructor embellishes and delves into interesting discussions and topics.

Sociological information is presented in an informal, conversational style at a reading level comfortable to many students. We are not out to impress the student with our knowledge but to have a dialogue in writing with the student and, in turn, we hope the student can mentally talk with us as they read the material.

Plan of the Book

In this textbook we start the learning process by leaving behind the introduction and scenarios. As delightful as these are, and as much fun as they are to write, through interviewing students, we have learned they do not read them anyway. Therefore, we just jump right in and get the student involved with active learning. In addition to the textbook, there is an accompanying Study Guide.

Chapter Organization

PART 1:

Each chapter is divided into seven sections.

    a. A series of questions outlining chapter objectives
    b. A list of important concepts and names
    c. A definition of the concepts
    d. Body of chapter
    e. What topics have been discussed in flow-chart forward
    f. Chapter summary
    g. Reading

By introducing the definitions at the beginning of the chapter, the student is provided with a tasty sample of the fare coming up in the chapter. This allows the student to read with greater comprehension because the student already has the beginning frame on which to build the chapter information.

PART 2: THE BODY OF THE CHAPTER

The active learning approach continues throughout the chapter because each topic head is a question. Starting with a question has several advantages:

    a. A question starts the student to thinking about the answer before he or she has even started to read.
    b. Known information about the topic is triggered by the question.
    c. Reading is focused in order to answer the question.

    d. Last, but not least, human beings hate not having closure; an unanswered question seeks to have an answer.

The answer to topic questions incorporates the instructor's individual experiences as they explain sociology, insight into current social issues and a cross-cultural perspective. It is hoped that when a student leaves a sociology course based on this book, they will not only have a greater understanding of their own culture but other cultures as well.

PART 3: CHAPTER SUMMARY

A chapter summary allows the students to bring all the ideas of the chapter into a cohesive whole and gives the student an overview of what is the important information in the chapter.

PART 4: ARTICLE OR BOOK EXCERPT

Each chapter contains an article from either the mass media or the professional literature. Each article was chosen for its interest and/or relevance. In the study guide there are questions concerning the material. These questions are designed to test information, provide a practical application of chapter material and stimulate critical thinking about the article and the world around the student.

PART 5: QUICK GLANCES, THINKING SOCIOLOGY, AND LEARNING TIPS

Each chapter contains "Quick Glances" as immediate reinforcement for text material. These are "true/false" questions which relate to the text material. "Thinking Sociology" contains critical thinking questions pertaining to text material. It is hoped that through application of material to student experience, retention of concepts will increase. "Thinking Sociology" questions can also be used to generate class discussions. "Learning Tips" are dispersed throughout the chapter to help with studying and text taking.

Textbook Organization

The textbook is divided into three sections. This division is used because instructors often use three tests during the course of the semester.

SECTION 1: THE FRAMEWORK

This section contains five chapters and provides the framework to develop the students' sociological thinking skills. The first chapter discusses the sociological perspective, the early history of sociology and the three basic theoretical perspectives. In Chapter 2 the student learns the importance of sociology as a science and how the sociologist conducts research. The third chapter gives the student insight into the important concepts of culture and society and the components of culture. The fourth chapter discusses how a society socializes its members into culture. Chapter 5 provides the basic information about the group such as what constitutes a group and what are the differences between primary and secondary groups.

SECTION 2: THE CURTAINS AND THE VALANCES

Five very important subjects are discussed in Section 2. Chapter 6 discusses collective behavior. Deviance from a sociological viewpoint, rather than a criminologist's viewpoint, is considered in Chapter 7. Social stratification is an interesting concept which is analyzed in Chapter 8. Chapter 9 takes a look at the very pertinent topic of minorities. This section ends, Chapter 10, by investigating population and ecology.

SECTION 3: THE VIEW VIA THE INSTITUTIONS

Each institution is discussed as a separate chapter. The structure, functions and trends are discussed for each of the basic institutions of government, economy, religion, education and the family. We end the book with the institution of the family, because this area is of wide interest to many college students in today's world.

Website

A website takes the place of the traditional paper bound study guide. This website offers much more than the traditional study guide. Each chapter has:

a. A chapter outline
b. Multiple choice questions
c. Fill-in-the-blank questions
d. Essay questions on textbook
e. Essay questions on reading
f. Critical thinking questions
g. Crossword puzzle
h. Word search
i. Practical application which reviews text information and stimulates critical thinking
j. A "What about Me" assignment for the student to use to apply sociology to their own lives and to stimulate critical thinking
k. Interest/mass media research questions or issues. This is "Internet Intrigue."

Outstanding Features of the Book

READABILITY

The purpose of this book is to impart knowledge not to inflate the instructor's ego so writing style is unpretentious and conversational. Content is not masked by overuse of jargon and large words.

ILLUSTRATIONS

Charts and pictures add information, please the eye, and break up the text material, we hope.

INTRODUCTORY OBJECTIVES AND CONCEPTS

Each chapter begins with objectives and important concepts. We introduce the guideposts of student reading at the beginning of the chapter rather than at the end.

BIBLIOGRAPHY

A bibliography provided at the end of every chapter gives additional sources of information for student and instructor on the material covered in the chapter.

LENGTH

The book is short for an introductory text but the text builds a good framework for sociological information. We would rather have the student learn the basics and enjoy reading the material than give a comprehensive overview of the total field of sociology.

USE OF THE SQ3R METHOD OF PRESENTATION

The question format stimulates student learning and critical thinking skills. The key to the SQ3R method is repetition and repetition. The "S" stands for "survey," "Q" equals "questions." The "Rs" represent "read," "recite," "review."

MATERIAL PRESENTATION

Important concepts are written in **boldface** throughout the textbook.

CROSS-CULTURAL REFERENCES

In our ever shrinking world today, knowledge of other cultures is critical. We have incorporated cross-cultural information as part of explanations and examples rather than making the information "different" or "not important" through boxes and readings.

We have enjoyed writing this textbook, we hope you enjoy reading and using the material.

Peeking at Sociology

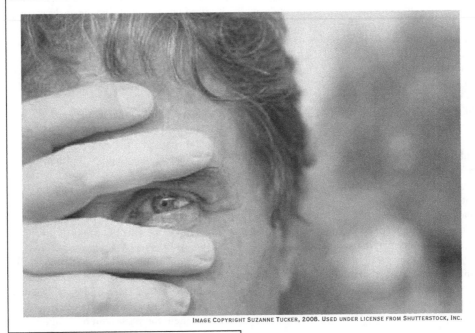

IMAGE COPYRIGHT SUZANNE TUCKER, 2008. USED UNDER LICENSE FROM SHUTTERSTOCK, INC.

CHAPTER OBJECTIVES

1. What is sociology?
2. What is the sociological perspective?
3. What triggered the birth of sociology?
4. Who were the founding fathers of sociology?
5. How did sociology mature in the United States?
6. What are the three basic sociological theories?

altruistic suicide: a suicide which occurs when a person feels a deep sense of moral obligation to society and is willing to give his/her life for the welfare of the group

anomic suicide: a suicide which occurs when a person lacks clear rules of social behavior and commits suicide

anomie: a feeling of not knowing the rules of society

conflict theory: a sociological theory that stresses interest groups, power and change rather than the cohesiveness of society

dysfunction: the result of a social structure that has a negative impact on societal stability

economic determinism: the statement that an economic system influences all other social institutions and interpersonal relationships within a society

egoistic suicide: a suicide which occurs when an individual feels little connection with the larger society and takes his/her own life

fatalistic suicide: a suicide which occurs when a person feels powerless in his/her life and, therefore, takes his/her own life

function: the result of social structure that has a positive effect on the stability

ideal type: a pattern or model used for analytical purposes

latent dysfunction: the unintended by-product of social structure or policy within a society that has a negative impact on social stability

latent function: the unintended by-product of social structure or policy within a society

macro level of analysis: the analysis concentrating on large-scale phenomena

manifest dysfunction: the intended purpose or result of a social structure or policy within a society that has a negative impact on social stability

manifest function: the intended purpose or result of a social structure or policy within a society

mechanical solidarity: a society held together because of sameness of member's roles and a collective conscience

micro level of analysis: the analysis concentrating on small groups or smaller units of analysis

organic solidarity: a society held together because of mutual needs of members and diverse skills

social sciences: a set of sciences dealing with human affairs such as economy, government, psychology, sociology and anthropology

social dynamics: that which gives movement to a social system

social statics: building blocks of society

social structure: the recurring patterns of relationships

sociological imagination: the ability to see ourselves as part of a society existing in a period of history and to be able to identify personal problems as public issues

sociological perspective: the awareness of the influence of structure on individual behavior

sociology: the scientific study of human behavior in social groups, i.e. social structure

structural functional theory: a model that stresses patterns of organization and the purposes of social structure

symbolic interactionism theory: a model that stresses the importance of human interaction and the use of symbols

verstehen: the possession of an interpretative understanding of behavior

▼ KEY PEOPLE

Auguste Comte, Talcott Parsons, Herbert Spencer, Emile Durkheim, Karl Marx, Albine Small, W. I. Thomas, Robert Merton, Max Weber, Georg Simmel, C. Wright Mills, Robert Park, Lester Ward

WHAT IS SOCIOLOGY?

We experience the subject matter of sociology every day as we watch people entering elevators, as we goggle fans screaming at football games, and as we stand in lines at the grocery store to purchase food. Sociology, however, is systematic rather than casual observation (This is further explained in the reading for this chapter). As a discipline, sociology methodically tries to understand the social world by analyzing the social structure in which people conduct their lives. **Social structure** is the recurring patterns of relationships that we deal with every day. These relationships can be between people, two or more groups, or a group and a person. We can now define **sociology** as the scientific study of social structure.

Since sociology is concerned with people, sociology is a social science. Sociology has much in common with other social sciences such as psychology, history, political science, economics and anthropology. By comparing and contrasting these fields with sociology, a better understanding of sociology can be gained.

Let's begin with a comparison of sociology and psychology. The psychologist focuses on the individual rather than the group. If a psychologist analyzes the phenomena of the battered child, he might ask such questions as what impact has the battering had on the child's intellectual and emotional development. The sociologist, on the other hand, might ask, what factors in society have contributed to the rising incidence of battered children.

In our society, we tend to think psychologically rather than sociologically. We look to the individual rather than the group influence to determine why we do what we do. It should be pointed out that the field of psychology is based on sociological thought. For example, the definitions of adjustment and mental illness are culturally determined. This semester we want to help you to develop the ability to think in terms of sociology. We would like for you to view your surroundings using the sociological perspective. The sociological perspective will be discussed in more detail in a later section of this chapter.

History is a social science concerned with the past of humankind. Sociological theory helps to explain history, and sociology is illustrated and tested through the use of historical incidents and events. For example, the current incidence of child abuse can be analyzed by tracing the history of child abuse. What constituted child abuse during the Victorian era? How was child abuse defined during the Industrial Revolution? Both these periods of history contained behavior that at the time was not considered to be child abuse. During the Industrial Revolution children frequently worked long, hot hours in textile factories. In today's society, these working conditions are unacceptable for adults, let alone children. How can sociology account for this change in definition of child abuse?

Political science is interested in the use of power and the distribution of power within the state. Sociology, rather than directly analyzing the workings of the political system, looks at the impact of government on group life and the effect of group action on the government. Our government has passed many laws on child abuse. Failure to report known abuse, for example, is a crime and subject to fine and/or imprisonment. What effect has this law had on reporting and prevention of child abuse?

Economics deals with the production, distribution and consumption of goods and services. Sociology is concerned with the way these economic factors affect the everyday lives of people. The discipline of sociology might ask, for example, about the cost of child abuse to society, the impact of child abuse on future development and earning potential of the abused child or the effect of unemployment on the rates

THINKING SOCIOLOGY

How would a sociologist study dating? How would this differ from the way a psychologist would study dating?

A SOCIOLOGIST IS A SCIENTIST WHO BLAMES CRIME ON EVERYTHING AND EVERYONE, EXCEPT THE PERSON WHO COMMITS IT.

ANONYMOUS

Quick Glance

Sociology is a social science.	T	F
Sociology studies individual actions.	T	F
Our society is psychologically oriented.	T	F
History is a social science but political science is not.	T	F

EVERY MAN IS THE CREATURE OF THE AGE IN WHICH HE LIVES; VERY FEW ARE ABLE TO RAISE THEMSELVES ABOVE THE IDEAS OF THE TIME.

VOLTAIRE
(FRANÇOIS MARIE AROUET, 1694–1778)

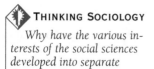

THINKING SOCIOLOGY

Why have the various interests of the social sciences developed into separate disciplines?

🐦 *Quick Glance*

Sociology is an Eastern science.   T F

Sociology focuses on preindustrial societies. T F

Russia and the People's Republic of China do not have programs in sociology.   T F

▲ SOCIOLOGY STUDIES THE IMPACT OF MONEY ON EVERY DAY LIVES OF PEOPLE.

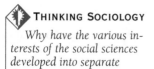

THINKING SOCIOLOGY

Why is it beneficial for Russian and Chinese students to attend colleges and universities in the U.S.A. in order to study sociology?

🐦 *Quick Glance*

The sociological perspective is a way of viewing the world.   T F

The sociological perspective is interested in the individual.   T F

There is a sociological bias in the U.S.A.   T F

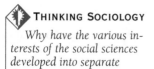

THINKING SOCIOLOGY

Why do Americans believe love comes before marriage?

of child abuse. A current and important issue shared by both economics and sociology is the cost to society for the care and support of crack babies and HIV positive babies.

Anthropology studies some of the same topics as sociology but the focus is on pre-industrial societies. Sociology has traditionally studied technologically advanced societies or industrialized societies. The anthropologist for example, might look at the incident of child abuse among such groups as the Yanomamo Indians who live in Brazil and Venezuela. Among this group of people, with their fierce reputation, wife rather than child abuse is quite common and expected.

Until recently, sociology was primarily a Western science but now the discipline is widely accepted over a much broader base. Both the People's Republic of China and the Soviet Union deemed sociology an irrelevant science. When the Communist Party took over China in 1949, the departments of sociology were closed. The Communists believed that Marxist theory was sufficient to explain the world and further analysis of society was unnecessary. That left sociology out of the realm of acceptable sciences. There was no need for a sociologist to study social problems because with a communistic system, the problems would disappear. Sociology has since been reintroduced into the People's Republic of China. When the Communist Party took control of the Soviet government during the middle 1900s, they cut back funding and enrollment in sociology. This situation has since shifted because of the political and economic changes that occurred during 1991 and 1992. Since this point in time, starting with the Gorbachev administration, the field of sociology has gained importance in Russia. Both Russian and Chinese students are now applying to study sociology in the colleges and universities of the United States.

WHAT IS THE SOCIOLOGICAL PERSPECTIVE?

The **sociological perspective** is a way of viewing the world. In the American society, we are more apt to view the world from a psychological rather than a sociological viewpoint. For example, I eat cereal for breakfast (it must go snap, crackle and pop) because that is what I like: I wear a blouse and slacks because that is what I prefer to wear. We do not step back and say, "I eat cereal, rather than blood, for breakfast because that is what my country eats for breakfast," or "I wear slacks and a blouse rather than a sarong because that is what the women in my country wear." Looking at the influence of the world around us on our thoughts and behavior would be using the sociological perspective.

There are several assumptions that need to be clarified in order to understand the sociological perspective.

First, when a number of individuals are brought together to interact and communicate, the group phenomena becomes different from the individuals who make up the group. This follows the philosophical principle that the whole is greater than the sum of its parts. For example, people ask us if we ever get bored teaching principles of sociology year in and year out but we can honestly say, "no." This is true because each class is very different from every other class. In fact, during the first week of class you can frequently hear instructors talking about their various classes. The conversation goes something like this:

"Oh, I just love my 7:30 a.m. class but I hate that 10:00 a.m. class," or "My class is such a lively one."

Second, by being a member of a group, I have different experiences than if I am by myself. For example, I hate to go shopping for birthday and Christmas presents. Therefore, I do my shopping via catalogs from my kitchen table with phone in one hand and credit card in the other or I shop via the Internet. This is a much different shopping experience than battling my way through the crowds at the mall on a Saturday afternoon.

▲ SOCIOLOGISTS STUDY GROUPS.
IMAGE COPYRIGHT MWPRODUCTIONS, 2008. USED UNDER LICENSE FROM SHUTTERSTOCK, INC.

Another very good example of being part of a group involves one of my cousins. She decided that she wanted to home school her children rather than send them to public school. She wanted her children to avoid coming in contact with language she deemed inappropriate, drugs and values different from their religious background. She taught the children through the high school years. Academically the children were very well prepared for college, but they had not learned the social skills of getting along with a group of strangers nor had they made the cluster of friends that we generally make through our school years.

Third, participation in the group changes my behavior. Confession time. I hate baseball. Every year my husband gets free tickets to an Astros game so off I go with *Reader's Digest* in hand. I read happily along until an Astro player hits a home run. Everyone stands up and cheers—right along with me asking what is going on and standing up and cheering!

The authors of your textbook attended a musical production of Scrooge in December 2005 at a local theater. We commented at the intermission that the production was so-so and all four of us thought the music was boring. However, at the end of the musical, several people stood up for a standing ovation. You can guess what happened! Everyone stood up—including us—to give a standing ovation! What we were part of was sociology in action because the behavior of just a few people altered the behavior of a theater full of people.

Furthermore, an individual can change the behavior of the group. One aspect of the antidrug campaign—"just say no"—hopes that one individual not using drugs will deter drug usage by their friends. At my daughter's high school graduation in May, three people threw their mortar boards in the air and very quickly the air was filled with two hundred fifty-seven sailing missiles symbolic of graduation.

Fourth, we are, in reality, a creation of our group. This sums up what we have said earlier in the chapter. What we like, what we wear, what we consider beautiful is directly due to the group. Individual variation, such as funky clothes and hair styles, are a reflection of the people with whom we interact. My son, for example, wears his hair clubbed in a pony tail rather than short like his father would prefer because that is the way his friends wear their hair. He likes his concert T-shirts because that is what his friends prefer.

As part of this sociological perspective, we need to be aware of the difference between personal problem and public issue. Does the American society view unem-

≋ *Quick Glance*

Our actions are
influenced by the
group.   T   F

The group can change
my behavior.   T   F

I can change the
behavior of the group. T   F

I determine what I
eat and what I wear. T   F

SOCIOLOGICAL PERSPECTIVE

1. INDIVIDUALS BELONG TO GROUPS.
2. GROUPS INFLUENCE OUR BEHAVIOR.
3. GROUPS TAKE ON CHARACTERISTICS INDEPENDENT OF ITS MEMBERS, I.E. THE WHOLE IS GREATER THAN THE SUM OF ITS PART.
4. SOCIOLOGISTS FOCUS ON BEHAVIOR PATTERNS OF GROUPS.

≋ *Quick Glance*

Beauty is relative to
time and place.   T   F

Personal problems
may be public issues. T   F

C. Wright Mills analyzed
the place of society in
history.   T   F

ployment as a personal problem or a public issue? If I personally experience unemployment, I probably would define it as a public issue. If unemployment strikes someone else, I tend to view unemployment as a personal problem. When the economy is in a down swing, it no longer is a personal problem when a person is without work but, in many cases, it is beyond the individual's control, thus unemployment becomes a public issue.

In conclusion, the sociological perspective is a way of analyzing our own and other's behavior by focusing on patterns within society rather than looking at individual decision making.

> TWO MAY TALK TOGETHER UNDER THE SAME ROOF FOR MANY YEARS, YET NEVER REALLY MEET.
> MARY CATHE WOOD

WHAT TRIGGERED THE BIRTH OF SOCIOLOGY?

The birth of sociology began during a period of history called the Age of Enlightenment. During the late eighteenth century, society was undergoing tremendous change. The power of the Catholic Church was challenged by Protestantism. New forms of economic organization arose. The village system was replaced by mass production as the Industrial Revolution started and gained strength. The French and American Revolutions proclaimed the rights of citizens and said that people were capable of ruling themselves without benefit of monarchy.

From these catastrophic changes occurring in society, several important ideas emerged.

1. *The idea of progress became important.* Events were no longer viewed as static; the idea that change could cause improvement in the human condition emerged.

🕮 *Quick Glance*

The idea of progress did not emerge until the twentieth century. T F

The American Revolution stated the principle that citizens had rights. T F

Sociology, as a discipline, emerged during the Age of Enlightenment. T F

The scientific method emerged in the Age of Enlightment as a way to study the world. T F

2. *The idea of skepticism lurked around the corners of people's minds.* One of the important questions was "why?"
3. *The idea of order and repetition entered the scene.* Events were no longer viewed in isolation but rather analyzed in terms of what patterns emerged.
4. *Based on these previous ideas, the idea of the scientific method became very important.* Scientists asked questions then sought valid answers.
5. *A strong belief was fostered that human beings could solve human problems.* Through the study of society, laws could be developed explaining human behavior. Since there are laws of human behavior, a more perfect society could be designed. This belief in analyzing society gave birth to sociology as a discipline.

The founding fathers of sociology emerged out of this Age of Enlightenment.

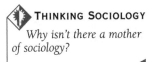

THINKING SOCIOLOGY
Why isn't there a mother of sociology?

WHO WERE THE FOUNDING FATHERS OF SOCIOLOGY?

Henri de Saint-Simon

The first thinker to identify society as a unit of study was a man by the name of Count Henri de Saint-Simon. He was born into a noble French family in 1760 and died in 1825. His primary focus was towards making a more perfect, balanced society and he wanted to replace the existing theological and feudal powers of society with leaders who came from the fields of science, philosophy and industry. He was the prophet of a planned industrial society.

Quick Glance

During the Age of Enlightenment, progress was not important.   T   F

Order and repetition is important for the scientific method.   T   F

Prior to the Age of Enlightenment, we believed humans could solve human problems.   T   F

▲ COMTE

Auguste Comte

The Father of Sociology was a personal secretary to Saint-Simon. This secretary was a Frenchman by the name of Auguste Comte (1798–1857). Comte agreed with Saint-Simon that we needed to study society as a separate discipline, not as part of religion or philosophy. Since Comte wrote that we needed to separate the study of society from that of religion or philosophy, he tried to make this new field a science using observation, measurement and comparison. Comte initially named his science "positive philosophy" but he soon felt that name was not appropriate and renamed the field "sociology." The word sociology comes from the Latin word *socio* meaning companion or companionship and the Greek word *logy* meaning "the study of." Literally, sociology means the study of companions or companionship.

THINKING SOCIOLOGY
What stage of development would Comte say Iraq occupies? Why?

Auguste Comte had some very interesting ideas about this new field called sociology. First, he divided his study of sociology into two parts, social statics and social dynamics. **Social statics** analyzed how and why society held together and endured. It analyzed the building blocks of society. **Social dynamics** gave action to the system; social dynamics dealt with change and the influences causing social change. This division still exists in sociology, but we now call the division social structure and social process.

DISCOVERIES ARE OFTEN MADE BY NOT FOLLOWING INSTRUCTIONS, BY GOING OFF THE MAIN ROAD, BY TRYING THE UNTRIED.
FRANK TYGER

THINKING SOCIOLOGY

What type of suicide would be the suicide bombers in Iraq and Israel? Explain your answer.

Second, he proposed an evolutionary theory for the growth and development of society. He said that preliterate society is governed by religion. At this stage, people worry about the spirits in the stones or the animals. He called this the Theological Stage. The second stage of society is the Metaphysical or Philosophical Stage. At this stage, people start to question the world around them. The third stage is the Scientific Stage. At this stage, cause and effect are sought. He also ranked the sciences and he said that sociology, of course, was the queen of the sciences; he would have liked to see the world run by a board of enlightened sociologists.

▲ **DURKHEIM**   ©BETTMANN/CORBIS

Emile Durkheim

Emile Durkheim (1858–1917) was another of the founding fathers of sociology. Like Comte, Durkheim was born in France. He was the first to receive employment as a full-time professor of sociology. Durkheim made several important contributions to the field of sociology.

First, he said that sociology should study social facts. **Social facts** are identifiable items which relate to the nature of a social relationship. These social facts include such things as laws, customs, institutions and organizations. He felt that these social facts were external to each of us but that they controlled us. He argued that social phenomena could not be reduced to individual behavior or psychology.

Second, Durkheim became very interested in how people integrate with the rest of society and, more particularly, how a lack of integration within a society resulted in anomie. **Anomie** is the feeling of not knowing the rules. He took his interest in anomie into an extensive scientific study on suicide. He collected data from public records and statistical analysis.

From his study of public records, he determined that there were four types of suicide. First is **altruistic suicide**. The person feels a deep sense of moral obligation to his society and is willing to give his life for the group's welfare. When James Bond gets captured, he will flip his poisoned dart ring rather than let the enemy get his secrets. This type of suicide characterized the Japanese suicide pilot during World War II and the terrorists who flew commercial airliners into the New York Twin Towers and the Pentagon on September 11, 2001.

The second type of suicide is egoistic suicide. **Egoistic suicide** is the opposite of altruistic suicide. The individual feels so little connection with the larger society that he or she engages in self-destructive behavior. A bag lady or an elderly man living alone might commit egoistic suicide.

The third type of suicide is anomic suicide. **Anomic suicide** occurs when a society lacks clear rules of social behavior. Anomic suicide is apt to happen during drastic social changes, such as during the Stock Market Crash of 1929. Upper level managers of Enron might have considered economic suicide after the collapse of Enron in February 2002.

The fourth type of suicide is **fatalistic suicide**. When a person feels powerless in his or her life and when he or she feels that his or her life is regulated to an extreme, he or she may commit suicide. A prisoner of war sometimes commits this kind of suicide because he or she feels powerless about their living conditions.

🕮 *Quick Glance*

Emile Durkheim is the Father of Sociology.   T   F

Sociology had its birth in the Middle Ages.   T   F

August Comte named sociology.   T   F

Durkheim analyzed types of suicide.   T   F

Social facts are the same as social structure.   T   F

Anomie means knowing the rules.   T   F

IF YOU DON'T MAKE MISTAKES, YOU'RE NOT WORKING ON HARD ENOUGH PROBLEMS. AND THAT'S A BIG MISTAKE.

FRANK WILCZEK

Third, Durkheim, like Comte, had an evolutionary view of society. He believed that some societies are held together by **mechanical solidarity**. These societies are held together as units because there is a sameness in everybody's roles and a collective conscience. People conform to tradition and most property is communally owned. Religion controls their daily lives and opinion is controlled by community beliefs. This is the kind of solidarity that Durkheim said holds together primitive or preliterate societies such as the Yanamomo Indians in Brazil and Venezuela. These people use slash-and-burn agricultural techniques and hunt for animals such as monkeys. They live in extended kinship groups.

The opposite pole of mechanical solidarity is **organic solidarity**. These societies are made up of a series of complex, interdependent parts. The society holds together because of mutual needs of one another because we each have specialized tasks. There is moral and social diversity, and formally institutionalized religion. The nuclear family of mom, dad and children, rather than the extended family, is very important. There is little community control over individual thought and action. This is the type of solidarity found in countries like Great Britain, the United States and other industrialized nations.

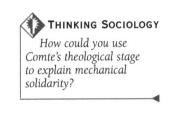

▶ **THINKING SOCIOLOGY**

Are people more dependent upon one another in mechanical solidarity or organic solidarity? Why?

▶ **THINKING SOCIOLOGY**

How could you use Comte's theological stage to explain mechanical solidarity?

Herbert Spencer

▲ SPENCER ©HULTON-DEUTSCH COLLECTION/CORBIS

Herbert Spencer (1820–1903) was Great Britain's claim to fame in the early history of sociology. He wrote a textbook called *Principles of Sociology* which was published in 1877. This was the first true principles text that included a systematic description of sociology as a science.

Spencer said that society was like a living organism. He believed that society, like living organisms, had important parts and each part was needed for survival. Like the living organism, the parts of a society interrelated and served a function for the society.

Spencer thought societies evolved from simple to more complex forms. His ideas of social evolution were parallel to Charles Darwin's theory of biological evolution. He felt that those societies better adapted to their surroundings were more likely to survive and develop than those which were poorly adapted. Thus, those societies that faced extinction were not adapted and should not be saved. This thinking pattern has come to be known as *social Darwinism* or social evolutionism. Spencer was against planning a more perfect society by active intervention because he believed that this would interfere with social evolution and allow unfit elements to survive.

These three men agreed on several important points. First, they stated that society should be studied as a separate phenomena and that a science needed to be created in order to do so. Second, each of these men asserted that society was made up of a series of interrelated parts. These beliefs were the foundation of the sociological school of thought called structural functional theory.

Max Weber

Max Weber (1864–1930) was another of the founding fathers of sociology. Weber was not only influential in sociology but in other fields such as economics, history,

🦅 *Quick Glance*

Comte proposed a typology of suicide.   T   F

The United States has organic solidarity.   T   F

Spencer wrote a Principles of Social Sociology textbook.   T   F

A society which has mechanical solidarity would be in Comte's Theological Stage.   T   F

Fatalistic suicide would most likely happen in a society with organic solidarity.   T   F

▶ **THINKING SOCIOLOGY**

Does current government policy in the U.S.A. support social evolutionism? Why or why not?

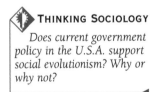

Learning TIP
Before you first read a chapter or parts of a chapter in a textbook, survey the chapter by looking at words or headings in **bold**, *italic* or larger print.

philosophy and political science. He is considered one of the greatest thinkers of the period and made a profound contribution to sociology.

First, Weber studied the larger dimensions of society such as organizations and institutions. He did extensive research into the structure and functioning of the bureaucratic organization. Another contribution was his research and thoughts on the impact of religion on the economic system. His particular interest was the impact of Protestant thought on the development and growth of capitalism; he utilized the words Protestant Ethic and Spirit of Capitalism. His concern with capitalism provided the basis for his analysis of social stratification.

▲ WEBER ©HULTON-DEUTSCH COLLECTION/CORBIS

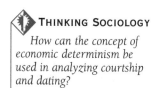
Second, he believed that the sociologist should study all aspects of society in a value-free approach. According to Weber the sociologist should not consider his own values in doing research and in drawing conclusions. He felt that we must be objective observers of society; therefore, he was very important in the development of sociology as an empirical science. His method of study included what he called **verstehen**. Weber used this term to mean that human behavior and structure should be studied by using a sympathetic or interpretative understanding of social behavior.

Another important idea of Max Weber was that of ideal type. An **ideal type** does not involve a judgmental statement but rather is a constructed model that is used to analyze the real world. Weber designed an ideal type for a bureaucracy which included the characteristics of division of labor, hierarchy of command, universal rules and regulations, impersonal relationships, advancement and hiring based on competency, and efficiency and specialization. We rarely find a bureaucracy that fulfills all of the characteristics but the ideal type provides a tool to analyze the bureaucracies that exist in a society. By using ideal types, we can contrast different events in society, we can compare the real world with the ideal type, and we can use the ideal type as a basis for measurement.

Karl Marx

Karl Marx (1818–1883) contributed a great deal to early sociological thought. Marx did not see the parts of society working together in harmony; he focused on the conflict occurring within the society. He believed in the *dialectic*. This means that change occurred through conflict among two or more ideas rather than through evolution. He explained history in terms of this conflict and the struggle for an end to oppression.

He supported **economic determinism**; that is, he contended that the economic system influences all the other social institutions as well as the interpersonal relationships within the institutions. He argued that the economic sector determined the shape of the other major organs of society's body, rather than the

▲ MARX   ©BETTMANN/CORBIS

parts being interrelated into a whole. Structures such as the family and religion supported the division of labor into owners and workers. Families would raise their children such that they accepted authority if they were in the working class and taught them to be managers if they were of the owner class. Religion, according to Marx, was the opiate of the people thus discouraging the workers from asserting control. The core values of the culture served to support the interests of the economically privileged.

His view of history was not that of continual perfection of humankind, but of continual struggle for equality and justice that would end only when there was no longer a distinction between owner and worker. The workers would eventually realize their common interest and a class struggle would result in the overthrow of the owners. After this revolution, the society would go through a period of history when government would control the means of production for the good of everyone (socialism). Eventually the state would die away and we would enter communism. In a communistic society, everyone would receive what they needed and would contribute what they were able.

Marx's analysis led to another school of sociological theory. He was one of the founding fathers of a second theoretical school in sociology called conflict theory.

Georg Simmel

Georg Simmel (1858–1918) thought that Marx, Spencer and Comte were wrong in their approach. According to Simmel, sociologists did not study society, they studied the people that made up society. Rather than trying to study larger units, smaller units should be analyzed. Thus, patterned interactions among people were the subject matter of sociology rather than larger institutions. He believed the study of people should occur in natural settings. Some of the topics he studied included flirting and playing games. He is one of the founders of the third major theory of sociology called symbolic interactionism theory.

HOW DID SOCIOLOGY MATURE IN THE UNITED STATES?

After sociology had its beginning in Europe, the field grew more quickly in the United States. There were several reasons for this.

1. Our universities were not isolated from society like those in Europe.
2. We were a nation of creative thinkers. We had a new country and wanted a new way to look at the world.
3. Our universities were in urban centers which abounded with the subject matter of sociology.
4. We were a country of great ethnic and racial diversity. This was a perfect laboratory for sociology. The early focus of sociology in the United States was one of solving social problems.

The University of Chicago is considered to be the Mother Institution of Sociology. In 1892, the University of Chicago was the first university in the world to offer a doctorate in sociology. By the 1920s, sociology had become an important element in the academic world and was an accepted discipline in colleges and universities all over the United States. We were interested in such social problems as ghettos, immigration, race relations and urbanization.

Several important men emerged from the early history in the United States. Lester Ward was considered the American Father of Sociology. He was born in 1841 and died in 1913. He followed the basic ideas of Auguste Comte. Albine Small established

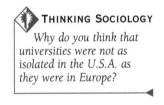

A LITTLE CHARM AND YOU ARE NOT ORDINARY.
YIDDISH PROVERB

▲ WARD

the first department of sociology at the University of Chicago, wrote the first American sociology textbook in 1894, and founded the *American Journal of Sociology*. Robert Parks was also at the University of Chicago. He was a news reporter, social activist, ghost writer for Booker T. Washington, researcher and theorist. He wrote the first major principles of sociology textbook. W. I. Thomas was one of the first Ph.D. recipients at the University of Chicago. Thomas established the method of participant observation that will be discussed next chapter. Thomas is responsible for the Thomas Theorem, "if we define a situation as real, it is real in its consequences."

After the beginnings at the University of Chicago, the center for sociology shifted to Harvard and Columbia. Here was the home of important abstract systems builders such as Talcott Parsons (1902–1979) and Robert Merton (1910–). Other top universities in the field of sociology include University of Wisconsin, University of Michigan, Stanford University, University of Texas and Ohio State University. These are just a few!

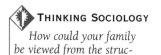
WHAT ARE THE THREE BASIC SOCIOLOGICAL THEORIES?

We have introduced you to the names of the three major sociological theories—structural functional theory, symbolic interactionism theory and conflict theory. These theories are either classified as macro or micro theories. The structural functional theory and conflict theory are considered a **macro level of analysis** because they analyze the larger units of a society; while the symbolic interactionism theory is considered to be at the micro level of analysis. The symbolic interactionism theory is not the only micro level theory in sociology, but it is utilized most often to study society from the micro level. The **micro level of analysis** concentrates on small groups or smaller units of analysis.

Structural Functional Theory

The **structural functional theory** asserts that society is like a living organism. Society is made up of a series of parts, or organs, like an animal. Just as a cat is made up of a series of organs such as the heart and the lungs, society has a series of parts referred to as institutions. The five institutions or parts are family, religion, education, government and economy. In a living organism, when one of the major organs is completely destroyed, the organism dies. To extend the analogy to sociology, if the religious system is destroyed, then the society will cease to exist in the same form. For example, among the Tiwi of Australia the introduction of Christianity and trade goods accounted for a major shift in many of the Tiwi's way of life. Some of the Tiwi gave up their traditional farming and hunting-gathering practices which involved frequent moves to that of settled communities around the mission center.

Like a living organism, parts of society try to maintain an equilibrium position. In the case of a human being, if the lungs become diseased and do not pump enough oxygen; the heart, in turn, is enlarged and beats faster to compensate. The same is true in a society. When one part changes, the other parts must come back into a balance point. We say that the system seeks equilibrium. We have had many changes in the economic system. One of those changes is that women with children are working. This has created new needs in the education system such as child care before and after school, children eating lunch at school rather than at home and the development of preschools and daycare.

Structural functionalists state that the people who make up a society believe in basic values (consensus). The common faith in basic values forms the cement that holds a society together. This belief in basic values, such as belief in universal literacy, means that there is a core of the society that remains constant.

Structural functional theory maintains that change disrupts society. This theory prefers slow, gradual change in society which allows the basic society to maintain an equi-

▲ RELIGIOUS BEHAVIOR IS STUDIED BY SOCIOLOGISTS.

librium position. As one part changes, the other parts can come into balance. Iraq during the early 2000s would be a good example of society quickly changing. The drastic change in government with the fall of Saddam Hussein caused chaos in the economic sector.

After the early writings by Comte and Spencer on structural functional theory, Talcott Parsons gave further insight into the social structure by identifying that each of the parts or institutions have functions. Just as the heart has the function of pumping blood through our body, each of the institutions have functions. The family has the function of replacing members, or of reproduction; education has the function of transmitting skills necessary for an individual to be productive in our society; religion helps us to understand the spiritual realm of our society; government protects us from outside forces; and the economy provides us with a marketplace whereby we can exchange goods and services.

Robert K. Merton, a student of Parsons who died in 2003 at 92, identified that functions can be either manifest or latent. A **manifest function** is obvious, and may even be stated. A manifest function of the automobile is to get us from home, to school, to work, and back home again. However, the automobile may have a latent function. Are we happy with just any automobile to take us from home, to school, to work and back home again or do we want a brand new red Mitsubishi 3000GT to drive? Our automobile provides us with social status. **Latent functions** are not stated and may be less obvious than manifest functions. Sociologists often feel that if latent functions are identified, we may better understand why our society experiences social problems.

The automobile can also be dysfunctional. A **dysfunction** has negative effects for the stability of the system or causes difficulties for the operation of the social system. A car has a habit of breaking down and needing repair, thus it is dysfunctional. The automobile contributes to pollution; people have accidents that may seriously harm them or someone else.

There are several criticisms of this theory.

1. The structural functional theory lacks concern for the individual personality.
2. The theory is unable to explain social changes that occur suddenly in a seemingly peaceful system.
3. The theory can easily be used to legitimize the status quo.

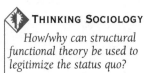 **THINKING SOCIOLOGY**

What is the difference between a manifest and latent function? How do these two concepts apply to the Social Security System?

☞ *Quick Glance*

Manifest functions are unintended.   T F

Structural functional theory supports rapid change.   T F

Structural functionalism explains individual personality.   T F

THINKING SOCIOLOGY

How/why can structural functional theory be used to legitimize the status quo?

☞ *Quick Glance*

Structural functional theory takes individual interests into consideration.   T F

The family can be analyzed with structural functional theory, but not the economy.   T F

Merton disagreed with Parson's analysis of society.   T F

≈ Quick Glance

Conflict theory says society is like a living organism.	T F
Conflict theory is a micro theory.	T F
Conflict theory stresses change.	T F
Conflict theory is a good theory to explain social integration.	T F

> THE MUTUAL AND UNIVERSAL DEPENDENCE OF INDIVIDUALS WHO REMAIN INDIFFERENT TO ONE ANOTHER CONSTITUTES THE SOCIAL NETWORK THAT BINDS THEM TOGETHER.
>
> KARL MARX
> (1818–1883)

▲ COMPETITION IS FOUND IN ALL SOCIAL GROUPS.

The family can be viewed in terms of structural functional theory. With structural functional theory, we can ask what impact the family has on the other institutions. What can the family do for the institution of religion? The family is frequently based on a religious belief system and teaches the children religious principles. The family is an economic unit because families consume many products and services. We learn many of our political views within the family. In many preliterate societies, the family is also the economic and the political organization. Within the family we start many of the socialization processes such as learning our alphabet and learning the important rules of society. We can also view the functions of the family in a larger sense when we say that the family provides new members for the society.

The structural functionalist looks at the impact of the rest of society on the family. The family is affected by economic changes within the society. This is one of the reasons why, in our culture, we have many dual-career families. As underemployment and unemployment go up, more and more women return to the work force to help support families. One of the largest groups experiencing poverty in our country is single-mother families. The low education and low availability of jobs for this group contributes to the high rates of poverty. The government also makes laws that affect the family. Here we could discuss the cost of private education or the laws concerning abortion.

Through the influence of the four institutions on the family, and the family's influence on the other four institutions, we can better understand how and why a society is integrated into a social unit. Structural functional theory looks at the social structure providing basic human needs through harmony, stability and social order. The parts of society are easily identified in this theory because each part, such as the family, serves a function to the whole society and also functions for the good of the society. On the other hand, the conflict theorist looks at the distribution of power within a society and the influence of interest groups on the operation of society. The conflict theorist accuses the structural functionalists of looking at society through rose-colored glasses.

Conflict Theory

The **conflict** theorist contends that society is like a sports arena with groups in competition with one another for scarce resources. The social structure is not based on an interrelation of parts, as the structural functionalist contends, but rather produces patterns of inequality. This inequality is perpetuated by unequal access to power and thus rewards. The conflict theorist argues that change is inevitable and desirable. In fact, the basic focus is on competition, conflict and dissension. Furthermore, for the conflict theorist, there is no agreement on basic values of society. The conflict theorist says that any agreement is because some people have more power than others and can force their beliefs on their less powerful comrades. For example, among the Tiwi of Australia, Tiwi males competed with other men in order to have the most wives because wives were viewed as political capital. With more wives a man could control more food and thus win favor and goodwill of others. Another example of conflict theory in action is the competition between older males to keep control over their young wives versus the younger males who would like to lure the women away from the control of the older married males.

There are several criticisms of the conflict theory.

1. The conflict theory pays too little attention to what holds a society together.
2. The conflict theory takes an overly critical view of society.

The conflict theory is a very good theory for explaining change, particularly sudden and dramatic change. For example, the institution of the family is going through a period of change right now with the increase in single mother families, high divorce rates and dual career families. These shifts have created changes in the economic, political and educational system. Single mothers are often in conflict with the educational system because of the need for extended child care and reasonably priced child care.

The conflict theory supports change and a shifting in power structures. Women, for example, are becoming more common in government, religion and economic organizations. These areas used to be predominantly white male but now women serve important functions in many areas of life. These shifts in power structures are often easily traced and analyzed.

Symbolic Interactionist Theory

Symbolic interactionism is the third major theory we are going to discuss. The basic unit of study for the symbolic interactionist is the social act rather than society as a whole. In this level of analysis, we analyze interaction patterns in terms of a message being received by individuals, individual interpretation of message, and response to message. For example, among the Tiwi an older married male would accuse a younger male of adultery. The older married man could respond to the extra marital affair by calling on surrounding camps dressed in white paint in order to gain support for his side against that of the younger male. This community support could result in a duel. The older male would have ceremonial spears in one hand and a bundle of hunting spears in the other. The older man would then—via gestures such as stamping of feet and chewing of his beard—tell the young man what he thought about his disrespectful behavior. After twenty minutes or so of this angry tirade, the

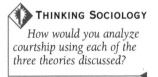

THINKING SOCIOLOGY
How would you analyze courtship using each of the three theories discussed?

THEORY SUMMARY TABLE				
Theory	*Premise*	*Theorists*	*Type*	*Concepts*
Structural functional	Society is like a living organism.	A. Comte H. Spencer E. Durkheim T. Parsons R. Merton	Macro	equilibrium, stability, social integration, manifest function, latent function, functional, dysfunctional
Conflict	Society is like a sports arena.	C. Mills H. St. Simon K. Marx R. Dahrendorf	Macro	class conflict, power, supremacy, competition, interest group
Symbolic interactionism	Society is like a theater.	G. Mead I. Goffman W. Thomas C. Cooley G. Simmel	Micro	role taking, presentation of self, definition of situation, role, script

LET GO OF YOUR ATTACHMENT TO BEING RIGHT, AND SUDDENLY YOUR MIND IS MORE OPEN. YOU'RE ABLE TO BENEFIT FROM THE UNIQUE VIEWPOINTS OF OTHERS WITHOUT BEING CRIPPLED BY YOUR OWN JUDGMENT.

RALPH MARSTON

older man would throw his hunting spears at the younger man. The younger man tried to avoid the spears. Generally no serious injury occurred and the older man was appeased.

The interpretation and response to the message depends upon both verbal and nonverbal symbols. Social life depends upon each of us learning the symbols that we are supposed to learn, interpreting them and acting as society dictates. We learn these meanings from others. For example, a slap on the face could be an insult, a punishment or a playful gesture. Change occurs when we change the meaning of the symbols and our interactions with other people.

According to the symbolic interactionist, we develop a self or personality through the symbolic process of learning to treat ourselves as both a subject and an object. (This is the topic of the reading for chapter 4) Once a person has developed a self and has mastered a language system, he or she can begin to classify behaviors into categories rather than simply view them as discrete and unrelated events. In this way a person can define a situation and operate a societal interaction that vary from, but are also similar to, other situations previously encountered. We shall discuss the development of the self in chapter 4.

The symbolic interactionist faces several problems.

THINKING SOCIOLOGY

Which of the three perspectives do you most prefer? Why?

1. Symbolic interactionist find it difficult to identify the important variables.
2. Symbolic interactionists have difficulty determining what symbols should be studied.

The family can be studied through symbolic interactionism. The symbolic interactionist would look at the scripts that we teach girls and boys for their job as parents. Traditionally, girls are taught to like to wash dishes and take care of the baby; boys are taught to be family providers and to repair the car. When we are very young, we encourage girls to play with dolls but tend to downplay males playing extensively with the same type of toys.

⊛ *Quick Glance*

Interpretation of symbols is based only on verbal communication.   T   F

The identification of variables is easy for the symbolic interactionist.   T   F

Any of the three approaches can be used to analyze education.   T   F

In conclusion, we have given you the basic information about three major theoretical schools of thought in sociology. A social situation or event can be analyzed using any one of these three approaches. Some sociologists are predominantly conflict theorists, others are structural functionalists, and some are symbolic interactionists. This textbook is eclectic in its approach but the structural functional and symbolic interactionism point of view are predominant.

Before we conclude this chapter we would like to take a peak in the side-window of Postmodernism.

Modernity was first addressed by early sociologists with the changes brought about by the Industrial Revolution. The buzz word of Postmodernity emerged in the 1990s. Postmodernity refers to the social patterns found in Post Industrial societies which have experienced the Information Revolution. Several themes are important in Postmodernism:

Learning TIP
Do not sleep in class—it is rude and shows a lack of interest and attention.

1. Postindustrial society experiences changes in all five of the institutions. With the emphasis on ideas, people have more choices to make. For example, in Chapter 15 we discuss several different family types. The "Leave It to Beaver" family is no longer the only correct family.
2. We no longer are focused as much on material goods which were important in Industrial societies. There is increasing emphasis on ideas such as social justice and human rights.
3. Reality and truth are relative. These terms are social constructs.
4. The future is not necessarily going to be a better place to live.

5. The Industrial Revolution and the 20th Century did not live up to its promise. We still have a plethora of social problems such as poverty, lack of medical care and discrimination.

▼ CHAPTER SUMMARY

1. Sociology is the scientific study of human interaction.
2. The sociological perspective focuses on how social structure affects the way we act and feel. The sociological perspective explains how the discipline of sociology views the world.
3. Sociology had its birth in eighteenth century Europe but experienced rapid development in the United States during the twentieth century.
4. There are three major theories in sociology. Structural functionalism views society as a living organism; conflict theory views society like a sports arena; and symbolic interactionism theory views society as individuals interacting with one another.

▼ REFERENCES

Babbie, E. 1988. *The Sociological Spirit*. Belmont, CA: Wadsworth.

Berger, Peter L. 1963. *Invitation to Sociology: A Humanistic Perspective*. New York: Anchor Books.

Bernstein, Richard J. *The New Constellation: The Ethical Political Horizons of Modernity/ Postmodernity*. Cambridge, MA: MIT Press, 1992.

Durkheim, Emile. 1951. *Suicide*. Translated by John A. Spaulding and George Simpson. New York: Free Press (Originally published in 1897).

Fine, G.A. 1990, *Talking Sociology*. Boston: Allyn & Bacon.

Greer, Ann and Scott Greer. 1974. *Understanding Sociology*. Iowa: Wm. C. Brown Company Publishers.

Hall, John R., and Mary Jo Neitz. *Culture: Sociological Perspectives*. Englewood Cliffs, NJ: Prentice Hall, 1993.

Hart, C. W. M., Arnold R. Pilling and Jane C. Goodale. 1988. *The Tiwi of North Australia*. Fort Worth: Holt, Rinehart and Winston, Inc.

Levin, J. 1993. *Sociological Snapshots*. Newbury Park, CA: Pine Forge Press.

Marx, Karl and Fredrich Engels. 1965. "The Communist Manifesto." In Arthur Mendel (Ed.), *Essential Works of Marxism*. New York: Bantam Books. (Originally published in 1848).

Merton, Robert. 1957. *Social Theory and Social Structure*. New York: Free Press.

Mills, C. Wright. 1959. *The Sociological Imagination*. London: Oxford University Press.

Parsons, Talcott. 1951. *The Social System*. New York: Free Press.

Rudel, Thomas K., and Judith Gerson. "Postmodernism, Institutional Change, and Academic Workers: A Sociology of Knowledge." *Social Science Quarterly*. Vol. 80, No. 2 (June 1999): 213–28.

Timasheff, Nicholas S. and George A. Theldorson. 1976. *Sociological Theory*. 4th ed. New York: Random House.

READING

"SOCIOLOGY AS AN INDIVIDUAL PASTIME" BY PETER L. BERGER FROM INVITATION TO SOCIOLOGY: A HUMANISTIC APPROACH*

The sociologist is someone concerned with understanding society in a disciplined way. The nature of this discipline is scientific. This means that what the sociologist finds and says about the social phenomena he studies occurs within a certain rather strictly defined frame of reference. One of the main characteristics of this scientific frame of reference is that operations are bound by certain rules of evidence. As a scientist, the sociologist tries to be objective, to control his personal preferences and prejudices, to perceive clearly rather than to judge normatively. This restraint, of course, does not embrace the totality of the sociologist's existence as a human being, but is limited to his operations as a sociologist. Nor does the sociologist claim that his frame of reference is the only one within which society can be looked at. For that matter, very few scientists in any field would claim today that one should look at the world only scientifically. The botanist looking at a daffodil has no reason to dispute the right of the poet to look at the same object in a very different manner. There are many ways of playing. The point is not that one denies other people's games but that one is clear about the rules of one's own. The game of the sociologist, then, uses scientific rules. As a result, the sociologist must be clear in his own mind as to the meaning of these rules. That is, he must concern himself with methodological questions. Methodology does not constitute his goal. The latter, let us recall once more, is the attempt to understand society. Methodology helps in reaching this goal. In order to understand society, or that segment of it that he is studying at the moment, the sociologist will use a variety of means. Among these are statistical techniques. Statistics can be very useful in answering certain sociological questions. But statistics does not constitute sociology. As a scientist, the sociologist will have to be concerned with the exact significance of the terms he is using. That is, he is interested in understanding for its own sake. He may be aware of or even concerned with the practical applicability and consequences of his findings, but at that point he leaves the sociological frame of reference as such and moves into realms of values, beliefs and ideas that he shares with other men who are not sociologists.

We daresay that this conception of the sociologist would meet with very wide consensus within the discipline today. But we would like to go a little bit further here and ask a somewhat more personal (and therefore, no doubt, more controversial) question. We would like to ask not only what it is that the sociologist is doing but also what it is that drives him to it. Or, to use the phrase Max Weber used in a similar connection, we want to inquire a little into the nature of the sociologist's demon. In doing so, we shall evoke an image that is not so much ideal-typical in the above sense but more confessional in the sense of personal commitment. Again, we are not interested in excommunicating anyone. The game of sociology goes on in a spacious playground. We are just describing a little more closely those we would like to tempt to join our game.

We would say then that the sociologist (that is, the one we would really like to invite to our game) is a person intensively, endlessly, shamelessly interested in the doings of men. His natural habitat is all the human gathering places of the world, wherever men come together. The sociologist may be interested in many other things,

Quick Glance

The nature of sociology is scientific. T F

The sociologist is allowed to use their own experience in analyzing society. T F

If a sociologist uses his knowledge for practical purposes, he is following the sociological frame of reference. T F

*From An Invitation to Sociology by Peter Berger, copyright © 1963 by Peter L. Berger. Used by permission of Doubleday, a Division of Random House, Inc.

but his consuming interest remains in the world of men, their institutions, their history, their passions. And since he is interested in men, nothing that men do can be altogether tedious for him. He will naturally be interested in the events that engage mens ultimate beliefs, their moments of tragedy and grandeur and ecstasy. But he will also be fascinated by the commonplace, the everyday. He will know reverence, but this reverence will not prevent him from wanting to see and to understand. He may sometimes feel revulsion or contempt. But this also will not deter him from wanting to have his questions answered. The sociologist, in his quest for understanding, moves through the world of men without respect for the usual lines of demarcation. Nobility and degradation, power and obscurity, intelligence and folly—these are equally interesting to him, however unequal they may be in his personal values or tastes. Thus his questions may lead him to all possible levels of society, the best and the least known places, the most respected and the most despised. And, if he is a good sociologist, he will find himself in all these places because his own questions have so taken possession of him that he has little choice but to seek for answers.

It would be possible to say the same things in a lower key. We could say that the sociologist, but for the grace of his academic title, is the man who must listen to gossip despite himself, who is tempted to look through keyholes, to read other people's mail, to open closed cabinets. Before some otherwise unoccupied psychologist sets out now to construct an aptitude test for sociologists on the basis of sublimated voyeurism, let us quickly say that we are speaking merely by way of analogy. Perhaps some little boys consumed with curiosity to watch their maiden aunts in the bathroom later become inveterate sociologists. This is quite uninteresting. What interests us is the curiosity that grips any sociologist in front of a closed door behind which there are human voices. If he is a good sociologist, he will want to open that door, to understand these voices. Behind each closed door he will anticipate some new facet of human life not yet perceived and understood.

The sociologist will occupy himself with matters that others regard as too sacred or as too distasteful for dispassionate investigation. He will find rewarding the company of priests or of prostitutes, depending not on his personal preferences but on the questions he happens to be asking at the moment. He will also concern himself with matters that others may find much too boring. He will be interested in the human interaction that goes with warfare or with great intellectual discoveries, but also in the relations between people employed in a restaurant or between a group of little girls playing with their dolls. His main focus of attention is not the ultimate significance of what men do, but the action in itself, as another example of the infinite richness of human conduct. So much for the image of our playmate.

In these journeys through the world of men the sociologist will inevitably encounter other professional Peeping Toms. Sometimes these will resent his presence, feeling that he is poaching on their preserves. In some places the sociologist will meet up with the economist, in others with the political scientist, in yet others with the psychologist or the ethnologist. Yet chances are that the questions that have brought him to these same places are different from the ones that propelled his fellow-trespassers. The sociologist's questions always remain essentially the same: "What are people doing with each other here?" "What are the collective ideas that move men and institutions?" In trying to answer these questions in specific instances, the sociologist will, of course, have to deal with economic or political matters, but he will do so in a way rather different from that of the economist or the political scientist. The scene that he contemplates is the same human scene that these other scientists concern themselves with. But the sociologist's angle of vision is different. When this is understood, it becomes clear that it makes little sense to try to stake out a special enclave within which the sociologist will carry on business in his own right. Like

☞ *Quick Glance*

A sociologist is interested in the human habitat. T F

The sociologist is not interested in the mundane world. T F

The sociologist may study areas of the human condition that are against his morals. T F

☞ *Quick Glance*

The economist and the political scientist share interest with the sociologist. T F

The sociologist asks different questions than other social scientists. T F

The sociologist likes to study topics others might find boring. T F

Wesley, the sociologist will have to confess that his parish is the world. But unlike some latter-day Wesleyans he will gladly share this parish with others. There is, however, one traveler whose path the sociologist turns from the present to the past, his preoccupations are very hard indeed to distinguish from those of the historian. However, we shall leave this relationship to a later part of our considerations. Suffice it to say here that the sociological journey will be much impoverished unless it is punctuated frequently by conversation with that other particular traveler.

Any intellectual activity derives excitement from the moment it becomes a trail of discovery. In some fields of learning this is the discovery of worlds previously unthought of and unthinkable. This is the excitement of the astronomer or of the nuclear physicist on the antipodal boundaries of the realities that man is capable of conceiving. But it can also be the excitement of bacteriology or geology. In such discovery, when undertaken with passion, a widening of awareness, sometimes a veritable transformation of consciousness, occurs. The universe turns out to be much more wonder-full than one had ever dreamed. The excitement of sociology is usually of a different sort. Sometimes, it is true, the sociologist penetrates into worlds that had previously been quite unknown to him—for instance, the world of crime, or the world of some bizarre religious sect, or the world fashioned by the exclusive concerns of some group such as medical specialists or military leaders or advertising executives. However, much of the time the sociologist moves in sectors of experience that are familiar to him and to most people in his society. He investigates communities, institutions and activities that one can read about every day in the newspapers. Yet there is another excitement of discovery beckoning in his investigations. It is not the excitement of coming upon the totally unfamiliar, but rather the excitement of finding the familiar becoming transformed in its meaning. The fascination of sociology lies in the fact that its perspective makes us see in a new light the very world in which we have lived all our lives. This also constitutes a transformation of consciousness. Moreover, this transformation is more relevant existentially than that of many other intellectual disciplines, because it is more difficult to segregate in some special compartment of the mind. The astronomer does not live in the remote galaxies, and the nuclear physicist can, outside his laboratory, eat and laugh and marry and vote without thinking about the insides of the atom. The geologist looks at rocks only at appropriate times, and the linguist speaks English with his wife. The sociologist lives in society, on the job and off it. His own life, inevitably, is part of his subject matter. Men being what they are, sociologists too manage to segregate their professional insights from their everyday affairs. But it is a rather difficult feat to perform in good faith.

The sociologist moves in the common world of men close to what most of them would call read. The categories he employs in his analyses are only refinements of the categories by which other men live—power, class, status, race, ethnicity. As a result, there is a deceptive simplicity and obviousness about some sociological investigations. One reads them, nods at the familiar scene, remarks that one has heard all this before and don't people have better things to do than to waste their time on truisms—until one is suddenly brought up against an insight that radically questions everything one had previously assumed about this familiar scene. This is the point at which one begins to sense the excitement of sociology.

People who like to avoid shocking discoveries, who prefer to believe that society is just what they were taught in Sunday School, who like the safety of the rules and the maxims of what Alfred Schuets has called the world-taken-for-granted, should stay away from sociology. People who feel no temptation before closed doors, who have no curiosity about human beings, who are content to admire scenery without wondering about the people who live in those houses on the other side of that

☥ *Quick Glance*

The sociologist frequently studies what he is part of.   T F

The everyday life of people is interpreted differently when studied by a sociologist.   T F

Sociology is deceptively simple.   T F

Sociology appeals to people who are nonjudgmental.   T F

river, should probably also stay away from sociology. They will find it unpleasant or, at any rate, unrewarding. People who are interested in human beings only if they can change, convert or reform them should also be warned, for they will find sociology much less useful than they hoped. And people whose interest is mainly in their own conceptual constructions will do just as well to turn to the study of little white mice. Sociology will be satisfying, in the long run, only to those who can think of nothing more entrancing than to watch men and to understand things human.

THINKING SOCIOLOGY

According to Berger, should you be studying sociology? Explain and support your answer.

Looking at Sociological Research

CHAPTER OBJECTIVES

1. What is science?
2. What is the scientific method?
3. What is involved in identifying the problem?
4. What is involved in surveying the literature?
5. How do we formulate hypothesis?
6. What are the research designs?
7. How are the time frames used for sociological research?
8. How do we collect data?
9. How do we analyze data?
10. Why make conclusions, formulate theories and write reports?
11. What are the difficulties in conducting sociological research?
12. What are the ethics in conducting sociological research?

content analysis: the objective coding and recording of data based on mass media

cross-sectional study: a study which compares two or more groups at a single point in time

data: the information gathered concerning hypothesis

debriefing: respondents are told about the research methods and goals

dependent variable: the variable receiving the change

ex post facto study: the research design which takes a current situation backwards to an earlier point in time

Hawthorne effect: the individual's awareness of being studied alters their behavior to conform to what he or she feels the researcher is looking for in their behavior

hypothesis: a tentative statement about the relationship between two or more variables

independent variable: a variable a researcher controls

interview: sample survey based on oral collection of data

longitudinal study: a collection of data over an extended period of time

nonobtrusive measures: a type of research design in which the researcher does not actually come into contact with the persons or groups being studied

nonparticipant observation: a type of research design in which the researcher does not take part in the group that he/she is studying through observation

operational definition: defining the variable in measurable terms

physical traces and artifacts: a type of research design which studies human behavior by studying items which have been used in human activities

planned experiment: a research design based on the systematic examination of cause and effect utilizing both a control group and an experimental group

population: a group of people (or objects) that share a common characteristic

questionnaire: sample survey based on written answers

random sample: a sample in which everyone in a population has an equal chance or probability of being included in the sample

research design: a blueprint for testing the hypothesis

sample: a subset of the population

sample survey: a research design which questions respondents about variables of interest either by using a questionnaire or interview

science: a body of organized, verifiable knowledge based on the scientific method

scientific method: the process of collecting information such that the information is objective, precise and fully disclosed for public usage

theory: a way of explaining some phenomenon or the relationship between phenomena

variable: the property or characteristic of something that can take on different values

▼ **KEY PEOPLE**

Shere Hite, Laud Humphreys

WHAT IS SCIENCE?

As stated in Chapter 1, sociology is one of the social sciences. Science is divided into two major categories which are referred to as the physical sciences and the social sciences. Both physical and social sciences use the same scientific method to find their truths or facts. Sociology is a social science because it deals with people and because of its development of a body of organized, verified knowledge based on the scientific method.

Science is a structured process of seeking the truth, but there are other ways to analyze the world around us. *First, we can make conclusions based on intuition.* For example, at the company's annual picnic, I told my husband that his boss and wife were having marital difficulty. He told me that I was totally wrong; if there had been any problems, he, and the rest of the work force, would know. The following Monday the boss let it be known that he and his wife were separated. *A second technique often used to find truth is to make conclusions via tradition*; what has been correct in the past will continue to be right in the present and future. If this were true, we still should be farming with horse-drawn plows instead of the huge machinery that is used today! *Third, an authority can be a source of knowledge.* We have been taught for generations that Columbus discovered America. The Vikings and Asian groups were in the New World centuries before Columbus set foot in the Americas. In fact, he did not even set foot on the mainland. *A fourth way of getting the truth is to use common sense.* One of the adages in our society has been "spare the rod and spoil the child." We have since learned that teaching a child the consequences of his behavior and to think out behavior is better for guiding a child's behavior. These methods, however, may lead to questions to study.

Pseudoscience, under the guise of science, violates the basic assumptions of science. For example, Shere Hite in her book *Women and Love: A Cultural Revolution in Progress* concluded that American women are unhappy in their love and sexual relationships, but this finding was based on a very small sample of women who took the time to respond to a questionnaire sent to various organizations such as feminist clubs and church groups. She sent out 100,000 questionnaires but only 4,500 women responded. In other words, her conclusions about American women's love and sex life was based on a self-selected sample of women.

Science, unlike other sources of information, has some very important characteristics:

1. *Science is based on verifiable, objective evidence confirmed by the human senses.* We are trained to make objective observations. As social scientists, we have to be able to quantify or make factual observations about the information we seek.
2. *Personal feelings and values must not influence our findings.* We must let the facts speak for themselves. Our values can influence the subject we choose to study, but values cannot influence the results of a study. We introduced the word "value-free" in Chapter 1.
3. *Any findings are subject to change as new information comes to light.* Once we have a finding, we must remain flexible and be willing, even anxious, to discover new information and relationships in the social world.
4. *Science is cumulative.* Each research project should add to the explanation of social phenomena. After a research project is completed, the results and conclusions stimulate further hypothesis both for the original researcher and for other researchers in their reading of professional journals.
5. *Scientific information forms the basis for making future predictions.* With sociological research we make predictions for the group rather than for the indi-

THINKING SOCIOLOGY
What type of information did you use in selecting your college major?

Quick Glance

The physical and social sciences do not use the same scientific method.　T　F

Intuition is equivalent to science for finding the truth.　T　F

The past can be used as a basis for science.　T　F

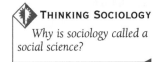

THINKING SOCIOLOGY
Why is sociology called a social science?

Quick Glance

Science is based on verifiable evidence.   T   F

The social researcher should remain value free.   T   F

Replication suggests that another researcher repeats the research.   T   F

Reliable refers to the ability to measure the variable intended.   T   F

vidual. For example, statistical research indicates that one out of two marriages end in divorce. Therefore, we can predict that out of every 100 marriages, there will be approximately 50 divorces. We can also say that when a person gets married he/she stands a 50/50 chance of getting a divorce. Sociology does not, however, say which 50 out of 100 will get a divorce, nor does it make a prediction of any given person getting a divorce. Sociologists can only help the individual be aware of factors which contribute to marital success or failure.

6. *Our information can be validated through replication.* Someone else can repeat what we have discovered through science and either refine, reject or accept what we have concluded. If another researcher repeats our findings, this means that the study is *reliable*.

The scientific method ensures that these characteristics of scientific thinking are carried out. Only with training can we develop the skills needed to use the scientific method.

REACH HIGH, FOR STARS LIE HIDDEN IN YOUR SOUL. DREAM DEEP, FOR EVERY DREAM PRECEDES THE GOAL.

PAMELA VAULL STARR

WHAT IS THE SCIENTIFIC METHOD?

The **scientific method** is a way of collecting information such that the information is objective, precise and fully disclosed for public usage. This method will be presented to you in linear steps, but the process is ongoing. The steps in the scientific method are:

1. Identify the problem.
2. Research the literature.
3. Formulate one or more hypothesis stated in terms of independent and dependent variables.
4. Plan the research design and consider the time frame.
5. Select the sample.
6. Collect the data.
7. Analyze the data.
8. Formulate conclusions and theories.
9. Write reports.
10. Start the research process all over again.

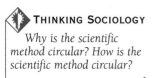

THINKING SOCIOLOGY

Why is the scientific method circular? How is the scientific method circular?

WHAT IS INVOLVED IN IDENTIFYING THE PROBLEM?

The first step in the scientific method is to identify a problem. Issues to be studied can be based on previous research, theoretical articles, intuition, common sense, brainstorming or just a moment of insight. Frequently, ideas for a problem emerge from what is going on around us or from an observation we make. One of the authors is an avid baseball card collector, so one morning we decided it would be interesting to do a research project on collecting.

The next step in deciding on a problem to study is to narrow the problem down to manageable proportions. Collecting is obviously too broad of a topic to study. We had the task of narrowing it down to a specific aspect of collecting. We decided to analyze the different types of collections and the impact that type of collection had on behavior and attitude toward the collectible. The researcher also has to beware of getting so small a problem that it becomes meaningless.

When we narrowed our problem about collecting to manageable proportions, we also identified our variables and presented theoretical definitions of these variables.

Quick Glance

Science does not have any identifiable characteristics.   T   F

Sociologists are trained to make objective observations.   T   F

The scientific method is an ongoing process.   T   F

Part of identifying the problem is delineating and defining the variables we wish to study.

We now had the general idea for our research, but we needed to know what else had been written and researched about collecting. This takes us to the second step of the scientific method.

WHAT IS INVOLVED IN SURVEYING THE LITERATURE?

The next step in the formulation of the problem is doing a comprehensive review of the existing knowledge on the chosen subject. We need to look for possible books regarding the subject matter and/or journal articles that have been published addressing the topic. This is where you develop eye strain, dirty fingers and a tolerance for frustration. We went to the library and looked up such topics as *collections, collectibles, baseball cards* and *collective behavior*. We questioned and talked with people who had collections. This investigation of the literature has two rewards for the researcher. First, the material found on the variables will help in the formation of the hypothesis; second, researched material will help the researcher in writing a research report. Each scientific or professional journal article begins with a section on a comprehensive survey of existing literature and research findings.

After we completed our comprehensive search of the literature, we took the next step in the scientific method, stating the hypothesis.

HOW DO WE FORMULATE HYPOTHESES?

After reviewing the literature, we need to refine the variables in which we are interested. A **variable** is a property or characteristic of something that can take on different values. For example, one of the variables we analyzed was the person's appraisal of the collection's value. Collections were valued all the way from $0 to $150,000.

Based on our survey of the literature, we make a statement about the relationship between two or more variables. This is the hypothesis. A **hypothesis** is a tentative statement of the relationship between two or more variables. If we want to investigate "is America virtuous?", do we have a hypothesis? No, because there is a lack of a tentative statement about the relationship between two variables in this statement. As researchers, we can investigate the relationship between women working and divorce. Perhaps we feel that if married women are employed in the job market, then the marriage is more likely to end in divorce. This is a tentative statement concerning the relationship between two variables.

There are two types of variables in the hypothesis; there is an independent and a dependent variable:

1. The **independent variable** is the one that the researcher controls; it is sometimes called the causal variable.
2. The **dependent variable** is the outcome or the result of the independent variable.

The dependent variable is the variable receiving the change or it is thought to be influenced by the independent variable. Thus, the independent variable is thought to be responsible for influencing another variable (dependent variable).

We can now state our hypothesis in terms of the independent and dependent variables. A very convenient way to state the hypothesis is in an "If _____, then _____" statement. The independent variable is the "if" clause and the dependent variable is the "then" clause. We hypothesized that if people viewed their collections

🕮 *Quick Glance*

Hypothesis must come from existing theory. T F

The first step of the scientific method is the formation of the hypothesis. T F

Surveying literature gives ideas for possible hypotheses. T F

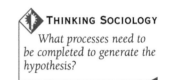
THINKING SOCIOLOGY

What processes need to be completed to generate the hypothesis?

🕮 *Quick Glance*

A hypothesis is a tentative statement of one variable. T F

The independent variable receives the change from another variable. T F

The hypothesis must be true. T F

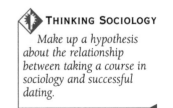
THINKING SOCIOLOGY

Make up a hypothesis about the relationship between taking a course in sociology and successful dating.

Quick Glance

The hypothesis is a type of research design. T F

The dependent variable is in the "if" part of a hypothesis. T F

The best way to state the hypothesis is an "if _____, then _____" format. T F

The subject must be the same in the two clauses of the hypothesis. T F

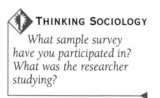

THINKING SOCIOLOGY

How would you operationally define "successful dating?"

as valuable, then they would want to spend more time reading and working with their collectible. Therefore, our hypothesis could have read, "If a person views their collection as an investment, then he/she spends time reading magazines about their collectible," or "If an individual views their collection as a hobby, then he/she does not read magazines about their collectible." The feeling that the collection is an investment or a hobby is the independent variable and the reading of magazines is the dependent variable. The subject should be the same for both clauses.

In order to investigate the variables, each variable must be measurable. This is the operational definition of our variables as opposed to the theoretical definition. An **operational definition** is defining the variable by the way it is measured. A juvenile delinquent, for example, could be defined as any male or female who was listed as truant from school for seven or more days per semester. Or a juvenile delinquent could be defined as any male or female who had been arrested for at least a misdemeanor offense. In our case, we asked people whether they viewed their collection as a leisure time activity or as an investment. In order to measure magazine reading, we asked how much time he or she spent reading magazines about their collection. Then we divided the time into three categories which were 0 time, 1–3 hours per month and 3 or more hours per month. The breakdowns of times were based on the results of an earlier questionnaire given to a large number of people.

The concept of operational definition is a very important one. Sometimes in the literature, a student or a professional will read very contradictory results about a particular issue. Many times differences in operational definition accounts for the divergent research findings.

WHAT ARE THE RESEARCH DESIGNS?

The next step in the scientific method is to decide how to test the hypothesis. The way we test the hypothesis is referred to as a research design. The **research design** is the blueprint for our research; the research design tells us how we are going to carry out the gathering of our information.

Quick Glance

Operational definitions are not important. T F

Operational definitions remain the same no matter who does the research. T F

The operational definition is defining the variable by the way it is measured. T F

THINKING SOCIOLOGY

What sample survey have you participated in? What was the researcher studying?

Opinion Research or Sample Survey

There are many types of research designs. The first type is called **opinion research** or **sample survey**. Sample surveys are a popular method in sociological research. With this type of design, a large number of people are questioned about the variables of interest. We used a sample survey for our project on collecting. We designed a three-page questionnaire that 325 people completed. Then we compared those people who were investors with those people who were hobbyists. With this research design, data is collected through questionnaires, telephone interviews and personal interviews. Thus, there are two types of sample survey: interview or questionnaire.

A **questionnaire** is a pen or pencil test that a subject completes. The questions may be structured; the respondent must choose

▲ SAMPLE SURVEY IS MOST OFTEN USED IN SOCIOLOGY.
IMAGE COPYRIGHT GALINA BARSKAYA, 2008. USED UNDER LICENSE FROM SHUTTERSTOCK, INC.

from a limited number of responses. The questions may also be unstructured; the respondent answers an open-ended question. A structured questionnaire would be like a multiple choice exam; an unstructured questionnaire would be like an essay exam.

An **interview** involves a researcher asking a respondent the questions. Sometimes interviews are done face to face, but telephone interviews also may be conducted. With the interview, the researcher asks the question of the respondent and records their replies.

The sample survey has several advantages:

1. It is very precise and permits the use of statistical techniques.
2. It allows for the comparison of responses because findings can be quantified.
3. A large amount of data can be collected in a relatively short period of time.

However, the sample survey also has several disadvantages:

1. It can be expensive when large samples are involved.
2. The questions may miss unanticipated information.
3. People may not want to fill out questionnaires or be interviewed, or they may give you incorrect information.
4. There are problems designing questionnaires and interviews.
5. It does not allow probing for the context of social behavior.

Planned Experiment

The second type of research design is the planned experiment. The **planned experiment** is a systematic examination of cause and effect. In order to complete the research using the planned experiment, we need to establish a control group, which shows what changes occur due to the passage of time, and we need one or more experimental groups. The experimental group receives the stimulus, or the independent variable, that we are interested in studying. A comparison of the differences between the two groups will yield evidence that our hypothesis is accepted or rejected.

For example, we might wish to determine if a new way to teach research method would be more effective than the traditional method. We would take all of our principles of sociology classes and randomly assign the students to either the experimental group or the control group. The experimental group would learn research methods by actually conducting a research project; the control group would learn by the traditional manner of lecture and textbook. At the end of the semester, we would test knowledge about the scientific method in order to determine if the new method had a positive effect on learning or not.

The planned experiment can either be in the laboratory or in the field. The laboratory experiment is the least used research design in sociology simply because it is very difficult to bring a group's social variables into the laboratory and be certain that all variables are included. The field experiment is occasionally used in sociology. In the field experiment, the researcher manipulates the independent variable in the real world. If we used our classes to test the new way of teaching research, we would be doing a field experiment. If we brought a group of students into the laboratory and divided them into two groups and gave one group the new way of learning research methods and the other group a textbook and then tested retained knowledge four days later, we would be doing a laboratory experiment.

There are several advantages to the planned experiment:

🜁 *Quick Glance*

The research design is a blueprint for research. T F

A sample survey is the same as an opinion survey. T F

There are no advantages to the sample survey. T F

The multiple choice exam is a structured questionnaire. T F

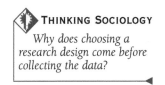

THINKING SOCIOLOGY

Why does choosing a research design come before collecting the data?

◄

🜁 *Quick Glance*

Sample Surveys are a cheap way to collect data. T F

Questionnaires are easy to write. T F

Sample surveys are good to find out the "why" of human behavior. T F

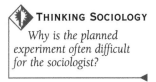

THINKING SOCIOLOGY

Why is the planned experiment often difficult for the sociologist?

◄

SCIENCE IS NOTHING BUT DEVELOPED PERCEPTION, INTERPRETED INTENT, COMMON SENSE ROUNDED OUT AND MINUTELY ARTICULATED.

GEORGE SANTAYANA

1. Cause and effect can be determined.
2. Other researchers can readily repeat the experiment.
3. Contamination from other variables is eliminated, minimized or controlled.

There are several disadvantages of the planned experiment:

1. It is expensive.
2. There are ethical questions of experimentation using people.
3. People have the option to cooperate or not.
4. When people know they are being studied, their behavior may change.
5. The experimental situation may be very artificial.
6. Research is limited to a well-defined, narrow topic.

Observation

Observation can either be **nonparticipant observation** or **participant observation**. In nonparticipant observation, the researcher does not take part in what he or she is studying; they kick back and watch what is going on in the group. This is an example of Weber's verstehen method that was mentioned in Chapter 1. Jean Piaget's theory of cognitive development is an example of nonparticipant observation because he observed children at play and recorded the information in his journal.

Another example of nonparticipant observation is a study I conducted of the Young Republican Club at Ohio State University. I hung around the office; I listened in on telephone conversations; and, without pride, I went through garbage cans. I tried to be as unobtrusive as I could be and waited for what would happen. Jane Goodall, starting summer of 1960, observed the chimpanzees at Gombe National Park in Tanzania. At first she had to watch them through binoculars but she gradually gained their trust and could watch at a closer distance. The observation continues to this day.

In **participant observation**, the researcher actually takes part in what he or she is studying. Several studies of mental institutions and prisons have been done using this method. Rosenhan's article "Being Sane in Insane Places" is an example of participant observation. Graduate students checked into mental hospitals as patients in order to study the interaction patterns between staff and patient, and patient and patient. Part of our research on baseball card collectors has involved participant observations because one of the authors is an avid baseball card collector who likes to go to baseball card shows and shops. We went to more than our fair share of these shows watching people trade, con and buy cards! Dean Fossey, like Jane Goodall, studied primate behavior. At first she just watched the mountain gorillas which would have been nonparticipant observation but then she started to sit with the gorillas and play with the babies so she became a participant. She stated her observations in 1967 in Rowanda.

There are several advantages of observation:

▲ PRIMATE BEHAVIOR OFFERS CLUES TO HUMAN BEHAVIOR.
IMAGE COPYRIGHT ERIC ISSELÉE, 2008. USED UNDER LICENSE FROM SHUTTERSTOCK, INC.

1. Observations take place in a natural setting.
2. The method is good for studying interaction among people.
3. Dynamics of change can be analyzed.
4. The context of the behavior can be analyzed.
5. The method is flexible and direction of observation can be altered to meet changed circumstances.
6. It is relatively inexpensive.

There are several disadvantages to this method:

1. Findings may depend on the researcher's insight and judgment.
2. A single observer may not yield reliable information.
3. Findings may apply only to the group studied.
4. The presence of an observer may alter the way people behave.
5. Ethical questions arise about informing or not informing people that they are being observed.
6. Replication of research is often difficult.

Nonobtrusive Research

Sociologists also use what is called nonobtrusive research designs. With nonobtrusive measures, the researcher does not actually come into contact with the people being studied. One nonobtrusive method is **secondary analysis**. This is getting data from already existing sources of information. There are several sources of secondary analysis data. Official data contains information just waiting to be analyzed. The census data has a treasure of data just waiting to be analyzed. Courthouses and other legal agencies keep many records. If we wanted to study the number of misdemeanors that were happening in the College District, I would contact the local police department. Durkheim's study on suicide mentioned in Chapter 1 used official data.

The use of official data has several advantages:

1. Data is collected on nearly everyone in the defined population or a representative sample drawn from that population.
2. It is a less expensive way to collect data.

THINKING SOCIOLOGY

After reading "Humphreys At a Glance," what research design do you feel Humphreys should have used in his study of homosexual males? Why?

Quick Glance

Replication is easy with nonparticipant observation.　　T　F

Observation is an expensive way to collect data.　　T　F

Secondary analysis is the same as nonparticipant observation.　　T　F

Learning TIP
Ask questions about text material. Write these questions on index cards. Use one card per question.

HUMPHREYS AT A GLANCE

Sociologist Laud Humphreys was responsible for a controversial book, *Tearoom Trade*. Humphreys used deception in his study as the men Humphreys observed were not aware that they were participating in a sociological study. Humphreys used participant observation to study the lifestyles of homosexual males who frequented public restrooms for the purpose of obtaining sex. The public restrooms were often referred to as tearooms because of the homosexual use. Humphreys served as a "watchout" in these restroom encounters alerting the participants if any intruders were approaching. This would be participant observation. Humphreys wanted to know who the homosexuals were and what kind of private lives they had. Humphreys collected his data by recording the license plate numbers of the participants. From this information, he was able to obtain home addresses. A year later, after altering his appearance, he went to their homes and interviewed them. Some social scientists view this research as a violation of professional ethics. Humphreys' research grant and teaching contract were terminated.

TRUTH HAS NO SPECIAL TIME OF ITS OWN. ITS HOUR IS NOW—ALWAYS.
ALBERT SCHWEITZER

There are several disadvantages to using official data:

1. Essential data such as religion may be omitted.
2. The variables may not be measured in the form needed by the researcher.
3. Information may be dated or incomplete, nonsystematic or inaccurate.

The mass media is a fruitful source of data. A method used to analyze the mass media is called **content analysis**. We used content analysis in our study of romance novels. We wanted to know the incidence and type of sexual contact that occurred between heroine and hero in these books. We wrote up an analysis form which included such variables as length of time of foreplay, number and rating of passionate scenes, marital status of couples, number of acts of intercourse, and the number and timing of pregnancies. It made for a rather spicy paper!

There are several advantages to using content analysis:

1. Data is accessible and relatively inexpensive.
2. Data can cover a long time period.
3. Data can study real culture rather than reported culture.
4. Data can pick up on shifts occurring within the society.

There are several disadvantages to using content analysis:

1. Almost all the material, such as newspapers and magazines, have already gone through the selection process of an editor or publisher.
2. It is very time consuming.
3. It is difficult to avoid judgment and subjectivity in the coding process.
4. Information is provided only about symbolic behavior.

A third nonobtrusive method is **physical traces and artifacts**. This type of research design studies human behavior by studying items which have been used in human activities. This method is frequently used in anthropology, but is becoming more popular in sociology. If we wanted to study people's drinking habits, we might look through their garbage cans to see how many beer cans and bottles they throw away; if I want to study brand name buying, I could sort through garbage cans to determine what brands households are buying.

There are several advantages to this method:

1. People are not aware they are being studied so they cannot change their report or alter their responses.
2. It is a relatively cheap way to collect data.

There are several disadvantages to this method:

1. Many behaviors do not leave physical traces.
2. A great deal of work must be done to sort out the data.

There is no one correct research design for any question. We can study juvenile delinquency by designing a questionnaire and asking teenagers to assess what unlawful activities they engage in; we can use content analysis of the newspapers to see how many articles contain juvenile delinquents and what kind of delinquency occurs; we could become teachers in a high school and be a nonparticipant observer of the teens' behavior; we could go to the county courthouse and ask for information; we could take a group of juveniles and put one group in special classes and

🕮 *Quick Glance*

Nonparticipant observation is a nonobtrusive measure but participant observation is obtrusive.   T   F

Findings in a participant observation study may be colored by researcher bias.   T   F

Secondary analysis is based on official data.   T   F

Information for secondary analysis is complete and valid.   T   F

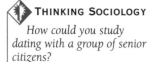
THINKING SOCIOLOGY

What information could be gained by doing a content analysis of children's books?

🕮 *Quick Glance*

Content analysis is based on the mass media.   T   F

Content analysis is an obtrusive measure.   T   F

Physical traces and artifacts are frequently used by anthropologists.   T   F

There is only one correct research design for any hypothesis.   T   F

THINKING SOCIOLOGY

How could you study dating with a group of senior citizens?

leave another in the regular classroom to see what changes occur in juvenile delinquency rates between the two groups; we could talk with a group of convicted felons and ask them to trace their history back to see what type of juvenile activities they did. What research design you use ultimately depends on what hypothesis you use and how you want to gather information about those variables.

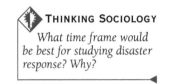

WHAT ARE THE TIME FRAMES USED FOR SOCIOLOGICAL RESEARCH?

Before continuing with the collection of the data, we need to determine the time frame for studying the selected variables.

There are three basic types of time frames. *A cross-sectional study compares two or more groups at a single point in time.* This type of research design frequently uses standardized questionnaires or interviews in order to collect information on a comparatively large number of people. When we compared hobbyists with investors, we were using a cross-sectional study.

The second possible time frame is an ex post facto study. This takes some current situation backwards in time. For example, we might take a sample of juvenile delinquents and trace backwards into their childhood to see if there were any serious head injuries or to determine the type of discipline their parents used. Studies of mental illness and alcoholism frequently use this time frame.

The third time frame is the longitudinal study. This provides us with a framework to collect data over an extended period of time. A famous study, *Termain's Gifted Children*, would be an example of a longitudinal study. Dr. Lewis Termain started his study in 1921 with a sample of gifted children. He wanted to disprove the belief of his time period that the child gifted early in life was "rotted in adulthood." He followed these children to their adulthood. After his death, one of his students picked up the project and followed all the people who were still in the study until their deaths. The data from this research project showed that very high intelligence did not necessarily lead to extraordinary accomplishments, but these gifted children did not "rot."

The research designs can be "mixed and matched" with the time frames. For example, if I wanted to study juvenile delinquents I could use a sample survey with the ex post facto study. I would have questions in my questionnaire tracing their history back to their early childhood. I could use a longitudinal study. I could interview a group of twelve year old boys and then continue to interview them once a year for the next fifteen years.

THINKING SOCIOLOGY
What time frame would be best for studying disaster response? Why?

Quick Glance
The ex post facto study compares two or more groups at a single point in time.   T   F
A longitudinal study collects data over a wide geographical area.   T   F
There is only one correct time frame for any given research design.   T   F

HOW DO WE COLLECT DATA?

After we have decided on our game plan for collecting data, we need to push up our sleeves and get to work. We have to get the information to analyze our hypothesis; in other words, we have to gather our data. **Data** is the information that we gather concerning our hypothesis. For example, the information documenting the number of hours people read magazines is data. The first issue we have to determine before we go out and collect our data is "who or what are we going to sample?"

There are two concepts that you must understand before we begin this section. First, you need to know what a population is. The **population** is a group of people (or objects) who share a common characteristic. The researcher defines what he or she wants the population to be. In the research we mentioned on romance novels, our population was "all romance novels." This is a very broad population. A **sample**

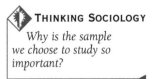

THINKING SOCIOLOGY
Why is the sample we choose to study so important?

is a subset of the population. The researcher also specifies how many he or she wants in the sample. In our research on romance novels, for our first paper, we read 100 romance novels; that was our sample.

There are two basic types of samples. A **random sample** is a sample in which we can list everyone or everything that could potentially be in the study. Based on this list, we draw a sample of a predetermined size. This means that each individual has a known probability of being included in the sample. For example, we want to study the student body at North Harris College. We would go down to the registrar and get a listing of all the students enrolled at the college, approximately 13,000 students. We have decided that we want a sample of 50 students. Each student would have a 1 in 13,000 chance of being selected for our sample. We could draw our sample by cutting every student's name into a slip of paper, putting them in a drum, rolling the drum, and drawing out fifty names (rolling the drum each time). An easier way would be to have a computer randomly generate a sample of 50 students registered at North Harris College.

The second type of sample is called a **nonrandom sample**. We frequently use a nonrandom sample when we are unable to list everyone or everything in the population or it would be too expensive to draw a random sample. There are several types of nonrandom samples. The first type is a **snowball sample**. We drew a snowball sample for one of our projects on collecting. We asked students to give a questionnaire to somebody they knew who was a collector. Then that collector, in turn, gave a questionnaire to someone else. A second type of nonrandom sample is an **accidental sample**. We could stand in the courtyard and stop students on the way through to complete a questionnaire. This was the type of sample we used for our paper on romance novels; we read the novels that we could find in our homes and at the new and used book stores. We did not stand a chance of listing every romance novel ever published or even listing a year's worth of romance novels. A **purposive sample** has a method in its madness. When I did research on nursing homes, I went to the phone directory and picked out three homes in a lower income area, three homes in a middle income area, and two homes in an upper income area; this was a purpose sample. A fourth type of nonrandom sample is a **quota sample**. We might divide our books between historical romance, bodice rippers and modern romance and choose an equal number of books from each category.

After we have determined our population and drawn our sample, it is time to collect data. After we have accumulated our data, we have to make order out of chaos by analyzing the data in light of our hypothesis.

▲ AN ACCIDENTAL SAMPLE WOULD RESULT FROM STOPPING RUNNERS AND REQUESTING THEY COMPLETE A QUESTIONNAIRE.
IMAGE COPYRIGHT IGOR KARON, 2008. USED UNDER LICENSE FROM SHUTTERSTOCK, INC.

🐚 *Quick Glance*

Data is information gathered for research.   T   F

A sample is the same as a population.   T   F

A random sample does not depend on listing a population.   T   F

HOW DO WE ANALYZE DATA?

After we collect the data, we analyze it. This means that the data is organized by tabulating, making tables and calculating statistics. I shall calculate such statistics as percentages, rates, means and measures of association. (You will need to take a course in statistics and research design to fully understand what is involved in analysis of

	Types	Example	Definition
Random Sample	Simple	The winning of a lottery drawing.	List all elements of population and select sample using random numbers.
	Systematic	Listing all the students in your school, i.e. 6,000. You want a sample of ten students. Randomly select first student then choose every 600th student.	List all elements of population and select first element by using a table of random numbers and select every "x" element after that.
	Stratified	Divide the student body into male and female and randomly select a sample of fifty from each group or strata.	Divide population into homogenous units and take a simple random sample from each unit.
	Cluster	Take a random sample of voter districts in your state. Get a list of all the registered voters in the selected districts and take a random sample from the appropriate list.	This involves several layers of random sampling from several population units.
Nonrandom Sample	Snowball	Get a number of people to fill out a questionnaire about baseball card collecting. Then ask these people to recommend people of like interests.	A "ripple effect" sample in which one respondent suggests other respondents.
	Purposive	Interviewing people exiting a trial to gather opinions of the legal process.	Sampling elements which fulfills certain criteria.
	Quota	Dividing romance novels into historical and contemporary and reading a hundred books of each type.	Divide population into certain categories and sample within each category.
	Accidental	We want a sample of fifty students enrolled in your college or university. We stand in the middle of campus and talk with fifty students.	Sample whatever is convenient for the researcher and fits the requirements for the research.

data but it is like solving a mystery to see what is going to happen.) The analysis of our data gives us the basis on whether to accept, reject or modify our hypothesis.

THINKING SOCIOLOGY

Why do you think so many college curriculums are requiring a course in statistics?

WHY MAKE CONCLUSIONS, FORMULATE THEORIES AND WRITE REPORTS?

The last step of the scientific method is drawing conclusions and writing reports. After we have analyzed the data, we need to either accept or reject our hypothesis and fully explain our findings. This step involves the statement of the problem we have done in step one, then adding our information to what has already been determined. The final report will take the reader through the complete scientific method so that he or she can understand just exactly how you arrived at your results.

Part of drawing conclusions is either supporting an already existing theory or designing a new theory. A **theory** is a way of explaining some phenomenon or the relationships between phenomena. A theory is a way of binding together a multitude of facts into a comprehensible whole. There are two different levels of theory: **micro** and **macro**. We introduced these two concepts in Chapter 1. Do you remember what they mean?

IF WE WOULD NOT BE SATISFIED UNTIL WE HAD PASSED A SHARE OF OUR HAPPINESS ON TO OTHER PEOPLE, WHAT A WORLD WE COULD MAKE!

LAURA INGALLS WILDER

Measures of Central tendency	mean	average i.e. $\dfrac{5 + 5 + 6 + 7 + 8}{5} = 6.2$
	median	middle score, i.e. 6
	mode	most frequent score, i.e. 5
Measures of Variability	range	top and bottom score, i.e. 5 to 8
	standard deviation	average variability around the mean
Measures of Association	Correlation (Spearman/ Pearson)	relationship between 2 variables based on scores
	analysis of variance	relationship between more than 2 variables based on means
	multi variate analysis	relationship between more than 2 variables based on scores
	Chi square	relationship between 2 or more variables based on observed scores
	t-test or z-test	relationship between 2 variables based on differences in means

🕮 *Quick Glance*

You will probably need a course in statistics to do research.　T　F

The last step in the scientific method is formulating theories.　T　F

A theory is a way of explaining research facts.　T　F

A good theory need not help make predictions.　T　F

Research is a neverending cycle.　T　F

THINKING SOCIOLOGY

Which of the difficulties of conducting sociological research do you think presents the most problems for the researcher? Why?

◀

🕮 *Quick Glance*

The Hawthorne effect is not a difficulty in conducting research.　T　F

It is not ethical to do some types of research on human subjects.　T　F

A correlation always yields cause and effect between variables.　T　F

What makes a good theory?

1.　logical consistency
2.　consistency with existing theories
3.　production of predictions
4.　stimulation of further research

As you can see, research is a cyclical process. We have tied our results with theory or perhaps written theory, and that takes us right back to the first step of our research method. Research is an ongoing process and every research project always generates more questions than it answers.

WHAT ARE THE DIFFICULTIES IN CONDUCTING SOCIOLOGICAL RESEARCH?

There are several difficulties in conducting research. *One difficulty that is bothersome is the issue that studying behavior often alters behavior.* If an individual realizes he or she is being watched, he or she may alter his or her behavior to conform either to community standards or to what he or she thinks the researcher wants. The term for this is **Hawthorne effect**. The Hawthorne effect is based on a study done at the Western Electric Company in Hawthorne, Illinois in the mid-1920s. They were studying such factors as lighting and other environmental factors on the morale of workers. What they found was that no matter what they did, production remained high and morale remained good. They decided it was the act of studying these people that made the changes rather than the actual environmental conditions.

A second difficulty is that people, unlike bacteria or other lower life forms, have emotions, motives and highly individual personality characteristics. Human behavior can be very unpredictable. How many animals would deliberately walk on fire or even come very close to a hot bed of coal? I have seen people, however, walk over beds of coals either for fun or profit—probably for profit. Look at the different reactions of people to horror movies. Some people will not watch horror flicks; other people hide their faces at every scary scene; and other people, like me, laugh at them.

A third difficulty is the ethical issues. It is not permissive to do some types of research on human subjects. For example, I would like to study the impact of isolation on infant development. I could not take a sample of twenty children and raise them in isolation with nothing more than a food source. A psychologist by the name of Harry Harlow did conduct such an experiment with baby monkeys.

A fourth difficulty is that the facts and information we are interested in are frequently not directly observable. Intelligence, for example, is measured by a test rather than by an observation. Prejudice is often measured by use of a questionnaire. In many studies, we use indicators in the form of questions or attitude scales in order to get the information that we need.

A fifth difficulty is that many social behaviors are influenced by many variables. Marriage or divorce patterns contain more than just one set of variables.

A sixth difficulty is that we can rarely make a definitive statement of cause and effect. We can make a statement of association, but we cannot, in many cases, say that one variable causes another variable. A correlation is found when a change in one variable occurs with a change in another variable. Only through a planned experiment can a researcher make a statement of cause and affect. The other research designs yield correlational results.

A seventh problem is that we, as sociologists, are part of what we study. We have to be very careful to be objective in our observations and conclusions.

Learning TIP
Be on time for class and do not leave early.

WHAT ARE THE ETHICS IN CONDUCTING SOCIOLOGICAL RESEARCH?

According to the American Sociological Association, the following ethics should be followed:

▶ *We must be objective in our research.* We cannot let our own preference or personal opinions influence our final results. Our values will direct us into what type of research we do or the topics that we choose; but, our values cannot influence our findings.

▶ *We must respect the rights of research subjects.* Subjects have the right to know what is going on, to not be physically or psychologically harmed and to be informed of results if they desire to be so. We use **informed consent** to ensure that people know that they are being studied. When a person is going to be in a project, he/she acknowledges that they will be filling out a questionnaire or he/she signs a paper acknowledging that he/she is willing to participate in the experiment. We also use **debriefing** at the end of an experiment to let the respondents know what was going on and what we hope to find out from the research.

▶ *We must respect the subject's right to privacy.* All information must remain private and confidential.

▶ *We must acknowledge all authors and researchers of the project,* and we must list sources of financial support.

THINKING SOCIOLOGY

Have you ever been in an experiment in which you felt that your privacy or rights had been violated? Why or why not?

Quick Glance

Values never have a place in research.   T F

A subject, by virtue of being a subject, has no privacy.   T F

Informed consent means telling research subjects about the goals and methods of the research project.   T F

▼ CHAPTER SUMMARY

1. Science is based on verifiable, objective evidence; the researcher does not influence findings; findings are subject to change, and forms the basis for making future predictions; and scientific information can be validated through replication.

2. The scientific method includes identifying the problem, researching the literature, forming the hypothesis, completing the research design, planning the time frame, selecting the sample, collecting data, analyzing data, making conclusions, writing reports and starting the process again.

3. Research designs may be sample surveys, nonobtrusive measures, planned experiments, nonparticipant observation and participant observation.

4. Three time frameworks are used in research: cross sectional, longitudinal and ex post facto.

5. A sample is a subset of the population. A sample may be either a random sample or a nonrandom sample.

6. There are difficulties conducting sociological research including the Hawthorne effect, unpredictable human behavior, ethical issues, information which may not be directly observable, the problems making a definitive statement of cause and effect and professional objectivity.

7. The American Sociological Association recommends that sociologists remain objective in conducting research, respect and rights of subjects and the subject's right to privacy and acknowledging all sources of research support and financial support.

▼ REFERENCES

Goleman, Daniel. February 1980. "1528 Little Geniuses and How They Grew." *Psychology Today*. vol. 13, no. 9, 28–34.

Hite, Shere. 1987. *Women and Love: A Cultural Revolution in Progress*. New York: Alfred A. Knopf.

Humphreys, Laud. 1975. *Tearoom Trade: Impersonal Sex in Public Places* (enlarged ed.). Chicago: Aldine.

Liebow, Elliot. 1967. *Tally's Corner: A Study of Negro Streetcorner Men*. Boston: Little, Brown.

Machlup, Fritz. 1988. "Are the Social Sciences Really Inferior?" *Society* (May/June): 57–65.

Marsha, Linda. 1992. "Scientific Fraud." *Omni* (June): 39+.

Piaget, Jean. 1952. *The Origins of Intelligence in Children*, M. Cook, Trans. New York: International University Press.

Rosenhan, David L. 1973. "On Being Sane in Insane Places." *Science* 179, January, 250–258.

Walton, J. 1990. *Sociology and Critical Inquiry*. Belmont, CA: Wadsworth.

READING

"NOT SO SILI: SOCIOLOGY INFORMATION LITERACY INFUSION AS THE FOCUS OF FACULTY AND LIBRARIAN COLLABORATION" BY LYNDA DODGEN, SARAH NAPER, OLIA PALMER AND ADRIAN RAPP

ABSTRACT. In summer 2001, librarians and Sociology faculty members at the North Harris College embarked on a collaborative project designed to improve the information literacy skills of Principles of Sociology students. Other goals were the improvement of student grades on a particular Sociology assignment and overall improvement of the students' library research skills. Students were instructed in basic literature analysis skills and were given hands-on training in database searching techniques. While results of the study were mixed, students learned some important concepts and the professors and librarians count the collaboration as successful. Follow-up studies are planned.

KEYWORDS. Information literacy, bibliographic instruction, faculty collaboration, library research skills.

THE LIBRARIANS' STORY

Like most academic librarians, North Harris College (NHC) librarians had been trying for many years to ensure that students who came to the library left with some transferable strategies for finding information. We hoped that students would be able to transfer information locating skills learned here to meet other information searching needs, both in school and in their lives. We especially hoped that students would learn to think critically about information that they found.

Primarily, we sought to achieve these goals by instructing students in first-year English classes that were brought to the library by their instructors. Additionally, we taught some Internet searching workshops. We also tailored instruction to meet other instructor needs as requests occurred.

In Fall 1999 librarians identified three possible methods of achieving information literacy at our campus:

* Create a credit course in library skills
* Partner with other campus areas to create a mandatory Freshman Orientation course: information literacy as one module of this course, computer literacy, study skills, and other campus services as other modules of this course
* Promote information literacy by a concentrated integration into a new key target course, ideally a high-enrollment course.

Initially, the credit course in library skills was the option that was most exciting to us. We relished the prospect of having a course that was entirely our own. How-

Quick Glance

The librarians initiated this project.　　T　F

The librarians were interested in students knowing how to check out books.　　T　F

This study was about a class on databases.　　T　F

© 2003, The Haworth Press, Inc., Binghamton, NY. "Not So SILI: Sociology Information Literacy Infusion as the Focus of Faculty and Librarian Collaboration" from *Community and Junior College Libraries*, vol. 11, no. 4, pp. 27–33. Article copies available from The Haworth Document Delivery Service: 1-800-HAWORTH. E-mail address: docdelivery@haworthpress.com

Lynda Dodgen is Professor of Sociology, North Harris College, Houston, TX. Sarah Naper is Business Reference Librarian, James A. Michener Library, University of Northern Colorado, Greeley, CO. Olia Palmer is Reference/Instruction Librarian, North Harris College, Houston, TX (E-mail: olia.h.palmer@nhmccd.edu). Adrian Rapp is Professor of Sociology, North Harris College, Houston, TX. Community & Junior College Libraries, Vol. 11(4) 2003, http://www.haworthpress.com/store/product.asp?sku=J107. © 2003 by The Haworth Press, Inc. All rights reserved. 10.1300/J107v11n04_05

The librarians successfully started a course on finding information.   T   F

The study began using four English classes.   T   F

Sociology was chosen to test out the database information technique because it had no prerequisite.   T   F

ever, when we began to seriously examine this avenue, we discovered that it was not a realistic option. First, we had trouble identifying an appropriate course number for such a credit course, and second, we were unsuccessful in finding enough Texas four-year colleges that would accept such a transfer course. Lacking a clearly identifiable transfer potential, we feared that students would have no reason to take our course. Pursuing such an option began to seem like a tremendous expenditure of effort that probably would not be rewarded.

We began instead to tackle concentrated integration into key target courses. Our first effort emerged as a three-part instruction for first-semester English classes. After securing agreement from lead English faculty, we created three modules (library catalog, databases, and Internet research) of instruction. Each module consisted of key concepts, a worksheet to complete in class, and a post-test. Though some faculty still ask us to use this 3-module approach, most English faculty members believe that it takes too much time away from subject instruction.

Librarians also made specific overtures to Developmental Studies English faculty. This effort was rewarded by Developmental Studies faculty recognizing library activities as one of the ways that students could achieve their required laboratory hours.

In Spring 2001 we decided that, though English faculty continued to be excellent partners, we needed to forge new information literacy partnerships with faculty in other departments.

We wondered if we could prove that library research instruction, with its emphasis on information literacy skills, makes a positive difference in the academic lives of students. Our interest turned to students at greatest risk of dropping out, those who were at a disadvantage for varied reasons, e.g., poor academic background or non-English primary language. Because such students can register for several courses that have no pre-requisites, we chose to approach the professors teaching one of these courses, SOCI 1301–Principles of Sociology.

THE SOCIOLOGISTS' STORY

During the summer of 2001 two NHC librarians approached us, the two faculty members of the Sociology department, with both a concern and proposition. Their concern was NHC students who experience academic difficulties as a result of information illiteracy. In the sociology department, we have made a commitment to students entering the college environment who have not passed the TASP (Texas Academic Skills Program) test, thereby proving they can function in a college-level course. We believe such students deserve an opportunity to be enrolled in a college-level course. We are convinced that students deserve better than the self-fulfilling prophecy inherent in the practice of TASP reading prerequisites for college-level courses. Because of our philosophy, we wanted to cooperate with the librarians to study the benefits of library information skills instruction.

The librarians approached us with the idea that the sociology students would benefit from presentations on the use of the library at the beginning of their college experience rather than waiting until they were enrolled in their English composition classes. During the summer, we mapped out when the presentation of the library skills would take place. For the sociology instructors it was important that the least amount of time be taken from the class. The decision was made that at the beginning of the semester the librarians would present a general overview of information skills and would also administer a pretest of such skills at the beginning of their presentation. A few weeks later the students would go to the library for a hands-on activity.

🦅 *Quick Glance*

The sociologists thought students would benefit from information databases.   T   F

Students were pretested in the class room.   T   F

Twelve Principles of Sociology classes were used for this study.   T   F

Research Design

Students enrolled in eight sections of Principles of Sociology during Fall 2001 and in seven sections during Spring 2002 were the subjects of the study. Two librarians came to each SOCI 1301 class to administer a pre-test and lead a Scholarly Literature Evaluation Class consisting of a lecture and demonstration followed by a small group exercise applying the principles taught. Later in each semester, the classes came to the library for a hands-on Database Searching Workshop followed by the post-test.

The pre/post-test was developed to measure student comprehension of the basic information about scholarly articles provided during the Evaluation class and later reinforced during the Database Searching Workshop. An assignment for SOCI 1301 was used as the basis for the Scholarly Literature Evaluation Class. The assignment was chosen because the sociology professors wanted to encourage a greater number of students to successfully complete the assignment. In the assignment, students must identify a scholarly article that is a report of original research and summarize the article.

The content of the Database Searching Workshop was based on a SOCI 1301 assignment that focuses on a theory in deviant behavior (Merton). The student must give an example of each of the five responses of the theory and include printed support of their example. Past sociology students had experienced difficulties with the assignment and it was thought that this particular assignment would be a good springboard for a discussion of how library literacy would benefit the student. The instructors would discuss the theory in class and during the library visit the librarians would discuss the theory and demonstrate how students would be able to do library searches for the assignment. Librarians would also review the basic information presented in the first session regarding scholarly literature. The post-test would be given at the end of the Database Searching Workshop.

Quick Glance

The students were given a pretest to measure their library skills. T F

Librarian would give general information about research but no specific help with course work. T F

It was hypothesized that improving library skills would improve course grade. T F

Hypothesis

The first hypothesis is concerned with teaching students to use databases in the library. We felt that if a student were introduced by a knowledgeable person to the use of library resources, the learning curve would be a steep upward curve. This initial introduction was followed with a hands-on experience in the library working with the databases. Thus, the first hypothesis states: If a student is exposed to information about databases, then the student will learn how to use these databases.

The second hypothesis deals with the practical utilization of the ability to use the databases. SOCI 1301 has assignments that need research and the library databases are a perfect tool for this. Thus, the second hypothesis states: If a student learns how to use the databases, then the student will earn a higher assignment grade.

HYPOTHESES

1. If a student is exposed to information about searching databases the student will learn how to search those databases.
2. If a student learns how to use databases the student will earn a higher grade on class assignments.

🜂 *Quick Glance*

Only students who
completed a pre- or post-
test were included in
the sample.   T F

Past semester grades
were used to test the
second hypothesis.   T F

Assignment grades
improved the exposure
to databases.   T F

Subjects

In order to test the hypotheses, the 8 sections of SOCI 1301 taught by the two full-time sociology faculty members were used as the experimental group. These classes met either on a Tuesday-Thursday format or a Monday-Wednesday-Friday format.

Measurement

In order to test the first hypothesis, current SOCI 1301 students received a pretest at the beginning of the instructional session and a posttest at the end of the library workshop. Only those students who completed both tests were included in the data analysis. Those students who failed to take either the pre- or the post-test were eliminated from the sample. The final sample totaled 294 students.

In order to test the second hypothesis, current (academic year 2001–02) assignment grades were compared to past semesters (academic year 2000–01) in which the student did not have exposure to the library. We compared the two spring classes and the two fall classes. For Hypothesis 2, our experimental group was current SOCI 1301 student assignment grades, and our controls consisted of assignment grades from previous semesters' SOCI 1301 students.

RESULTS

A matched pair t-test was used to evaluate the first hypothesis. This test was significant at the .001 level. The sessions and the hands-on experience definitely had a positive outcome for the students.

We calculated two t-tests for Hypothesis 2. One t-test compared the Spring 2001 classes (control group) with Spring 2002 classes (experimental group). The second t-test compared Fall 2001 classes (control group) with Fall 2002 classes (experimental group). Neither t-test was significant. The assignment grades were not higher with training in the use of databases.

DISCUSSION

🜂 *Quick Glance*

It is best for a student to
be introduced to library
research methods and
quickly put the skills
to use.   T F

More students completed
the assignment when they
had the data research
sessions.   T F

This article is the first
phase of a larger
project.   T F

Results for Hypothesis 1

The library database intervention had a greater impact during the fall semester than the spring semester. We believe that several critical events happened that made the two semesters different. First, during the fall semester there was only a one-week lag time between the first and second sessions. For the spring semester, there was a month lag between the first and second contact sessions, with spring break occurring during that month. We think that there is an optimum time between the student being introduced to database searches and the hands-on experience. One week appears to be much more advantageous than a greater length of time.

Results for Hypothesis 2

The Sociology professors believed the assignment grades should have been higher among those students having the database experience. To get a clearer picture of what happened with our data, we did some further exploration. During Fall 2001, of 111 students, 47 students (42%) did not complete the assignment and 19 (17%) received 0s on the assignment. During Fall 2000, 76 out of 110 students (69%) did not do the assignment and 2 (2%) received 0s. More students completed the assignment during the fall semester with librarian intervention, but, unexpectedly, a greater number of the completed assignments earned zero grades.

We got very different results for the comparison between Spring 2002 and Spring 2001. During Spring 2001, 57 did not complete the assignment and 8 earned 0s. This means that 77% did not do the assignment and 11% earned 0s. The results of Spring 2002 were very much the same. Sixty-six percent (66%) did not complete the assignment and 10% earned 0s. There were 83 students in Spring 2002 and 74 students in Spring 2001. There was no significant difference between assignment results for the Spring semesters. Because these results were contrary to expectations, the research design will be examined for validity (see Table 1).

CONCLUSIONS

In conclusion, for Phase 1 of the study, the first hypothesis is accepted but the second hypothesis is not. Library instruction in basic information literacy concepts resulted in improved scores on the pre/post-test. There was no corresponding improvement in assignment grades (see Table 2).

RECOMMENDATIONS

In the next phase of our study, we plan to further explore the second hypothesis by giving a quiz on Merton's typology of deviance (which is the topic of the assignment) to a control group and to the classes with the library database exposure. Both control and experimental groups will take a quiz after discussing the chapter and completing the homework. The quiz will be an objective quiz. Grading of the homework assignment could be influenced by "person factors" and giving an objective quiz would eliminate this factor.

In addition, the pre- and post-test will be revised to eliminate the two questions which most of the students miss; this includes the last of the 12 questions on the instrument. We surmise that the 5 minutes allowed for the 12-item test is an inadequate period and we assume that trimming the test to ten items will eliminate the problem.

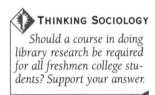

THINKING SOCIOLOGY

Should a course in doing library research be required for all freshmen college students? Support your answer.

TABLE 1				
	Fall 2000	*Spring 2001*	*Fall 2001 (SILI)*	*Spring 2002 (SILI)*
No assignment	69%	77%	42%	66%
0 grade	2%	11%	17%	10%

TABLE 2	
Hypothesis	*T-test*
If a student is exposed to information about databases, then a student will learn how to use these databases.	Significant at the .001 level of probability
If a student learns how to use the databases, then the student will earn a higher assignment grade.	Not significant

Gazing at Culture

IMAGE COPYRIGHT RONALD SUMNERS 2008. USED UNDER LICENSE FROM SHUTTERSTOCK, INC.

CHAPTER OBJECTIVES

1. What is society?
2. Why is society important?
3. What are the characteristics of a society?
4. What is culture?
5. What are the characteristics of a culture?
6. What are the components of culture?
7. What is the difference between ideal and real culture?
8. What are subcultures and countercultures?
9. How does a culture change?

counter culture: a group that goes against the basic values and norms of a society

cultural lag: the time of maladjustment between adoption of society's material culture and nonmaterial culture

cultural relativism: the analysis of a culture in terms of the culture's internal standards and conditions

cultural universal: the practices found in all cultures, i.e. dancing

culture: the way of life of a society; totality of what is learned by being a member of a society

culture shock: the feeling of disorientation that is experienced when people experience a culture very different from their own or when people experience very quick cultural change within their own culture

custom: a norm sustained by group opinion or tradition

diffusion: the spread of an idea or technology from its point of origin

discovery: the recognition of something not previously known

ethnocentrism: the belief that one's own culture is the correct and best way to live

folkway: a norm which a society would like its members to follow but does not insist upon

future shock: the human feelings which result from rapid change

ideal culture: a model of what culture states should exist or happen in a culture

ideology: the ideas, beliefs, folklore, legends, proverbs and philosophy of a culture

innovation: the process of introducing a new element into a culture

institution: a cluster of norms centered around a major human need

invention: the creation of something new

language: a symbolic system of communication used to transmit culture

law: norm written down through the political process

linguistic relativity hypothesis: the relationship between understanding a language and a culture

material culture: the objects which humans create and use; part of culture that results from technology

more: a norm considered essential to the well-being of the group

nonmaterial culture: the adaptations of a culture to physical conditions such as norms, values and sanctions

norm: a group-shared expectation

popular culture: culture composed of activities enjoyed by the populace

real culture: the manner in which people actually carry out the norms of a culture

sanction: the reward or punishment used to enforce a norm

social change: a process which causes/contributes to alterations in the structure of society

society: a fundamental group of social organization

subculture: a group that shares the total culture but has a set of norms or beliefs that set them apart from the rest of the society

urban legend: a story that develops in modern times

value: a sentiment or ideal that is at the core of a culture and tells the culture what is correct and important

---

▼ **KEY PEOPLE**

Ruth Benedict, George Murdock, Horace Miner, William Ogburn, William Sumner, Alvin Toffler

What Is Society?

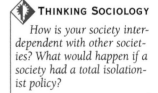
THINKING SOCIOLOGY

What would happen to the individual if he/she were outcast from his/her society?

Society is the fundamental group of social organization. A **society** is that group in which we live and work. We have defined a society in terms of human beings, but other animals also have societies. For example, bees and ants both have complex societies. We are, however, concerned only with human society.

Why Is Society Important?

If humans did not live in a society, we could not survive. Human beings are basically defenseless social animals. We need the group to help us get food to eat. Men in hunter-gatherer societies frequently hunt together as a unit, particularly for the larger animals, in order to maximize the chance of making a successful kill. Women in these societies go as a group to gather fruits and tubers. Then, when each gender returns from their day's activities, the extended family members combine the food from their collective efforts into one cooking pot in order that individuals may have some food in each of the major food groups. In pastoral societies, a unit of people herd animals such as cattle or reindeer.

Humans cannot defend themselves very well as individuals. We cannot run quickly, we do not have sharp teeth or claws to defend ourselves, and we do not possess overly keen eyesight or hearing. Only through the group effort are we able to protect ourselves. This is also true of other primates such as chimpanzees and gorillas. Watch a troop of baboons or chimps being threatened by an enemy; the males and childless females form a protective circle around the young and mothers with young.

Humans need the group to develop normally both physically and psychologically. Babies raised in isolation have a higher death rate and develop motor skills less competently than do those children raised in the group.

Quick Glance

We live but do not work with people in our society.	T	F
Society exists only among human beings.	T	F
Humans need their society in order to survive.	T	F
Humans need the group to develop psychologically.	T	F

What Are the Characteristics of a Society?

First, society is the breeding ground of culture. Within the society, a culture develops and changes. For example, the Masaii are pastoral people living in Kenya and Tanzania. Originally, they used gourds for collection containers for blood and milk and animal skins for their clothing. Their clothes still have the same basic pattern as those made of animal skins, but the clothes are now made from cotton material purchased at a store. They no longer use gourds as much, but have added the plastic bucket to their tools. I bought a pair of "native" earrings while in Kenya; bits of aluminum soft drink cans decorated the earrings.

Second, a society occupies a definite geographical territory. The Masaii occupy a territory called "Masaiiland" that cuts a kidney-bean-shaped area in Tanzania and Kenya. Masaiiland is not an official governmental country but gained the name since the Masaii occupy this area. The Kurds in Iran, Iraq and Russia have occupied this land for centuries, but modern governments have carved their domain around and over the Kurds. The Kurds are looking for an area to call their own. The geographical boundaries of the United States are the Pacific Ocean to the west, Atlantic Ocean to the east, Gulf of Mexico and the Rio Grande River to the south and the Great Lakes and 49th parallel to the north. When we were originally talking about making Alaska and Hawaii the 49th and 50th states, one of the issues brought up was that these two areas would not connect with the other 48 states.

Third, societies maintain themselves primarily through sexual reproduction. The Oneida tried to increase and maintain numbers by recruiting and adopting, but they

> THE OPTIMIST SEES THE DOUGHNUT. THE PESSIMIST SEES THE HOLE.
> McLandburgh Wilson

THINKING SOCIOLOGY

How is your society interdependent with other societies? What would happen if a society had a total isolationist policy?

George Murdock compiled a list of what he referred to as cultural universals or practices found in all cultures. The activities identified as cultural universals serve to meet the basic human needs of its members. Examples identified by Murdock include the following:

Athletic sports	Attempts to influence weather
Bodily adornment	Calendar
Cooking	Courtship
Dancing	Dream interpretation
Family	Folklore
Food habits	Funeral ceremonies
Games	Gift giving
Language	Laws
Medicine	Music
Myths	Numerals
Personal names	Property rights
Religion	Sexual restrictions
Toolmaking	

Not all cultures will participate in a cultural universal in the same manner. Medicine in the United States is based on the concept of physician care with the doctor prescribing a medication, while in other cultures the shaman will give their patient a particular herb to take. Medicine seen as acceptable in one culture at one particular time in history may also change. For example, cocaine was used for medicine at the turn of the century, but we do not consider it to be appropriate medication today.

☥ *Quick Glance*

A society is the same
as a culture.　　　　T　F

A society has definite
geographical
boundaries.　　　　 T　F

Societies maintain
themselves through
conquering.　　　　 T　F

Societies are
becoming increasingly
interdependent.　　 T　F

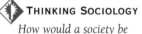

THINKING SOCIOLOGY

How would a society be studied scientifically from a macro level of analysis? From a micro level of analysis?

have not maintained themselves as a viable society. Societies like the Cheyenne Indians married women of certain other tribes and adopted the captured children, but this was not their primary method of meeting the reproductive needs of the society. Some modern societies such as France and Canada are concerned about their very low birth rate and are trying to encourage families to have more children.

Fourth, societies are relatively independent. This is much less true now than it used to be. Until recently, the Yanomamo of Brazil and Venezuela supplied most of the daily needs through their own efforts. Some groups of Native Americans have moved around mission centers and are now depending on the stores for much of what they need to eat and wear. The United States used to have an isolationist policy, but now economies all over the world are becoming more interdependent. I drive, for example, a "foreign" car made in the United States.

Fifth, society is organized around a complex division of labor. If I look at the Masaii, the basic division of labor is based on gender and age. If I look at a society such as the United States, I see a very complex division of labor based on age, sex, skill and education. In conclusion, a society is a fundamental group that profoundly influences our life choices. Culture is the basis for society.

▲ DIVISION OF LABOR AMONG THE MASAII IS LESS COMPLEX THAN IN THE U.S.A.

WHAT IS CULTURE?

Culture has a different meaning in the popular everyday English language from that of the sociological definition. We frequently consider a person to have culture when he or she likes the ballet and opera. The ballet and the opera are a part of the American culture; however, so is country and western music and the two step. A **culture** is the way of life of a society; a culture is the totality of what a member learns in a society. Culture gives me the skills I need to know in order to survive. For example, every day when I drive home from school, I drive past a herd of cattle. I brake my car, jump out with my knife, and butcher three fat juicy steaks! I think not! My culture has not taught me how to kill the cattle, let alone butcher it for steaks. Plus, I would be arrested for stealing another person's property. My culture teaches me the survival skills of going to the grocery store, picking out the meat for my family, and standing in line to purchase the food. In my culture, I learned how to operate a stove, rather than start a fire, and to prepare the food via the can opener, food processor and the microwave rather than in a brick oven or in a cauldron over an open fire.

▲ EACH CULTURE HAS ITS OWN ARTIFACTS.

THINKING SOCIOLOGY

How well do you think you would survive without electricity? What would happen to the U.S.A. culture without electricity?

WHAT ARE THE CHARACTERISTICS OF A CULTURE?

First, culture is not innate to humans, but rather learned. We are not born knowing a culture. When I get home from school, I like to have a crunchy snack. I have a readily available source of large wood roaches that I could fry and eat; roaches are high quality protein, nutritious, readily available and very cheap! I also have a plentiful supply of rats for my daughter's snake food; rats breed often and have large litters. I would not have to buy meat very often if I would eat rat. I could solve the cat and dog problem in our country; agencies such as Citizens for Animal Protection and the Humane Society have to euthanize a large number of homeless animals. If we would eat cat and dog in our culture, there would be a shortage rather than a surplus of these animals.

Americans eat oysters but not snails. The French eat snails but not locusts. The Zulus eat locusts but not fish. Jews eat fish but not pork. The Hindus eat pork but not beef. The Russians eat beef but not snakes. The Chinese eat snakes but not people. The Jale of New Guinea once found people delicious to eat. We learn from our culture what is appropriate food. No plant and animal can be defined as a proper diet innately, rather we learn what a proper diet consists of through living in a given culture.

We learn about our culture through the socialization process. Our parents reward us when we exhibit behavior that is acceptable for our culture. When I caught my two year old daughter eating dry cat food, I told her that was not acceptable food for her. The broccoli we find on our plates is what we are supposed to eat. When we learned to eat our broccoli with a fork, our parents told us what a great little girl or little boy we were. This reinforces appropriate behavior. However, when we talk with

Quick Glance

A culture is a way of life of a society.	T	F
Culture is innate.	T	F
Culture is shared by members of a society.	T	F
Culture is the same for every society.	T	F

food in our mouths, Mom may stare at us and call us by our entire given name rather than a favorite nickname. We learn what is and is not acceptable behavior for living in our culture. Socialization will be discussed in depth in the next chapter of *Sociology: Looking through the Window of the World*.

Second, members of a society share a culture. The American flag is a part of the American culture, along with the Liberty Bell and the Statue of Liberty. These items are symbols of the American culture and Americans share the knowledge of their meaning. The importance of these American symbols are passed down from one generation to another in families, schools, political organizations and religious groupings.

Third, culture is gratifying. We are very proud of our culture and feel that our culture beliefs and actions are the correct way. For example, I feel like my religion is the right religion, my form of dress is the most logical, and my food preferences are correct. The belief that my culture can be used as a yardstick by which to judge all other cultures is referred to as ethnocentrism. **Ethnocentrism** is the belief that one's culture is the right and the best way.

Horace Miner, in 1956, wrote an article entitled "Body Ritual among the Nacirema" to give Americans a parody on the American way of life. Nacirema is "American" spelled backwards! He described a daily barbaric Nacirema ritual of inserting bundles of bristles and magical powders into the mouth and then moving the bundle in a highly formalized series of gestures. "Strange and primitive," we might respond if we did not know that Miner was discussing the United State's culture. Many men daily scrape their faces with sharp instruments. We take people into a shrine to die. Females bake their heads in hot ovens with chemicals rubbed into the hair. This all sounds primitive, but Miner wanted Americans to step back from their culture and view American ritual from a different perspective.

In order for a culture to operate, we need to feel that our culture is the best, but we also need to understand other cultures and understand why other cultures are the way they are. One of the goals of this course is to enhance the student's awareness of cultural relativism. **Cultural relativism** is understanding and analyzing other cultures in terms of that culture's internal standards and conditions.

Fourth, culture is the basis for social solidarity. When we Native Texans are on a family vacation and stop at a tourist trap, we may find that the car parking next to us has Texas license plates too. We get out of our car and begin to talk with them, asking them where they live in Texas. We feel that this family shares a common interest and that provides us with a feeling of familiarity or solidarity as we share these elements.

Fifth, culture is adaptive. As conditions change, either social or physical conditions, a culture is modified. For example, as women have become more involved in sports and the economic world, our dress has changed. Scarlet O'Hara in "Gone With the Wind," looked beautiful in her gowns with the large hoops and crimped waist, but it would be rather difficult to get in and out of a car with such a skirt on the floor with a group of small children.

Sixth, culture is cumulative. The introduction of technology changes cultures. Black and white television sets changed the entertainment pleasures of the American culture; now we not only watch television but the picture is colored and large screen television sets with stereo sound have further changed entertainment. We now have an added choice of do we use a satellite dish, do we use digital or, like my daughter, do we use rabbit ears. Sports bars with large screens appeal to people as a place to combine television viewing with meeting people. Television viewing has brought about a concern for the amount of violence that our children become exposed to in any given day.

▲ TELEVISION VIEWING IS A PART OF THE AMERICAN CULTURE.
IMAGE COPYRIGHT IVAN JOSIFOVIC, 2008. USED UNDER LICENSE FROM SHUTTERSTOCK, INC.

During the past fifteen years, a new area of culture has emerged on the sociological scene. That is the idea of **popular culture**. Sociologists recognize that Americans identify variations in the enjoyment of dance and music according to social classes. Thus, a distinction can be made between high culture or that enjoyed by the upper class Americans and popular culture, activities enjoyed by the populace or middle class Americans. Someone frequenting the ballet and opera would be participating in high culture, while those who enjoy dancing the two step to country and western music would be participating in a form of popular culture. Examples of popular culture include baseball, movies, soap operas, wrestling and bubble gum chewing. Popular culture has become an endless source of study with some universities offering studies in popular culture. Bowling Green State University in Bowling Green, Ohio, has been a pioneer in the area of popular culture.

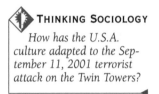

THINKING SOCIOLOGY

How has the U.S.A. culture adapted to the September 11, 2001 terrorist attack on the Twin Towers?

WHAT ARE THE COMPONENTS OF CULTURE?

A culture includes both material and nonmaterial culture. **Material culture** is the physical objects that people create and use. This includes everything from a straight pin to a complex computer system. There are several assumptions we need to be aware of when we talk about material culture. *First, we assume the use of our material culture.* If I had a gourd, I would more than likely use it as a centerpiece or make a bird house out of it. If I were a Masaii woman, I would use the gourd to collect milk or blood from my animals. *Second, we assume the value of material culture.* I can remember when we visited a small native village along the Amazon River. These people had little contact with the modern world. Several people gave dollars to the children, but the children just threw them on the ground. The children who were around the age of 10 much preferred a piece of gum or candy to the money, yet an American child of that age would have taken the money. *Third, we assume the meaning of material culture.* In our culture, a gold band on the left hand signifies marriage, but in other cultures they wear the bands on the right hand. If an American male saw a woman with a gold band on her right hand, he would figure that it was alright to date her, but her husband might have other ideas on the subject!

The wedding ring would be material culture, but the custom of the marriage ceremony would be nonmaterial culture. **Nonmaterial culture** is the adaptation of a culture to physical conditions. We shall discuss nonmaterial culture in the following paragraphs.

🔖 *Quick Glance*

Popular culture is a specialized part of culture.   T F

Different social classes may participate in different forms of popular culture.   T F

Ohio State University and Sam Houston State University are the founders of popular culture.   T F

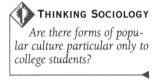

THINKING SOCIOLOGY

Are there forms of popular culture particular only to college students?

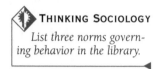

THINKING SOCIOLOGY

List three norms governing behavior in the library.

Quick Glance

Material culture is expensive culture.	T F
We assume use but not meaning of material culture.	T F
We always have to think about our norms.	T F
Norms never become automatic.	T F

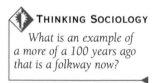

THINKING SOCIOLOGY

What is an example of a more of a 100 years ago that is a folkway now?

Quick Glance

A candle is an example of nonmaterial culture.	T F
A more is a norm.	T F
A folkway and a more are the same.	T F
Auguste Comte said there were two types of norms.	T F

Norms

Norms are expectations that are shared by members of a culture; norms are standards of conduct. An awareness of the norms in a society helps us better understand what acceptable behavior would be in a given situation. A student norm, for example, is that students will come to class prepared to take notes. Thus, the instructor expects that each student will come with a pencil and paper. Students can violate this norm by attending class and not taking notes during lecture, but both the instructor and other students might feel uncomfortable.

Norms serve three functions. *First, much of our behavior becomes automatic because we have learned the norms for our society.* We do not have to think about whether to drive on the right or left side of the road. The norm becomes internalized and this same thinking carries on into walking into the main school doors and walking down the mall corridor. We generally go to the right. *Second, we can predict the behavior of others because we know that they, too, have learned the norms.* We expect people to drive down the right side of the road; we do not worry about being served dog meat for dinner; we do not expect our students to get up and walk out of class or argue with us constantly. *Third, knowledge of the norms in my society helps me to survive.* If I were a Masaii woman, I would have to learn how to draw blood from a cow without killing it, but in my culture I have to learn how to manipulate through the drive-through window at KFC or McDonald's.

Folkways

William Sumner said that there are two types of norms: folkways and mores. **Folkways** are norms that our society would like us to follow but does not insist upon. I learn to eat my peas with a fork but my pudding with a spoon. If I grew up in the People's Republic of China, I would learn how to eat with chop sticks. I learn in the United States to clean my plate of all food or my hostess will think I did not like it. In China, however, if I clean my plate that means that I did not get enough to eat! Folkways include rules such as table manners and traditions. Folkways are generally transmitted in a culture informally and are usually informally enforced.

When getting on an elevator, we learn to turn and face the door. Because the child has often been taken on the elevator with Mom or Dad on shopping trips, the child internalizes the rule that when an individual enters an elevator, she/he turns around and faces the door opening of the elevator. If you are on an elevator and it stops on the third floor and a gentleman enters but remains facing the back of the elevator, everyone on the elevator is made very uncomfortable by this person's behavior. How would you respond? Would you get off the elevator on the fourth floor? The local police will not arrest this gentleman for the violation of this norm. However, the occupants on the elevator may well think of him as strange, maybe even dangerous.

Mores

Mores are norms that we consider essential for the survival of the society; our society insists that we follow the mores. We feel that if people do not follow the mores, we cannot maintain our culture, other cultures feel just as strongly about their mores. In our culture, the fundamental basis of mores originates from Judaic Christian beliefs. Some of the mores in our culture include not killing other people, not stealing, and honoring our mother and father.

Acceptance of folkways and mores may either be by custom or written down through the political process. When norms are written down through the political process, the norm is a **law**. For example, driving 20 miles per hour in a school zone is a law. Having a Christmas tree or eating turkey for Thanksgiving is a custom. Use of the English language is a custom in our country. (Use of the English language is also a more.) In Kenya, English is the official language so it is a law. If we should pass an amendment making English the official language of the land, then use of English would be law. Getting married and having about two children is a custom (and a more) in our country. Having one child has become public policy in the People's Republic of China; family size in China has become part of the law.

Many of our mores have become laws because we consider it extremely important that people follow them. A good example of this is child abuse. Parents have the responsibility of taking care of their children, both physically in the form of food, clothing, and housing and also emotionally—with much importance placed on a bond developing between the child and parent or parents. A father who drinks excessively, leaving very little money for his children to have shoes, may be viewed by his neighbors as an unfit father and neighbors may keep a watchful eye on the father for signs that he may be physically abusing the children. Failure to care for children is punishable by fine or jail sentence. Failure to report suspected child abuse is also part of our laws.

	Folkway	More
Law	Do not litter. Bicycles must stop at stop signs.	Do not commit child abuse. Do not steal a diamond ring.
Custom	Eat your peas with a fork. Open the door for an elderly person.	Speak the English language. Have children after marriage.

Sanctions

Folkways and mores are enforced through **sanctions**. Sanctions are rewards and punishments used to enforce the norms. There are four types of sanctions:

1. Informal positive: I praise my child when she cleans up her room.
2. Informal negative: I frown at a student who is disruptive in class.
3. Formal positive: I give a trophy to the high point winner of the swim meet.
4. Formal negative: I get a fine for exceeding the speed limit (when I get caught!).

We can now further explain folkways, mores, laws and customs in terms of sanctions. If you break a folkway, you are not severely sanctioned. For example, if I slurp my coffee or eat my peas with a spoon, I will not suffer serious consequences. You might frown at me for bad table manners, but I will not be ostracized from the group or put in prison. On the other hand, if I break a more, I face serious consequences. If I steal a four-carat diamond ring at gun point (and get caught), I face a prison term. A jury sentenced Andrea Yates to life in prison for the deaths of her five children in March, 2001.

A law is formally sanctioned. Or society has established punishments for breaking the laws. My son-in-law is either going to have to take defensive driving or pay a fine because he drove through a red light. Knowingly and deliberately killing another person results in life in prison or a possible death penalty as in the conviction of Andrea Yates. A custom is informally sanctioned. If I get on an elevator and look at other people, I will get funny looks and people might get off the elevator but I will

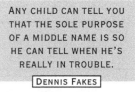

not be arrested. If I do not speak English, I will have more difficulty in conducting business but I will not receive any formal punishment through government process.

Values

Values are sentiments or ideas that form the core of every culture. Values tell us what is right and important for the culture. This word is used differently than in the popular language. I say that I value my diamond ring, but this is not the same sense of value for the sociologist.

Some of the identifiable values in our culture are:

1. belief in individual material comfort
2. belief in literacy and education for everybody
3. belief in hard work and efficient use of time
4. belief in rational thinking rather than philosophical thinking
5. belief in patriotism and democracy
6. belief in humanitarianism
7. belief in the ability to solve problems through rational thinking
8. belief in equality of all people
9. belief in moderation in all actions
10. belief in progress

The United States has existed for over 200 years plus with an idea of progress. Two hundred years ago, progress meant traveling to California or to the Alaskan gold mines. Our pioneer spirit has moved away from "go west young man, go west." The spirit now has us traveling to outer space.

There are some sociologists who believe that there has been an erosion of values today. According to Patterson and Kim, authors of *The Day America Told the Truth*, we, as a nation, do not have a moral concensus. Patterson and Kim believe that people are devising their own moral code and Ten Commandments. Here are the rules that many people actually live by according to Patterson and Kim:

1. I don't see the point in observing the Sabbath.
2. I will steal from those who won't really miss it.
3. I will lie when it suits me, so long as it doesn't cause any real damage.
4. I will drink and drive if I feel that I can handle it. I know my limit.
5. I will cheat on my spouse, after all, given the chance, he or she will do the same.
6. I will procrastinate at work and do absolutely nothing about one full day in every five. It's standard operating procedure.
7. I will use recreational drugs.
8. I will cheat on my taxes, to a point.
9. I will put my lover at risk of disease. I sleep around a bit, but who doesn't.
10. Technically, I may have committed date rape, but I know that she wanted it.

A set of values form the core of every culture. As the values differ, so do the cultures. For example, the Japanese culture stresses the importance of age and wisdom. As a consequence, the elderly in Japan are looked up to for knowledge and treated with great respect. Nursing homes or retirement homes for the elderly are not a viable option in Japan. In the United States, the value is on youth. We engage in a constant quest to try to remain young; we exercise, we dye our hair, we use all sorts of cosmetics and, if all else fails, we have a face lift.

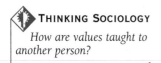

Learning TIP
After reading your text, write the answers to your questions on the backs of the index cards. Be sure to use your own words. Use these cards to study the material.

THINKING SOCIOLOGY
How are values taught to another person?

Quick Glance

Values remain the same over long periods of time.　　T　F

Some sociologists believe that values have eroded in recent time.　　T　F

Values form the core of every culture.　　T　F

Values are based on norms.　　T　F

THINKING SOCIOLOGY
Do you agree with Patterson and Kim? Why or why not? Take one value and list five norms based on your chosen value.

Our norms are based on our values. We value patriotism in our culture. As a consequence, we have such rules as when the National Anthem is played, we are to stand. When the flag is presented, we are to stand. Every school child has recited the Pledge of Allegiance many times. Our norms, in turn, determine our behavior. When the flag is presented, I stand up, just like everybody else does.

Language

Language is an abstract system of meanings and symbols for interacting within a culture. We learn the language of our culture just like we learn norms and values. For example, a father coaxing his year old son to say "daddy" will say "come on, say dada." The child finally utters something that resembles "dada" and dad is excited and praises the child (informal positive sanction); he may even taunt mom by saying that junior said "dad" before "mama." Does junior realize that the sound "da-da" stands for one individual in his life? The next day in the grocery store junior suddenly loudly mutters "da-da" and the one and only male on the grocer aisle reports, "No, I am not your father." Only through teaching does a child associate the sound "dada" with his father. A random sound comes to have a definite meaning. Parents and other people in a child's environment actively try to broaden a child's vocabulary and the child, himself, takes an active part in learning how to communicate.

The sounds in a language are arranged in what is referred to as grammar. For most individuals, grammar may be formally studied for almost 15 to 16 years of our life during the education process, but the study of grammar begins with the first learning of a language. For example, in English we have a subject such as "he" followed by the verb, but in many languages, such as Spanish, the subject is indicated by the ending on the verb. In English, the adjective comes before the noun, but in the Romance languages such as French and Spanish, the adjective frequently follows the noun.

Language includes not only the spoken language but body language as well. For example, the peace sign in our country means a vulgar sign in Great Britain. Space norms are another interesting aspect of body language, or kinetics. In our culture, the norm for space is arms length unless we are close friends or lovers. In many Spanish-speaking and Middle Eastern countries, space norms are much closer. A person reared in the United States of America may keep backing up, for example, while talking with a Cuban person; the Cuban keeps trying to close the space by walking towards us. And the two people proceed to dance across the floor with one taking a step forward and the other a step back.

Language serves several functions for a culture:

1. Language allows us to communicate ideas.
2. Language can stand for concepts and objects not physically present.
3. Language allows us to make judgments about events around us.
4. Language serves as a means of storing culture.
5. Language allows us to think, learn and plan for the future.
6. Language binds a society together.

Is there a relationship between understanding a given language and a culture? The **linguistic relativity hypothesis** (sometimes referred to as the Sapir-Whorf hypothesis) suggests that there is such a relationship. An example of this hypothesis would be chocolate mousse. Yum! We imagine this scrumptious dessert and we can almost taste it now in our imagination. However, to a small child the term "a chocolate mousse" might bring the perception of literally "a big brown moose." The book *A Chocolate Mousse for Dinner* aptly illustrates this hypothesis.

Quick Glance

Language is based on symbols.   T   F

Nonverbal language is not a part of culture.   T   F

Linguistic relativity hypothesis was written by Ogburn.   T   F

Sounds of a language are arranged according to grammar.   T   F

Language transmits but cannot store culture.   T   F

> TO BE AMIABLE IS TO BE SATISFIED WITH ONE'S SELF AND WITH OTHERS.
> WILLIAM HAZLITT

AUSTRALIAN WORD	U.S. WORD
LOLLY WATER	SODA/COKE
DODGER	BREAD
SAMMIE	SANDWICH
CACKLEBERRIES	EGGS
ICY POLE	POPSICLE

Quick Glance

Kinetics is not important in communication.   T   F

Understanding the rules of grammar is important in learning a new language.   T   F

Language forms one of the cements of culture.   T   F

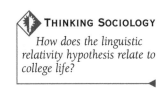

THINKING SOCIOLOGY

How does the linguistic relativity hypothesis relate to college life?

A second example would be verb tenses and idioms. English is a language rich in verb tenses. Spanish has even more tenses than English, but in active usage, Spanish-speaking citizens generally simplify the verb tenses. Spanish literature, however, is rich with the different verb tenses. The English-speaking people seem to have a compulsion about time. In English, the idiom says "time flies"; the idiom in Spanish is "time walks."

Color reflects the linguistic relativity hypothesis. The Navahos have two words for "black" but only one word for the colors we refer to as "blue" and "green." As a result, we are not sensitized to variations of black, and they do not easily differentiate between colors that we separate into blue and green.

Ideology and Urban Legends

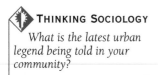

THINKING SOCIOLOGY

What is the latest urban legend being told in your community?

Every culture has an ideological system. **Ideology** is the ideas, beliefs, folklore, legends, proverbs and philosophy of a culture. We stress honesty with the story of George Washington telling the truth about cutting down the cherry tree; we stress achievement when we use the maxim, "A penny saved is a penny earned." We believe in romantic love, rather than financial advantage, in the choice of the marital partner.

An interesting new folklore that has emerged is called **urban legends**. These are legends that grow and develop in modern times. There was one legend floating around about the man who bought the Porsche for twenty-five cents. He was shocked at getting such a good deal, and asked the woman why she had sold it for so little. She responded that her ex-husband told her to get what she could for the car and send him the check. This is just one of the variations on the story. Perhaps you have heard another of the variations to this legend! There has even been several movies produced in the last several years based on urban legends.

Institutions

Quick Glance

Ideology is a cultural universal.　T　F

An example of ideology is the story of Paul Bunyan.　T　F

An institution is an organ of the culture.　T　F

There are six institutions in every society.　T　F

Institutions, which are the organs of the body of a culture, are clusters of norms centered around major human needs. These major human needs have to be met or we do not survive as a society. The needs include:

1. replacing of the population and maintaining health
2. distribution of goods and services
3. maintaining social order
4. providing meaning to our lives
5. socializing members into the culture

There are five basic institutions found in every society: family, education, economy, government and religion. We shall devote one chapter to each of these five major institutions.

Learning TIP
Talk to yourself about course information when you study.

WHAT IS THE DIFFERENCE BETWEEN IDEAL AND REAL CULTURE?

When we watch people, we discover that people show two types of uniformities. The first of these may be called *ideal* patterns. These are the models of exemplary conduct which are held up as standards of perfection. They represent what one "should do" or "ought to do" if he/she is to behave ideally. Suppose one were at a party at which inferior food was served and where the guests were dull and it was a bad evening. At the end of the evening, when paying the hostess the customary compliment, should one lie and be diplomatic, or tell the truth and offend her? Either choice violates a social code or norm. It is probable that in most cases diplomacy takes precedence over the truth.

There is a second set of behavior patterns. These are called *real*. They are real in the sense that they are what people actually do, irrespective of what they are ideally supposed to actually do, or what they, themselves, believe they should do. One notes that most people agree with the ideal that it is wrong to steal, but many compute their income tax in such a way as to pay the government less than they know they ought to, without regarding such behavior as theft. Having children after marriage (custom, more) is an ideal in our society. In reality, over half the babies born today are born to unwed parents. It is not as if ideal patterns are of no significance, but rather so long as ideal patterns exist, they tend to serve as checks upon real patterns, even though at times the checks seem not to be very effective. There always seems to be some morally sensitive people in a society who take ideal standards seriously. Such people perform the function of periodically reminding the members of the society of the inconsistencies between the real and ideal behavior patterns, and frequently they have originated significant changes making for a greater agreement between real and ideal patterns.

🕮 *Quick Glance*

Ideal culture is important, but real culture is not.   T F

Adultery is an example of real culture.   T F

Sociologists study real culture rather than ideal culture.   T F

◆ **THINKING SOCIOLOGY**

What are the differences in the ideal and real behavior patterns for people who cohabitate?

Ideal culture	Real Culture
Thou shalt not steal.	It is not really bad to take ashtrays from a motel room. It is okay to use the company xerox to copy three recipes. Most of us do not report a few cents extra in change from the grocery store.
Thou shalt not kill.	It is okay to kill if defending self or loved one. Capital punishment is okay. It is okay to kill in time of war. Police officer kills in the line of duty.

When there is a widespread discrepancy between what we do and what we say we do, it is a patterned evasion. We say we have children after marriage but many children are born outside of marriage. This is a patterned evasion. Driving speed is another good example of patterned evasion. Except in school zones, we routinely drive five to ten miles an hour over posted speed limits. In my neighborhood, for example, the major street is posted 35 mph but most of us drive right past the peace officer at 39 mph with no consequence.

WHAT ARE SUBCULTURES AND COUNTERCULTURES?

Within a large society such as the United States, subcultures develop. A **subculture** shares the common culture but has norms, and perhaps values, that set a number of people apart from the rest of society. We have subcultures based on social class. When I see someone drive up in a Rolls Royce, wearing a ten carat diamond, and having lunch with Condoleezza Rice, Secretary of State or Prince Charles, I can identify the subculture of "the upper crust." Subcultures can be based on occupations. When I see someone walking around our school halls with a ceramic mug, folder of notes and a lectern, I put them in the subculture of "teacher." Subcultures can be based on ethnic differences. In Texas, there is a very large group of Germans. Every

🕮 *Quick Glance*

A counterculture goes against the basic values of the society.   T F

The Royalty of Great Britain is an example of a subculture.   T F

Subcultures are based only on ethnic or racial characteristics.   T F

Jewish Americans form a counterculture in the U.S.A.   T F

THINKING SOCIOLOGY

What subcultures and counter cultures do you belong?

Learning TIP
Sit in the first row. There are less distractions.

Quick Glance

Social change occurs rapidly in all societies. T F

Social change happens only in industrial societies.　　T F

Social change is always deliberate.　　T F

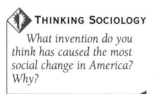

THINKING SOCIOLOGY

What invention do you think has caused the most social change in America? Why?

fall, Octoberfests are celebrated. Each year in Houston, we have a Greek Festival featuring dancing, music and food of the Mediterranean area. Subcultures can be based on religion. For example, if I celebrate the religious day on Friday, wear a star of David, and celebrate Hanukkah and Yom Kippur, I probably am Jewish. Subcultures can be based on region. Texas, for example, has even threatened several times to form their own country. There is a dictionary on how to speak "Texan" and we are very proud of our Tex-Mex food.

A **counterculture** goes against the basic norms and values of the culture. For example, the Moonies or the Hippies of the fifties are examples of counter cultures. The Hippies did not believe in individual success and felt that mainstream culture was entirely too materialistic. The Al-Qaida is a counter culture of Islam. The Branch Davidians and Heaven's Gate were religious counter cultures here in the United States. Counter cultures can bring about social change but they can also be disruptive of the social order.

HOW DOES A CULTURE CHANGE?

Social change is the process which is caused by alterations in the structure of society. All societies are changing, some societies are just changing faster than others. For example, for many years the Yanomamo Indians had a very slow rate of change. But now that they have come into contact with missionaries and industrialists, the rate of change has escalated among these Indians as they add new religious ideas, steel axes and hoes to their culture base.

Sometimes change is a deliberate event; sometimes it is accidental. Sometimes it is harmful, and sometimes it is beneficial. For example, we have slowly changed the English language as we have introduced more words from the space and computer age into the language such as "byte." We have also planned for change; the research done on tuberculosis and heart disease is setting out to lower death rates from these diseases. During the 1940s and 1950s, many children died or were crippled from polio, while children of the 1960s to present time no longer worry about polio. Scientists around the world are now trying to come up with a cure or a vaccine to control AIDS.

There are several processes of social change. The first process of change is innovations. **Innovation** is the process of introducing a new element into a culture. There are two types of innovation. First is invention. **Invention** is the creation of something new. A ceramic which could withstand all sorts of temperature variation from the very cold to the very hot could be an invention. Second is discovery. **Discovery** is the recognition of something not previously known. This would include such things as the use of this ceramic in cookingware and stove tops. The distinction between invention and discovery is not always clear cut.

The amount of innovation in a culture is affected by several variables. *First, innovation is influenced by the mental ability of a group of people.* If the people are desperately trying to get enough food to eat or large numbers of them are suffering from ill health, there is little time or energy left to come up with something new.

Second, demand impacts the amount of innovation. Women used to not wear much makeup nor did they engage in physically stressful sports. But both those factors have changed and they wanted a mascara that did not run in black rivers down their faces when it got wet with perspiration or swimming pool water. They now have waterproof mascara! Then there was a demand for something to take off the mascara and industry provided mascara removers!

Third, existing knowledge predisposes a culture to more or less innovations. The larger the culture base of technology, the more innovations there will be. The rate of innovation seemed very slow for early humans, but that is because they had a primitive technology with stone tools. In modern society, we have a very broad technological base and a rapid and constant increase in innovations. Just look at the multiplication of services and gadgets associated with the telephone.

Fourth, the slant of the culture controls how many innovations and what kind of innovations there are. Societies like our own encourage social change, but traditional societies do not want a great deal of change. An example of this is the feelings about the roles of women. In the United States, we are striving for equal pay and jobs, but in Iraq there is strong pressure to keep women in traditional roles.

The second process of social change is diffusion. **Diffusion** is the spread of an item of culture from its place of origin. This spread can be between individuals, groups or societies. Diffusion is influenced by several factors. *The first element is the form of the culture.* Material culture generally diffuses much more quickly than does nonmaterial culture. For example, Western suits are worn in many areas of the world. Western television shows are watched all the way from Italy to the People's Republic of China. *Second is the amount of coercion involved.* During the reigns of Elizabeth I and Mary, Queen of Scots, each tried to force their religion onto the people they ruled. More than one royal lost titles and land due to disagreeing with the ruler. *The third catalyst is the intensity of culture contact.* Along the Mexico-Texas border, there is much exchange of food and language. We say a party is a "fiesta" and we like "Tex-Mex" food. *The fourth factor is the amount of culture inertia.* Some cultures do not want to adopt new ideas either from internal forces or from other cultures.

Even in our own culture, certain areas are slow to change. Spelling is a good example of this. Many of the words in our language would really be better spelled in alternative ways. For example, "through" would make more sense spelled as "thru" or "intuition" would make more sense spelled as "intuishun." If you try spelling these words the way they sound, it would result in several wrong marks on an English paper!

Fifth, a crisis situation contributes to people and societies adopting a new idea or material trait. For example, during World War II we invented and used artificial rubber. Native peoples are more apt to accept Western medicine during a measles or mumps epidemic. A crisis situation can include changes in the physical environment. If there has been a long drought, people might change their food preference. The Cheyenne Indians moved from their hunting and gathering existence in the forest lands onto the prairie as a result of forces pushing them out of their traditional lands. Once on the open ranges, they changed their hunting pattern to using horses and started to hunt buffalo as a major staple in their diet.

Societies which are stationary, or nonchanging, differ from changing societies. A stationary society tends to avoid experimentation, while a changing society likes to try something new in as many areas as possible. A stationary society believes in the inevitable nature of events, while the changing societies maintains the belief in progress. In a stationary society, elders are more apt to hold the reins, but in a changing society, younger people control the society. The past guides the behavior in a stationary society, but convenience governs behavior in a changing society. In a stationary society, the past is held in great esteem. This contrasts with the changing society's belief that the past is a burden and needs to be conquered.

Several other factors need to be considered when we talk about the amount of change in a culture. If an item of culture is compatible with the existing culture, we are much more accepting of that material or nonmaterial culture. For example, we have many more women in our country than men, particularly in the older age groups. For social and financial reasons, it might make sense to allow for polygyny among our elderly by allowing elderly men to marry more than one woman. How-

🜩 *Quick Glance*

Social change comes about through invention and diffusion.   T F

Invention and discovery are the same process. T F

Diffusion involves borrowing from other cultures.   T F

THINKING SOCIOLOGY
What foods have been diffused into U.S.A. diets?

🜩 *Quick Glance*

In the U.S.A., we accept all sorts of change.   T F

Coercion slows the rate of social change.   T F

Changing societies avoid experimentation.   T F

The past governs a stationary society.   T F

A crisis situation handicaps social change.   T F

THINKING SOCIOLOGY
Which age group do you think is most apt to try or do something new? Why? What social class do you think is most apt to try or do something new? Why?

Quick Glance

The introduction of a new antibiotic in the U.S.A. is substitutive. T F

Cultural lag is the same as future shock. T F

We experience future shock from rapid change. T F

People moving from a Third World Country into the U.S.A. may experience future shock. T F

Society and culture form the foundation of society. T F

THINKING SOCIOLOGY

When have you suffered from "future shock"? What caused you to feel this way? How did you feel?

ever, as a culture, we have a strong belief in monogamy. We are more than willing to accept ball games such as soccer and rugby into our cultures because we have a strong cultural liking for ball games.

If an item of culture is additive, we are much more apt to accept it into our culture. Additive means that we can keep what we already have and add something new. If an item of culture is substitutive, we may or may not accept it. This means I have to give up something in my own culture and bring in something new. When modern medical personnel have gone into preliterate society and tried to supplant the local medicine man, they often met with resistance. However, when modern medical people were willing to work with the local medical person or shaman, people were more accepting. This made the help additive rather than substitutive. Bringing in new ball games in our culture is additive but changing the form of marriage would be substitutive.

▲ CULTURAL CONFIGURATIONS DIFFER FROM CULTURE TO CULTURE.
IMAGE COPYRIGHT INGVALD KALDHUSSATER, 2008. USED UNDER LICENSE FROM SHUTTERSTOCK, INC.

There are several effects from cultural change. First, a society may experience cultural lag. This term was introduced by William Ogburn. **Cultural lag** occurs when any one aspect of a culture lags behind another aspect to which it is related. Many airports do not meet the needs of modern aviation travel; our highway system in the cities cannot utilize the power in the cars that we drive today. Our electoral college was developed in the time of horse and buggy; with changes in technology, we could now use a popular vote for electing a president rather than the electoral college system.

In the process of cultural change, we may experience future shock. Alvin Toffler said that **future shock** often results from rapid change. When we are victims of future shock, we feel like the changes are happening too fast for us to adjust. These feelings include bewilderment, frustration and disorientation.

We can also talk about **culture shock**. Anthropologist, Ruth Benedict, referred to "cultural configurations" suggesting that when people encounter a new culture, there are differences that can be seen, heard and felt. Thus, people can sense the existence of a culture that differs from their own. When these differences are vast, we can experience "culture shock." It may take some time to adjust to these differences in religion, food, dress and/or language.

Society and culture form the foundation of all that we study in sociology. Society is the basic unit of social organization and culture is the way of life of a society. In the next chapter, we shall discuss how you learn to operate in your society by learning your culture.

▼ Chapter Summary

1. Society is the fundamental group of social organization. Characteristics of society are: breeding ground of culture, occupation of a definite geographical territory, maintenance primarily through sexual reproduction, relative independence, organization around a complex division of labor.
2. Culture is the way of life of a society. Characteristics are: learned, shared by members of society, gratifying, basis for social solidarity, adaptive and cumulative. Subcultures and counter cultures may exist within a society.
3. The components of a culture include both material culture (objects people create and use) and nonmaterial culture (norms, values, sanctions, language, ideology, institutions). The distinction needs to be made between real and ideal culture.
4. There are two types of norms: folkways and mores. Other terms to analyze norms are law and custom.
5. Four types of sanctions are important for enforcing the norms: informal positive, informal negative, formal positive and formal negative.
6. Characteristics of language include: communicating ideas, standing for concepts and objects, allowing for judgments, storing culture, allowing for thinking, learning and planning and binding a society together.
7. Institutions meet human needs: replacing of population, distributing of goods and services, maintaining order, providing meaning and socializing members.
8. Two processes of social change are innovation and diffusion. Innovation includes invention and discovery while diffusion is the spread of an idea or technology from its point of origin.
9. People experience cultural lag, future shock and culture shock when social change is rapid.

▼ References

Benedict, Ruth. 1946. *Patterns of Culture*. New York: Mentor.

Chagnon, Napoleon. 1983. *Yanomamo: The Fierce People*. Fort Worth, Texas: Holt, Rinehart and Winston.

Gwynne, Fred. 1976. *A Chocolate Mousse for Dessert*. New York: Prentice-Hall Books for Young Readers.

Hall, Edward T. 1959. *The Silent Language*. Garden City, New York: Doubleday.

Hoebel, E. Adamson. 1978. *The Cheyennes: Indians of the Great Plains*. Fort Worth, Texas: Holt, Rinehart and Winston.

Kephart, William. 1987. *Extraordinary Groups*. New York: St. Martin's Press.

Kluckhohn, Clyde. 1949. *Mirror for Man: Anthropology and Modern Life*. New York: McGraw-Hill.

Lamb, David. 1987. *The Arabs: Journeys Beyond the Mirage*. New York: Random House.

Murdock, George. 1965. *Social Structure*. New York: Free Press.

Ogburn, W. F. 1922. *Social Change: With Respect to Culture and Original Nature*. New York: B.W. Huebsch.

Park, Myung-Seok. 1979. *Communication Styles in Two Different Cultures: Korean and American*. Seoul: Han Shin.

Patterson, James and Peter Kim. 1991. *The Day America Told the Truth*. New York: Prentice Hall.

Summer, William Graham. 1907. *Folkways*. Boston: Ginn.

Toffler, Alvin. 1970. *Future shock*. New York: Bantam Book.

Williams, Robin. 1970. *American Society: A Sociological Interpretation, 3rd Edition*. New York: Knopf.

READING

EXCERPT ("MOTHER COW") FROM COWS, PIGS, WARS, AND WITCHES
BY MARVIN HARRIS*

Whenever I get into discussions about the influence of practical and mundane factors on lifestyles, someone is sure to say, "But what about all those cows the hungry peasants in India refuse to eat?" The picture of a ragged farmer starving to death alongside a big fat cow conveys a reassuring sense of mystery to Western observers. In countless learned and popular allusions, it confirms our deepest conviction about how people with inscrutable Oriental minds ought to act. It is comforting to know— somewhat like "there will always be an England"—that in India spiritual values are more precious than life itself. And at the same time it makes us feel sad. How can we ever hope to understand people so different from ourselves? Westerners find the idea that there might be a practical explanation of Hindu love of cow more upsetting than Hindus do. The sacred cow—how else can I say it?—is one of our favorite sacred cows.

Hindus venerate cows because cows are the symbol of everything that is alive. As Mary is to Christians the mother of God, the cow to Hindus is the mother of life. So there is no greater sacrilege for a Hindu than killing a cow. Even the taking of human life lacks the symbolic meaning, the unutterable defilement, that is evoked by cow slaughter.

According to many experts, cow worship is the number one cause of India's hunger and poverty. Some Western-trained agronomists say that the taboo against cow slaughter is keeping one hundred million "useless" animals alive. They claim that cow worship lowers the efficiency of agriculture because the useless animals contribute neither milk nor meat while competing for croplands and foodstuff with useful animals and hungry human beings. A study sponsored by the Ford Foundation in 1959 concluded that possibly half of India's cattle could be regarded as surplus in relation to food supply. And an economist from the University of Pennsylvania stated in 1971 that India has thirty million unproductive cows.

It does seem that there are enormous numbers of surplus, useless, and uneconomic animals, and that this situation is a direct result of irrational Hindu doctrines. Tourists on their way through Delhi, Calcutta, Madras, Bombay, and other Indian cities are astonished at the liberties enjoyed by stray cattle. The animals wander through the streets, browse off the stalls in the market place, break into private gardens, defecate all over the sidewalks, and snarl traffic by pausing to chew their cuds in the middle of busy intersections. In the countryside the cattle congregate on the shoulders of every highway and spend much of their time taking leisurely walks down the railroad tracks.

Love of cow affects life in many ways. Government agencies maintain old age homes for cows at which owners may board their dry and decrepit animals free of charge. In Madras, the police round up stray cattle that have fallen ill and nurse them back to health by letting them graze on small fields adjacent to the station house. Farmers regarding their cows as members of the family, adorn them with garlands and tassels, pray for them when they get sick, and call in their neighbors and a priest to celebrate the birth of a new calf. Throughout India, Hindus hang on their walls calendars that portray beautiful, bejeweled young women who have the bodies of big fat white cows. Milk is shown jetting out of each teat of these half-women, half-zebu goddesses.

Quick Glance

Americans are ethnocentric when judging the Indian's attitude towards the cow.   T F

Hindus like cows so much because they symbolize life.   T F

It is more serious to kill a cow than a person according to the article.   T F

Cows have more freedom in India than the U.S.A.   T F

Quick Glance

The government helps provide for homeless cattle.   T F

The cows are well fed and healthy in India.   T F

Zebu cows are good milk producers.   T F

Starting with their beautiful human faces, cow pinups bear little resemblance to the typical cow one sees in the flesh. For most of the year their bones are their most prominent feature. Far from having milk gushing from every teat, the gaunt beasts barely manage to nurse a single calf to maturity. The average yield of whole milk from the typical hump-backed breed of zebu cow in India amounts to less than 500 pounds a year. Ordinary American dairy cattle produce over 5,000 pounds, while for champion milkers, 20,000 pounds is not unusual. But this comparison doesn't tell the whole story. In any given year about half of India's zebu cows give no milk at all—not a drop.

To Western observers familiar with modern industrial techniques of agriculture and stock raising, cow love seems senseless, even suicidal. The efficiency experts yearn to get his hands on all those useless animals and ship them off to a proper fate. And yet one finds certain inconsistencies in the condemnation of cow love. When I began to wonder if there might be a practical explanation for the sacred cow, I came across an intriguing government report. It said that India had too many cows but too few oxen. With so many cows around, how could there be a shortage of oxen? Oxen and male water buffalo are the principal source of traction for plowing India's fields. For each farm of ten acres or less, one pair of oxen or water buffalo is considered adequate. A little arithmetic shows that as far as plowing is concerned, there is indeed a shortage rather than a surplus of animals. India has 60 million farms, but only 80 million traction animals. If each farm had its quota of two oxen or two water buffalo, there ought to be 120 million traction animals—that is, 40 million more than are actually available.

The shortage of draft animals is a terrible threat that hangs over most of India's peasant families. When an ox falls sick a poor farmer is in danger of losing his farm. If he has no replacement for it, he will have to borrow money at usurious rates. Millions of rural households have in fact lost all or part of their holdings and have gone into sharecropping or day labor as a result of such debts. Every year hundreds of thousands of destitute farmers end up migrating to the cities, which already teem with unemployed and homeless persons.

The Indian farmer who can't replace his sick or deceased ox is in much the same situation as an American farmer who can neither replace nor repair his broken tractor. But there is an important difference: tractors are made by factories, but oxen are made by cows. A farmer who owns a cow owns a factory for making oxen. With or without cow love, this is a good reason for him not to be too anxious to sell his cow to the slaughterhouse. One also begins to see why Indian farmers might be willing to tolerate cows that give only 500 pounds of milk per year. If the main economic function of the zebu cow is to breed male traction animals, then there's no point in comparing her with specialized American dairy animals, whose main function is to produce milk. Still, the milk produced in zebu cows play an important role in meeting the nutritional needs of many poor families. Even small amounts of milk products can improve the health of people who are forced to subsist on the edge of starvation.

Agriculture is part of a vast system of human and natural relationships. To judge isolated portions of this "ecosystem" in terms that are relevant to the conduct of American agribusiness leads to some very strange impressions. Cattle figure in the Indian ecosystem in ways that are easily overlooked or demeaned by observers from industrialized high-energy societies. In the United States, chemicals have almost completely replaced animal manure as the principal source of farm fertilizer. American farmers stopped using manure when they began to plow with tractors rather than mules or horses. Since tractors excrete poisons rather than fertilizers, a commitment to large-scale machine farming is almost of necessity a commitment to the use of

☙ *Quick Glance*

India has too many oxen and too few cows.   T   F

Oxen are used like tractors.   T   F

The small farmer needs at least two teams of oxen.   T   F

☙ *Quick Glance*

The manifest function of the cow is different in India than the U.S.A.   T   F

If India moved toward agribusiness, many jobs would be lost.   T   F

Cow waste is good fertilizer.   T   F

Cow dung makes a good substitute for wood and coal.   T   F

chemical fertilizers. And around the world today there has, in fact, grown up a vast integrated petrochemical-tractor-truck industrial complex that produces farm machinery, motorized transport, oil and gasoline, and chemical fertilizers and pesticides upon which new high-yield production techniques depend.

For better or worse, most of India's farmers cannot participate in this complex, not because they worship their cows, but because they can't afford to buy tractors. Like other underdeveloped nations, India can't build factories that are competitive with the facilities of the industrialized nations nor pay for large quantities of imported industrial products. To convert from animals and manure to tractors and petrochemicals would require the investment of incredible amounts of capital. Moreover, the inevitable effect of substituting costly machines for cheap animals is to reduce the number of people who can earn their living from agriculture and to force a correspondence increase in the size of the average farm. We know that the development of large-scale agribusiness in the United States has meant the virtual destruction of the small family farm. Less than five percent of U.S. families now live on farms, as compared with 60 percent about a hundred years ago. If agribusiness were to develop along similar lines in India, jobs and housing would soon have to be found for a quarter of a billion displaced peasants.

As I have already pointed out, cows and oxen provide low-energy substitutes for tractors and tractor factories. They also should be credited with carrying out the functions of a petrochemical industry. India's cattle annually excrete about 700 million tons of recoverable manure. Approximately half of this is used as fertilizer, while most of the remainder is burned to provide heat for cooking. The annual quantity of heat liberated by this dung, the Indian housewife's main cooking fuel, is the thermal equivalent of 27 million tons of kerosene, 35 million tons of coal, or 68 million tons of wood. Since India has only small reserves of oil and coal and is already the victim of extensive deforestation, none of these fuels can be considered practical substitutes for cow dung. The thought of dung in the kitchen may not appeal to the average American, but Indian women regard it as superior cooking fuel because it is finely adjusted to their domestic routines. Most Indian dishes are prepared with clarified butter known as *ghee*, for which cow dung is the preferred source of heat since it burns with a clean, slow, longlasting flame that doesn't scorch the food. This enables the Indian housewife to start cooking her meals and to leave them unattended for several hours while she takes care of the children, helps out in the fields, or performs other chores. American housewives achieve a similar effect through a complex set of electronic controls that come as expensive options on late-model stoves.

Cow dung has at least one other major function. Mixed with water and made into a paste, it is used as a household flooring material. Smeared over a dirt floor and left to harden into a smooth surface, it keeps the dust down and can be swept clean with a broom.

Because cattle droppings have so many useful properties, every bit of dung is carefully collected. Village small fry are given the task of following the family cow around and of bringing home its daily petrochemical output. In the cities, sweeper castes enjoy a monopoly on the dung deposited by strays and earn their living by selling it to housewives.

From an agribusiness point of view, a dry and barren cow is an economic abomination. But from the viewpoint of the peasant farmer, the same dry and barren cow may be a last desperate defense against the moneylenders. There is always the chance that a favorable monsoon may restore the vigor of even the most decrepit specimen and that she will fatten up, calve, and start giving milk again. This is what the farmer prays for; sometimes his prayers are answered. In the meantime, dung-making goes on. And so one gradually begins to understand why a skinny old hag of a cow still looks beautiful in the eyes of her owner.

Quick Glance

Cow dung can make a good building material. T F

Cow dung provides a useful occupation for children. T F

City sweepers cannot make money selling dung. T F

THINKING SOCIOLOGY

We tend to be ethnocentric when we think about keeping skinny, barren cows. What are three things we use routinely in the U.S.A. or do in the U.S.A. that other cultures might think odd?

Seeking the Self

4

IMAGE COPYRIGHT JASON STITT, 2008. USED UNDER LICENSE FROM SHUTTERSTOCK, INC.

CHAPTER OBJECTIVES

1. What is socialization?
2. What are the functions of socialization?
3. What are the socialization processes?
4. What is the nature versus nurture debate?
5. What impact does biological inheritance have on socialization?
6. What are the social factors in the socialization process?
7. What is self-concept?
8. What is the sociological perspective of the self or me?
9. What is anticipatory socialization?
10. What is adult socialization?
11. What are the differences between adult and childhood socialization?
12. What is resocialization?
13. What are the agencies of socialization?

adult socialization: the socialization occurring during the adult years

agencies of socialization: the groups and institutions which have an influence on socialization

anticipatory socialization: the learning of skills and values needed for future roles

bonding: the process of meeting human emotional needs

dramaturgical approach: the analysis of interaction based on learning scripts and acting out the roles in the different stages of life

face-work: the striving to maintain the proper image in social interaction

feral child: a child raised in isolation

generalized other: the term for generally held beliefs, attitudes, viewpoints and expectations of society as a whole

impression management: an individual's effort to try to guide and control impressions other people form

looking-glass self: the self as the product of our interaction with other people

marker event: an event that dramatically alters an individual's life or thought patterns

modal personality: a personality type characteristic of the members of a culture

nature versus nurture: a long-standing debate over whether personality results from genetic basis or socialization

resocialization: the unlearning and relearning, basic and rapid change within the self concept

role-taking: the process whereby we learn the norms necessary to perform a role

self-concept: that personality component which helps us to understand who we are, what we are worth, and even where we are going

significant other: the specific person in our social environment whose approval and affection are very important to us

socialization: the process by which we internalize our culture

sociobiology: the systematic study of the biological basis of social behavior

total institutions: a highly controlled social environment

▼ KEY PEOPLE

Orville Brime, Charles Cooley, Kingsley Davis, Irving Goffman, Harry Harlow, Marvin Harris, Daniel Levinson, George Herbert Mead, Wilburt Moore, Rene Spitz, Edward Wilson

WHAT IS SOCIALIZATION?

After approximately a nine-month incubation period, we arrive into the world as a screaming blob of protoplasm. We scream all night, we sleep most of the day, we have thin white stuff put in a cavity at the front and either regurgitate it out the same cavity or make a mess at the other end of a long muscular tube. Some way or another we have to get this little organism to realize that we sleep during the night, we do not throw up all over near adult organisms and bodily wastes can only be put in certain places. The process by which the organism learns these rules, or norms, is through the process of socialization. Socialization is that process whereby we learn to live in a particular culture. It is during the socialization process that we learn the attitudes, norms, values and behaviors that are necessary to function in our respective culture. The socialization process has at least two identifiable outcomes:

1. *It is during the socialization process that sociologists assert that we create human beings.* It is during this socialization process that humans develop the capacity and skills to think, love and communicate.
2. *It is the socialization process that is the means by which a society is maintained.* Through the socialization process, individuals learn the culture in which they were born or to which they immigrated. It is only through this very important process that a society is able to maintain itself from one generation to another.

When discussing the socialization process, the tendency is to see it as a perfect process. However, the socialization process is not always a perfect one. On any given day, our local radio, television and printed news will offer us numerous indications that there are individuals who exist in our society who have not totally learned the norms. Unfortunately, the United States, and other cultures as well, has adults who physically, sexually and psychologically abuse their children; spouses physically and psychologically mistreat each other; and people commit robberies, assaults and other crimes.

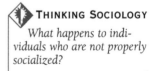

I WANT TO BE ABLE AS DAYS GO BY, ALWAYS TO LOOK MYSELF STRAIGHT IN THE EYE.
EDGAR A. GUEST

WHAT ARE THE FUNCTIONS OF SOCIALIZATION?

Through the socialization process the child will master the major elements of his/her culture:

1. *The child will learn the language of the culture.* Not only will the child learn the written and spoken language, but he/she will also learn the body language or nonverbal language.
2. *The child will enter a network of social relationships as he/she learns to live in the respective culture.* He/she will learn how to get along with others in his/her culture. If I am a Yanomamo male, I will learn to be fierce; if I am a Zuni male, I will learn to be very cooperative.
3. *The child will learn the norms of her/his society.* In the United States' culture, she/he will learn to eat with a knife, fork and spoon rather than with fingers or chopsticks.
4. *The child will determine what should be his/her goals and ambitions.* Through socialization we teach the child what is worth achieving. Let us share with you several examples. We might teach our children that some of their goals include obtaining a good job and family. These were some of the goals taught in my family. I was to get a good education so that I could get a good job. I

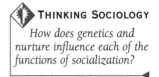

THINKING SOCIOLOGY
What happens to individuals who are not properly socialized?

THINKING SOCIOLOGY
How does genetics and nurture influence each of the functions of socialization?

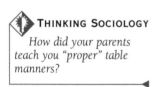

THINKING SOCIOLOGY

*How did your parents
teach you "proper" table
manners?*

needed a good job because I expected to marry and have children; I would need to help support a family. Marrying, having children, getting an education and obtaining a good job are important goals in the United States' culture. We frequently teach our children to be competitive and high achievers; these are also goals. If I were a Coahuiltecan Native American of South Texas, I would have taught my children not how to be competitive and get a good education, but, rather, how to be top notch fisherpersons, hunters and gatherers. Rather than stressing competition, I would have emphasized cooperation.

5. *The child will master technological skills needed to operate within the culture.* I learned, for example, how to drive a car and how to use a computer. If I am an Amish girl, I shall learn how to can fruits and vegetables and make and design quilts.

6. *The child will need to become familiar with the territory of his/her culture.* I need to know as a female that I do not go into the men's restroom at a football game; I learn that I do not laugh outrageously at a funeral or act somber at a wedding.

WHAT ARE THE SOCIALIZATION PROCESSES?

Socialization does not take place innately but rather is learned through several different social processes:

1. *Explicit instruction is an important means for socializing the child.* Teachers, religious leaders and parents use this technique. For example, I had my daughter watch my hands in order to show the motions of crocheting an afghan and gave her verbal instructions on how to turn on the ignition switch and turn the lights on in the car.

2. *Socialization can take place through conditioning.* If I associate a reward with a behavior, I shall continue with that behavior; if I am punished, I might stop the particular behavior. When my daughter was swimming competitively, we would give her a stuffed animal when she swam faster than she had the week before. This is a positive reward. This could be a formal or informal positive sanction. As we grow older, we start to reward our own behavior. When I sit down and grade a complete stack of papers, I mentally pat myself on the back and tell myself how great I am! When I make the four year old take "time out," when she hits her two year old sister, I am punishing her. I am hoping that this will stop the abusive behavior. My oldest child keeps up with her homework and maintains good grades because she does not want us to "get on her case." This would be negative reinforcement. In summary, conditioning can involve positive reinforcement, negative reinforcement or punishment. Positive reinforcement is something pleasant. Negative reinforcement is preventing something bad from happening to us. Punishment is something negative being done to us. Through all three avenues, we hope to have a change in behavior.

3. *Socialization can result from role modeling.* A child watches another person's behavior and begins to act like the other person. One of the things that I do when I cook is put the empty egg shell back in the carton; my daughters both follow the same behavior pattern. I might also add that children very quickly pick up their parents "naughty words" and personal mannerisms.

4. *Socialization can occur through innovation.* If I come upon a behavioral pattern through experimentation or chance that solves my problem, I will continue

in this behavioral pattern. My daughter "threw kisses" when she was a toddler. She came upon this behavior herself, but it got her plenty of attention, so she continued on with it!

WHAT IS THE NATURE VERSUS NURTURE DEBATE?

Biological inheritance influences how we are socialized. We have a very long period of infant dependency and this gives adult figures among humans a long time to teach us everything we need to know. In some cultures, a child remains dependent on an adult figure until age eleven or twelve, but, in cultures like our own, child dependency on the parents may last well into the twenties.

▲ IT IS DURING THE SOCIALIZATION PROCESS THAT A FEELING OF SELF IS FORMED.
IMAGE COPYRIGHT DARREN BAKER, 2008. USED UNDER LICENSE FROM SHUTTERSTOCK, INC.

It is during the socialization process that a feeling of self is formed. There is, of course, a controversy concerning how much of a part nurturing plays during that socialization and how much nature plays. This debate over **nature versus nurture** is longstanding and is the same as the concern of genetic basis versus socialization. These are actually two opposite ends of the continuum and many social scientists suggest that both nature and nurture are important for the formation of personality.

Sociobiology stresses the nature side of the long-standing debate. **Sociobiology** views our social behavior as having a biological base. Edward O. Wilson, a Harvard professor, coined the term sociobiology. According to Wilson, sociobiology is the systematic study of the biological basis of social behavior. He argues that a study of human behavior must begin with our genetic heritage. The discipline of sociobiology makes two basic assumptions:

1. Social behavior is partly determined by genetic factors.
2. Social behavior is partly innate; social behavior is influenced by evolution through natural selection.

Sociobiologists view social behaviors such as friendship, aggression, altruism, parental care and parental affection as having a genetic base. For example, I shall fight harder to save my child than my cousin because my child will more directly carry on my genetic structure. I shall care for my child because that child carries my genes. Research has indicated that when a new male chimpanzee becomes "head chimp," he may kill existing babies because he wishes the females to conceive with his sperm and, thus, genetic structure. This supposition has been the basis of the theory of child abuse against step children.

Wilson has been harshly criticized. One criticism has come from anthropologist, Marvin Harris (you read his article in the reading for Chapter 3). Harris suggests that there is too much cultural diversity to explain human behavior biologically. Another criticism of Wilson comes from Lewontin, Rose and Kamin in the book *Not in Our*

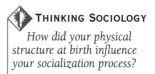

ALWAYS LISTEN TO EXPERTS. THEY'LL TELL YOU WHAT CAN'T BE DONE AND WHY. THEN DO IT.
ROBERT A. HEINLEIN

THINKING SOCIOLOGY
Is altruism learned? or innate? Support your answer.

THINKING SOCIOLOGY
How did your physical structure at birth influence your socialization process?

Genes. They suggest that the first principle of developmental genetics is that every organism is the unique product of the interaction between genes and environment at every stage of life.

Quick Glance

Reflexes play a role in the socialization process.   T F

Our gender influences the way we are socialized.   T F

Weight and height of child influence the socialization process.   T F

Personality is genetically determined.   T F

WHAT IMPACT DOES BIOLOGICAL INHERITANCE HAVE ON SOCIALIZATION?

In the face of the nature-nurture argument, let's take a look at what factors make up our biological inheritance and how these factors affect and are affected by socialization. *First, we arrive in the world with a set of reflexes.* For example, we start to make sucking motions in the womb, and even suck our thumb, before we are born. Society responds to this reflex. If we go back into the 1940s and 1950s, children were fed on a strict schedule and thumb sucking was not permitted. Parents would put nasty tasting solutions on children's hands to keep them from sucking. The attitude now is, "orthodontists are cheaper than psychiatrists." We have a much more permissive attitude about feeding schedules, thumb sucking and pacifiers.

Second, we arrive in the world with a gender. Whether a child is born male or female influences how we socialize the child. We tend to be rougher with our boys and tend to hold our girls closer to our bodies for longer periods of times. We dress little girls in frilly dresses, and maybe pants, but we would never dress a little boy in a pink dress.

Third, we also arrive in the world with a physical structure. If the child looks hearty, we treat the child more roughly than if a child has a very low birth weight. A friend of mine had a baby that weighed 5 pounds and was 21 inches long. Everyone treated the baby like it was made of glass; the child was never sick but everyone treated the baby like it was very delicate. If a child is large for its age, we tend to treat it as if it were in fact older and perhaps hold unrealistic expectations for the child's behavior.

▲ EVERY ORGANISM IS THE UNIQUE PRODUCT OF THE INTERACTION BETWEEN GENES AND ENVIRONMENT.
IMAGE COPYRIGHT JAMEY EKINS, 2008. USED UNDER LICENSE FROM SHUTTERSTOCK, INC.

Fourth, some research indicates that the child arrives in the world with some basic inborn behavioral and personality differences. Some of the traits targeted as being influenced by genetics include intelligence, extroversion and aggression. Intelligence, for example, could be accounted for by as much as 70% genetic differences but the impact of socialization is still tremendously important. Forty percent of job interest variation, according to studies, can be attributed to genetics; the other 60% is due to socialization factors. These personality and behavioral differences are genetically influenced, not genetically caused.

THE PRESSURE OF SOCIAL INFLUENCE ABOUT US IS ENORMOUS, AND NO SINGLE ARM CAN RESIST IT.
FELIX ADLER

THINKING SOCIOLOGY

Is it possible for a society to reach androgyny? Would this be good? Why or why not?

WHAT ARE THE SOCIAL FACTORS IN THE SOCIALIZATION PROCESS?

A culture must respond to the physical environment in which the culture develops. What a culture uses to gain a livelihood and uses for physical protection will influence to a great deal the skills that are needed for existence. Physical environment limits, rather than causes, socialization. If I live in an area where it is very difficult to get enough to eat, the socialization process is going to be very different than if I grow up in a tropical paradise. The same environment, however, can lead to different responses. If I live in an arctic area, I may learn to hunt walruses and seals, or I may learn to herd reindeer.

The culture we are born into influences the types of interactions which we experience. We are all born into a group, learn a language and receive certain rewards and punishments. As a consequence of these shared group experiences, each culture develops what is called a modal personality. A **modal personality** is that personality type which is characteristic of the members of a culture. If I were a palm reader, I could tell you that you are ambitious, willing to work hard for goals that you have set yourself, feel compassionate for people and like the good life. I would be correct the vast majority of the time because I know the personality characteristics of the American people. The modal personality of a North American includes (among some of the personality traits) ambition, assertiveness and aggressiveness.

The Dobuan of Melanesia has a very different modal personality from the North American. The main person who participates in the caretaking of the child is the mother's brother; the father resents the child and the child is frequently unwanted by its mother. The child is raised with little warmth or affection. As a consequence, the child grows up very hostile, suspicious and distrustful. In our culture we would call this paranoid, but in this culture it is a logical reaction. In fact, the Dobuan would probably want to check out our sanity for leaving scraps of hair at the beauty parlor or giving clothes to charity. Someone might put a curse on us based on these items!

The group experience is very important for the socialization process; we need the group experience in order to develop both physically and psychologically. The child raised without the group experience is called a **feral child**. This term literally means raised by wolves such as in Tarzan and Jungle Boy. Kingsley Davis conducted some of the early research on children raised in isolation. One girl by the name of Anna was discovered by social workers in early 1938. She was living in an attic room of her grandfather's house. Her unwed mother was retarded and had given her minimal care because she worked very long hours. When Anna was found at age six, she could not speak, sit up, walk or feed herself. Anna was taken into protective custody and given an enriched environment. When she died four and a half years later, she had made developmental progress but she had the intelligence of about a two and a half year old.

The second case history was a girl by the name of Isabelle. Isabelle had been locked in a darkened room with a deaf mother. When she was found at age six, she acted more like a child of six months. Due to the fact that she had been kept in a darkened room she had bad health. She was brought to an institution to be nurtured. She eventually reached a maturation level of an eight year old but continued to behave wildly. These two cases give an idea of how important the group is for the normal development of a child.

The classic research concerning nurturing is Harlow's study with rhesus monkeys. Psychologist Harry Harlow, in a planned experiment, gave baby monkeys two "mothers." One mother was covered with soft terry cloth but did not provide food; the other mother was a wire mother with no soft covering, but did provide food. The rhesus monkeys preferred the physical contact with the soft cloth mom. When introduced to an upset in their environment, the infant monkeys went to the cloth mom. These infant monkeys, undoubtedly, needed a feeling of warmth, contact and comfort. We must be careful in generalizing studies done with animals to human beings. However, studies of socially isolated children yield much the same findings as Harlow's study with isolated monkeys.

In 1945, Rene Spitz observed 91 children living in a foundling home. He observed these 91 children for two years. He looked at variables such as diet, clothing, bedding and room temperature. These children's physical needs were met each day.

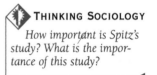

THINKING SOCIOLOGY

Why is the role of parenting so important?

☙ *Quick Glance*

Modal personality develops due to group processes.   T   F

A feral child is raised with a minimum of human interaction.   T   F

Physical environment limits the socialization process.   T   F

THINKING SOCIOLOGY

How important is Spitz's study? What is the importance of this study?

☙ *Quick Glance*

Bonding is only important in the lives of infants.   T   F

Harlow used elephants in his classic study.   T   F

Rene Spitz found bonding can mean the difference between life and death.   T   F

Bonding meets emotional needs.   T   F

THERE MUST BE MORE TO LIFE THAN HAVING EVERYTHING.
MAURICE SENDAK

THINKING SOCIOLOGY

When does the need for bonding stop?

The diet was sufficient, bedding was changed on a routine basis, clothing was adequate, and medical care was provided. At the end of his two year observation, Spitz noted that some thirty children had died and another twenty-one displayed slow physical and social development. A small staff took care of their physical needs, but social interaction was lacking. The staff did not have time to hold, rock, sing or talk to these children.

▲ BONDED RELATIONSHIPS FOR US AS HUMANS IS IMPORTANT THROUGHOUT THE SOCIALIZATION PROCESS.
IMAGE COPYRIGHT SONYA ETCHISON, 2008. USED UNDER LICENSE FROM SHUTTERSTOCK, INC.

Spitz compared these children to another institution in which mothers were being held for delinquency. The mothers took care of their children and, because they had little else to do, they spent many hours with their children. The development of these children was quite normal. In fact, many of the children walked and talked at early ages.

The process of meeting human emotional needs is referred to as **bonding**. The study done by Spitz illustrates that bonding can mean the difference between life and death. There are several types of bonded relationships for us as humans:

1. parent and child
2. married couple or friendship between two people of the opposite sex
3. two friends of the same gender

Not all parents bond with their children and the following are some reasons why this could happen:

1. genetic defect or brain damage of the child
2. illness of the child or the parent during the early years of the child
3. prenatal drug use
4. poor parenting from a drug-addicted parent
5. depressed parent

The last factor in socialization we need to consider is unique social experiences. We each have experiences that make us different from everyone else. A **marker event** is an event that influences an individual. Each of us have had individual marker events that have had a profound effect on our self-concept and our life. Someone might have said something or done something for you that made a difference in your life. For example, my daughter always wanted to be a singer. She sang every chance she had; she belonged to both the junior church choir and the choir at school; she always volunteered to be in talent shows. Then, one Monday morning the school music teacher asked her if something was wrong with her vocal cords. She came home and asked me "what was wrong?" I pondered a minute and then remembered that my daughter had been swimming at a swim meet all weekend long. She had chlorine on her vocal cords, plus she had screamed for her teammates to swim faster for four days. It did not matter that there were reasons for her voice sounding raspy, the damage had been done. My daughter no longer wanted to be a singer.

There are also generational marker events which affect whole groups of people. My aunt saves all the plastic bags that bread or vegetables are packaged in. She

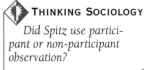

✦ THINKING SOCIOLOGY
Did Spitz use participant or non-participant observation?

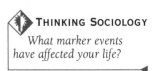

✦ THINKING SOCIOLOGY
What marker events have affected your life?

washes them out and reuses them. She carefully saves every piece of aluminum foil for several uses. She likes to buy large amounts of groceries on sale, she purchases many of her clothes and household goods at garage sales and second-hand stores. She has plenty of money, but she grew up during the Great Depression. There is a generation of people in their seventies and eighties who think the same way as my aunt due to these impoverished times. The Great Depression of the 1930s was a generational marker event.

Another generational marker which affected all age groups in the United States was the terrorist attack of September 11, 2001. Most of us watched with horror as two planes were deliberately flown into the Twin Towers and one into the Pentagon. After this event, patriotism escalated. Our lives were changed with increased security. We, for example, have to open our car trunks when parking at airports and have to allow extra time for boarding. We also had to make other adjustments such as I no longer carry a pocket knife and I travel even in the United States with my passport to use for identification.

A more recent generational marker event happened on August 29, 2005. On this date, one of the largest hurricanes ever recorded devastated the Central Gulf Coast. In further devastation, storm surges breached the levee system that protected New Orleans from Lake Pontchartrain and the Mississippi River causing the city to be flooded. Over 1.2 million people were evacuated and over a million people found themselves without homes. This storm caused major changes in the lives of those people who lived in New Orleans. Their belongings, homes and memories were destroyed. Many had to start new lives in new cities and states. This hurricane and subsequent flooding, radically changed their physical lives and many suffered emotional and psychological problems due to the devastation.

▲ SELF-CONCEPT IS FORMED DURING THE SOCIALIZATION PROCESS.
IMAGE COPYRIGHT JGW IMAGES, 2008. USED UNDER LICENSE FROM SHUTTERSTOCK, INC.

Learning TIP
Utilize the small units of time you have throughout the day to study. If you have 5 or 10 minutes waiting, use it to study your cards! We best remember what we study at the beginning and ending of a study session so the more beginnings and endings the better!

WHAT IS SELF-CONCEPT?

Sociologists offer insight on how the socialization process plays a part in the formation of our self-concept. Our **self-concept** helps us to understand who we are, what we are worth, and where we are going. The self-concept that we acquire can be either positive or negative depending on our experiences and how we internalize these experiences. Two sociologists, Charles Horton Cooley and George Herbert Mead, have developed theories to help us understand better the formation of this self-concept. Irving Goffman used a **dramaturigal** approach. These three men are a part of the symbolic interactionist perspective and thus look at the interaction among humans.

THINKING SOCIOLOGY
Is it possible to improve your feeling of self-concept? How?

WHAT IS THE SOCIOLOGICAL PERSPECTIVE OF THE SELF OR ME?

Cooley

Charles Horton Cooley's theory is known as the looking-glass self. The **looking-glass self** looks at the role that others may play in the formation of who we are and how we feel about ourselves. Other people serve as a mirror for us and we internalize what we think we see reflected from them. Cooley's theory consists of three elements:

Quick Glance

Karl Marx is responsible for the looking-glass self.   T F

Misinterpretation is impossible in looking-glass self.   T F

Self-concept is developed through looking at ourselves through the eyes of others.   T F

Self-concept is constant.   T F

1. *We imagine how we appear to others.*
2. *We imagine how others perceive us.*
3. *We develop some sort of feeling about ourselves based on the previous two items.*

THINKING SOCIOLOGY

How is Cooley's looking-glass self applicable to the formation of your self-concept?

OF ALL THE JUDGMENTS WE PASS IN LIFE, NONE IS MORE IMPORTANT THAN THE JUDGMENT WE PASS ON OURSELVES.

NATHANIEL BRANDON

THINKING SOCIOLOGY

How can we misinterpret other people's reaction to us?

Quick Glance

Language is important in the development of self-concept. T F

Through role-taking, we learn norms. T F

Cooley developed the concept of role-taking. T F

Mead studied the play and game stage. T F

During the play stage, a child gains an overall view of the rules of society. T F

Cooley and Mead were symbolic interactionists. T F

THINKING SOCIOLOGY

Do all adults reach the game stage? Should they? Why or why not?

As an example of Cooley's theory, we'll use Mary and John, a couple attending a high school prom. John asks Mary to go to the prom and Mary accepts. She begins to prepare for the prom by purchasing a new dress, new evening handbag, necklace, earrings, makeup, nail polish and by going to the salon to get a tan and have her hair cut and styled. Her dad is amazed at what this one prom has cost him. As Mary prepares for the date that day, she looks in the mirror and thinks that the tan and new makeup really have improved her looks. She is pleased with her new hair style and she likes her nails. Mary thinks she looks good and begins to imagine how John will react when he sees her. She imagines that John will watch as she walks down the stairs after her dad has let him into the house. She thinks that John will tell her how gorgeous she looks. However, when John does ring the door bell and she makes her descent down the stairs, John says nothing and only opens the door for her to go out. If Mary's feeling of self-concept is positive, John's in trouble because Mary will confront John and tell him that he is a jerk. If John is smart he will respond with, "Mary, I didn't say anything because your beauty has left me speechless." However, if Mary's feeling of self-concept is negative, the evening is ruined. Mary's thinking will be that it doesn't matter how much time she spends trying to make herself beautiful and it doesn't matter how much money her dad spends, she'll never be beautiful. Her self-concept will not allow her to confront John because of her fear that he'll respond, "Yep, you're right, you'll never be beautiful."

We can, of course, misinterpret how others perceive us. However, whether we correctly or incorrectly interpret another's reaction to us, the formation of self-concept is affected. Self-concept is not static, it can be changed. To summarize, Cooley believes that the behavior of others toward us is the mirror in which we see ourselves; the people around us influence the way we see ourselves. We learn through interaction with other people what and who we are. This means that our perception of ourself is never direct; we see ourselves reflected in the reactions of others.

Cooley viewed language as an important part of a child developing the self. We respond to our children in terms of language. One of my pet peeves is to hear a parent tell a child, "You are so stupid." This is the looking-glass self in action. The child thinks to himself, "Gee, I'm stupid; I am not a worthwhile person." On the other hand, when a parent says, "You really did a nice job on the project," the child thinks, in terms of language, "I'm a conscientious worker." Language plays an important role in several aspects of the looking-glass self. We respond to people in terms of language; we reflect about ourselves in terms of language too.

Mead

To George Herbert Mead, the formation of self takes place in what he refers to as role-taking. Role-taking is that process whereby we learn the norms necessary to perform a role. Learning role-taking is a three-step process. *The first step is imitation or preparatory stage.* Young children often imitate or mimic the behavior of others without really understanding the role or roles that person may play. The child merely imitates the behavior. Dad is reading the newspaper and Junior sits beside him with paper in hand, but upside down. Junior is imitating the behavior of Dad, but does not understand why Dad reads the paper.

The second stage for the child is that of "play". This starts at about age four and lasts until approximately the age of seven. In this stage, the child plays a particular role. Children playing "house" will recreate the role of "Mommy" or "Daddy." This helps the child to imagine their world and themselves from the "Mommy's" point of view or the "Daddy's" point of view. The child learns the behavior to play a role as he has seen it played in real life.

A T-ball game can illustrate the play stage. A child finally hits the ball off the tee and begins to run to their left (towards third plate) and the coach and the audience are screaming "NO, go to first." The child has not internalized the rules for playing roles. Little Johnny may be playing right field and during play he bends down and takes his time to tie his shoe string, driving the coach crazy. The ball comes Johnny's way. He gets the ball and stands there not realizing that he is supposed to do something with the ball. He understands his role, but does not yet understand the role played by each of the other positions.

It is in the third stage, *the game stage, that the child begins to see the larger picture of not only the role he/she plays, but the role that other members play as well.* The child begins to internalize the rules to play games and begins to see not only their role but the role of others. Thus, in the game stage, the child learns several important aspects of roles:

1. Some roles are related to or may complement other roles (the catcher and the pitcher in baseball).
2. Games have rules that govern the relationships among the players.
3. Each player must follow the rules.

At this stage, the child must learn the behaviors required of each player, not just the behavior required of his/her particular role. At this stage, the child also becomes aware of the obligations that go along with social roles; he starts to take responsibility for his actions. He learns that he has to be a member of society by playing according to the rules. If he does not play by the rules, he learns that he will be sanctioned. Mead felt that this role-taking is an important process for the formation of self-concept.

Two other concepts were recognized by Mead in the socialization process: significant other and generalized other. Significant other are those people whose judgments are most important to our formation of self-concept. **Significant others** is a specific person in our social environment whose approval and affection are very important to us. In the imitation stage, family members are significant others, especially mom and dad. As the child moves on to the play stage, parents remain important but the child is beginning to desire to be with people his own age and thus peers become significant others as well. In the game stage, the most important significant others may be peers, but family still remains important. Significant others can also be role models, such as police officers, firefighters or teachers.

The **generalized other** is the term for generally held beliefs, attitudes, viewpoints and expectations of society as a whole. The term generalized other is actually referring to the child becoming aware of the norms, expectations, attitudes and behavior that are necessary for him/her to function in a society. With the formation of the generalized other, the child becomes capable of maintaining society. Our generalized other becomes very important because it guides our behavior in socially acceptable directions. We develop the generalized other by watching many people play their roles and we generalize the standards from this behavior. This is much like what

THINKING SOCIOLOGY

According to Mead, what stage of development occurs during grade school? High school?

LET ME HOLD YOU IN MY HEART, MY SOUL, AND IN MY DREAMS . . . EXPERIENCING YOU IN MY MIND . . . FOR LOVING YOU HAS GIVEN ME THE POWER TO KNOW WHO I REALLY AM.
SHARON WARREN

▲ SIGNIFICANT OTHERS ARE IMPORTANT IN THE FORMATION OF SELF.
IMAGE COPYRIGHT JAIMIE DUPLASS, 2008. USED UNDER LICENSE FROM SHUTTERSTOCK, INC.

THINKING SOCIOLOGY

Does everyone's generalized other develop to the same degree? What accounts for differences?

Sigmund Freud referred to as the superego, or the conscience, that is formed during socialization.

Goffman

Erving Goffman presents a **dramaturgical approach**. He says that life is like a series of stages and we must learn the scripts and act out the roles on the different stages of life. As we play out these scripts, we manage the impressions of others; this is called **impression management**. Through impression management, we try to guide and control impressions other people form; we try to get them to assume a definition which fits in with what we want. For example, we dress conservatively for a job interview for an accounting job even though our clothing style may generally be that of a total slob. Sometimes we "act dumb" in order to get help from someone else. He also says that we do what is called **face-work**. Face-work is striving to maintain the proper image in social interaction. We do not want to be embarrassed. I may give a lousy lecture but I shall say that the students were not responsive or that I had a very sore throat.

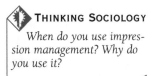

Quick Glance

Significant others are not important in our life. T F

We are born with a generalized other. T F

My father is a significant other. T F

The generalized other develops during the game stage. T F

THINKING SOCIOLOGY

When do you use impression management? Why do you use it?

WHAT IS ANTICIPATORY SOCIALIZATION?

Anticipatory socialization is learning the skills and values needed for future roles. This type of socialization begins, to a large extent, during adolescence. We prepare ourselves for future roles by working part-time jobs, taking special courses such as "Marriage and Family" in college, reading books and articles, talking with informed individuals, and trying out anticipated roles. Some young people cohabitate because they say that it prepares them for marriage. Teenagers babysit to earn money, but they may also be learning some of the skills needed to be a parent.

Several factors influence the effectiveness of anticipatory socialization:

1. *The visibility of the future role.* It is very easy to observe our parents in their parenting role, but it is much more difficult to watch them in all aspects of their spouse roles.
2. *The accuracy with which the future role is presented.* Many times parents do not disagree in front of the children or are not affectionate in front of the children, so children come to the conclusion that parents never disagree as spouses. Children also may think that their parents are nonsexual creatures.
3. *The agreement society has about the role.* For elderly people, for example, we tell them both to kick back and relax and to keep busy or they will vegetate. It is very difficult to do both at the same time!

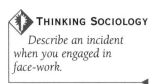

Quick Glance

We try to influence what people think about us. T F

We use face-work to maintain self concept. T F

Mead wrote the dramaturgical approach. T F

THINKING SOCIOLOGY

Describe an incident when you engaged in face-work.

THINKING SOCIOLOGY

How effective is anticipatory socialization?

WHAT IS ADULT SOCIALIZATION?

Adult socialization is the socialization occurring during the adult years. Since the late 1960s, we have started to look at the importance of adult socialization. We used to think that socialization ended when we "grew up," somewhere between the ages of 18 and 21. But many people kept feeling all sorts of changes within themselves and wondered what was wrong with them.

One of the leading pioneers in adult socialization, Daniel Levinson, addressed the concept that socialization continues into adulthood rather than stopping when we reach adulthood. Levinson studied thirty males for a period of ten years, thus the project was a longitudinal study. His conclusion was that there are four major stages in a person's life. Levinson also maintained that there are three major transitions as

Quick Glance

Anticipatory socialization ceases at adolescence. T F

The effectiveness of anticipatory socialization depends on several factors. T F

Anticipatory socialization involves learning for future roles. T F we move from one stage to the other. Each of these transitions takes at least 3 to 5 years to complete:

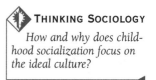

THINKING SOCIOLOGY

According to Levinson's theory, what stage of development are you in? Why?

1. *The first stage is childhood and adolescence (birth to 22 years).* The transition from this stage to young adulthood begins at about age 17 and ends at about age 22. During this time, we are gradually entering into the adult world. Some move out of the parental home, begin a career and some marry.
2. *The second stage is early adulthood (17 to 45).* The transition from early adulthood to middle adulthood begins at approximately the age of 40 and lasts to about 45. During this transition, the individual may experience a time of questioning his past goals and comparing those goals to what he feels he has accomplished. When there is a feeling that goals have not been accomplished, the individual may begin to make changes in his life, hence the term "mid-life crisis."
3. *The third stage is middle adulthood (40 to 65).* The transition from middle adulthood to late adulthood (60–65) is one of acceptance of retirement and issues of growing older.
4. *The fourth stage is late adulthood (60 to death).* In this stage, we come to an acceptance of what and who we are; we start to mentor people below us in our occupations. We start to limit occupational involvement and prepare for retirement. We become very interested in family and friends and realize that the next major transition point is death.

Levinson's research was conducted with a sample of males; Gail Sheehy did her interviews with both men and women. Her stages are found on the following page.

According to an article in *USA Today*, which appeared on February 16, 1999, Orville Brim and his research team showed that U.S. citizens forty to sixty years of age find life rewarding. This age group worries less, has a growing sense of job control and feels more financially secure compared to people under the age of forty. The MacArthur Foundation, directed by Orville, reported that the middle agers are in good health (but have destructive health practices that may affect future health), are able to handle stress well, and that they voice satisfaction with their marriage. This study paints an optimistic middle-age cycle for citizens of the United States.

Quick Glance

Anticipatory socialization is the same as adult socialization.	T F
We stop growing and changing at age 21.	T F
Levinson studied both male and female transition points.	T F
From the ages of 40 to 65, we question our life choices.	T F

THINKING SOCIOLOGY

How and why does childhood socialization focus on the ideal culture?

WHAT ARE THE DIFFERENCES BETWEEN ADULT AND CHILDHOOD SOCIALIZATION?

Orville Brim says that there are significant differences between adult and childhood socialization, or primary socialization. *Adult socialization focuses on overt behavior and childhood socialization concentrates on basic values.* In childhood we try to teach children how important education is and all the advantages of education. By the time young adults are in college, older adults are trying to help them learn material and to maximize their grades.

▲ CHILDHOOD SOCIALIZATION CONCENTRATES ON LEARNING BASIC VALUES.

IMAGE COPYRIGHT IOFOTO, 2008. USED UNDER LICENSE FROM SHUTTERSTOCK, INC.

Quick Glance

Childhood socialization is also called primary socialization.	T F
Primary socialization focuses on the informal nature of roles.	T F
Childhood socialization focuses on ideal culture.	T F
Adult socialization teaches us specific skills.	T F

Second, adult socialization stresses the informal nature of roles while childhood socialization focuses on the formal nature of roles. Remember when you were a child and saw

Learning TIP
Talk to other people about what you are studying. This is good review and practical application.

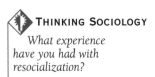

THINKING SOCIOLOGY

What experience have you had with resocialization?

your teacher in the store? You got very excited. Somehow, that teacher was not a real person; that teacher did not have any life outside of the classroom. But I hazard to guess you would think nothing of seeing one of your college instructors in the store. In fact, some of you have probably gone to social events with your instructors.

Third, adulthood socialization focuses on the real culture and childhood socialization focuses on ideal culture. We teach children the "shoulds," while as adults we do what is more expedient. I can remember my daughter at six being a terrible back seat driver. If the sign said 65 miles per hour, that is how fast she wanted me to drive. I knew, realistically, that if I drove exactly on the speed limit, if nothing else, I would obstruct traffic. We teach our children that taking other people's possessions is wrong, yet we use the copy machine at work, steal time by taking long coffee breaks, or take paper and pencils from places of business.

Fourth, adult socialization focuses on juggling many roles at the same time. I can still hear myself telling my children that they can not watch television and do their homework at the same time. This is the same woman who is grading papers, talking on the phone, and mixing spaghetti sauce at the same time. People drive, eat, shave, talk on the phone and read books in the car.

Fifth, adulthood socialization focuses on specific skills, childhood socialization concentrates on generalized skills. In primary socialization I teach you how to add and subtract, but in adult socialization I teach you how to balance a set of accounting books or a chemistry equation.

Sixth, there is a different relationship between the socializer and socializee. In primary socialization, or childhood socialization, the socializer generally is a very powerful figure; but in adult socialization, I have much more power. Children do not get up in the classroom and go to the restroom. They have to get permission first. In college, students do not have the same reticence about leaving a classroom. In primary socialization, the person is not being socialized voluntarily. I have no choice who my parents are or whether I attend school or not. As I get older, I make the choice to go to college and I have the freedom of changing my job if I do not like my boss.

WHAT IS RESOCIALIZATION?

Resocialization is an unlearning and a relearning; it is a fundamental and rapid change in thinking and behaving. Resocialization requires six conditions. *First, total control over the individual is necessary.* This means that we must isolate the person from the rest of society. Maximum security prisons, for example, are generally away from population centers and have walls and guards protecting the walls. Camp Pendelton is in Oceanside, California, but recruits are not allowed off base nor are they allowed to make or receive phone calls.

Second, there is the suppression of all past statuses. The person leaves behind his clothes and hair cuts. In prison, a person is issued clothes and given a number. In Marine boot camp, the recruits are issued clothes, given very short haircuts and even their money is seriously restricted.

Third, the moral worth of the old self is maligned. In boot camp, the "boys" are told that they are weaklings and sometimes worse. If a teenager goes into a cult, she/he is told that her/his old life was materialistic and she/he would not find inner peace.

Fourth, the individual participates in his own resocialization. In boot camp, the males march, chant cadence and spend many hours studying about the armed services. If they make a mistake, they are sanctioned accordingly.

Fifth, extreme sanctions are used in resocialization. In maximum prisons, prisoners can be put into solitary or total isolation. A Marine recruit may find himself doing a great number of pushups. Positive sanctions are also used. If a unit has the highest shooting score, everyone in the unit may be able to make a phone call. The recruits also work for special awards that they will receive at graduation.

Sixth, peer group pressure and support are intensified. If one person in a unit messes up, everyone gets punished. The movie "Full Metal Jacket" illustrates this. In this movie, one of the male recruits was caught sneaking food while he was on a special diet, so the drill sergeant punished the other men. That night the "guys" in the unit got revenge!

Much of the resocialization occurs in what is called a total institution. A **total institution** is one in which there is a highly controlled social environment. Some examples of total institutions are prisons, military bases, mental hospitals, convents and monasteries. These institutions control all aspects of life. They control when or what you eat, and where and when you sleep. Total institutions have four characteristics:

1. All aspects of life are in the same place and guided by a single authority.
2. Members share common conditions.
3. Authorities write and enforce rules.
4. All activities are designed to carry out the mission of the total institution.

🔾 *Quick Glance*

Resocialization is an unlearning and relearning.   T   F

Resocialization frequently occurs in a total institution.   T   F

Resocialization only happens in totalitarian countries.   T   F

Resocialization involves a breaking down of the self-concept.   T   F

Positive sanctions are never used in resocialization.   T   F

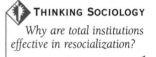

THINKING SOCIOLOGY
Why are total institutions effective in resocialization?

WHAT ARE THE AGENCIES OF SOCIALIZATION?

Agencies of socialization are those groups and institutions which have an influence on the way that we are socialized. Some of the socialization of these groups is deliberate; sometimes it is unconscious. Several factors contribute to these agencies in being effective:

1. Early access in terms of age is more effective than later access because ideas and interests are not as well formed.
2. Person-to-person interaction is more effective than indirect contact.
3. The individual must be physically and psychologically ready.
4. The more exclusive the access of the group to the individual, the more effective is its influence.

It is the family that is given the primary responsibility of socializing the young that they have procreated. It is the first and most important agency of socialization. Our family provides basic needs and teaches us the ways of society. Our family is subjective in socialization because it takes us into account as individuals. Some of us have family idiosyncrasies that make our socialization different from others in our society. For example, if our parents are considerably older than our friends' parents, we might not be able to play baseball or have running matches with our parents. My neighbors had their daughter late in life, and the girl is frequently asked if her mother is her grandmother. Another example was our neighbor's girl from across the street. The girl's household consisted of her mother and father but also her paternal grandmother and uncle! This girl faced another unique experience because she is a twin. There are also social class differences in raising children. To make a very general statement, there is a strong tendency for people in the middle and upper classes to use democratic child rearing practices and those in the working classes to be more authoritarian. People in the upper classes teach their children independence and high achievement and those in the lower classes teach cooperation and group effort. But no matter what the social class or unique family structure, the family teaches us fundamental values.

Very early in life we come in contact with the second agency of socialization, the peer group. Peer group does not mean "age cohort." Peer group refers to your circle of friends. The peer group consists of those people of our age group with whom we identify and interact. The peer group has become increasingly important in our society because our families are so much smaller. There usually are not several children in the family to interact with, so the child must go to his/her friends for companionship. Parents frequently are aware that the peer group can better serve some of their children's needs. Fashion changes may mean our children want input from peers rather than rely on information their parents can offer from twenty or more years ago. Technological changes may make parents feel they are unable to help their children with school work. For example, not all parents are versed in the ways of computers.

The peer serves several important functions for the child. *First, it is within the peer group that the child is introduced to impersonal authority.* Within the family, parents frequently make allowances for behavior because the child is the youngest or does not feel well. This does not happen in the peer group; play by the rules or take a hike. It is within the peer group that we start to test the limits of adult authority. Most of us snuck out when we were younger—and we did so with our group of friends. My daughters come to me with the statement, "Aw, Mom, everyone else is doing it, you're being mean. Why can't I?" Sound familiar?

▲ THE PEER GROUP IS AN IMPORTANT AGENCY OF SOCIALIZATION.
IMAGE COPYRIGHT WOLFGANG AMRI, 2008. USED UNDER LICENSE FROM SHUTTERSTOCK, INC.

The peer group may or may not support parental values. If the group does so, parents are happy people. If the friends go against what the parents believe in, there are periods of turbulence and family problems. The most difficult period for disagreement with adult values and norms is preadolescence and adolescence. Teens rebel frequently along very superficial lines like male's wearing earrings or the issue of length of hair or type of dress. Teens also go through periods of resentment against parents, but when teens go beyond this period, they may return to the family values that they were taught.

The next agency of socialization is the preschool and the day care center. This socialization agency is seen in today's modern world more often than ever before. Children who attend day care may develop independence more quickly than their peers who do not attend preschools.

By age six, all of us are in school; this is the next agency of socialization. Children spend an average of seven hours a day away from the home and in the educational process. The school does not take a subjective approach to socialization but rather has many rules for uniform indoctrination. When we attend school we prepare for adult rules but the school also teaches us attitudes and values that we need to operate in our culture.

The next agency of socialization is the mass media. The mass media has a tremendous impact on us since the average child spends more time in front of the television than he does in the school room. The mass media affects our values and behavior as social beings. Parents and other members of society are concerned about the impact that advertising and violence have on the development of our children. There has also been concern about the messages given in many shows because of the distorted images and sexual orientation. Parents can minimize the negative impact of television or make watching a positive experience by not using television as a baby sitter, turning off undesirable programs or sitting down with their children when they watch television in order to help the child develop a clearer picture of the inaccuracies and the techniques used in the mass media.

The sixth agency of socialization is organizations. These include the church that you attend and groups such as Girl Scouts and Boy Scouts. These groups frequently reinforce traditional values such as achievement and patriotism.

The work place is the last agency we are going to discuss. Wilbert Moore tells us that occupational socialization is a four-stage process:

1. *We have to make a career choice.* Based on that choice, we have to make decisions on where and how much training we shall need to enter our career.
2. *We experience anticipatory socialization.* This may last a few weeks or a few years and involves trying out different aspects of the future role.
3. *We experience conditioning and commitment.* This happens when we actually take our job of choice. We start out very excited about our new duties.
4. *The fourth stage is continuous commitment.* At this stage, the job becomes an integrated part of our self-concept.

In Chapter 5 we shall consider the importance of the group. The group is viewed as a fundamental part of what sociologists study as we assume that a human being is by nature a social animal.

EFFECTS OF WATCHING TV

1. FOSTERING OF AGGRESSIVE BEHAVIOR
2. LOUD MUSIC, FAST PACE FOSTERS AGGRESSION
3. DISTORTED VIEW OF AMOUNT OF VIOLENCE IN THE WORLD
4. DISTORTED VIEWS OF MINORITY PEOPLE
5. DESIRE FOR ADVERTISED GOODS
6. CHANGES IN DEVELOPMENT OF LANGUAGE AND IMAGINATION
7. LESS SENSITIVE TO VIOLENCE IN THE WORLD

Quick Glance

The peer group is the first agent of socialization.　T　F

The mass media influences children's attitudes toward violence.　T　F

The work place influences adult socialization.　T　F

Preschool is not considered an agency of socialization.　T　F

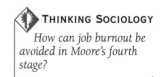

THINKING SOCIOLOGY

How can job burnout be avoided in Moore's fourth stage?

WHY SHOULD WE LIVE WITH SUCH HURRY AND WASTE OF LIFE? . . . . MEN SAY THAT A STITCH IN TIME SAVES NINE, AND SO THEY TAKE A THOUSAND STITCHES TODAY TO SAVE NINE TOMORROW. AS FOR WORK, WE HAVEN'T ANY OF ANY CONSEQUENCE. WE HAVE SAINT VITUS' DANCE, AND CANNOT POSSIBLY KEEP OUR HEADS STILL.

HENRY DAVID THOREAU
(1817–1862)

▼ CHAPTER SUMMARY

1. During socialization the individual will learn the language of the culture, gain a network of social relationships, learn norms of the society, set goals and ambitions, learn technological skills, and learn the territory of their culture.
2. Socialization occurs through explicit instruction, conditioning, role-modeling and innovation.
3. Biological inheritance, physical environment, culture, group experiences and unique experiences influence the socialization process.
4. Cooley's theory of looking-glass self consists of imagining how we appear to others, how others perceive us and how we develop some sort of feeling about ourselves.
5. Mead's theory of role-taking consists of the imitation stage, play stage and the game stage. He analyzes significant and generalized other.
6. The effectiveness of anticipatory socialization is influenced by the visibility of the future role, accuracy of role presentation and the agreement society has about the role.
7. The four stages of Daniel Levinson's theory of adult socialization are childhood and adolescence, young adulthood, middle adulthood and late adulthood.
8. Resocialization requires six conditions: total control over the individual, suppression of all past statuses, moral worth of the old self is maligned, individual participation in their own resocialization, use of extreme sanctions and intensification of peer group pressure and support.
9. The family, peer group, day care, school, mass media, organizations and the work place are agencies of socialization.

▼ REFERENCES

Brim, Orville. 1976. "Life Span Development of the Theory of Oneself: Implications for Child Development." In Hayne W. Reese (Ed.), *Advances in Child Development and Behavior (Vol. 2)*. New York: Academic Press.

Brim, Orville. 1980. "On the properties of life events." In Paul B. Baltes and Orville G. Brim Jr. (Eds.) *Life-Span Development and Behavior*. Vol. III. New York: Academic Press.

Buss, A. H. and R. A. Plomin. 1975. *A Temperamental Theory of Personality*. New York: Wiley.

Davis, Kingsley. 1949. *Human Society*. New York: The Macmillan Company.

Elias, Marilyn. 1999 (2/16). *What Midlife Crisis?* USA Today, 3A–3B.

Goffman, Irving. 1961. *Asylums*. New York: Anchor/Doubleday.

Goffman, Irving. 1959. *Presentation of Self in Everyday Life*. New York: Doubleday.

Harris, Marvin. 1978. *Cows, Pigs, Wars and Witches*. New York: Vintage.

Harlow, Harry. 1971. *Learning To Love*. New York: Ballantine.

Leo, John. 1987. "Exploring Traits of Twins." *Time*, 129 (Jan. 12):63.

Levinson, Daniel. 1978. *Seasons of a Man's Life*. New York: Knopf.

Lewontin, R. C., Steven Rose, Leon J. Kamin. 1984. *Not In Our Genes*. New York: Pantheon Books.

Maugh II, Thomas. 1990. "Study: Nature over Nurture: Personality Shaped More by Genetics than Upbringing." *Houston Chronicle*, Oct. 14, 27a.

Mead, George Herbert. 1934. *Mind, Self, and Society*. Chicago: The University of Chicago Press.

Moore, Wilbert. 1968. "Occupation Socialization." In David A. Goslin (Ed.). *Handbook of Socialization Theory and Research*. Chicago: Rand McNally, 861–83.

Plomin, R. 1989. "Environment and Genes: Determinants of Behavior." *American Psychologists*, 44, 105–111.

Plomin, R. 1990. "The Role of Inheritance in Behavior." *Science*, 248, 183–188.

Sheehy, Gail. 1976. *Passages: Predictable Crises of Adult Life*. New York: Dutton.

Wilson, Edward O. 1978. *On Human Nature*. Cambridge, Ma.: Harvard University Press.

READING

Life is constantly changing. Sometimes we accept the change and move on because the change is not perceived as life-altering for us. Some of the changes, however, are major ones that smack us in the face. The change may be expected or the change may blind side us. Regardless of whether we are expecting the change or not, it can leave us with a feeling of emptiness. We may think we will be better able to weather the storm of the expected loss because we will have time to adjust to the change. This is often not the case. Sometimes knowing is not better because we experience both the anticipated loss and the loss itself. Regardless of whether the loss is expected or sudden, our sense of security and confidence can be rocked to the very soul of our existence.

The type of loss we experience may differ depending on the stage of life we are living. Death is a loss that we avoid thinking about in modern America; death of a loved one such as a grandparent, parent, godparent, sibling, spouse or close friend is devastating. A death by suicide or murder is often thought to be even more shocking for us than a death by natural causes. However, our losses are not always due to a death. We can experience non-death losses as well. Non-death losses can also have serious ramifications on our lives. A near death experience by a loved one or an attempted suicide can have a traumatic effect on us. The loss of a pet may also be a major bereavement for us. Any major life event such as an unplanned pregnancy, loss of a friendship, divorce or separation of parents, end of a romantic relationship or a failure at school or job affects us as a loss. Being the victim of a crime such as a robbery or a rape is a non-death loss. Other losses such as moving to a new home, getting married or even graduation from college may seem like a positive change for us but these, too, involve loss. It is important to remember that what might be considered a major loss by one individual may not be considered a major loss for another individual. The same is true for minor losses, what might be considered a minor loss for one individual may be perceived as a major loss by another individual. Losses, both death and non-death, remind us that life is constantly changing and that life is fragile.

Loss, no matter from what source, must be dealt with through the process of grieving. If we do not appropriately grieve, these losses may continue to hold us hostage for a long time. Grieving for the losses must take place in order for us to move forward with our lives. When our losses are not resolved, then the emptiness turns into anger, blame, guilt, regret that can make us sick both physically and emotionally.

Culture is an important factor in how we will deal with the loss due to death or non-death losses. The American culture concentrates today on personal happiness. There is the idea that the secret in life is to attract happiness in our life. If we are not happy, then we are not trying hard enough and we are, therefore, attracting unhappiness. We find it very easy in our culture to put the label of "depressed" on a person who is, in fact, going through the grieving process. When we put the label of depressed on someone, the next logical step is for a chemical fix; the drug will take feelings of loss and grieving away.

Several authors have written about the process of dealing with losses. The three authors we would like to discuss are Elisabeth Kubler-Ross, J.W. Worden, and Alan D. Wolfelt. Kubler-Ross explains stages of grief experienced during the grieving process while Worden views the grieving process as tasks that must be accomplished. Many thanatologists (scientists that study death and non-death losses) criticize the theory of Kubler-Ross as being too rigid and stress theories dealing with tasks or phases. She has, however, had a profound influence on our cultures thinking about death and loss.

Quick Glance

Only negative change has negative consequences for us.   T   F

People experience losses in the same way.   T   F

Loss differs depending on stage of life cycle.   T   F

Quick Glance

Grieving is the process we use to deal with loss.   T   F

Culture has no effect on the grieving process.   T   F

Drugs make a beneficial substitute for the grieving process.   T   F

Elisabeth Kubler-Ross is often credited as a pioneer in the field of death and dying. Her work opened the dialogue for recognizing that empathy is needed when dealing with someone who is dying as well as with the surviving members of the family or circle of friends. Her work has since found application in the area of non-death losses as well.

In her book, *On Death and Dying*, published in 1969, Dr. Elisabeth Kubler-Ross outlined five stages of death and dying. The stages are denial, anger, bargaining, depression and acceptance.

▶ **D**enial ("I can't have lung cancer, it's not me!")
▶ **A**nger ("Why is it my Dad that is dying of cancer?")
▶ **B**argaining ("God, I'll be a better person *if*...")
▶ **D**epression ("Life pretty much stinks for me anyway.")
▶ **A**cceptance ("My life is in order")

Quick Glance

Elisabeth Worden has developed a typology of dealing with loss. T F

Thanatologists study life and life force. T F

Denial is the first stage in dealing with potential or actual death. T F

Sometimes we go through the five stages in an orderly manner; other times we bounce around through and back again with each stage. Or we step backwards or we can be in more than one stage at the same time. However, the stages must all be dealt with and resolved before we can complete the grieving process.

Stage One is denial. It is so easy to believe that our loss has not or is not happening. In the denial stage, we deny that the doctor was speaking to us about our dying or the surviving person denies that their loved one died or is dying. We may find ourselves picking up the phone to call our mother only to remember that we cannot because she is no longer alive. With a serious illness, we do not accept that we or our loved one is terminally ill. We can suppress thoughts about the robbery or rape. We deny death by saying we have "lost someone" or "the person has passed." Somehow, this leaves the feeling that the person can return.

In Stage Two, we become angry. We begin to face our loss and it makes us very infuriated. We become furious at the person for killing themselves, or dying. We become enraged at the wrongness of losing a job or all our possessions in a natural disaster. The angry stage may last for a long time. When other losses happen, we may find ourselves stuck in this stage and unable to move past it.

In the next stage, Stage Three, we begin to bargain. We swear we will change; we say to others and ourselves that we will make our lives or other people's lives better. It is at this stage that we may find ourselves feeling at fault because something we did or did not do caused the death or loss. By hook or by crook, if we can just strike up the appropriate bargain, everything will be alright yet again.

Stage Four is depression according to Kubler-Ross. In this stage we feel grief. There are some very real symptoms of grieving. Sometimes these symptoms are misdiagnosed as depression. People who grieve often feel like they just cannot move or do anything; they feel emotionally and physically drained. It is a real effort to get out of bed, be with friends or even to carry on with everyday activities like bathing or eating. The person may do harmful physical acts such as using too many prescription or illegal drugs or starting to drink too much. There are negative psychological symptoms such as guilt, destructive self criticism and thoughts of suicide. Sometimes a person cannot cry or will go to the opposite extreme, and cry all the time. Stage Four may be experienced by being short-tempered or frustrated. At times we just cannot concentrate as a result of the depression.

The last stage is acceptance. In this stage, we have worked through the other four stages; we have become angry, depressed and now we accept our loss. Sometimes this stage involves forgiveness and actively letting go of negative emotions. In this stage, we will find we are experiencing less pain and emptiness; we will become involved with our life once again. We can remember and cherish how our life was before our loss, but we are now ready to move forward with our lives.

The next theorist to be discussed is J. William Worden. In his book, *Grief Counseling and Grief Therapy*, he discusses expressions of what he calls normal or uncomplicated grief. He feels that grief happens with our feelings, physical sensations, thinking patterns and behaviors. The feelings which we undergo when we grieve include sadness, anger, guilt, anxiety, loneliness, fatigue, helplessness, shock, yearning, relief and numbness. He does mention, however, that there can be a positive feeling following a death. The survivor may be pleased that the person died because it may mean the end of abuse for them or a release from all the time they spent taking care of the dying person. According to Worden, the common physical sensations include emptiness in the stomach, tension in the chest and/or throat, oversensitivity to noise, a sense of depersonalization, weakness in the muscles, lack of energy and/or dry mouth.

Quick Glance

Grief is sometimes diagnosed as depression.   T F

Grief always involves a great deal of tears.   T F

According to Worden, the most common reaction to grief is thoughts of suicide.   T F

We also experience cognitive and behavioral reactions to loss. The thoughts we experience in the grieving process may last for just a short duration of time but, on the other hand, they may last for a long time and lead to depression. Some of the feelings according to Worden include disbelief, confusion, obsession with the loved one, a sense of the presence of the loved one, and/or hallucinations. Behavioral reactions to grief include sleep disturbances, changes in appetite, absentmindedness, withdrawing from friends and relatives, dreaming and searching about the loss, restlessness, crying, visiting places or carrying objects that remind us of the loss, and/or treasuring objects of the deceased.

Unlike Kubler-Ross, Worden thinks about the grieving process in terms of the tasks of mourning. He says that our first task is to accept the reality of the loss. We could say things such as "I didn't like that job anyway" or "he did not love me anyway." The non-acceptance of the loss is akin to the first stage identified by Dr. Kubler-Ross.

For his second stage, Worden says that we need to work through the pain of grief. Sometimes we can avoid this by consuming too much alcohol or doing too many legal or illegal drugs. It is sometimes avoided by staying busy or traveling. Working through the grief would involve giving ourselves permission to experience the normal symptom of grief. It would mean expressing our anguish rather than masking it. The cost of not working through the pain of grief can make us physically as well as emotionally ill. Not working through the pain of grief may make us a part of the "walking wounded" in our society. The "walking wounded" may account for incidences we have in our society such as the shootings at Virginia Tech University in 2007 and other homicide-suicide accounts in our society.

The third stage is to adjust to an environment in which the deceased, or the loss, is missing. Adjusting to this transformation in surroundings require many adjustments. Our life is different as a result of loss or the death of our loved one. It may mean we have to learn to change a light bulb or adjust to the celebration of holidays without our loved one. This task may mean adjusting to the fact that the roles we have played prior to the loss must be changed.

Quick Glance

A behavioral reaction to grief can include sleep disturbances.   T F

The walking wounded have resolved their grief.   T F

The last stage of grief according to Worden is to move on with life. T F

The last stage is to emotionally relocate the deceased or loss and move on with life. In this stage we need to realize that life is good. We can take on new projects, meet new people and approach life with meaning and passion once again.

Alan D. Wolfelt, in *Healing Your Grieving Heart*, takes a more practical approach to adjusting to loss and grief. He identifies 100 practical ideas for grieving. Some of these ideas embrace much of what has been suggested by Kubler-Ross and Worden but he puts a very practical twist to the grieving process. Some of his ideas include understanding the difference between grief and mourning, being compassionate to ourselves, acknowledging the reality of death, and embracing the pain of the loss. He gives some more practical suggestions such as being aware of how grief affects the physical, emotional and social reality of each of us, keeping a journal, creating a sanctuary, meditating, buying a book, taking care of a pet, calling someone or looking into support groups, and/or praying.

When grieving, there are steps to take to help deal with feelings of loss. Probably the most difficult step is to accept your loss. It is good to talk about our loss to other people and to yourself. Secondly, we must give ourselves permission to suffer sadness. If we do not deal with our loss, it will act like a dam to our emotional health. Thirdly, we must come to accept our loss and redefine our physical and social environment in terms of our loss. Fourthly, read literature written specifically for losses. There is a list of suggested books at the end of this paper. The books are divided into the categories of death, losses, suicide and grief. Lastly, explore new interests with the help of loved ones.

There are some activities that we can take to help us with the grieving process. If we are grieving, we might have to push ourselves to take steps to finish the grieving process and sometimes we may need help using some of these techniques. Do not be afraid to ask for help. Talking to family and friends about our loss and our feelings is important. It may be necessary to seek professional counseling or join a support group. A trusted religious leader may be very helpful. Make the effort to seek out friends, eat healthy food, listen to music and exercise. And, most important, be kind and patient with yourself.

In conclusion, coping with loss is a journey, but it is a journey that must be taken in order to heal from our loss. To choose healing may be the more painful fork in the road, but if we do not take it then the price is high for us as individuals as well as our society. The tears happen and help us in healing from our losses, but the only person who is with us our entire life is ourselves. Empathy (the ability to understand another person's pain from their perspective instead of ours) may be the best gift we can give others. Empathy is a skill that is learned. Hence, it is a skill that is teachable. Life is fragile with its many changes; help others by learning to show empathy.

Quick Glance

It is best to keep grief and sorrow personal and private. T F

Handle problems yourself; do not burden friends. T F

Coping with loss can be taught. T F

THINKING SOCIOLOGY

What losses have you experienced in the last year? How effective were you with dealing with these losses? What techniques or steps did you use in coping? Were they effective? Why or why not.

Book List

DEATH:

Kubler-Ross, Elisabeth (1975). *Death: The Final Stage of Growth*. New York: Simon & Schuster.

LOSSES:

Beattie, Melody (2006). *The Grief Club: The Secret to Getting Through All Kinds of Change*. Center City, Minnesota: Hazelden.

Boone, Peggy and Bonnie Headington (2003). *Our Walk With Elephants: surviving the loss of adult children*. Baltimore: PUBLISHAMERICA, LLLP.

Kuehn, Eileen (2001). *Loss: Understanding the Emptiness*. Mankato, Minnesota: Capstone Press.

Lightner, Candy and Nancy Hathaway (1990). *Giving Sorrow Words*. New York: Warner Books, Inc.

Sanders, Catherine M. (1992). *Surviving Grief . . . and Learning to Live Again*. New York: John Wiley & Sons, Inc.

Scarf, Maggie (1980). *Unfinished Business*. New York: Ballantine Books.

Smedes, Lewis (1996). *The Art of Forgiving: When You Need to Forgive and Don't Know How*. New York: Ballantine Books.

Tatelbaum, Judy (1980). *The Courage to Grieve: Creative Living, Recovery, & Growth Through Grief*. New York: Harper & Row.

Trozzi, Maria (1999). *Talking With Children About Loss: Words, Strategies, and Wisdom to Help Children Cope with Death, Divorce, and OtherDifficult Times*. New York: A Perigee Book.

Wright, H. Norman (2006). *Recovering from Losses in Life*. Grand Rapids, Michigan: Baker Publishing Group.

SUICIDE:

Fine, Carla (1997). *No Time to Say Goodbye: Surviving the Suicide of a Loved One*. New York: Broadway Books.

Smolin, Ann and John Guinan (1993). *Healing After the Suicide of a Loved One*. New York: A Fireside Book.

GRIEF:

Albom, Mitch (2006). *for one more day*. New York: Hyperion Books.

Baugher, Bob, Carol Hankins and Gary Hankins (2000). *Understanding Anger during Bereavement*. Newcastle, Washington: Robert Baugher.

Feinberg, Linda (1994). *I'm Grieving As Fast As I Can*. Far Hills, New Jersey: New Horizon Press.

Froehlich, Mary Ann (2000). *An Early Journey Home: helping families work through the loss of a child*. Grand Rapids, Michigan: Discovery House Publishers.

Ginsburg, Genevieve Davis (1995). *Widow to Widow: Thoughtful, Practical Ideas for Rebuilding Your Life*. Cambridge, Massachusetts: Da Capo Press.

Levang, Elizabeth (1998). *When Men Grieve: Why Men Grieve Differently & How You Can Help*. Minneapolis, Minnesota: Fairview Press.

Manning, Doug (1979). *Don't take my grief away from me*. Oklahoma City, Oklahoma: In-Sight Books, Inc.

Neeld, Elizabeth Harper (1990). *Seven Choices: Taking the steps to new life after loss shatters your world*. Austin, Texas: Centerpoint Press.

Rando, Therese A. (1988). *How To Go On Living When Someone You Love Dies*. New York: Lexington Books.

Tavris, Carol (1982). *Anger: the Misunderstood Emotion*. New York: A Touchstone Book.

VanDuivendyk, Tim P. (2006). *The Unwanted Gift of Grief: A Ministry Approach*. Binghamton, New York: The Haworth Pastoral Press.

Vincent, Erin (2007). *Grief Girl: my true story*. New York: Delacorte Press.

Wolfelt, Alan D. (2001). *Healing Your Grieving Heart: 100 Practical Ideas*. Fort Collins, Colorado: Companion Press.

Worden, J. William (2002). *Grief Counseling and Grief Therapy*, Third Edition. New York: Springer Publishing Company, Inc.

Focusing on the Group

CHAPTER OBJECTIVES

1. What is a group?
2. What do we call different sized groups?
3. What are the differences between primary group and secondary group?
4. What are the differences between in-group and out-group?
5. What are the differences between gemeinschaft and gesellschaft?
6. What is a formal organization?
7. What is a reference group?
8. What is a social process?
9. What is a status?
10. What is a role?
11. What are role strain and role conflict?

▼ KEY TERMS

achieved status: a position earned through one's own efforts

aggregate: the people gathered by chance at the same place at the same time

alienation: the state of feeling detachment, devalued

ascribed status: the status that is assigned at birth

coalition: an alliance among members who share a common goal

competition: a social process that exists when there is a struggle for scarce resources

conflict: a social process that involves a disagreement, inflicting harm to another in an attempt to destroy or thwart another's efforts

cooperation: a social process whereby members work together to achieve a goal

dyad: a two-member group

formal organization: a group designed to meet special purposes

gemeinschaft: a community-oriented society which has personal and informal relationships

gesellschaft: a society based on impersonal relationships

group: two or more people in patterned interaction with a feeling of membership and sharing of norms and values which builds a feeling of solidarity among the members

in-group: any group to which a person feels like he/she belongs

master status: an extremely important status which is a central focus for the individual

out-group: a group to which a person feels like he/she does not belong

peter principle: in a bureaucracy people tend to be promoted up to their level of incompetence.

primary group: a group characterized by intimate interaction among its members

reference group: a group which is used as a standard in evaluating or understanding ourselves

role: a cluster of norms which tells us how to carry out a status

role complex or role set: all the roles that we play

role conflict: the condition that exists when we can not meet the obligations of two or more roles at the same time

role strain: the condition that exists when we can not meet role obligations as defined within one role

secondary group: a group which is formal and impersonal

social category: a statistical collectivity which shares a social characteristic

social exchange: a social process that involves each person calculating what he/she wants and what he/she is willing to give

social process: the behavior pattern that characterizes interaction between people

status: a position in society

triad: a three-person group

▼ KEY PEOPLE

Charles Cooley, Emile Durkheim, Robert Merton, Georg Simmel, Ferdinand Tonnies, Max Weber

What Is a Group?

One assumption of sociology is that human beings are social animals. People interact with one another on a daily basis. People often cluster together in one location such as a beach, ball game or movie theater. On a college campus, students are gathered in a classroom, student area or club meeting. In all these situations, people are interacting with one another; this interaction is a subject of great interest to sociologists. Interaction is the focus of study for the sociologist because interaction is necessary for the continuation of a culture.

Popular language frequently uses a different definition of a group from that of the sociologist. In popular language, a group is defined as a number of people gathered at the same place at the same time. However, in sociological terms, people gathered at the beach at the same time do not constitute a group; this gathering, in sociological terms, is called an aggregate. An **aggregate** is two or more people who are gathered at the same place at the same time but are not communicating in patterned interaction. In popular language, we also talk about women or African Americans as being a group. To the sociologist, both would be considered a social category. A **social category** shares some social characteristic; it is a statistical collectivity. Other examples of social categories include men, singles, elderly or the unemployed. These people share a common characteristic, but they do not occupy the same territory, nor do they interact.

Sociologists search for patterned interaction among people. Thus, for sociologists, a number of people gathered together does not necessarily make for a group because patterned interaction is lacking. A **group**, in sociological terms, suggests that there is preplanning for interaction among its people; there is a feeling of membership, sharing of norms and agreeing on values thus building a feeling of solidarity among its members. College fraternities and sororities, members of a swim team, a high school debate team and members of a family are all examples of groups. This chapter will investigate characteristics and the types of groups formed by people in their interaction with one another.

Groups share some very important characteristics:

1. *Members of a group share interests, values and norms.* I belong to the Parent-Teacher Organization. We share the interest of trying to provide quality education for our children; we place a high importance on education; and we all work at the fund raisers in order to raise money to buy supplemental equipment.
2. *Members of a group interact.* Sometimes it is a very intimate interaction such as the physical contact among members in the family, but sometimes it is more impersonal such as the interaction at the Parent-Teacher Organization meeting which conforms to formal rules.
3. *People identify with the group.* I am a member of the Parent-Teacher Organization. I am a member of African Wildlife Federation. Part of my feelings about myself are involved with the groups to which I claim membership.
4. *Groups have structure.* The structure may be written or unwritten. We have a formal structure here at our college. The president is at the top of the hierarchy and he has several vice presidents beneath him. Then come the division heads, department heads and, finally, the faculty. We have an organizational chart to show everyone's position. Our families also have a structure, but it is not written down on some formal chart. Mom and Dad are head of households, children are next in line for power. The older the child, generally the more authority that child has. At the bottom of the power list are the family pets!

THINKING SOCIOLOGY

To what social categories do you belong? To what groups do you belong?

Quick Glance

A group is the same as an aggregate. T F

A social category shares a social characteristic. T F

We share interests and interaction in a group. T F

Groups have either a formal or informal structure. T F

THINKING SOCIOLOGY

Analyze your peer group according to the characteristics of a group.

 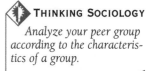

WHAT DO WE CALL DIFFERENT SIZED GROUPS?

Two or more people in interaction constitute a group. A German sociologist, Georg Simmel, is credited with being the pioneer in investigating the size of groups. Simmel identified the **dyad** as a two-member group. The dyad is identified as the simplest group because the membership is two members. A dyad may be two friends, an engaged couple or a married couple. Membership in a dyad means a close relationship in which there is a feeling of belonging and intimacy between the two. This intimacy is not possible when the group increases in number. We simply cannot develop a relationship with everyone who may be enrolled in our sociology course, but we may find that we develop a close relationship with the person sitting beside us in the class. A dyad, however, is the most fragile of any size group. Should one of its members decide to leave the group, it means the group dissolves and no longer exists. The dyad can become a larger group with the introduction of one other member.

▲ A TRIAD IS A THREE-PERSON GROUP.
IMAGE COPYRIGHT KISELEV ANDREY VALEREVICH, 2008. USED UNDER LICENSE FROM SHUTTERSTOCK, INC.

A **triad** is a three-person group. The addition of one member to the dyad alters the communication and structure of the group. An example of a triad is a married couple who have a child. In a triad, this third person may play a number of different roles. The third person may serve a unifying role which brings the group closer together. A husband and wife may find themselves seeking a professional marriage counselor serving the role as a mediator in order to facilitate a successful marriage. The third member may also be a divisive factor within the group. When I was in high school a male liked me; my best friend happened to like this same male. Needless to say, the friendship did not last between the girl and me.

As groups begin to grow in number of people, there begins to exist the possibility of coalitions. A **coalition** is an alliance among members who share a common goal. Coalitions can form in families. A dad can feel like a coalition forms between a child and a mother, mom can feel like a coalition forms between the child and the father. My husband felt that our teenager should be home at midnight, but I felt that was much too late. Our teenager, of course, felt like we had "ganged up against him."

WHAT ARE THE DIFFERENCES BETWEEN PRIMARY GROUP AND SECONDARY GROUP?

A contemporary sociologist, Charles Horton Cooley, addressed types of groups; he made a distinction between primary groups and secondary groups. He coined the term **primary group** to refer to a group which is characterized by intimate interaction among its members. Examples of a primary group would be members of our respective family, close friendship with people of our same gender, parent-child relationship and some teacher and student relationships. It is possible to be a part of more than one primary group at any time in our lives. The term **secondary group** refers to a formal and impersonal group.

The concept of ideal type was discussed in Chapter 1. Cooley designed a typology based on ideal types for the purpose of analyzing different types of groups; the two ends of the continuum are primary group and secondary group. The family is a good example of a primary group and we shall use this group to discuss the characteristics of a primary group:

1. *A primary group is relatively small.* This group generally does not include more than two to five people. If the primary group is a close friendship group, it will include no more than around ten people.

2. *A primary group is held together by strong ties of affection.* We usually have strong feelings of love and passion between spouses, we love our parents, we usually sign birthday cards to very close friends with something other than "Yours truly" or "Sincerely yours." The strong ties of affection also allow us to express other strong feelings within the primary group. In addition to feeling strong feelings of love, we also feel angry or hurt.

3. *We are emotionally invested in our primary group.* Within our family, for example, we love, hate, scream and pat on the back because we relate to these people in a bonded relationship.

4. *The primary group gives us emotional and social support.* We like to receive warm fuzzies at home when the workplace has been traumatic or we have had a fight with a friend or lover.

5. *We feel strong, personal identification with our primary group.* Since we identify with them, we want their approval for our actions. That is one reason why young people want their parents to like their choice of spouse. This close identification is also why our families have such a strong impact on the development of our self-concept.

6. *The primary group is characterized by multidimensional relationships.* The interaction we have, for example, with our family is extensive. By extensive we mean that within the family group you feel like you can be yourself and fully share your emotions, actions and attitudes without fear of permanent censure. If I have a bad headache when I am at home, I can act grumpy. If I am at school, I shall act as if I feel okay.

7. *The primary group depends on continuous face-to-face interaction.* We interact with our family frequently and for long periods of time. After children leave home, we call each other and get together for holidays and vacations if we want to maintain strong, primary ties.

8. *The primary group is a very durable group and can even be called a permanent group.* The family goes on until the death of its members. My mother has had some of the same friends, another example of a primary group, lasting for twenty-five years.

9. *The primary group is based on trust.* As a result of the long nature and strong feelings involved in the primary group, we feel that we can trust the people in our primary group, and that they can trust us. We do not think that our parents lie to us in any significant way, or that children lie to parents. That is the reason why parents get so upset when they catch their children lying to them.

10. *Within the primary group, social control is based on informal means.* In Chapter 3, we talked about informal negative and positive sanctions. These are the types of sanctions that are used in the primary group. We tell our children that they did a good job; our spouse says that the meal was really good; we tell the children that they can not go to the movies until their room is cleaned up and homework done.

Quick Glance

A primary group is usually small.	T	F
Primary group is one end of a continuum.	T	F
A family is a secondary group.	T	F
We are emotionally vested in a secondary group.	T	F
Primary groups are long-lasting groups.	T	F
We develop much of our self-concept in primary groups.	T	F
Human needs are met in primary groups.	T	F

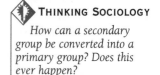
THINKING SOCIOLOGY

How can a secondary group be converted into a primary group? Does this ever happen?

Quick Glance

The secondary group is multidimensional.	T	F
A secondary group usually has about five people.	T	F
Emotions are important in a primary group.	T	F

A secondary group, in contrast, forms the opposite type of group from that of primary group. A work division in a large corporation is a good example of a secondary group:

🔆 *Quick Glance*

A secondary group is emotionally based.　T　F

People have extensive emotional bonds with people in a secondary group.　T　F

Informal sanctions are important for secondary groups.　T　F

◢ THINKING SOCIOLOGY

Do you spend more time within your primary groups or your secondary groups? What type of group do you most enjoy? Why?

1. *A secondary group is a relatively large collection of people.* The secondary group can include thirty or more people in it. For example, the division in which my husband works includes twenty-three people.
2. *The secondary group is held together by weak affectional ties.* We may like the people in our secondary group, but we do not love them or feel any real close emotional attachment to them. We maintain an impersonal involvement. When we leave a large college class, we say "goodbye" and go on our way. The next semester we enroll in another class and meet different people.
3. *The secondary group involves little or no personal identification.* One class setting is about like another. We do not say we are a permanent member of any given class like we do in our family.
4. *Secondary groups have one-dimensional relationships.* People in our secondary group do not know all about us; they only know that aspect of our behavior that is important for the functioning of the group. For example, students are not really interested in the physical health or the status of their instructor's family; they only want to know how good an instructor that person is.
5. *The secondary group is characterized by limited face-to-face contact.* We meet three hours a week in the average class. We rarely spend any degree of time with each other outside of the classroom. A dormitory floor forms a secondary group but if you become close friends with your roommate or the person down the hall, you start spending a great deal of time together, and then the group shifts to a primary group.
6. *The secondary group is not a permanent group.* At the end of the semester or year, our dorm floor breaks up and each person goes their own way. The class ends after fifteen weeks and each student goes on their way to another life adventure. We may say that we will get together for lunch or dinner, but chances are you do not or only do so for one or two times.
7. *We do not put the same trust in people in our secondary group that we do in our primary group.* For example, a salesperson is noted for misrepresenting his product in order to make a sale. That is the reason why some groups like to have home sales parties because primary groups are involved and you can trust someone with whom you are emotionally close.
8. *The secondary group uses formal sanctions to ensure conformity.* You are bound by rules of attendance and grading policy within the classroom. The corporate division has the right to fire you or not renew your contract.

In modern society much of our contact is secondary in nature. Our involvement with people in the workplace, at school and with our daily interaction at restaurants, hospitals and doctors' offices is secondary. We sometimes create the illusion of the primary group in the secondary setting. The hospital personnel who call people by their first name, rather than by a more formal title, and the salesperson who asks you about your spouse and kids are making an effort to generate the feeling of primary group. Within the secondary group, primary ties can emerge. Our division is a secondary

▲ IN MODERN U.S.A., MUCH OF OUR CONTACT IS SECONDARY IN NATURE.
IMAGE COPYRIGHT DMITRIY SHIRONOSOV, 2008. USED UNDER LICENSE FROM SHUTTERSTOCK, INC.

group, but the authors of this text form a primary group. We are in frequent face-to-face contact, know a great deal about each other's family, and, if we have a rotten day, it is all right to "cut loose."

Primary-secondary group forms a continuum. Some groups are more secondary than others. For example, a sociology class at a large university such as Stanford, Texas A & M or Ohio State University, may have 250 people in it and chances are you will know few, if any, people in the class and your instructor probably does not know the students' names. On the other hand, if the sociology class is small, students are more apt to get to know each other and the instructor can engage in face-to-face interaction. The smaller class is still a secondary group but does not as strongly share in all of the characteristics of the secondary group.

Some voluntary organizations may begin with small numbers and those members may form a primary group. However, as that organization grows in numbers, that feeling of closeness and intimacy may lessen thus developing into a secondary group. There can be, however, primary groups that form within secondary groups. Within a large sorority, there will be individuals who realize they have some things they share in common and begin to interact with one another forming a primary group.

Sociologists look very closely at the interaction differences within primary and secondary groups. Within primary groups, human needs are met with regard to people caring about us as people; while in secondary groups the concentration may be on people meeting the needs of the organization. Of concern to sociologists is the amount of time that people are now spending within secondary groups.

In Chapter 1, reference was made to Durkheim's study of the importance of groups. Durkheim's study of suicide scientifically viewed the importance of belonging to a group. In the egoistic suicide, Durkheim identified the need for belonging to a group and for feeling that someone cares about us as a person. That need is more likely to be met within a primary group. However, in post-industrialized America, we are spending more and more of our time in secondary groups. In secondary groups, lacking in intimacy and closeness, it is possible to feel loneliness even among a large number of people.

Both primary and secondary groups, and all types in between, are very important for the operation of our society. Much of our interaction takes place within the group and, the group as we discussed in Chapter 1, influences our behavior just as we often change the behavior of other members of the group. These groups also help to link us to the rest of society. For example, by being a member of the school faculty, I am networked with not only my fellow teachers, but with administration and faculty from other schools around the United States.

WHAT ARE THE DIFFERENCES BETWEEN IN-GROUP AND OUT-GROUP?

William Graham Sumner first identified the terms in-group and out-group. With these types of groups, we develop feelings of "we" and "them." An **in-group** is any group to which people feel they belong. The term in-group implies the existence of an **out-group**, or that group to which people feel they do not belong. We may have membership in many groups and come to have a feeling of "us" or "we" and consider those who do not belong to be "them." Many times there may be a feeling of "us" being the superior group and "them" being inferior. This can occur between football teams, fraternities, sororities, religions and families. Americans who have served their country in the armed services view "veterans" as superior because they have demonstrated their dedication to their country while they view nonveterans as inferior because they did not

🕮 *Quick Glance*

A group is either a primary or a secondary group. T F

Only primary groups are important for the operation of society. T F

Lack of integration into a primary group can lead to egotistic suicide. T F

Much of modern contact is secondary in nature. T F

Primary ties can exist within the secondary group. T F

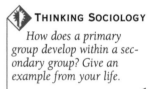 **THINKING SOCIOLOGY**

How does a primary group develop within a secondary group? Give an example from your life.

🕮 *Quick Glance*

I identify with my in-group. T F

Feelings of in-group can contribute to prejudice. T F

An in-group is the same as a primary group. T F

demonstrate their love for their country. For example, my father and his friends "looked down" upon males who avoided the drafts during World War II.

Sociologist Robert K. Merton took this idea one step further when he identified "in-group virtue, out-group vice." This term identifies that members of an in-group view their behavior as virtuous or good; however, when the same behavior is exhibited by members of the out-group, that behavior is viewed as a vice or bad. Proselytizing, or trying to bring in new members by distributing religious "tracts" at a street corner, is encouraged by mainstream religions. However, when various cults attempt to proselytize, or bring in new members by distributing their tracts, mainstream religion may try to have such evil stopped. This feeling of "in-group and out-group" may account for problems of prejudice and discrimination that exist in the society in which we live. These feelings can influence an individual's behavior and thinking.

IN-GROUP/OUT-GROUP AND PRIMARY/SECONDARY GROUP		
	In-Group	*Out-Group*
Primary Group	My family	"The Jones'"
Secondary Group	My college	Competing college

WHAT ARE THE DIFFERENCES BETWEEN GEMEINSCHAFT AND GESELLSCHAFT?

A German sociologist, Ferdinand Tonnies (1855–1936), analyzed types of societies by looking at the kind of ties within the community. He developed a polar typology of societies which he called gemeinschaft and gesellschaft. A **gemeinschaft** society is a community-oriented society in which the relations are personal and informal. Tradition is very important in holding the society together. Family life is very strong, and everyone knows, or knows of, everyone else. This is what we find in village and town life. In the **gesellschaft**, on the other hand, we find the relationships impersonal and based on contract. Because of this, the importance of the primary group has declined and social control is much more difficult. The gemeinschaft shares the characteristics of the primary group and the gesellschaft shares the characteristics of the secondary group.

WHAT IS A FORMAL ORGANIZATION?

Increasingly, people find themselves interacting more within large secondary groups. These large secondary groups are **formal organizations** and are designed to meet special purposes. The formal organizations are much different from the patterns of organization and interaction found in small groups.

The following are the differences between small groups and formal organizations:

1. *In small groups, members share many of the same activities.* In a family, for example, everyone might be wrapping presents for a birthday party. In a formal organization, however, members generally do specialized tasks.
2. *In a small group, the hierarchy is informal;* but when the group becomes larger, it is necessary to spell out everyone's job and to write job descriptions in order to ensure that all tasks are done.
3. *In a small group, norms are generally informal.* Everyone knows and accepts the norms. In a larger group, the rules and regulations are clearly defined. In fact,

Gemeinschaft	Gesellschaft
Tradition oriented	Future oriented
Resistant to change	Look to rapid change
Emphasis on customs	Emphasis on codified laws
Social relationships long-lasting	Social relationships more transitory
Social relationships personal, affectionate	Social relationships more impersonal, anonymous
Little division of labor	Complex division of labor
Interrelated roles	Segmental roles
Emphasis on ascribed roles	Emphasis on achieved roles
Agricultural and extraction industries	Manufacturing and service industries
Caste system of social stratification	Class system of social stratification
Homogeneous population	Population of diverse cultural backgrounds
Ascribed status important	Achieved status important
Economically self sufficient	Increasingly complex economic interdependence
Simple technology	Increasingly complex technology
"Folk" entertainment such as carnivals	More synthetic entertainment, i.e. spectator sports
Apt to be patriarchal	More gender equality
Informal education, illiteracy widespread	Emergence of mass education
Usually small in size	Usually large in size
Family is focal unit of society	Kinship group loses importance to economic and political relationships
Primary group emphasis	Secondary group emphasis
Family loyalty important	Society loyalty important
Society in harmony with nature	Society control of nature important
Religion is important unifying factor	Religion is separate and diverse
Little or no social disorganization	Raising rates of social disorganization/anomie
High social integration	Low social integration
Cooperation is an important social process	Competition is an important social process

frequently there are books of rules and regulations that we can refer to in order to determine correct behavior.

4. *In a small group, membership is based on personal affection or kinship.* This is not true for the larger organization. In the formal organizations, membership is based on competency or skill.

5. *In a small group, relationships are generally primary;* we value people for who they are. In a formal organization, we are more apt to have primary ties within the group, but others are judged on task orientation.

6. *In small groups, communication is face to face.* In the larger formal organization, communication frequently is by phone call, newsletter or some other form of written communication such as a memo.

THINKING SOCIOLOGY

Which do you prefer for problem solving? A small group or formal organization? Why?

Formal organizations develop characteristics of what Max Weber identified as a bureaucracy. Characteristics of a bureaucracy are division of labor, hierarchy of authority, rules and regulations, impersonality and job security.

First, bureaucracies develop a division of labor to ensure efficiency. Rather than one person performing all of the functions of the organization, there is an emphasis on becoming an expert in one area. If a person knows their particular part of the job well, then he or she can do a better job doing one job rather than several jobs. American factories started the assembly line so that consumer products could be produced faster. More cars could be produced using an assembly line rather than one person building one car. There has been a dysfunction based on this division of labor, loss of a feeling of craftsmanship. Workers rarely observe the raw product transformed into an actual product, but rather see only the stage at which the product passes them. For many of those on assembly lines, there is the fear of being replaced by automation.

Another characteristic of a bureaucracy is the hierarchy of authority. There is a chain of command in a bureaucracy. The members are aware of who is in charge. This chain of command clarifies who has power in decision making so that a worker knows to whom to take a problem for solutions. However, dealing with a bureaucracy can be frustrating when we cannot find the person who claims to be able to make a decision.

Within a bureaucracy, rules and regulations govern the group. This clarifies what procedures are to be followed. However, those rules and regulations may mean what is often referred to as "red tape" or that the procedures are so lengthy that an individual may become frustrated by the amount of paperwork involved.

A fourth characteristic is impersonality; this characteristic states that everyone is treated the same. We may be assigned account numbers to speed up efficiency. However, we come to feel that no one cares.

The last characteristic identified by Weber is security. An employee cannot be fired because of personal reasons but only for not conforming to the rules. Guidelines for hiring employees are established by impersonal qualifications rather than by whom we know. Thus, according to the guidelines of a bureaucracy, Hillary Clinton should not have been hired as part of President Bill Clinton's cabinet in January of 1993.

Life in the bureaucratic setting has some negative consequences:

1. *Bureaucracies potentially facilitate ritualism.* Sometimes in a bureaucracy we become so concerned with procedures that we lose sight of why the rules were put there in the first place. When we rigidly follow the rules, we stop looking at the needs of the people and do not adapt to changing circumstances. Ritualism also involves "passing the buck." People become afraid to make decisions because they do not know the procedure of the situation.

2. *Bureaucracies protect incompetent people.* They do this by hiding mistakes from people higher in the hierarchy, developing informal work loads, being hesitant to demote people and promoting on seniority rather than skill.

3. *Bureaucracies end up hiring and promoting people based on personality and personal relationships.* Who you know may be as important as what you know and promotions may be based on feelings of liking rather than qualifications. Such terms as "team player" come into play here. The **Peter Principle** may be a by-product. We see individuals promoted based on merit until they reach their level of incompetency. At that point, the person is no longer promoted. There is a strong tendency in a bureaucracy not to demote a person and as a consequence, the person remains in a position in which he or she is not really competent.

Quick Glance

A bureaucracy is based on job specialization. T F

A bureaucracy promotes a hierarchy of leadership. T F

Efficiency is important for a bureaucracy. T F

Rules and regulations govern a bureaucracy. T F

Quick Glance

A bureaucracy promotes ritualism. T F

A bureaucracy often stifles creativity. T F

Information tends to be generated by bosses. T F

THINKING SOCIOLOGY

Have you experienced some of the negative results of a bureaucracy? How? Which ones?

Quick Glance

Information flows freely in the bureaucratic system. T F

A collective organization is based on the bureaucratic model. T F

The Japanese have the same employment system as the U.S.A. T F

4. *Bureaucracies stifle creativity and may contribute to feelings of alienation.* Since I am performing a very narrow range of skills, I cannot put any of my own ideas into my work. And since I do this narrow range of skills, I become very much like a machine and may become very dissatisfied with my job; I develop feelings of alienation.
5. *There is strong pressure to keep an organization going no matter what.* There are jobs involved, and also egos, which demand that the group keep going even after the task has been accomplished.
6. *In theory, communication flows upward and downward in a bureaucracy, but in reality, information goes from the top to the bottom.* Management rarely listens seriously to people on the bottom rungs of the bureaucratic ladder. Because of the authoritarian nature of the bureaucracy, it is also in the best interest of people below the bosses of the bureaucracy to hide mistakes and problems because their promotions and evaluations depend on what and how the boss feels about them.

One response to the negative results of the bureaucracy is the collective model of organization. The collective model is based on achieving organization efficiency by worker commitment, ideology, dedication, technical competence, minimal division of labor, generalization of jobs rather than specialization, restriction on reward differentials, democratic control and stressing of primary ties.

Learning TIP
Essay questions are a better way to study for a multiple choice exam than the multiple choice questions in the study guide.

THINKING SOCIOLOGY
How do you think the collective model would work for an American bureaucracy such as your college or university?

Quick Glance
We use our reference group as a behavioral standard.   T F
Reference groups serve a normative function.   T F
I can belong to, or identify with, a reference group.   T F
I can only belong to one reference group at a time.   T F

WHAT IS A REFERENCE GROUP?

A special type of group is called a reference group. A **reference group** is a number of people that we use as a standard for evaluating or understanding ourselves. We look to the reference group for norms and symbols to guide our own behavior. There are several types of reference groups:

1. *A reference group can be one of which you are actually a member.* I am a member of the college faculty, and as such I follow certain norms like helping a colleague with information or substituting in their class if she/he is ill. If you belong to a fraternity or sorority, you will follow the dress and behavioral standards of the group.
2. *A reference group can be one which you aspire to join.* A young person may aspire to become a lawyer. Lawyers become a reference group for him as he learns what he must do to become a lawyer. He may try to become ac-

THINKING SOCIOLOGY
How are reference groups important to children? Who or what was one of your reference groups as a child?

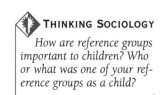

🐚 *Quick Glance*

Reference groups
can influence our
behavior. T F

Our reference group
can influence our self-
concept. T F

Reference group gives
us a reference for other
people in our group. T F

Learning TIP
Use your study guide questions as a trial test. Study
the material and then do
the study guide as a pretest.

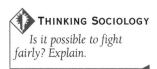
THINKING SOCIOLOGY
*Is it possible to fight
fairly? Explain.*

quainted with a lawyer to discover what a lawyer does, how a lawyer dresses and what income a lawyer can make. To this young person, "lawyers" have become a reference group.

3. *A reference group can be a mentor or famous figure that you emulate but have no illusions of becoming a part of their direct group.* Teenagers who idolize rock stars may dress in cut up, ragged clothes, wear long earrings and unusual hair styles in order to emulate their favorite stars. If a boy admires Garth Brooks or Clint Black, he may dress, cut his hair and act like the famous singer. Jesse, (played by John Stamos) on the television show *Full House*, makes Elvis Presley his reference group. Jesse wears his hair like the *King* and imitates his musical style. He has an Elvis guitar and has a large picture of Elvis on his wall.

Reference groups serve at least two functions:

1. *Reference groups serve a normative function by giving standards of behavior that are acceptable.* For example, a person who wishes to become a lawyer will have to successfully pass the entry exam for law school.

2. *Reference groups serve as a comparative function so that a person can judge themselves and others.* A person may feel that because she has done well on a debate team, she could easily become a lawyer. A person can be influenced by more than one reference group in his or her lifetime or by more than one reference group at any particular point in his or her life.

Reference groups are important because they give us a standard on which to model our own behavior, plus they give us insight into other people's behavior.

WHAT IS A SOCIAL PROCESS?

🐚 *Quick Glance*

A social process is the
way people interact. T F

Conflict is the same as
competition. T F

Conflict is the most
important social
process. T F

Competition can
shape the attitudes of
competitors. T F

NEVER DOES THE HUMAN
SOUL APPEAR SO STRONG
AND NOBLE AS WHEN IT
FORGOES REVENGE AND
DARES TO FORGIVE AN
INJURY.
E. H. CHAPIN

Regardless of the size or type of groups, social processes can be identified. A **social process** is a behavior pattern that characterizes interaction among people. Social processes are repetitive forms of behavior that are found within the group or social life. The interaction among the members may be identified as cooperation, competition, conflict and social exchange. All four processes can occur simultaneously. For example, episodes of cooperation, competition, conflict and social exchange can all be identified as occurring in one family. It is not as if one family practices only cooperation, another only competition, while another practices only conflict. We shall briefly discuss each of the four major social processes.

Conflict

Conflict is that social process that involves disagreement and inflicting harm

▲ ALL FOUR SOCIAL PROCESSES MAY BE IDENTIFIED IN ANY SOCIAL GROUP.
IMAGE COPYRIGHT KRISTIAN SEKULIC, 2008. USED UNDER LICENSE FROM SHUTTERSTOCK, INC.

on another in an attempt to destroy or to thwart another's efforts. Conflict can occur at a corporate level when labor unions go on strike against the managers. Conflict can be on a more personal level; for example, two siblings fighting over a toy. There are few rules governing conflict. The adage is that "all is fair in love and war."

Competition

Competition exists when there is a struggle for scarce resources. Competition also can be identified as a process that takes place in the family. Children may compete with one another for mom's or dad's attention. Competition occurs in the market place for the consumer to buy a Ford, Chevrolet or Chrysler. Competition on the political scene is obvious as politicians struggle for votes. Competition is related to conflict but there are rules governing competition. And the less you know your competitor, the more rules there are governing your behavior. If you are up for a job, for example, you do not slash your competition's tires so she/he cannot get to the job interview nor do you alter her records. You work on making yourself know more and appear better prepared. Competition is a very important social process in our culture; we compete for grades and jobs as well as compete on the job for promotions and raises.

Competition has some interesting consequences on human behavior:

1. *Competition can shape the attitudes of the competitors.* For example, when merit pay enters the academic world, there is a strong tendency not to share teaching methods and materials because there is only so much money to go around and each person would like to maximize their share. Children can be playing quite happily in a group until they divide into two teams. Then the children in the two groups may have disagreements over rules and have bitter quarrels.

2. *Competition increases productivity only if the task is repetitious.* For the creation of new ideas, the third social process, cooperation, is much more effective. If I want to get three bushels of peas shucked, competition would be good; if I wanted a new way to shuck the peas, competition would be counterproductive.

3. *Some people do not want to compete.* That baffles some parents when their children do not play to win at a game. I can remember when my daughter swam competitively, one set of parents kept pushing their child to swim faster and start bringing home ribbons. The child did not try any harder nor swim any faster. The parents finally realized the child really was not interested in winning but enjoyed the social aspects of the swim team.

4. *People, when they consistently lose, may drop out of the competition.* Another competitive swimmer tried very hard to improve her swimming times, but never consistently won. She dropped out two years later to try another sport.

5. *Competition can turn into conflict.* A football game is competitive and many a game has ended with fights on the field among players or among fans after a close game.

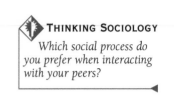

THINKING SOCIOLOGY

How has competition influenced your academic performance?

THINKING SOCIOLOGY

Which social process do you prefer when interacting with your peers?

Quick Glance

Everybody competes in America.	T F
Conflict turns into competition.	T F
Cooperation is the least common of the social processes.	T F

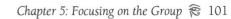

COMPETITION EXISTS WHEN THERE IS A STRUGGLE FOR SCARCE RESOURCES.
IMAGE COPYRIGHT ARTMANNWITTE, 2008. USED UNDER LICENSE FROM SHUTTERSTOCK, INC.

WIN-WIN IS NOT A TECHNIQUE, IT'S A TOTAL PHILOSOPHY OF HUMAN INTERACTION.
STEVEN COVEY

Cooperation

THINKING SOCIOLOGY

How would you analyze the four processes using the family?

The third, and most pervasive of the social processes, is cooperation. **Cooperation** is the process whereby members work together to achieve a goal. Without cooperation, there would be no society. Cooperation depends on people motivated to seek and share goals, to have knowledge of the benefits of cooperation, to have a favorable attitude towards working and sharing and to have the skills to cooperate. We start very early telling children that cooperation is good and giving them the skills they need to know in order to share toys and time. Cooperation can be identified in families with the members working together to get chores done within the household and then going to a movie together. I am on a committee to establish an alumni group for our college; we have divided up college and universities in the area to ascertain how they have established their organizations. Politicians can cooperate to get a bill passed.

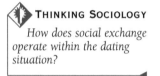

IF WE HAD NO WINTER, THE SPRING WOULD NOT BE SO PLEASANT.

ANNE BRADSTREET

Social Exchange

Social exchange is an important social process in modern society. This involves each person calculating what they want and what they are willing to give. It is a rational form of cooperation. Trade would be a good example. I shall watch your children tonight, if you watch mine tomorrow night. I shall drive you to school today because you picked up my dry cleaning last week.

THINKING SOCIOLOGY

How does social exchange operate within the dating situation?

There is a long list of important social processes which include consensus (terms of cooperation are laid down like in a court order), accommodation (conscious effort to gain a working relationship), exploitation (depriving someone else of goods and services such as in slavery), compromise (all parties renounce some of their demands and the decision meets at a mutually acceptable place), confrontation (strong pressures to change another person's opinion) and coercion (forcing someone to do something).

WHAT IS A STATUS?

Quick Glance

Social exchange is a rational form of cooperation.	T F
A status is a role in society.	T F
An achieved status is inherited.	T F
A master status is a minor status.	T F

Within our groups and organizations, we occupy positions. Each of these positions is called a **status**. There are two basic types of status: ascribed and achieved. An **ascribed status** is one over which we have no control. My position as female is an ascribed status; my race of Caucasian is an ascribed status. An ascribed role is assigned at birth and includes such factors as race, gender, nationality and, sometimes, religion. In an **achieved status**, on the other hand, I can take direct action to change. My position of female is ascribed but my status as mother is achieved. My position as college professor is also an achieved status.

Some of my statuses are more important in life than others, this is called a **master status**. For example, my status as female is a master status because it affects all of my other statuses. Without the status of female, I would not be mother, wife or even female professor who is generally perceived as being more nurturing than a male professor.

SOCIAL PROCESSES WITHIN THE FAMILY			
Conflict	*Competition*	*Cooperation*	*Social Exchange*
fist fight between brothers for telephone	two sisters trying to beat each other's swim time	parents and children decorating Christmas tree	parents paying a child money to mow lawn

WHAT IS A ROLE?

Each status has a role associated with it. A **role** is a cluster of norms which tell us how to carry out the status. The role is the dynamic part of the position. Each role has a set of rights and duties associated with it. I occupy the status of college instructor. Some of the norms associated with this role include being dressed appropriately and not eating breakfast in front of the class. Some of my duties include having a pertinent lecture planned, telling students my grading policy and announcing tests in a timely manner. I also have some rights. I have the right to expect my students to be prepared for class and not plagiarize their research papers. You occupy the status of student and you play the role. As a student, you have the duty to be on time to class and to read the chapter before entering the classroom. You have the right to receive appropriate material in the classroom. We learn about these roles through the socialization process.

Roles serve important functions for society:

1. *Roles regulate behavior.* When I drove to school this morning, I did not have to decide whether I would drive on the right- or the left-hand side of the road. I did not ask what that blinking red light meant. I have learned the role of driver, so much of my driving behavior is automatic.

2. *Roles allow me to predict your behavior.* This goes back to Mead's generalized other that we discussed earlier in Chapter 4. I assume that you, too, will drive on the right-hand side of the road. I know that most people even walk down the right hand side of the mall walkway. I do not think any of you will enter the classroom and start yelling nasty words at me.

3. *Roles facilitate social control.* We learn our roles at a very young age, and we carry them out. When I go to McDonald's, I know that I have to wait in line until it is my turn; very rarely do people just barge up ahead of us. We internally control our own behavior.

We each have a role complex or role array. A **role complex** or role set is all the roles that we play. My role complex, for example, includes college instructor, mother, wife, neighbor, daughter and volunteer worker for Citizens for Animal Protection. Since my earlier years, my role complex has become more elaborate. When I was five years old, I had a more limited number of roles to play but as I got older, I added roles. As I age, I shall probably give up some of my roles. My mother role will become less time consuming as my children get their driver's licenses, leave home for school and start their own families. I shall retire and give up my workplace role. Some of us during the middle years feel like our role complex has become much too involved; we feel like a pie divided into many small pieces. This is one of the reasons why so many people have high levels of stress.

Every role has an accompanying complementary role. In order to play the role of wife, there has to be a person playing the role of husband. In order for me to carry out my role of wife, I have to have a basic understanding of the role of husband. My husband also has to come to an agreement with me on what constitutes my role of wife. In order for a person to function with their own roles, she/he has to know the complementary role. The norms of the complementary roles should mesh into a harmonious whole. This is also part of what Mead called the generalized other that we studied in Chapter 4.

▼ **THINKING SOCIOLOGY**

What would you consider to be your master status?

Quick Glance

A role is a bagel.	T F
A role complex is the same as role array.	T F
We all play many roles.	T F
We learn our roles through socialization.	T F

WHAT TIME WOULD IT BE IF ALL THE CLOCKS WERE STOPPED?

ZEN SAYING

Quick Glance

Roles govern my behavior.	T F
Roles are important for social control.	T F
Roles have duties but no rights.	T F
We all have a role complex.	T F
We must understand complementary roles.	T F

▼ **THINKING SOCIOLOGY**

What roles make up your role complex?

 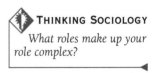

THINKING SOCIOLOGY

What roles bring you the most happiness? Which give you the least feeling of accomplishment? Why?

With each of us playing so many roles, we face problems fulfilling the obligations and duties within one or more of our roles. This is called role strain. **Role strain** is the difficulty we face in meeting our obligations within one role.

Role strain occurs in several ways:

1. *I may be inadequately prepared for the role.* We talked about this when we talked about deviancy. I may not fully understand the role of mother; therefore, if I do not understand how to care for diaper rash, I have a screaming child on my hands.
2. *I may feel a distaste for the role.* For example, a man can be very much the introvert and not like to get up in front of crowds to speak, but part of his job is to run company seminars. He faces role strain.
3. *There may be ambiguity with society's definition of the role.* When our doctor had her first baby, she faced role strain; her friends thought she should go back to work very quickly, but her in-laws felt she should stay at home with the baby. Society has not yet clearly defined the norms of what constitutes a "good mother." Can she work? Should she stay home? This is not a source of stress yet for the males in our society.
4. *A person may face role strain when there is a discontinuity in their roles.* We tell people to work hard all of their life, be productive and then we retire them at about age 65 and tell them to kick back and relax. We tell our teenagers to act like adults, make their own decisions; then, we tell them to be in by midnight and not to buy that leather jacket.

Role conflict happens when you cannot meet the obligations of two or more roles at the same time. For example, I get up on a Monday morning and my child has a fever of 100 degrees, do I fulfill my role of mother and stay home, or do I fulfill my role as instructor and teach my classes?

Role conflict and role strain can be eliminated or alleviated through several means. *First, we can ease the strain of role transition by having rites of passage.* A rite of passage ceremony takes a person from one status to another. Among the Masaii, for example, a boy goes through a circumcision ceremony, receives instruction on the ways of the culture, and enters the culture as an adult with all the rights and responsibilities of an adult. There is no definite period in our culture when we go from being an adolescent to an adult. There is also a ceremony among the older warriors that takes them to status of "elder." We have a similar situation if we have a retirement dinner for a person.

Second, anticipatory socialization can help minimize problems with role strain. Proper training in teaching courses and making public speeches might help the man who has to run company seminars. More courses in spouse roles and parenting roles would ease the transition into these new roles.

Third, delinquency and crime are sometimes used to ease role strain or conflict. A student who is working thirty hours a week and must produce a major term paper is suffering from role conflict. Rather than taking the time to do the research, he could buy a paper, or pay to have someone else write it.

Fourth, mental illness is occasionally used to ease role conflict. If I compulsively have to wash windows and scrub floors, I do not have time to worry about my other roles. If I become a catatonic schizophrenic, I withdraw from reality and thus leave many of my roles.

Quick Glance

Every status has a complementary role.	T F
Role strain occurs within a role.	T F
Role conflict happens between two roles.	T F
I can experience role strain because I am forced to retire.	T F
I can experience role strain because I dislike public speaking when I am president of a civics group.	T F
Going from student to worker can cause role strain.	T F
I can experience role strain because I lack knowledge.	T F

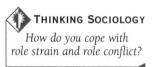

LIFE IS WHAT HAPPENS TO YOU WHILE YOU'RE BUSY MAKING OTHER PLANS.
JOHN LENNON

THINKING SOCIOLOGY

How do you cope with role strain and role conflict?

Quick Glance

Anticipatory socialization helps alleviate role strain.	T F
Rites of passage make role strain worse.	T F
Mental illness is a solution to role conflict.	T F
Substance abuse can help role conflict.	T F

Fifth, role conflict or strain can be solved by compartmentalizing. I put on my "mom hat" in the morning. After I drive the children to school, I put on my "teacher hat" and wear that until about 3 p.m. Then, on with my "chauffeur hat," quickly followed by "mom, cook, and dishwasher hat." In the evening, I put back on my "teacher hat" to grade papers and prepare lectures. We divide our days up so that we can fulfill the different roles that we must do.

Sixth, we set a hierarchy of role obligations. In the example I used earlier about my child being sick and having to teach class, I probably would stay home with the sick child. There is a strong tendency in our culture to put the mother role before the work role. If my husband was sick, however, I would go ahead and teach my classes. For a student in an evening class who is working full time to support a family, the work role probably would be placed before the school role. We all have certain roles that we feel are more important than other roles.

Seventh, physical illness can be used to avoid role strain or conflict. If I am sick, I have to stay in bed and take care of myself in order to get well again. I relinquish my roles or cut back on my roles for the period of time that I am sick. I had a neighbor who always either had a headache, backache or colitis so she never had to fulfill some of her other roles such as mother and neighbor.

Eighth, we can change the role definition to help resolve role conflict or strain. I grew up in a very traditional family which viewed the wife role as one who got up in the morning and fixed breakfast, packed all needed lunches, and had supper on the table. I have since redefined my wife role, and I no longer get up to fix breakfast and the evening meal no longer has to be on the table every time. Sandwiches at 7 p.m. are now okay. Part of redefining roles frequently involves delegation of responsibility. For example, I do not fix lunches; every child fixes their own lunch. My husband can do some of the tasks that were traditionally part of my wife role such as laundry and feeding the pets.

Ninth, we can give up some roles to relieve the stress or strain of roles. I might, for example, drop one of my courses, stop attending an organizational meeting or stop doing volunteer work.

Tenth, we can run away or selfhandicap. Running away includes substance abuse such as alcoholism all the way to the ultimate run-away of suicide. If I run away, I have no problem with role strain or conflict any longer.

Let us summarize the basic theme of this chapter. When we talk about levels of social organization, we have a continuum. At the micro level of organization we have social encounters: two or more people in interaction. From these social encounters, relationships develop and relationships form social groups. As the social groups become larger, associations develop. Associations become even larger in an urban, industrialized society. Associations are at the level of macro organization; they join together as parts of institutions and institutions combine to form societies.

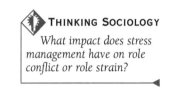

FOR FAST-ACTING RELIEF, TRY SLOWING DOWN.
LILY TOMLIN

THINKING SOCIOLOGY
What impact does stress management have on role conflict or role strain?

TIME MANAGEMENT IS REALLY A MISNOMER—THE CHALLENGE IS NOT TO MANAGE TIME, BUT TO MANAGE OURSELVES.
STEPHEN R. COVEY

Quick Glance

A dyad is a group at the micro level of analysis. T F

Institutions combine to form societies. T F

Associations are common in urban areas. T F

▼ CHAPTER SUMMARY

1. The sociological definition of a group is two or more people in interaction. This is unlike an aggregate or a social category which share a location or a social characteristic.

2. Groups differ in size. A dyad is a group of two people while a triad is three people.

3. A primary group is geared towards emotional needs in contrast to a secondary group which is task oriented.

4. The gemeinschaft is community-oriented while gesellschaft is like modern urban centers. Formal organizations are typical of a gesellschaft.
5. A reference group is used as a standard for evaluating or understanding our behavior. We can either identify or be a member of this group.
6. We identify with our in-group and feel indifference towards or hostility against out-groups.
7. Social process is the common means by which interaction takes place within a group. The four most common are conflict, competition, cooperation and social exchange.
8. Status is a position in society; achieved status is based on direct effort while ascribed status is based on characteristics that cannot be changed.
9. A role is a cluster of norms. Individuals face dilemmas in fulfilling requirements within a role which is role strain or between two or more roles which is role conflict. We address role conflict and role strain through anticipatory socialization, rite of passage, mental or physical illness, compartmentalization, hierarchy of role obligation, change of role definition and/or escapism techniques.

▼ REFERENCES

Cooley, Charles Horton. 1902. *Human Nature and the Social Order*. New York: Scribner's.

Cooley, Charles Horton. 1967. "Primary Groups." In A. Paul Hare, Edgar R. Borgotta, and Robert F. Bales (Eds.), *Small Groups: Studies in Social Interaction* (rev. ed., 15–20). New York: Knopf. (Original work published 1909).

Janis, I. 1991. "Groupthink" in L. Cargan, J. H. Ballantine (Eds.), *Sociological footprints*. Belmont, CA: Wadsworth.

Milgram, S. 1974. *Obedience to Authority*. New York: Harper & Row.

Morgan, G. 1986. *Images of Organizations*. Newbury Park, CA: Sage.

Sumner, William Graham. 1906. *Folkways*. Boston: Ginn.

Tonnies, Ferdinand. 1957. *Community and Society*. Translated and edited by Charles P. Loomis. East Lansing: Michigan State University Press.

Weber, Max. 1946. "Bureaucracy." In H. H. Gerth & C. W. Mills (Eds.), from Max Weber. *Essays in Sociology* (pp. 196–244). New York: Oxford University Press.

Weber, Max. 1946. *From Max Weber*. Edited by H. H. Gerth and C. Wright Mills. New York: Oxford University Press.

Weber, Max. 1964. *The Theory of Social and Economic Organization*. Translated by A. N. Henderson and Talcott Parsons. New York: The Free Press.

READING

EXCERPT FROM SOCIAL THEORY AND SOCIAL STRUCTURE
BY ROBERT K. MERTON*

To discover that ethnic out-groups are damned if they do embrace the values of white Protestant society and damned if they don't, we have first to turn to one of the in-group heroes, examine the qualities with which he is endowed by biographers and popular belief, and thus distill the qualities of mind and action and character which are generally regarded as altogether admirable.

Periodic public opinion polls are not needed to justify the selection of Abe Lincoln as the culture hero who most fully embodies the cardinal American virtues.

Even the inevitable schoolboy knows that Lincoln was thrifty, hard-working, eager for knowledge, ambitious, devoted to the rights of the average man, and eminently successful in climbing the ladder of opportunity from the lowermost rung of laborer to the respectable heights of merchant and lawyer.

Did Lincoln work far into the night? This testifies that he was industrious, resolute perseverant, and eager to realize his capacities to the full. Do the out-group Jews or Japanese keep these same hours? This only bears witness to their sweatshop mentality, their ruthless undercutting of American standards, their unfair competitive practices. Is the in-group hero frugal, thrifty, and sparing? Then the out-group villain is stingy, miserly and penny-pinching. All honor is due the in-group Abe for his having been smart, shrewd, and intelligent and, by the same token, all contempt is owing the out-group Abe for their being sharp, cunning, crafty, and too clever by far. Did the indomitable Lincoln refuse to remain content with a life of work with the hands? Did he prefer to make use of his brain? Then, all praise for his plucky climb up the shaky ladder of opportunity. But, of course, the eschewing of manual work for brain work among the merchants and lawyers of the out-group deserves nothing but censure for a parasitic way of life. Was Abe Lincoln eager to learn the accumulated wisdom of the ages by unending study? The trouble with the Jew is that he's a greasy grind, with his head always in a book, while decent people are going to a show or a ball game. Was the resolute Lincoln unwilling to limit his standards to those of his provincial community? That is what we should expect of a man of vision. And if the out-groups criticize the vulnerable areas in our society, then send 'em back where they came from. Did Lincoln, rising high above his origins, never forget the rights of the common man and applaud the right of workers to strike? This testifies only that, like all real Americans, this greatest of Americans was deathlessly devoted to the cause of freedom. But, as you examine the statistics on strikes, remember that these un-American practices are the result of out-groups pursuing their evil agitation among otherwise contented workers.

Once stated, the classical formula of moral alchemy is clear enough. Through the adroit use of these rich vocabularies of encomium and opprobrium, the in-group readily transmutes its own virtues into others' vices. But why do so many in-groupers qualify as moral alchemists? Why are so many in the dominant in-group so fully devoted to this continuing experiment in moral transmutation.

An explanation may be found by putting ourselves at some distance from this country and following the anthropologist Malinowski to the Trobriand Islands. For there we find an instructively similar pattern. Among the Trobrianders, to a degree which Americans, despite Hollywood and the confession magazines, have apparently

Quick Glance

Abraham Lincoln personifies American virtues. T F

Out-groups are supposed to adopt in-group virtues. T F

Out-groups are not supposed to adopt in-group virtues. T F

not yet approximated, success with women confers honor and prestige on a man. Sexual prowess is a positive value, a moral virtue. But if a rank-and-file Trobriander has "too much" sexual success, if he achieves "too many" triumphs of the heart, an achievement which should of course be limited to the elite, the chiefs or men of power, then this glorious record becomes a scandal and an abomination. The chiefs are quick *to resent any personal achievement not warranted by social position.* The moral virtues remain virtues only so long as they are jealously confined to the proper in-group. The right activity by the wrong people becomes a thing of contempt, not of honor. For clearly, only in this way, by holding these virtues exclusively to themselves, can the men of power retain their distinction, their prestige, and their power. No wiser procedure could be devised to hold intact a system of social stratification and social power.

The Trobrianders could teach us more. For it seems clear that the chiefs have not calculatingly devised this program of entrenchment. Their behavior is spontaneous, unthinking and immediate. Their resentment of "too much" ambition or "too much" success in the ordinary Trobriander is not contrived, it is genuine. It just happens that this prompt emotional response to the "misplaced" manifestation of in-group virtues also serves the useful expedient of reinforcing the chiefs' special claims to the good things of Trobriand life. Nothing could be more remote from the truth and more distorted a reading of the facts than to assume that this conversion of in-group virtues into out-group vices is part of a calculated deliberate plot of Trobriand chiefs to keep Trobriand commoners in their place. It is merely that the chiefs have been indoctrinated with an appreciation of the proper order of things, and see it as their heavy burden to enforce the mediocrity of others.

Nor, in quick revulsion from the culpabilities of the moral alchemists, need we succumb to the equivalent error of simply upending the moral status of the in-group and the out-groups. It is not that Jews and Negroes are one and all angelic while Gentiles and whites are one and all fiendish. It is not that individual virtue will now be found exclusively on the wrong side of the ethnic-racial tracks and individual viciousness on the right side. It is conceivable even that there are as many corrupt and vicious men and women among Negroes and Jews as among Gentile whites. It is only that the ugly fence which encloses the in-group happens to exclude the people who make up the out-groups from being treated with decency ordinarily accorded humans beings.

Checking Out Collective Behavior

6

IMAGE COPYRIGHT LARS CHRISTENSEN, 2008. USED UNDER LICENSE FROM SHUTTERSTOCK, INC.

CHAPTER OBJECTIVES

1. What is collective behavior?
2. What are the forms of collective behavior?
3. What is a social movement?
4. How do social movements start and what are the stages of a social movement?
5. What are the types of social movements?
6. How do sociologists explain collective behavior?
7. What does the future hold?

acting crowd: a crowd in action

casual crowd: the most loosely structured of all crowds consisting of a collection of individuals

collective behavior: the relatively spontaneous and unstructured behavior of people who are reacting to a common influence in an ambiguous situation

conservative movement: a social movement striving to keep conditions the way they are currently

contagion theory: the explanation of collective behavior suggested by Gustave LeBon which states that people become crazed and violent within a crowd

conventional crowd: a deliberately planned crowd engaging in relatively structured behavior

convergence theory: a crowd attracts participants who are ready to participate

craze: a collective behavior in which the behavior of participants is viewed as outrageous

crowd: a temporary gathering of people to share a common event

cultural drift: the process in which small changes in a culture occur over a period of time and eventually add up to change the whole way of life of a society

emergent-norm theory: the theory that states that what is considered appropriate or inappropriate norms is decided as collective behavior occurs

expressive crowd: a crowd organized to permit the personal gratification of its members

fad: a temporary episode of collective behavior that involves a large number of people centered around a behavior or object

fashion: a form of temporary collective behavior involving personal appearance or behavior

generalized belief: the shared view that something must be done to correct structural strain

goal displacement: the goals of the original social movement are translated into other goals in order to keep the formal organization in existence

mass hysteria: the irrational, compulsive behavior that spreads among people

migratory movement: a social movement in which discontented people move geographically

mob: a very emotional, disorderly crowd which may use destructive and violent behavior to achieve its goal

mobilization for action: the actual organization for participation in collective behavior

orgy: a proceeding marked by unbridled indulgence of passion, such as overeating or drinking

panic: the feeling of fear to an impending threat

precipitating factor: an event, incident or behavior that gives the generalized belief credence thus leading to collective behavior

public opinion: the attitudes expressed concerning matters of public policy

reactionary movement: a social movement that rejects the status quo

reform movement: a social movement that campaigns for change

revolutionary movement: a social movement in which a large number of people reject all or part of society and want to establish a new social organization

riot: the destructive outbursts in which participants experience a feeling of heightened arousal

rumor: an unconfirmed report of information given informally

separatist movement: a social movement which seeks to escape by setting up alternative organizations

social movement: an organized collective behavior designed to bring about or resist social change

structural conduciveness: the structure of society that tolerates collective behavior

structural strain: the feeling of social deprivation which is identifiable

value-added theory: the theory which explains how social conditions bring about collective behavior

▼ KEY PEOPLE

Herbert Blumer, Betty Friedan, Gustave LeBon, Neil J. Smelser

WHAT IS COLLECTIVE BEHAVIOR?

In 1938, H. G. Wells' novel, "The War of the Worlds," was broadcast over a New York radio station. Although the program began with an announcement that the broadcast was a fictional dramatization, some people tuned in late and some were fooled by an announcer who interrupted the music to say that strange disturbances had been observed in New Jersey. To further confuse listeners, music was interrupted by an apparent eye-witness account of a meteorite that had landed and from which a monster emerged. "Experts, scientists and public officials" made commentaries during the broadcast to further increase the reality of the airing. Then, the station announced that the Martian invader had destroyed an army unit and had moved to New York City where it had poisoned the population with toxic gas. By the time of the half-hour station break, panic had struck. Phone lines were swamped, crowds swarmed into bus and train stations, people hid in cellars or jumped into their cars and drove away. The "panic" caused by this broadcast was an example of collective behavior. There have been several movies based on both the book and the peoples reactions to the broadcast.

What is collective behavior? **Collective behavior** is the study of relatively spontaneous, unstructured social behavior and its products. Collective behavior frequently causes relatively rapid changes in people's behavior and brings about changes in ideas.

Collective behavior has several important characteristics:

1. *Collective behavior is not synonymous with all human social action*. Social action such as school registration or children piling into school the first day of school does not constitute collective behavior.
2. *The collectivities which are formed are distinct from organized human groups*. The family, the peer group and the work force are groups which we think of as a cohesive unit. However, in collective behavior, emotional contagion binds people together.
3. *Collective behavior depends on emotional contagion*. People "pick up" on other people's emotions and are influenced by them. We sense, for example, physical behaviors such as heavy breathing, perspiration and muscular tension. We look to others for cues on how to feel and what to do. An important *consequence of heightened suggestibility is the loss of critical thinking*. When tension dominates consciousness, the weighing of alternative courses of action recedes into the background. These common emotions form a common bond holding us together to act as a unit without critical thought. For example, in a very close football game, excitement builds from one person to another. Even if I am not very interested in the outcome of a game, I can hardly prevent myself from being swept up by the excitement.
4. *Participants in collective behavior usually do not behave according to the traditional norms*. Interaction in the newly formed collectivities may differ from routine social interaction. For example, during the duration of a fad (which we shall define later) I may dress in an unusual way; animal prints are currently a fad so I have several outfits that have zebra print or African animals on them. Another example of not acting according to traditional norms involves behavior about the pro-choice or pro-life movement. I was driving my child to school and a woman threw herself across the hood of my parked car protesting abortion. Women (there were fifteen of them) were doing this to all the cars and shoving signs against windshields. I knew these women as moderate people who usually conformed to society's expectations.

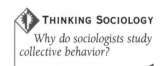

THINKING SOCIOLOGY

How do you think that you would have reacted to the broadcast of "The War of the Worlds?" Why?

Quick Glance

"The War of the Worlds" caused panic.	T	F
School registration is collective behavior.	T	F
Collective behavior can create rapid change.	T	F
Collective behavior is planned.	T	F

THINKING SOCIOLOGY

Why do sociologists study collective behavior?

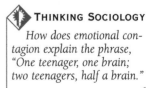

WHETHER SOCIAL CHANGE IS FAST OR LAZY, WHETHER IT IS ACHIEVED BY VIOLENCE OR BY FABIAN REFORM, IT LEADS FORWARD, BUT NEVER QUITE UP TO THE PERFECT SYSTEM OR THE PERFECT STATE.

LYNMAN BRYSON

THINKING SOCIOLOGY

How does emotional contagion explain the phrase, "One teenager, one brain; two teenagers, half a brain."

🕭 *Quick Glance*

Collective behavior is
the same as any other
social behavior.　　T　F

Collective behavior
depends on emotional
contagion.　　T　F

People engaging in
collective behavior often
act very emotionally.　T　F

Collective behavior
emerges when people
face a new problem.　T　F

THINKING SOCIOLOGY

*Analyze a situation in
your life in which emotional
contagion played a significant part.*

🕭 *Quick Glance*

Collective behavior is fluid
and unpredictable.　　T　F

Collective behavior
happens only when
people engage in face-to-
face interaction.　　T　F

Collective behavior is
always unstructured
behavior.　　T　F

Collective behavior is
always spontaneous.　T　F

Social change can come
about through collective
behavior.　　T　F

THINKING SOCIOLOGY

*What part did emotional
contagion play in the
suicides at Jonestown?*

5. *People engaged in collective behavior tend to act more emotionally*; they may cry, scream, run, shout or carry a protest sign. During the protest marches of the 1960s, civil rights workers marched on Washington, D.C.; people picket abortion clinics; and after a very close football game, people stream, yelling, onto the field to tear down the goal post.

6. *Collective behavior usually emerges when there is an unusual or unforeseen problem*. Collective behavior also emerges when the situation is ambiguous. We have norms in place to handle routine problems. Greenpeace became very frustrated about the slowness of the government system, so they came up with a new solution to stop animal killing and pollution. They took boats out and followed very closely those agencies they felt were hunting endangered species or were polluting the oceans.

7. *Collective behavior usually lasts a relatively short period of time*. A fad, such as dress, lasts for a couple of months; pickets in front of abortion clinics rarely last more than a couple of days. Even sustained rioting occurs sporadically rather than lasting for a long duration.

8. *Collective behavior is frequently marked by a sense of urgency*. People feel something is going to happen. Much collective behavior does not just happen without prior conditions. In the U.S.S.R., there were feelings of problems and tension that something was going to happen long before the actual breakup came during the winter of 1991.

9. *Collective behavior is fluid and unpredictable*. Fashion, for example, cannot be readily predicted from the previous year. Hems go up, hems go down; hats are in style, hats are not in style. Rioting also is unpredictable. Law enforcement, for example, cannot predict where a riot will break out in areas such as Los Angeles during the summer of 1992 or the spring of 2002 in Pakistan until it does. The times and places for high activity are not predictable.

10. *The boundaries of emotional contagion, and thus collective behavior, are not set by physical proximity or even group membership, but rather by the limits of effective communication*. To the extent that feelings are transmitted through mass communication; press, radio and television can cause an entire nation to be caught up in collective excitement. An example of this is the Neo-Nazi movement during the 90s that have gained strength in Germany and the United States, even in the 2000s.

11. *Collective behavior forms a continuum from spontaneous behavior to very structured behavior*. Examples of spontaneous behavior include such phenomena as hysterical outbursts; crowds and riots are more structured; the most structured types of collective behavior are social movements and revolutions. We shall talk about social movements in another section of this chapter.

12. *Collective behavior is important not only because it makes headlines and sometimes affects great events, but also because spontaneous activities may give rise to new norms and values*. Some of the religious denominations originated in collective behavior. Denominations such as Methodist and Baptist originated in a religious social movement.

WHAT ARE THE FORMS OF COLLECTIVE BEHAVIOR?

What qualifies as an episode of collective behavior is diverse; therefore, there are many different kinds or types of collective behavior.

Crowds

Crowds are a very important type of collective behavior. A **crowd** is a temporary gathering of people joined to share a common event. People who gather at a baseball game and participate in the "wave" would be a crowd. A "heavy metal" concert, a Garth Brooks concert or a Michael Bolton concert would qualify as a crowd.

Crowds are a good source of collective behavior for several reasons:

1. *People in a crowd tend to be suggestible to ideas and actions from other people.* We mentioned emotional contagion in an earlier section of this chapter. People are more apt to go along with feelings and actions of the rest of the group. I can remember my mother saying that "one person has a whole brain, two people half a brain, and three people, no brain at all." The statement may not be totally accurate, but it does point out that discretionary action decreases in the presence of other people.

2. *People in a crowd feel insignificant and unrecognized because they are a member of a group.* A crowd acts in unison rather than as individuals and, for this reason, an individual does not feel like they are easily identifiable.

3. *People of a crowd are more apt to behave in a more spontaneous manner.* Individuals are not as apt to reflect on their actions and the consequences of their actions.

4. *People in a crowd feel invulnerable.* Because they feel like they cannot be identified, they behave in ways that would be less likely if social control mechanisms were in place. This is true because a crowd is a temporary social group; it may last only a matter of minutes or hours before it disperses. Within a crowd, I do not make a life-long commitment to the other participants and I am not concerned with their knowing me in several hours, let alone several days.

5. *A crowd is largely unorganized.* Leadership may develop, but there is not a hierarchy of leadership and no socially sanctioned norms have been established.

6. *There are loose internal controls within a crowd.* Behavior is not controlled by authority formally vested in certain members of a crowd. The group pressure may be powerful within a crowd.

Quick Glance

A crowd is a temporary gathering of people. T F

People in a crowd are more suggestible. T F

People in a crowd often feel unrecognized. T F

People in a crowd feel invulnerable. T F

THINKING SOCIOLOGY

Think about the last time you went to a concert or sporting event. How did the 6 characteristics of a crowd influence your behavior?

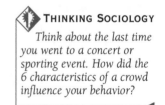

▲ WHO KNOWS WHAT IS GOING TO HAPPEN IN THIS CROWD WITH SUCH A LARGE NUMBER OF PEOPLE BECAUSE PEOPLE FEEL INSIGNIFICANT AND INVULNERABLE.

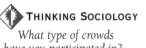

THINKING SOCIOLOGY

*What type of crowds
have you participated in?
Analyze your behavior in
terms of collective behavior.*

Herbert Blumer came up with several different types of crowds. **Casual crowds** are the most loosely structured of all crowds and consist of a collection of individuals such as an ordinary crowd in a street who have little or no purpose in common. The individual members have little emotional involvement in the crowd and can easily detach themselves from it. Their physical closeness implies some social interaction, however, and a precipitating incident such as a traffic accident or attempted suicide leap from a nearby building can produce greater structure and more social cohesion for the members. When we waited to buy our tickets to the Michael Bolton concert, we were part of this type of crowd.

Conventional crowds are deliberately planned and relatively structured; they are "conventional" in the sense that their behavior follows established social norms or conventions. An audience in a theater, for example, is a conventional crowd, although circumstances such as an emergency can disrupt the crowd's conventional behavior. Once we got to the Michael Bolton concert and found places on the hillside, we became part of a conventional crowd.

Expressive crowds are usually organized to permit the personal gratification of its members, an activity that is viewed as an end in itself. A college dance, a religious revival meeting and a rock festival are all examples of expressive crowds. When Michael Bolton came out into the audience during the second half of the concert, we were all yelling and screaming; this made us a part of an expressive crowd. In some religious services, emotional contagion is encouraged and results in a relatively uncontrolled and predominantly expressive behavior such as the speaking in tongues and enthusiastic dancing. Mass meetings and deliberate assemblies form crowds. Besides conducting business, meetings are also designed to stimulate feelings of solidarity. Political conventions and Amway meetings could become expressive crowds.

Acting crowds are crowds in action. There are three basic types of acting crowds: mobs, riots and orgies. A mob is a very emotional, disorderly crowd which may use destructive and violent behavior to achieve its goal. It refers to one crowd that is fairly unified and singleminded in its aggressive intent. Mob aggression is the most goal-oriented and dependent upon leadership for its direction. Acts of mob behavior include lynching, looting or destroying property. The storming of the Basteille during the French Revolution in 1789 is a very good example of mob behavior. The lynching of a horse thief in Texas during the 1800s would be another example of mob behavior.

Riots are destructive outbursts of collective behavior with the participants usually experiencing a feeling of heightened arousal. A riot does not involve the focus of a mob; a riot, even though destructive, involves a wide range of activities and goals. Rioting tends to express generalized resentment and rebellion rather than definite purpose. The riot occurring in Los Angeles after the trial of the police officers accused in the beating of Rodney King in 1992 is an example. The looting and destruction of buildings and homes will take years to rebuild. The race riots that happened in Miami in 1980 is another example. There were riots in March 2002 in Venezuela when a general strike was called during political turmoil. Riots are apt to happen during times of political problems and changes.

An orgy is an example of an acting crowd. An **orgy** is any proceeding marked by unbridled indulgence of passion. This includes such behavior as a Thanksgiving feast where we eat ourselves into a total couch potato, New Year's Eve where we drink and eat too much, and Halloween when we beg and eat too many sweets. Tension is released through shared fun. However in some cases the behavior of the participants may exceed what is assumed to be the cultural norm.

Mass Hysteria and Panic

Mass hysteria and panics are forms of collective behavior. **Mass hysteria** is irrational, compulsive behavior which spreads among people. Mass hysteria is based on false beliefs. Hysteria has been provoked by the excitement of sporting events, fear of phantom attackers, fear of practice of witchcraft and Orson Welles' 1933 broadcast of "The War of the Worlds" which we mentioned earlier. Several years ago there was great concern about satanic cult groups killing chickens and cattle. In late 1973, Johnny Carson reported on his show that the federal bureaucracy had not budgeted enough money for the purchase of toilet paper in government buildings. Carson mentioned that it would be possible for the people of the United States to experience a shortage of toilet paper. His comments were taken seriously by millions of his viewers and they stockpiled toilet tissue for their families. The run on toilet paper, of course, led to a shortage of this supply, the self-fulfilling prophecy in action.

A **panic** happens when a number of people react to a threat in the environment with fear and anxiety. A panic occurs in the face of danger and this danger usually is in relationship to physical survival. In panic we see an immediate and severe danger but we do not know what to do because we can only see a limited number of escape routes and, in many cases, these escape routes do not get everyone out of the situation; disorganization then happens when people become preoccupied by their own personal safety and totally disregard the safety of others. Lack of information or of existing communication channels contribute to this feeling of entrapment. This is the reason why institutions such as high schools, colleges and hospitals have fire or safety drills; if people know what to do in an emergency, they are less apt to panic. When I was a child we used to have tornado drills; the teachers would tell us to go to the central hall, if possible, and place our arms over our heads as we sat in a crouched position.

A panic, interestingly enough, does not usually occur during natural disasters such as the mass flooding as California experienced in 1993 or the hurricanes that struck Homestead, Florida in 1992 or the flooding in Texas, 2001 caused by Allison. Behavior rapidly becomes structured as people react to the natural disaster.

Fad, Fashion and Craze

A **fad** involves the quick spread of an unusual pattern of behavior through a large number of people. A fad generally involves some relatively superficial and external pattern of behavior such as a way of dress. Fads seem to spread primarily among individuals in similar social circumstances; they represent heightened cue-taking from other members of one's own social group or from members of some group to which one would like to belong. One of the underlying emotions seems to be anxiety concerning social status. Some of the past and present fads include collecting "pet rocks" and giving them personal names, wearing a "mood ring," possessing Cabbage Patch dolls, swinging with children's "hoola hoops" and the recent fad of collecting Power Rangers. This, of course, also includes eating the appropriate cereal for breakfast and wearing the appropriate logo t-shirt! A fad provides a market for entrepreneurs who strike it lucky with their invention. Americans rush out to purchase the newest fad. Fads usually appear and then die without building on the next fad. Fads sometimes are reborn such as with troll dolls.

Fashion is also a form of temporary collective behavior involving personal appearance or behavior. A fashion reflects a society's interests and motives and changes more slowly than do fads. We accept a fashion and we expect it to change periodically. Clothing styles, for example, are expected to change from season to season and year to year. The wearing of the "mini skirt" or the sideburns made popular by Elvis were in fashion in the 60s. Mini skirts appeared again in 1990. Other current fash-

▶ **THINKING SOCIOLOGY**

Have you ever panicked? Why?

Quick Glance

A riot is goal oriented. T F

An orgy is an acting crowd. T F

Mass hysteria is the same as a panic. T F

Natural disasters cause panic. T F

▶ **THINKING SOCIOLOGY**

Can you think of a current fad? What is it?

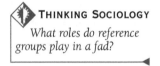

EVERY GENERATION LAUGHS AT THE OLD FASHIONS, BUT FOLLOWS RELIGIOUSLY THE NEW.

H. D. THOREAU

▶ **THINKING SOCIOLOGY**

What roles do reference groups play in a fad?

Quick Glance

A fad is a superficial behavior pattern. T F

A fad spreads between people within a peer group. T F

A fashion is expected to change. T F

A craze has more emotional connotation than a fashion. T F

Fads change more quickly than fashions. T F

ions include wearing gold chains and having pierced ears and noses. A nonclothing fashion is drinking bottled "gourmet" water. The colors of gold and olive green of the 60s have given way to the blue, mauve and cream of today's well-decorated house.

A craze has more emotional connotations than a fad or fashion. **Crazes** are a form of collective behavior in which the behavior of the participant may be viewed as outrageous by observers because the behavior consumes so much time and energy. Crazes range all the way from aerobics, country and western dancing and rap music to solving jigsaw puzzles. The distinction between fad and craze is not definite. For example, I collect baseball cards; is this activity a fad or craze? The activity certainly occupies a great deal of time in sorting and cataloging cards, attending shows and going to shops in quest for the needed card!

Rumor and Public Opinion

Rumor occurs in dispersed groups of people. A **rumor** is an unconfirmed communication usually transmitted by word of mouth in a situation of anxiety or stress. Rumors are reports of information that travel from person to person on an informal basis. Rumors spring up in unstructured situations when information is needed but reliable channels do not exist. Because rumors are so readily influenced by emotions, rumors tend to be rapidly disseminated and distort or falsify the facts. Rumor both contributes to and is a product of emotional contagion. The rift between the royal couple, Prince Charles and Princess Di, in 1990, began as a rumor that filtrated through the media because of speculation about the lack of the two being seen together in a happy fashion. The Watts riots of 1965 were partly due to a rumor that European American police officers had beaten a pregnant African American woman. Michael Jackson claims that he has long been beset by rumor. Rumors circulated that he had multiple plastic surgeries to change his face, that he had undergone a process of bleaching his skin and that he and his siblings were victims of child abuse. In February of 1993, Michael Jackson went on a televised interview with Oprah Winfrey and attempted to set the rumors to rest.

Public opinion is the attitude expressed concerning matters of public policy. Talk shows on television and radio have become important means for Americans to express their public opinion. In the presidential election of 1992, media came into its own concerning public opinion. Voters in the United States expressed the public opinion that changes in health care, unemployment and the economy were desired. Candidates for election responded to these issues utilizing the media for influencing the public opinion.

The last form of collective behavior to be discussed is social movement. A **social movement** is an organized form of collective behavior designed to bring about or resist social change. The Civil Rights Movement and the Women's Movement in the 1960s would be examples of social movements desiring to change conditions in a society which offered unequal opportunities to some of its members. A more detailed discussion of social movements follows.

Houston, Texas was a collective behavior laboratory during the week of September 19, 2005. The Houston area was in the potential path of hurricane Rita. After the devastation caused by hurricane Katrina, Houston residents panicked. Millions of people evacuated the city. There were traffic jams beyond belief. Some people gave up leaving and decided it was safer to turn around and return home. Commutes that normally took forty minutes were sometimes taking 10 or more hours. People spent two days just getting out of the city. Mass hysteria happened in the stores. Lines were long and shelves were empty of water, batteries, plywood! Those of us who stayed put, stayed glued to our television for 3 days! Rumors were flying about where water or gasoline could be purchased. Public opinion differed on whether evacuation

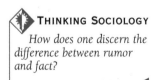

FORMS OF COLLECTIVE BEHAVIOR

Type	Example
Mob	The crowd outside The Summit after the Houston Rockets won the NBA Championship
Riot	The Boston Tea Party
Orgy	Rose Bowl Day Party when Ohio State is playing!
Mass hysteria	Fear of Disease in the book *Hot Zone*
Panic	Disorganization at College under bomb threat
Fad	Power Rangers
Fashion	Spiral Permanents
Crazes	Aerobic exercise
Rumor	"Tom Cruise will run for president."
Public opinion	Feelings about Welfare Reform
Social movement	Women's rights

ALL THINGS ARE CONNECTED. WHATEVER BEFALLS THE EARTH BEFALLS THE SONS OF THE EARTH. MAN DID NOT WEAVE THE WEB OF LIFE. HE IS MERELY A STRAND ON IT. WHATEVER HE DOES TO THE WEB HE DOES TO HIMSELF.

CHIEF SEATTLE

was necessary or not. Many people evacuated due to emotional contagion. Even your authors, who had decided to stay, wondered if we had made the correct decision with so many friends and neighbors leaving.

WHAT IS A SOCIAL MOVEMENT?

THINKING SOCIOLOGY
What social movement have you participated in?

A **social movement** is a conscious striving by a relatively large group of people to bring about or resist societal change. A social movement is a lasting form of collective behavior. When there is widespread dissatisfaction with certain conditions within a society, people try to change the conditions. A social movement emerges with goal-directed behavior and attempts to create change concerning some aspect of the social institutions. Some examples of social movements include women's liberation, black liberation, the peace movement, Zionism, Young Republicans, League of Women Voters, pro-bussing movement, anti-bussing movement, equal rights for the handicapped, pro-choice, anti-abortion, and the Marriage Encounter Movement.

The distinction needs to be made between social movement and cultural drift. **Cultural drift** is the process in which small changes in a culture occur over a period of time and these changes eventually add up to changing the whole way of life of a society. Examples of cultural drift include early urbanization, the Industrial Revolution and, possibly, the Women's Movement.

A social movement has several basic features that distinguish it from other forms of collective behavior:

1. *The members always share values and goals with an underlying ideology.* For example, as an environmentalist, I support saving the environment and the belief that we have the obligation to save our planet from ecological disaster. In the early history of our culture, we had a "cowboy mentality;" we felt that we always had another stream or another acre of land to use or abuse. Now we think in terms of our planet being a spaceship with a limited number of resources and, once these resources are depleted or polluted, there is no other source.

2. *The members of a social movement share a sense of belonging with those who agree with their viewpoint (in-group) and a sense of opposition to those who do not share their ideology (out-group).* I get very angry at people who throw trash out their car window or who do not recycle aluminum cans and newspapers.

3. *The members know how they should behave as supporters of a social movement.* I tell people where they can recycle material; I belong to several environmen-

Quick Glance

A social movement is a form of collective behavior.   T F

A social movement develops when people are unhappy about some aspect within the society.   T F

People involved in a social movement share norms and values.   T F

Members of social movements are idealistic.   T F

Social movements are made up of many organizations.   T F

Social movements come into existence when a sufficient number of people are dissatisfied with a condition in society.   T F

talist groups, I send money to support environmental causes, and write letters to my congressman and representative.

4. *There is a division of labor between the leaders and the followers.* Audubon was one of the early leaders of the environmentalist group as was Gloria Steinem for the Women's Movement.

5. *The members are idealistic and this idealism helps maintain loyalty, especially during periods of opposition from other groups.* There was a bumper sticker that said, "Let the Yankees Freeze in the Dark" during the oil crunch of the 1980s. Strong advocates of social movements want change now and quickly. Many of the environmentalist groups, such as Greenpeace, have active lobbies in Washington, D.C.

6. *The members are convinced that a particular condition or situation requires change and they are therefore committed to the activity.* Every session of Congress and state legislatures bring a host of new bills related to air and water pollution, waste disposal, the control of dangerous chemicals and other environmental issues.

7. *Social movements are pluralistic.* There may be several groups supporting the same ideology. For example, I belong to African Wildlife Federation, American Farmland Trust, Audubon, Houston Zoological Society, Nature Conservancy and Archaeological Conservancy.

8. *A social movement comes into existence when a sufficient number of people want to change some aspect of social life and take action to do so.* People must discover that they are not isolated in their unhappiness in order to develop a sense of collectivity.

HOW DO SOCIAL MOVEMENTS START AND WHAT ARE THE STAGES OF A SOCIAL MOVEMENT?

The first stage is called *social unrest.* A social movement starts at a time when a large number of people are deeply dissatisfied with a certain condition within the society. There is deep and widespread discontent. This discontent is in response to either absolute or relative deprivation. In absolute deprivation, we look at factors like poverty or political oppression such as those that existed in Haiti in 1991 through 1993. In relative poverty, there is a sense of being poor or oppressed in comparison to other people within the culture or with a society different from our own. At this stage, the structure is informal and the presence of a charismatic leader may be very important.

The second stage is the *excitement or popular stage.* During this stage, attention is focused on an enemy and there is widespread feeling that the condition should be eliminated by direct action. Prophets, leaders and slogans emerge. This is the stage when enthusiasm is developed. There has to be an understanding among members in the society that there is agreement that a condition is undesirable and needs to be changed and that through the collective effort, the condition can be changed. At

▲ **SOMETIMES DIRECT ACTION BY MEMBERS OF A SOCIAL MOVEMENT RESULTS IN INTERVENTION BY LAW ENFORCEMENT.**
IMAGE COPYRIGHT RTIMAGES, 2008. USED UNDER LICENSE FROM SHUTTERSTOCK, INC.

this stage an ideology is developed and a plan of action evolves. Different local groups develop and so do groups in opposition. For example, there are both pro-life and pro-choice groups discussing their viewpoints.

The third stage is *formalization*. At this stage, the grass root supporters form a collective effort to change a condition within the society. During this stage, definite organization takes place, including a characteristic bureaucratic structure, with a hierarchy of officials, definite goals and a network of local leaders and workers. It is at this stage that the "cause" is proclaimed and effort is made to attain the desired goal. Resources such as money come in and organizations are formed. These organizations are national groups such as the NAACP. The organization has to maintain commitment.

Stage four is the *institutionalization* of the social movement. When the goals of the movement are accepted by society, the social movement has met its objective. The pro-life group feels that when there is an amendment passed, they will have accomplished their goal. The pro-choice group felt that they had met their goal with the case of Roe versus Wade. If the change is specific, the goal is easily recognized as being accomplished. For example, women's suffrage happened with the passing of an amendment which legalized voting rights for women. When the movement is concerned with more general goals such as civil rights, it may take some time for acceptance by members of society.

The last stage is *dissolution*. This is the stage in which the movement dies because it has achieved its objective. Rather than disappearing, however, many social movements engage in *goal displacement*; the goals of the original social movement are translated into other goals in order to keep the formal organization going. This is what happened with the March of Dimes for polio. With the polio vaccine, the March of Dimes stopped asking for money for polio and now focuses on birth defects.

Several factors cause the demise of a social movement. External factors contribute to the downfall of a movement. *Cooptation* is the process of winning a truce by bringing the opposition's leadership or platform into the governing seat of power. This can be accomplished by the government inviting the movement's leader to become part of the ruling body. The opposition leader then becomes a part of the establishment. This technique is frequently used in grammar schools when a troublemaker is made the class monitor, or protest absorption in which those in power take over the ideology or program advocated by the movement. President F. D. Roosevelt during the Great Depression successfully coopted many programs from the American left. Social Security was taken from the Townsend Movement. Another external factor is the process of labeling an individual or movement as operating on false premises and not in the public interest. Movements are usually discredited by respected social institutions. Internal factors also cause the dissolution of a social movement. Fragmentation of the movement occurs. In stressing uniformity or total agreement on leadership, ideology and tactics, movements may be ripped apart. In institutionalization, a movement that survives for any length of time begins to develop a social bureaucracy, with leaders and followers, rules, privileges and all of the other trappings of an institution. When this happens, the organization may become more concerned with maintaining itself as a unit than with the changes it is proposing.

WHAT ARE THE TYPES OF SOCIAL MOVEMENTS?

There are several types of social movements:

1. A **reactionary movement** rejects the status quo and would like to go back to conditions as they were at an earlier point in time. This includes organizations such as the Ku Klux Klan and John Birchers. John Birch died at age 85 in 1985. He tried to rid the world of Communism.

☙ Quick Glance

During the popular stage of a social movement, formal organization takes place.　T　F

Institutionalization means the goals of a social movement have been met.　T　F

Cooptation means dissolution.　T　F

Social movements may break apart due to internal disagreements.　T　F

◆ THINKING SOCIOLOGY

In what type of social movement have you participated? Explain your answer.　▶

ACCEPTANCE IS NOT SUBMISSION; IT IS ACKNOWLEDGEMENT OF THE FACTS OF THE SITUATION, THEN DECIDING WHAT YOU'RE GOING TO DO ABOUT IT.

KATHLEEN CASEY THEISEN

☙ Quick Glance

A reactionary social movement wants to go backwards in history.　T　F

A revolutionary movement wants to change a significant part of a society.　T　F

An expressive social movement focuses on people changing themselves.　T　F

The National Rifle Association is part of a reactionary social movement.　T　F

2. A **conservative movement** would like to keep conditions the way they are now; an example of this type of movement is the National Rifle Association. The NRA wants to maintain the right of private citizens to own and use guns.

3. A **reform movement** campaigns for change. The civil rights movement and women's movements are this type of social movement. The destruction along the Gulf Coast due to hurricane Katrina and the serious problem with the evacuations of both New Orleans and Houston during the fall of 2005 has stimulated a social movement to improve both natural and man-made disaster response.

4. The **revolutionary** or **radical movement** rejects part or all of society and wants to replace it with something new; the revolutionary movement of 1776, the Black Muslim movement and the French Revolution are examples.

5. The **separatist** or **withdrawal movement** seeks to escape by setting up alternative organizations and societies. Farming communes are examples of this type of movement.

6. In a **migratory movement** discontented people may wish to move. When many move to the same place at the same time, they create a migratory social movement. Migration of the Irish to the United States following the great potato famine, the back-to-Israel movement of the Jews known as Zionism, the flight of the East Germans to West Germany before the Berlin Wall locked them in, the escape of Cuban refugees to the United States and the American migratory turn around from big cities to small towns and country are examples.

7. The **expressive movement** occurs when people cannot easily move and cannot easily change things; they may change themselves. In expressive movements, people change their reactions instead of trying to change the reality itself. Expressive movements range from the relatively trivial such as forms of dance, art, music and dress to the serious such as religious movements. Expressive movements may help people to accept a reality they despair of changing.

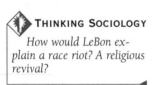
HOW DO SOCIOLOGISTS EXPLAIN COLLECTIVE BEHAVIOR?

There are several important theories which try to explain the emergence of collective behavior within a society or group.

It was Gustave LeBon's interest in crowds that was responsible for the beginning of a study of collective behavior and one of the first theories trying to explain this phenomena. His book, *The Crowd: A Study of the Popular Mind*, was an attempt to examine those who participated in mobs. LeBon suggested a **contagion theory** of collective behavior. His belief was that people became crazed and violent when they are within a group or a crowd. Because people could participate more anonymously within a large number of people, LeBon assumed that they would participate in behavior that they might otherwise consider unacceptable. A charismatic leader might be able to bring followers to a heightened level and the emotions become contagious. The followers of the Jim Jones cult drank their cyanide-laced "kool-aid" in a contagion fashion. The contagion theory helps to explain why a person might commit an otherwise undesirable behavior within a group of people.

Convergence theory says that collective behavior involves a collective response to a situation which is encouraged because of the shared cultural and personality characteristics of the members of the collectivity. The **convergence theory** suggests that crowds attract participants who are ready to participate in collective behavior. Participants in an anti-abortion rally come prepared with protest signs and carefully

▲ PEOPLE COME TO A ROCK CONCERT
WITH SHARED CULTURAL AND SOCIAL
CHARACTERISTICS.
IMAGE COPYRIGHT ANDREAS GRADIN, 2008. USED UNDER LICENSE FROM
SHUTTERSTOCK, INC.

plan and advertise the time and place for the rally. Many fans, when purchasing their Garth Brooks tickets, know that they will participate in screaming and know that they will leave with sore throats.

The **emergent-norm theory** suggests that what is considered appropriate or inappropriate norms are decided as the form of collective behavior occurs. A crowd is ruled by norms which are developed and validated by group processes within the crowd. The crowd experience, according to this theory, is just an extension of the social processes that occur every day, but that these processes take control of the crowd situation. The conduct of fans at a Ministry concert may mean that the fans stampede the stage and participate in "moshing" or "riding the pit." This behavior suggests that participants hold up both of their arms and a person is thrown from one person to another. This behavior is accepted as the participants share in mutual enjoyment of the concert.

🦜 *Quick Glance*

LeBon devised the contagion theory of collective behavior. T F

Convergence theory focuses on norm agreement. T F

Emergent-norm theory states that collective behavior is very similar to other behaviors occurring within a society. T F

Convergence theory is a better theory than emergent-norm theory. T F

The **value-added theory** seeks to explain how social conditions bring about episodes of collective behavior. Neil J. Smelser is responsible for this theory of collective behavior. Smelser's theory is referred to as value-added because each time one of the six "ifs" or determinants is brought into the episode, it adds value to the likelihood that collective behavior will occur. One of the "ifs" in Smelser's theory actually arches over the other five and can intervene at any time during the formation of the collective episode and stop the collective behavior from occurring, or, in some cases, intensify the episode. This sixth "if" is social control. We have defined formal social control in Chapter 7 as the police, courts and the criminal justice system.

The first determinant of Smelser's theory is **structural conduciveness**; this refers to the social conditions that allow a particular type of collective behavior to occur. The structure of the United States allows for episodes of collective behavior. If citizens want to protest planned parenthood clinics or stores that are reported to sell pornographic materials, they are allowed to participate within established guidelines for their behavior. The United States' citizens are free to criticize the policies of the government without fear of reprisal. However, until recently, Soviets were not free to protest because the structure of their society was not conducive to collective behavior. Violators in the U.S.S.R. who may have protested an action taken by their government would have found that the KGB (agent of social control in the U.S.S.R.) intervened in the episode of collective behavior and stopped it immediately. The participants might be jailed or placed in mental institutions. Structural conduciveness may exist and we still might not witness episodes of collective behavior. The structure of the U.S.A. was conducive for collective behavior long before the Civil Rights Movement and the Women's Movement of the 1960s. Neither movement had taken much advantage of this first determinant. However, the existence of this determinant does add value to the likelihood that collective behavior will occur.

When the second determinant appears and is added to the first determinant, then the society is closer to witnessing an episode of collective behavior. *This second deter-*

◆ **THINKING SOCIOLOGY**
Explain a social movement that you participated in using the value-added perspective.

THE ULTIMATE MEASURE OF A MAN IS NOT WHERE HE STANDS IN MOMENTS OF COMFORT, BUT WHERE HE STANDS AT TIMES OF CHALLENGE AND CONTROVERSY.
MARTIN LUTHER KING, JR.

Value-added theory looks at conditions that bring about collective behavior.   T F

Value-added states that conditions in society have to be appropriate for a social movement to occur.   T F

Structural strain is a feeling of identifiable social deprivation.   T F

A precipitating factor triggers collective behavior.   T F

THINKING SOCIOLOGY

How would you analyze the high interest in Beanie Babies using Smelser's theory?

minant identified by Smelser is that of structural strain. **Structural strain** is a feeling of social deprivation which is identifiable. When people in the United States say that all men are created equal, people come to expect that equality will exist for all people. However, although this idea is expressed, it is the ideal pattern. Reality suggests that some people are created more equal than others, resulting in deprivation for those who are not equal. For both African Americans and women, the structural strain prior to the 1960s was in the areas of unequal opportunity for equal education, equal housing and equal opportunity for employment. The structural strain was there before it was acted on in the 1960s. However, in the 1960s a generalized belief was added to structural conduciveness and structural strain thus bringing further value to the likelihood that collective behavior would occur.

A *generalized belief is a shared view that something must be done to correct the structural strain*. A generalized belief suggests that the structural strain has been identified and recognized as a problem. This precipitates the view that action must be taken. Speeches of Martin Luther King underlined the belief that inequalities existed and must be corrected. Malcolm X also became a spokesperson bringing about the identification of the inequalities that existed in the United States. The Women's Movement caught on to the skirt tail of the Civil Rights Movement and identified that women experienced the same inequalities. A generalized belief can occur and be added to the other two, and collective behavior does not have to take place. However, when the generalized belief is added to a precipitating factor, we have added value to the possibility that collective behavior may occur.

A **precipitating factor** *is an event, incident or behavior that gives the generalized belief credence*. For the Women's Movement, the 1963 book by Betty Friedan, *The Feminine Mystique*, acted as a precipitating factor because it identified the plight of being

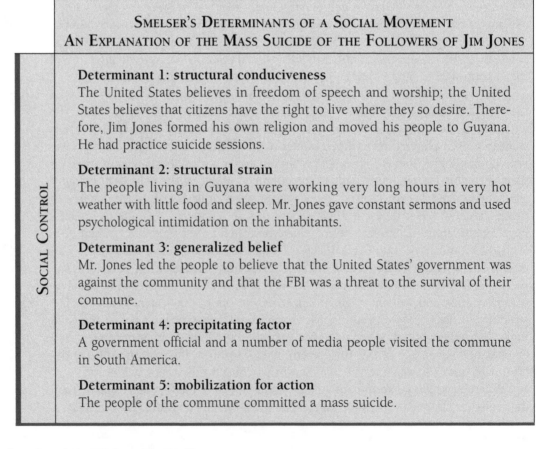

SMELSER'S DETERMINANTS OF A SOCIAL MOVEMENT
AN EXPLANATION OF THE MASS SUICIDE OF THE FOLLOWERS OF JIM JONES

SOCIAL CONTROL

Determinant 1: structural conduciveness
The United States believes in freedom of speech and worship; the United States believes that citizens have the right to live where they so desire. Therefore, Jim Jones formed his own religion and moved his people to Guyana. He had practice suicide sessions.

Determinant 2: structural strain
The people living in Guyana were working very long hours in very hot weather with little food and sleep. Mr. Jones gave constant sermons and used psychological intimidation on the inhabitants.

Determinant 3: generalized belief
Mr. Jones led the people to believe that the United States' government was against the community and that the FBI was a threat to the survival of their commune.

Determinant 4: precipitating factor
A government official and a number of media people visited the commune in South America.

Determinant 5: mobilization for action
The people of the commune committed a mass suicide.

female in the United States. Women began to meet in informal "consciousness raising" groups, talking about this "feminine mystique." Women burning their "bras" began to raise the consciousness of Americans that women were serious about demanding equal rights. For the Civil Rights Movement, Rosa Parks, refusing to move to the back of the Birmingham city bus, was a precipitating factor that led to the Birmingham Bus Boycott. Once these four factors are in place, there is added value to the chance that collective behavior will occur. How long it will last or the intensity of it is determined by the addition of the mobilization for action.

Mobilization for action refers to the actual organization for participation in collective behavior. If a leader is named and the desire for change is given a name, further collective behavior will probably occur. The Civil Rights Movement experienced mobilization for action with the creation of the NAACP and, for women, the formation of NOW with Betty Friedan as its first president. The collective behavior for both African Americans and women was in the form of a social movement.

Quick Glance

A generalized belief is the last step in collective behavior.   T   F

A precipitating factor is a feeling of social deprivation.   T   F

A formal organization forms in the stage of mobilization for action.   T   F

Modernization involves changes in institutions.   T   F

WHAT DOES THE FUTURE HOLD?

Collective behavior and social movements are ways that social change is enhanced. We discussed social and cultural change in more general terms in Chapter 3. We stated that every society is in the process of change, but though the degree and the direction may vary from society to society, change, however, is a continual process. Change comes about through alterations in the physical environment; changes in the size, density and composition (such as age and gender) of a population; changes in technology, war and revolution; and social inequality. In response to these factors, the United States will see a continuation of industrialization and urbanization, more mass communication and education, high energy consumption, technological diffusion, increase in material goods, increase in services, increase of media, equalization of the sexes, erosion of traditional cultures, expansion of government and an aging world as birth rates decline. One of the changes that we are seeing throughout the world is the continuing process of modernization.

Modernization involves changes in old patterns of social and economic commitment, shifts from generalized to specialized roles—and increased dependency upon technology and the world market place.

THINKING SOCIOLOGY
Describe what you think our society will be like in 2093.

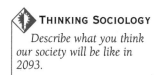
HISTORY REPEATS ITSELF, THAT'S ONE OF THE THINGS THAT'S WRONG WITH HISTORY.
CLARENCE DARROW

Learning TIP
Read appropriate textbook material before coming to class.

▼ CHAPTER SUMMARY

1. Collective behavior is the study of relatively spontaneous, unstructured social behavior. It frequently produces relatively rapid change in people's behavior and brings about change in ideas.
2. Crowds, riots, orgies, mass hysteria, panics, fads, fashion, crazes, rumors, public opinion and social movements are all forms of collective behavior.
3. The stages of a social movement include social unrest, excitement, formalization, institutionalization and dissolution. External factors and/or internal factors may bring the demise of a social movement.
4. Social movements include reactionary, conservative, reform, revolutionary, separatist, migratory and expressive.
5. Theories that seek to explain collective behavior include contagion, convergence, emergent-norm and the value-added theories.

▼ REFERENCES

Almquist, Elizabeth M., Janet S. Chafetz, Barbara J. Chance and Judy Corder-Bolz. 1978. *Sociology: Men, Women and Society*. St. Paul: West Publishing Co.

Blumer, Herbert. 1969. "Collective Behavior." In Alfred M. Lee (Ed.), *Principles of Sociology*. 3rd. ed. New York: Barnes and Noble.

Dawson, Carl and W. E. Gettys. 1934. *Introduction to Sociology*. New York: The Ronald Press Company.

DeFronzo, J. 1991. *Revolutions and Revolutionary Movements*. Boulder, CO: Westview.

Faludi, S. 1991. Backlash. *The Undeclared War Against Women*. New York: Crown.

Friedan, Betty. 1963. *The Feminine Mystique*. New York: Dell.

Herskovitz, Melville J. 1946. *Man and His Works*. New York: Alfred A. Knopf, 581.

LeBon, Gustave. 1943. *The Crowd: A Study of the Popular Mind*. London: Unwin (originally published in 1895).

Lofland, J. 1981. "Collective Behavior: The Elementary Form." In M. Rosenberg and R. H. Turner (Eds.) *Social Psychology: Sociological Perspectives*. New York: Basic Books.

Merton, Robert. 1957. *Social Theory and Social Structure: 2nd ed*. New York: The Free Press.

Michener, H. A., J. D. DeLamater, S. H. Schwartz. 1986. *Social Psychology*. San Diego, CA: Harcourt Brace Jovanovich.

Persell, Caroline Hodges. 1984. *Understanding Society: An Introduction to Sociology*. New York: Harper & Row, Publishers, Inc.

Piven, F. F. and R. A. Cloward. 1977. *Poor People's Movements: Why They Succeed, How They Fail*. New York: Vintage.

Smelser, Neil. 1962. *Theory of Collective Behavior*. New York: Free Press.

Turner, R. Q. and L. M. Killian. 1987. *Collective Behavior*. Englewood Cliffs, NJ: Prentice Hall.

Zurcher, L. A. and D. A. Snow. 1981. In M. Rosenberg and R. H. Turner (Eds.) *Social Psychology: Sociological Perspectives*. New York: Basic Books.

READING

During the many years that we have been writing and researching about collectors and collecting behavior, we have been baffled as to what exactly constitutes a collector and a collection. When we looked at collectors and their collections, there seemed to be a great diversity in what people considered to be a collection and how people approached their collectible. Some people collect what is generally called collectibles such as Precious Moments Figurines, baseball cards or coins. Other people, however, collect a variety of other objects such as anything with a frog as part of it, saltshakers, baskets, earrings, precious gems, rocks or comic books and they consider this to be their collection! With such a wide diversity of types of objects that people collect and of the approach people take to collecting these objects, we need a tool with which to analyze these differences in collectible and collecting behavior. We want some framework with which to make the distinction between different types of collections such as coins or anything with frogs. Furthermore, we require a tool with which to analyze different the way people collect their objects. We propose that collections and collecting behavior does not form a single type of activity but is a much more complex phenomenon. There are actually different types of collections and different types of collectors. We have developed two typologies with which to address these distinctions: the first typology focuses on the collectible and the second typology concentrates on the manner of collecting.

The first typology involves the nature of the collectible. The objects that people collect can be based on a particular topic or the objects that people collect can be an item. A topic collector has a theme in which he or she is interested. My daughter collects cats. It does not matter in what form the cat comes. Her Christmas tree is decorated with cat ornaments; her drinking glasses have cats on them, her shower curtain has cats on it and she has many ceramic, china, crystal and resin cat figurines as well as stuffed cats, cat jewelry and clothes with cats. She has cat pictures on the walls, cat floor mats, cat music boxes and cat bathroom accessories in two of her bathrooms. When she travels, she always comes home with cat souvenirs. To celebrate her honeymoon to Italy, she bought a Moreno glass cat. Many of her baby's clothes have a cat design on them. In fact, if she finds an outfit with a cat, she buys it! It does not matter what the object is as long as it is a cat or has a strong cat theme. My son collects Mickey Mouse in any form. He delights in wearing clothes with the Mickey Mouse insignia such as shirts and ties. He has a Mickey Mouse clock and a Mickey Mouse watch as just part of the Mice that have the roam of house and closet. Many people who have teapot collections are topic collectors. They not only have teapots, but they like objects such as teapot shaped trivets and collector plates with teapots on them.

An item collector focuses on a particular object. My mother-in-law collected thimbles. She had several racks of thimbles. These thimbles were in the shape of birds, elves and clowns. Some of the thimbles had pictures on them while others had small objects such as hats perched on top of them. But no matter the shape or decoration on the thimble, each and every collectible was classified as a thimble. Most of the thimbles were purely decorative and would have been hard pressed to use in the function for which thimbles were intended. Here are some other examples of item collections. One of my friends collects first edition books by Stephen King. I collect stamps that are used with inkpads. I have a special cabinet built to hold the different stamps. Several people

---

*By Adrian Rapp and Lynda Dodgen.

A collection is a series
of a particular item.   T F

People have to actively
collect something in order
to be a collector.   T F

The cat-collector in the
article was an item
collector.   T F

I know collect Beanie Babies. A person who tries to get a whole set such as a particular baseball card series would be an item collector.

Sometimes a person can actually have several collections making up a single collection. This could include both topic and item collections. The focus of the collectible would be topic but within the collectible there might exist as a sub collection which is an item collection. My daughter the cat collector would classify herself as a topic collector. But Lenox China issued a series of spice jars featuring cats. She was bound and determined to collect all the spice jars in their special spice rack. When the spice rack got knocked off the wall and about half the spice jars were broken, she wrote to the company and made arrangements for her set to be complete again. The opposite could also happen. The person could be an item collector. Then for various reasons the person might add a topic collection to the item collection. This might happen because the item in question might no longer be available or the item set was complete or the item might be more difficult to find. Or just because of the fun of it, the person could take some aspect of an item collection and become a topic collector. This has happened among some Beanie Baby collectors. The woman I am thinking of collects Beanie Babies but she also has other Beanie Baby collectibles such as Beanie Baby trading cards. The Tye Company itself encourages people to add to their item collections. The company has now issued small stuffed dolls and larger stuffed animals to encourage people to expand on their collection. I collect baseball cards which would be an item collection but I have, over the years, also become a topic collector because I also collect signed baseballs and autographed pictures of the players. In summary, there are topic collections and there are item collectors: topic collectors focus on many different types of objects centered on a central theme, item collectors have many different themes centered on a particular type of object.

The second typology to be discussed delves into the way the collectible is approached. The person may be an active collector or a passive collector. The passive collector does not take an active interest in their collectible. The passive collector relies on other people to add to his or her collection. My mother-in-law's thimble collection is a good example of this type of collecting. She never bought a thimble for herself but people would buy her thimbles when they traveled and wanted to bring her back a souvenir. When her birthday or Mother's Day came along, it was very typical for her to receive one or more thimbles as gifts. We always made it a point to buy her a collectible thimble for Christmas. My daughter now has the thimble collection and it still continues to be a passive, but growing, thimble collection. When I travel, I always bring her back a thimble. It is nice that thimbles are so readily available!

Passive also refers to how the person interacts with their collectible. The passive collector puts their objects on a shelf or cupboard and does not worry about the general upkeep or value of the collectible. My daughter's cat collection is displayed in a series of cases and bookshelves but she does not know the value of her collectible nor does she catalog or research the value of any of her cats.

The second style is the active collector. This type of collector takes an active interest in acquiring the collectible and interacting with their collectible. They may go to flea markets, shop the auctions, visit special shops or garage sales or anywhere else the collectible might be found. In pursuit of my baseball memorabilia, I have attended many baseball card shows as well as visiting shops specializing in cards and other collectibles. My daughter is an active cat collector. For example, on her European trip she bought a wooden cat puzzle in Switzerland and a cat carved from olive wood in Spain. In France she bought a picture of a black cat which she had framed in the United States. In Belgium she bought a lace scarf with a cat design in the middle.

The active collector tries to complete a set of some object or to obtain as many examples of the item as possible. Some sets may be unlimited or constantly expanding such as baseball cards. Other sets might not have known parameters. For example, one person collected antique breadboxes with the German word for bread on the box because that was their last name. Since they collect antiques, there are a finite number of these boxes available but they do not know how many there are. Hence, they get very excited with they find a new box at a flea market or auction house. Other collectibles are finite and known such as a special issue of plates or music boxes. The Lenox spice jars mentioned earlier would be a finite collection. Once the jars were all issued, that was all there was! The free display case is full and no more will be made.

There is also a mind set for the active collector. The active collector would be a person who would study the value of their collectible or be aware of the increasing or decreasing value of their collectible. A gun collector, for example, is usually very aware of what the value of his/her collection is and, in many cases, has insurance on the collection. My son-in-law is a knife collector. He can tell you to the dollar what the current value of his collection is. He also has many of the other characteristics of an active collector. He subscribes to a magazine for knife collectors and reads it cover to cover. Not only does he read the magazine, he goes to the bookstores looking for books dealing with knives. He also spends at least an hour a day looking for information on the Internet and e-mailing with other knife enthusiasts. People who are active collectors form a community with other collectors. They share a common interest, a passion, that holds them together.

Based on these two typologies, four ideal types of collectors can be discussed:

- Item active
- Item passive
- Topic active
- Topic passive

The item active collector is perhaps the person that we might call the true collector. This person actively seeks specific items with which to complete or round out his or her collection. Coin and stamp collectors are relatively common item active collectors. Baseball card collecting is also popular. Other item active collections would be the collection of Christmas Village houses and accessories or Hummel figurines. Coin and stamp collectors are collecting a specific item and, due to the expense, they purchase the item for themselves. The element of knowing exactly what is desired also plays a role in acquiring objects. These collectors take an energetic interest in his or her collection. He or she may spend time organizing his or her items, reading magazines and books about his or her collection and have special storage for the collection.

The item passive collector has an interest in a particular item but does not seek to actively complete a collection. For example, a woman collected thimbles for forty years but she rarely, if ever, purchased a thimble for herself. Thimbles came from friends who picked up thimbles as souvenirs for her of their trips and relatives purchased her thimbles for presents. It seemed that the people around her took a more active interest in her thimble collection than she did. This type of collector probably does not spend a great deal of time of reading or researching about their collection.

The topic active collector seeks a particular case such as cats or unicorns. The active subject collector actively looks for items that fulfill his or her requirements but the choice of object can be very diverse. For example, a man who collects frogs tried to find items with frogs to add to his new house when he decorated it. The bathroom

Quick Glance

If a person is a passive collector he or she reads books and magazines about his/her collectible.   T F

In order to be an active collector, the person must seek out an item.   T F

The item active collector is not really interested in their collection.   T F

Quick Glance

The topic active collector collects a particular item such as thimbles. T F

Collecting is a unidimensional activity.   T F

Collecting is part of high culture.   T F

wallpaper has frogs on it. When he travels he always tries to bring back a frog souvenir.

The topic passive collector has a theme for objects but the person makes little or no effort to accumulate these objects. A woman we know is very interested in turtles. She cares for turtles that are injured and she has an area in her backyard devoted to the care and raising of turtles. Based on this, people started to buy her things with turtles. These included such objects as turtle trivets, turtle jewelry and turtle figurines. When people traveled, it became standard to try to bring her back something having to do with turtles. She likes her turtles and her turtle collection but it is not something that she actively seeks for herself. I have a topic passive collection of flamingos. Several years ago my daughters bought me a gag gift of a flamingo that could be dressed in different clothes. The joke ended up on them because I proceeded to buy a total wardrobe for the flamingo and change his/her clothes on a monthly basis. Since then there has been a steady stream of flamingoes coming into the house including fountains, door mats, dishes, pitchers, glasses, all sorts of yard art and, this year, earrings which were custom made and a t-shirt.

In conclusion, we have stated that we believe that collecting and collections should not be dealt with as a uniform type of popular culture. Rather, we need to look at the several dimensions of behavior and objects. Two sets of criteria were suggested. We need to identify whether a collection deals with a single type of item or is broader in what is considered part of the set. This would be a topic collection. The approach to acquiring the items also needs to be addressed. Some people are very active in pursuit of their collectibles and the collection forms an important interest in their life. To other people a collection grows passively. To these people the collection probably would not be an addictive behavior nor would the analogy of the hunt be applicable. When writers start to discuss such factors as Freudian implications in collection behavior, these writers are probably dealing with the active collector. Collecting behavior has very much become part of the American way of life and part of popular culture. The typology that we have suggested will be a beneficial tool in the analysis of any and all collections and collectors.

> ▶ **THINKING SOCIOLOGY**
>
> *What do you collect? According to this article, how would you classify your collecting behavior? Explain and justify your answer.*

Bibliography

Belk, R.W. 1982. Acquiring, possessing, and collecting: fundamental processes in consumer behavior. In R.F. Bush and S.D. Hunt (Eds.) *Marketing Theory: Philosophy of Science Perspectives* (pp. 185–190). Chicago: American Marketing Association.

Belk, R.W. 1988. Possessions and the extended self. *Journal of Consumer Research* 15 (September), 139–167.

Belk, R.W. 1995. *Collecting in a Consumer Society*. NY: Rontledge.

Danet, B., Kariel, T. No two alike: play and aesthetics in collecting. *Play and Culture*, (2) 1989, 253–277.

Olmsted, A.D. The Hunting Metaphor. 1992. Paper presented at the Popular Culture Annual Meeting.

Olmsted, A.D. Collectors and collecting. 1988. Paper presented at the Popular Culture Annual Meeting.

Rotenstein, D. Bending Contexts: A Historical Perspective on Relic Collection. 1997. Paper written for Folklife Studies, University of Pennsylvania.

Slater, J. Dissertation: From Trash to Treasures. 1/1/01. Internet Site.

Turner, G.I. 1/1/01. Internet Site.

Warren, L., J. Ostrom. Pack rats: world-class savers. *Psychology Today* (February) 1988, 58–62.

Analyzing Deviance

IMAGE COPYRIGHT ERIC CHARLES PHOTOGRAPHY, 2008. USED UNDER LICENSE FROM SHUTTERSTOCK, INC.

CHAPTER OBJECTIVES

1. What is deviance?
2. What is considered deviant?
3. What is criminal behavior?
4. How does the structural functional theory explain deviance?
5. How does the conflict theory explain deviance?
6. How does the symbolic interactionist theory explain deviance?
7. What is social control?
8. What is a social problem?

anomie theory of deviance: the theory of deviance proposed by Robert Merton that explains deviance as a gap between goals of society and the approved means for achieving those goals

conformist: a behavior which conforms to both the goals of society and the approved means for achieving those goals

conformity: a behavior according to the social norms

criminal behavior: a deviant behavior which breaks the formal norms as established by the society

deviance: a behavior that varies significantly in direction or degree from the social norm for that behavior

differential association theory of deviance: a theory proposed by Edwin Sutherland that states deviance is learned in the same way that conformity is learned

formal social control: the enforcement of formal norms based on society's authorized agencies such as law enforcement officers and judges

informal social control: the enforcement of norms based on informal positive and negative sanctions

innovator: a behavior that follows the norms concerning the goals set by society but not the means

labeling theory: a theory proposed by Howard Becker that explains the process of a person receiving the deviant identity

primary deviation: the deviation by which the person is not labeled as being a deviant because the act of deviation is trivial, tolerated or well hidden

rebel: a behavior that rejects the goals of society and the means for achieving those goals but substitutes new goals and means

retreatist: a behavior that rejects both the goals and the approved means for achieving the goals of society

ritualist: a behavior that rejects the goals set by society by conforming rigidly to the means thus losing sight of the goals

schismatic community breakdown: a situation in which the bonds that hold a society together are broken apart

secondary deviation: a deviation that is publicly labeled deviant

social control: the means and processes used by a society to ensure conformity to the group norms

social problem: a deviance that is recognized by society as a condition needing correction through group effort

▼ KEY PEOPLE

S. E. Asch, Howard Becker, William Chambliss, Albert Cohen, Stanley Milgram, Robert Merton, Edwin Sutherland

WHAT IS DEVIANCE?

Behaviors of conformity and deviance are found in all societies. **Conformity** implies that the behavior adapts to the expectations of society. On the other hand, deviance implies the opposite. **Deviance** is behavior that varies significantly in direction or degree from the social norm for that behavior. Examining properties of deviance may better explain the concept of deviance.

First, deviance does not always mean negative behavior even though in the popular language deviance carries with it a negative connotation. Florence Nightingale was just as deviant as Jack the Ripper. She was doing a very unfeminine type of activity in 1854 when she started caring for sick and injured males during the Crimean War. Deviance that is acceptable to society includes high intelligence, special aptitudes such as athletic or artistic ability and motivation for success. Another form of positive deviance is physical courage which is rewarded in times of war; earning the Medal of Honor is a coveted honor among service people.

Second, there is not an absolute standard of what constitutes deviant behavior. The definition of deviance may vary depending on several factors. *First, deviance may vary because of different perceptions.* Is homosexuality considered deviant behavior? Some members of our society may answer "yes" while others may define homosexuality as an alternative life style. No longer is homosexuality listed on the DSM-IV (the official source for diagnosing and labeling mental disorders) as a mental disorder. There have been changes in the perception of homosexuality as deviant behavior. *Second, deviance may vary with historical time periods.* Cohabitation is much more acceptable today than forty years ago. However, for many of our parents and grandparents, cohabitation is still not an acceptable life style because it violates their ideas of right and wrong. Gambling was once unlawful in the state of Texas; however, in 1992 a lottery was put into effect and now certain types of gambling are legal. What would have been against the law in 1990 now has government sanction! *Third, deviance may vary with the culture or subculture.* Illegal drug usage may be the norm for members of the drug subculture. But for many Americans, drug usage would be considered deviant behavior. In Amsterdam and Hamburg, prostitutes can operate openly in certain areas: it is legal behavior. In specified areas in the state of Nevada, prostitution is legal. But in the rest of the United States there is no area which is legal for prostitution. *Fourth, deviance varies with the situation.* In times of war, soldiers are given guns and instructed to shoot the enemy. This is considered patriotic. However, it is not considered patriotic for individuals in the cities of the United States to kill other human beings. Many murders occur every year in the United States.

The third property of deviance involves a labeling process; until society or significant other labels a person a "deviant," an individual would not be considered "deviant." Whether a person is labeled deviant or not depends on several factors. *First, how far away from the behavioral norm the person is acting.* It is very common in our society for people to take a few extra minutes at lunch or coffee break, people frequently use the copy machines at work for personal business, we take pens and pencils from work to use at home. These behaviors are all actually stealing, but we accept it as "normal." If, however, I take the copy machine and get caught, then I become deviant! I can borrow several pieces of paper, but if I take reams of it and am caught, then I am considered deviant. *Second, circumstances of the behavior are considered.* If I appear to be an able-bodied person and I do nothing constructive with my time, you probably would say that I was deviant. If I told you that I had tuberculosis and was under doctor's orders to rest, then you would not put the deviant label on me. *Third, we need to consider the persistence in acting out the behavior.* If I get drunk one time, most people would not label me deviant. But if I got drunk every day, then others would be more apt to say that I was deviant.

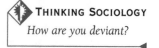

Quick Glance

Deviance is always negative behavior.	T	F
There is always an absolute standard for deviance.	T	F
Some deviant behavior is considered beneficial to society.	T	F

THINKING SOCIOLOGY

How are you deviant?

Quick Glance

Deviance may vary because of different perceptions.	T	F
Deviance does not vary with the situation.	T	F
Different time periods view the same behavior as deviant.	T	F
A subculture may have a different definition of deviancy.	T	F

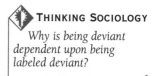

THINKING SOCIOLOGY

Why is being deviant dependent upon being labeled deviant?

Learning TIP
Form a study group!

TECHNIQUES OF NEUTRALIZATION

There are certain techniques that we use in order to deny that we are a deviant:

1. denial of responsibility
   I shall blame my low grades on my high school rather than admit to myself that I need to study.

2. denial of injury
   When my son took my car without permission, he told me that no one got hurt. The car was fine, he was fine, and all of his friends were fine. He admitted that it was technically against the law, but he "only borrowed it."

3. denial of victim
   Sometimes when a large major store undercharges us, we do not say anything because we feel that the large stores make too big a profit anyway. If I cheat on a test, I shall say that I did not hurt the other students because the teacher does not curve grades anyway.

4. condemnation of condemners
   A person could justify his crime by saying that "everybody's crooked." What's the difference between holding up a gas station and what the oil companies are doing? They are all in it for the money just the same as I am.

5. appeal to higher loyalties
   With the increasing incident of gang behavior, we see in newspapers violence done for the purpose of becoming members or staying members of a gang. Many of these people feel that they have to uphold the loyalty to the gang. If the gang has a fight, the gang member feels he has to go along with the gang even if laws are broken.

THINKING SOCIOLOGY

Is the mass media interested in primary or secondary deviation? Why?

THINKING SOCIOLOGY

Which of the techniques of neutralization do you commonly use?

Quick Glance

Deviance involves a labeling process.	T	F
Primary deviance is labeled deviance.	T	F
Secondary deviance is a misdemeanor.	T	F
A label of deviant may become a master status.	T	F
Deviants follow many of society's norms.	T	F
People who cannot distinguish between right and wrong are considered deviant.	T	F

The concepts of primary and secondary deviation address the issue of labeling. **Primary deviation** is when the person is basically a conforming person who is deviant in small aspects of his or her life. His deviation is so trivial, tolerated or very well hidden that the society does not label the person as deviant. **Secondary deviation** occurs when a person is publicly labeled a deviant. This can come about through arrest for a crime such as rape or murder. An accusation of deviance may also lead to a person being labeled deviant. A girl on my daughter's swim team accused the coach of sexually inappropriate behavior in a diary. School officials were given the diary by some angry swimmers. The school officials acted on the diary by dismissing the coach. It took him several years to clear the label of deviant from his record, and five years later I talked with people who did not know that he was cleared of all charges and still think him guilty.

When we label someone deviant, the label becomes a master status in many cases. This is interesting because even deviants conform to most social norms. The mass murderer still wears clothes, eats what we eat, sleeps in a bed and answers the telephone. It is in just one area of behavior that he/she receives the label of deviant. Charles Manson, killer and cult leader now in prison on a life sentence, still eats socially prescribed foods, dresses in appropriate clothing, speaks the English language, watches television and reads books. Even though he has been labeled a deviant, in many areas of his life he acts very much like you and me. We are all deviant to a greater or lesser degree. It is just a matter of how much and in which direction. If a person just tries a behavior such as cocaine at a party one time or acts deviant in the course of acceptable behavior, we regard him as a primary deviant. If, however, he or she continues to act out the socially unacceptable behavior, he or she engages in secondary deviance and he or she carries the label of deviant.

WHAT IS CONSIDERED DEVIANT?

THINKING SOCIOLOGY

Are the physically challenged considered deviant? Is this changing?

Mental differences can be regarded as deviant. For example, someone with an extremely high intelligence score can be said to be "weird" or "eccentric." More commonly, we think of people with subnormal intelligence as being deviant even though we excuse their deviant behavior because of conditions that they cannot help or prevent. These people do not have the mental ability to fully understand the roles they are expected to play.

The mentally and emotionally disturbed are considered deviant in United States' culture. These people have lost the ability to fully comprehend their roles and to interact in society. For example, someone with schizophrenia may not show any emotional response and a distorted perception of reality. A paranoid schizophrenic may view the world as out to assassinate him even though this is not true. The person is considered ill and in need of treatment in order to bring him/her into a grasp of reality as defined by society.

People can also be deviant because of physical attributes. This classification includes people with certain identifiable physical or social characteristics that are often perceived and treated as deviant. This includes people such as midgets, dwarfs, blind and wheelchair-bound people. It is interesting that many people talk louder to a blind person or a wheelchair-bound person.

▲ SINCE THE HOMELESS BREAK THE NORMS OF RESIDENCY, THEY ARE CONSIDERED DEVIANT.
IMAGE COPYRIGHT JON LE-BON, 2008. USED UNDER LICENSE FROM SHUTTERSTOCK, INC.

WHAT IS CRIMINAL BEHAVIOR?

TRAVELER THERE IS NO PATH; PATHS ARE MADE BY WALKING.

SPANISH PROVERB

A very particular type of deviance is criminal behavior. **Criminal behavior** is that behavior which breaks norms as established by the society. Criminal behavior can include the following:

1. index crimes: murder, rape, robbery, assault, burglary, theft, motor vehicle theft, arson
2. professional criminal: safecracking, hijacking, pickpocket
3. organized crime: enterprises involved in narcotics wholesaling, prostitution, gambling
4. white collar crime: income tax evasion, embezzlement and misrepresentation in advertising
5. victimless crimes: gambling, substance abuse, prostitution

☞ *Quick Glance*

Criminal behavior is a form of deviant behavior.   T   F

Murder is an index crime.   T   F

Gambling is a victimless crime.   T   F

NUMBER OF OFFENSES (1000)					
Crime	*1980*	*1990*	*2000*	*2003*	*2005*
Murder	23	23	16	17	17
Forcible Rape	83	103	90	93	94
Robbery	566	639	408	413	417
Aggravated Assault	673	1055	912	858	863
Burglary	3795	3074	2051	2153	2154
Larceny Theft	7137	7946	6972	7022	6956
Motor Vehicle Theft	1132	1636	1160	1260	1235

U.S. Census Bureau, Statistical Abstract of the United States, 2006, Table No. 299.

HOW DOES THE STRUCTURAL FUNCTIONAL THEORY EXPLAIN DEVIANCE?

Each of the three major theories has a different perspective on deviance. The structural functionalist believes that deviance is found in all societies and serves certain functions. *First, deviance may help to bring about needed social change.* For example, Dr. Martin Luther King, Jr. and some of his followers were jailed many times by local authorities in the late 1950s and early 1960s for attempting to enter and be served at white-owned restaurants, theaters, etc. Rosa Parks, a black female, sat on a front seat of a city bus in the 1960s. Her deviant behavior brought attention to the discrimination that had taken place for many years in the United States. Episodes of deviant behavior may help groups feel that they can bring attention to issues. She died in 2005. Actions such as those by King and Parks furnished the basis for the civil rights movement which in turn resulted in much needed civil rights legislations during the mid and late 1960s.

Second, deviance may act to promote a sense of group identity and cooperation. When citizens band together to fight the dumping of toxic waste in their neighborhood, they begin to interact with each other more often. Bonds are built between them as they unite together in a common goal. Those feelings of solidarity begin to develop against those perceived as deviants. A particular group or community may be brought closer together by its disapproval of a certain kind of deviance. Neighborhood watches for preventing crime have brought many neighborhoods closer together.

Third, deviance helps to clarify certain norms. Only when a law has been broken and the system has reacted to it, do we know if a behavior is deviant or not. Our child does this when we set a curfew of midnight; he or she come in at 12:15 AM, and nothing happens, thus the teenager figures we really mean 12:15. Next time when a curfew is set at midnight, the teenager comes home at 12:20 and is grounded. The rule has now been clarified to mean 12:15 AM. Our school rules say that faculty should dress appropriately. If I wear gold high-heeled sandals and get funny looks from my colleagues, I shall know that sandals are not appropriate attire and I should cease with my deviance. When a child breaks a rule in a family, Mom may exert her informal social control by giving the child that stare that all members understand to be "you had better straighten your behavior." That child and the other children may realize that Mom means business. It strengthens that rule for the disobedient child and for the other children as well.

Fourth, deviance allows for diverse forms of expression. For example, homosexual desires that may be difficult and even painful to suppress can be fulfilled by playing this clearly defined deviant role.

Fifth, deviance can help cut the red tape. If a student has problems with an instructor, rules state the student should first go to the instructor, but every now and then a student goes right to the head of the department or the president of the college.

Sixth, deviance can act as a safety valve. We party on the Fourth of July, New Years Eve and Friday afternoons. By allowing a little deviance, we can prevent more serious problems at a later point in time.

Seventh, deviance provides for innovation and creativity. If we did not have deviants in the world of art, we would still be doing cave painting!

Eighth, deviance acts as a barometer of social strain. Deviance can be symptomatic of greater social ills, a signal of strain within a social system. For example, a sudden increase in theft, drug taking, or exhibitionism can be taken as a sign that young adults are not taking an interest in school or lacking parental supervision.

Finally, deviance provides a source of employment and income. Without deviance, what would become of the millions of law enforcers, social workers, health officials and related professionals who work to prevent deviance and treat deviant persons?

THINKING SOCIOLOGY

What type of crime do you think creates the most problems for society? Why?

IN SOME CASES NON-VIOLENCE REQUIRES MORE MILITANCY THAN VIOLENCE.

CESAR CHAVEZ

Quick Glance

Deviance can be functional.   T F

Deviance can promote feelings of being in an in-group.   T F

Deviance causes problems defining norms.   T F

THINKING SOCIOLOGY

What family rule in your household has been clarified by you or a sibling through being deviant?

Quick Glance

Deviance cuts red tape.   T F

Deviance can let us know that there are problems in the society.   T F

Deviance cost the society jobs.   T F

According to the structural functionalist, deviance is also dysfunctional. *Deviance disrupts the social order of a society, community or family.* High crime rates, high suicide rates and high drug use cause problems within the society. The deviant individual that drives by and shoots innocent individuals generates the concern of other citizens living in that society. People reading their daily newspapers, listening to the news on the radio or television may begin to be fearful to venture out of their homes as a result of the concern for drive-by shootings. The burglaries taking place in the suburbs may result in the homeowners placing burglar bars on their windows and doors. Communities take on the look of fortresses as its members protect their personal belongings. Residents may resent the fact that they cannot trust others and desire the days when one did not lock windows or doors. The social order of the community is disrupted. A husband who becomes intoxicated and batters his wife and children has disrupted the social order of that family. This, of course, has a snowball effect for the society. Social services to provide centers for battered women and children cost money to maintain.

Deviance can destroy the motivation of other people to conform; we can become confused about what is normal and of value. If I see other people cheating on their tests, why should I earn a lower grade by not cheating? The act of cheating on an exam in a school classroom is perceived as deviant. However, if a student cheats and the teacher does not punish the behavior, other students may begin to cheat. A resulting good grade rewarding their behavior may mean that deviance during exams becomes the norm. If all of my peers are shoplifting, if I want to feel part of the crowd, maybe I better do it too!

Deviance is expensive; deviance results in a diversion of resources. When malicious deviant behavior occurs, it is generally going to cost the society. For adolescents writing graffiti on the side of the local high school, the cost will be in monetary terms to that school district. My husband and I recently had a box of personal checks taken from our home mailbox. We were unaware that there were individuals writing over $2,000 a day on our account. What was the cost or the diversion of resources? Merchants have to make good on the checks which they honor in their establishments resulting in a loss for them. You and I as consumers pay for this. However, it also means that local police agencies and the judicial system will spend time and effort to apprehend the deviant individuals. Each of us pays extra money because of the shoplifting that happens in grocery stores and department stores. We all pay added insurance rates to cover accidents due to substance abuse and arson. We all pay for the people who operate the criminal justice system through our taxes.

Deviance destroys the trust in the workings of the system. The Watergate Affair of 1973–75 in Washington resulted in a tremendous temporary loss of confidence by many Americans in the existing political system. This was compounded in the William Clinton administration from 1993–2001 with the Travelgate and Monicagate. When deviants stole a box of checks from our mailbox, my husband and I experi-

▲ CRIME IN NEIGHBORHOODS INCREASES FEELINGS OF FEAR AND DISTRUST.

◆ THINKING SOCIOLOGY

Have you ever been negatively affected by someone cheating on an exam? What was the negative result for you?

☥ *Quick Glance*

Deviance contributes to social change.   T   F

Deviance can undermine the trust in the social system.   T   F

Deviance causes an increase in cost to society.   T   F

THE WINNERS IN LIFE THINK CONSTANTLY IN TERMS OF I CAN, I WILL AND I AM. LOSERS, ON THE OTHER HAND, CONCENTRATE THEIR WAKING THOUGHTS ON WHAT THEY SHOULD HAVE OR WOULD THEY HAVE DONE OR WHAT THEY CAN'T DO.

DENIS WAITLEY

◆ THINKING SOCIOLOGY

How would you define academic integrity?

enced feelings of violation of trust. We concluded that we could not trust our mailbox to be left unguarded. Now the mailperson places a lock on our mailbox after delivering our personal mail. There is a feeling of a violation of trust experienced by victims of rape. For rape victims, of course, there are other feelings: anger, shame, confusion, rage, and psychological and physical pain.

Merton's Anomie Theory

One of the well-known structural functional theories explaining deviance was proposed by Robert Merton. Merton explained deviance using the **anomie theory of deviance**. Merton proposed that deviance resulted from a gap between the goals of society and the means for achieving those goals. The goals of society can be seen in what may be called status symbols in our society. We know there are differences in automobiles, in jewelry, in homes and in schools. Because prestige and power also are a part of these status symbols or goals, they are widely sought after. Merton concluded that there were five possible responses in considering deviant behavior. Each response is approached in terms of goals of society and the means for achieving those goals.

The first of Merton's five responses is the conformist. The **conformist** accepts both the goals of society and the approved means for achieving those goals. Conformity is the only nondeviant response in Merton's typology of deviant behavior. Conformity is also the most common response. The truth is that conformity is the norm. That may be difficult to conclude when most of us are accustomed to hearing and reading about the deviant acts that take place in our society. In our social psychology class, we ask students to find five examples of deviant behavior in one newspaper. This poses no problem! We also ask that they find five examples of prosocial behavior in the same newspaper. This usually does pose a problem. Our newspapers have found that reporting on positive or prosocial behavior does not sell newspapers. Of course, our reading about the deviant behavior reinforces for us the belief that only bad and terrible things are happening in our society. There is, of course, the concern for the rise in crime. Most students are conformists because they have accepted the goals of society. Goals for most students are to succeed in obtaining a degree that has market value so that other goals of society may be within their grasp. We want to achieve our degree in order to earn the money to feed our spouse and children. Goals such as fancy sports cars, homes, Rolex watches also are desired. For students there is the acceptance of the approved means for achieving those goals. Students are devoting four to five years of their lives to attending college and studying long hours to achieve that degree. This is acceptable behavior for our young people.

The second response identified by Merton is the innovator. The **innovator** accepts the goals of society but rejects the approved means for achieving those goals. The innovator is like the conformist in that he accepts the goals of society. Innovators want the same status symbols of fancy sports cars, homes and Rolex watches. Innovators are unlike conformists in that they do not accept the approved means for achieving these goals. A burglar desires a VCR, but is not willing to purchase a VCR and put it on his or her credit card. The innovator steals the VCR from possible conformists. Merton does suggest that not everyone has equal opportunity to achieving goals by approved means. The cost of college may prevent some from achieving goals by the approved methods.

The third response is a ritualist. A **ritualist** response is the opposite of the innovator. The ritualist rejects the goals of society but accepts the means for achieving those goals. An example of a ritualist may be a bureaucrat. When the person working within a bureaucracy becomes disenchanted with the goals of that bureaucracy but continues to work there, adhering to all the rules and regulations, he or she becomes a ritualist. They may make certain every "i" is dotted and every "t" is crossed. Almost

🐦 *Quick Glance*

Deviance can weaken the trust in the social system.   T F

Auguste Merton explained deviance.   T F

"Conformist" is a type of adaptation to societal goals and means.   T F

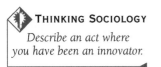

THINKING SOCIOLOGY

Why is conformity the most common response of individuals?

🐦 *Quick Glance*

Conformists accept goals and means of society. T F

Robert Merton is a conflict theorist.   T F

Anomie means a conformist.   T F

THINKING SOCIOLOGY

Describe an act where you have been an innovator.

MERTON'S ANOMIE THEORY OF DEVIANCE		
Response	*Goals*	*Approved Means*
conformist	accepts	accepts
innovator	accepts	rejects
ritualist	rejects	accepts
retreatist	rejects	rejects
rebel	substitutes	substitutes

🕮 *Quick Glance*

An innovator tries new means to goals.	T F
A ritualist establishes new goals.	T F
A skidrow alcoholic is a retreatist.	T F
A rebel accepts society's goals.	T F

eight years ago, a student enrolled in a social problems class and began to habitually miss class. She was reached by phone and made aware that she needed to attend class. However, her response was "Don't drop me from class." My response was "Fine, then I'll see you in class." To which she responded "Oh no, I'll not be in class." My final response was "Then that means that you choke up an 'F.'" "Fine," she responded. This student had rejected the goals, but accepted the means. It turns out that she was concerned with being on her father's insurance.

▲ MERTON WOULD CONSIDER THIS MAN A RETREATIST.
IMAGE COPYRIGHT LISA F. YOUNG, 2008. USED UNDER LICENSE FROM SHUTTERSTOCK, INC.

The fourth response identified by Merton is that of retreatist. The **retreatist** rejects both the goals and the approved means for achieving the goals of society. A typical example of the retreatist is a street person, hobo or bum. The homeless would not be examples of the retreatist. They have not made conscious decisions to reject the goals and means of society. Another distinguishing factor between the homeless and the retreatist is the fact that many of the homeless are children who have not made a rational decision of rejecting goals and the means for achieving those goals.

The last response in Merton's typology is the rebel. The **rebel** is like the retreatist in that he/she has rejected the goals of society and the means for achieving those goals. However, for the rebel, there is the substitution of his/her own goals and his/her own means for achieving goals. This would include the anarchist or the fascist. The hippies of the 1950s would be this type of deviant.

Merton's theory has been criticized because of its limited application in the field of criminology. It simply does not explain all deviant behavior. What about serial murderers? What about passion killings or drive-by killings?

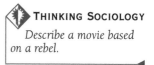

TELEVISION HAS PROVED THAT PEOPLE WILL LOOK AT ANYTHING RATHER THAN EACH OTHER.
ANN LANDERS

🔺 THINKING SOCIOLOGY
Describe a movie based on a rebel.

HOW DOES THE CONFLICT THEORY EXPLAIN DEVIANCE?

The conflict theorist believes that people become deviant because laws and norms reflect the interests of powerful members of a society. People who threaten the status quo are likely to be defined as deviant. Deviation by the powerful is not viewed as negatively as that of the powerless. For example, white collar crime is not punished as seriously as robbery. Several examples of conflict theory will now be given.

IN ORDER TO GET WHAT WE WANT, WE MUST SAY WHAT WE MEAN. IN ORDER TO SAY WHAT WE MEAN WE MUST KNOW WHAT WE WANT. WHEN WE KNOW WHAT WE WANT, WE CAN THINK AND SPEAK POSITIVELY WITH GREAT EXPECTATIONS.
IYANLA VARIZANT

THINKING SOCIOLOGY

How would gangs be delinquent subcultures according to Cohen?

Albert Cohen devised a theory based on delinquent subcultures. He said that whether a person became deviant or not depended on the sociocultural environment and social interaction. A delinquent subculture develops among people, primarily teenagers, who are unable to compete in a middle-class environment. There is, in other words, a gap between what they see as being desirable and what they can hope to obtain.

Three types of delinquent subcultures may develop from this blocked opportunity structure (Cloward and Ohlin, 1960):

1. criminal: property and wealth
2. conflict oriented: violence
3. retreatist: withdrawal from deviant and conformist behavior

Based on data from the U.S. Census Bureau, Statistical Abstracts of the United States, 2006, the states with the highest violent crime rate (murder, forcible rape, robbery and aggravated assault) are Delaware, District of Columbia, Florida, Illinois, Maryland, Louisiana, Nevada, New Mexico, South Carolina, and Tennessee. The states with the highest property crime (burglary, larceny/theft and motor vehicle theft are Alaska, Arizona, Florida, Georgia, Hawaii, Louisiana, Missouri, Nevada, New Mexico, Oklahoma, Oregon, South Carolina, Tennessee, Texas, Utah, and Washington.

Disorganization within the community can bring about deviant behavior. This happens when the community subsystems do not work efficiently. Both man-made and natural disasters cause problems within the system. When teachers go on strike, parents may be forced to leave their children unsupervised at home. When medical personnel go on strike, it may be necessary to diagnose our own illnesses and seek other types of treatment. When a natural disaster strikes, and telephone and electrical lines are out of commission, crime rates often escalate. After natural disasters such as a flood strike a community, bogus repair services emerge such as de-molding and carpet cleaners who do not have the proper equipment or skills. Or people might start being more generous than the norms require. One lady, when the hurricane struck Homestead, Florida in 1992, took in homeless pet ferrets and sent out a newsletter asking for donations to pay for food and medical care. She also asked for volunteers to adopt a ferret.

Another form of community dysfunction is schismatic community breakdown. **Schismatic community breakdown** occurs when the bonds that hold a society together are broken apart. This happened during the Salem Witch Trials and the McCarthy Era of the 1950s. People, when schismatic community breakdown occurs, look around them and wonder who is squealing on whom, who is the witch or communist. We become very suspicious and secretive in our behavior and people in power can put to trial and convict people in relatively powerless positions.

Community disorganization such as violence, race riots and political riots cause community social disorganization. This type of behavior generally occurs when a subgroup within the society feels powerless and would like to shift the balance of power. (This topic was discussed in Chapter 6 of this text.)

⊛ *Quick Glance*

Albert Cohen studied delinquent subcultures.   T F

There are three types of delinquent subcultures.   T F

Schismatic community breakdown brings the members to feelings of more solidarity.   T F

Community disorganization does not exist.   T F

Violence is not a form of community disorganization.   T F

Learning TIP
E-mail your instructor—this is another way to get to know you! Ask questions via e-mail.

THINKING SOCIOLOGY

Does the current pattern of race relations in our society constitute schismatic community breakdown? Support your view.

HOW DOES THE SYMBOLIC INTERACTIONIST THEORY EXPLAIN DEVIANCE?

The symbolic interactionist can look at several different aspects of human behavior in order to explain deviant behavior.

The first type of explanation deals with the socialization process teaching us how to function within the society according to the norms and roles. People can become deviant because of inappropriate socialization; the person has failed to learn the appropriate norms of behavior for her/his respective culture. For example, in our

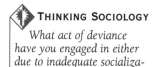

country, if I eat a large meal and give a roaring belch, I would be considered deviant. But in many eastern cultures, my belch is a compliment to the hostess. If that eastern person belched in the North American culture, they would be considered deviant.

Inadequate socialization contributes to deviance. If I have not learned the role through anticipatory socialization, I can become deviant. For example, we find that some people who abuse their children lack child rearing and discipline skills. In order to help the battering parent, the intervening agency provides them with child rearing courses in order to help them cope with the frustrations of parenthood.

Role conflict and stress can cause deviant behavior. For example, if I know that my daughter needs good grades to get into college, and that all the other students in her chemistry class are cheating on the exams, I shall have a mental battle of whether my role of honest citizen wins over my role of wanting the best

▲ THIS MAN HAS NOT LEARNED THE ROLE OF A LAW-ABIDING CITIZEN.
IMAGE COPYRIGHT THOMAS SZTANEK, 2008. USED UNDER LICENSE FROM SHUTTERSTOCK, INC.

for my child. Other forms of deviance which help alleviate role stress include mental illness, substance abuse and suicide.

A second aspect that the symbolic interactionist is interested in concerns the labeling process. The symbolic interactionist believes that it is through society defining a person as deviant that a person becomes deviant. Once a person gets the label, then he further acts out on these by committing other deviations.

Becker's Labeling Theory

Howard S. Becker, a sociologist, views deviance from the labeling perspective. The **labeling theory of deviance** attempts to explain the process of a person receiving the deviant identity. Becker's conclusion is that there are three major elements of the deviant act:

1. Someone exhibits a behavior.
2. A guideline established for deviance and conformity says "that is deviant behavior."
3. A person or a group of people decide that because deviant behavior has been exhibited, that the person is a deviant; a label is now established.

Once a person has been labeled, other deviants accept him into their groups which may lead to more deviant behavior. According to Becker, it is the very act of labeling a person that accounts for deviant acts occurring. There are three important principles of the labeling perspective:

1. *Behavior by itself is not always criminal or normal.* The "criminality" of a behavior is determined by people and how people react to it. Deviance is rela-

THINKING SOCIOLOGY

What act of deviance have you engaged in either due to inadequate socialization or role conflict?

◀

Quick Glance

People can become deviant because of inappropriate socialization. T F

Lack of anticipatory socialization contributes to deviance. T F

Role conflict can cause deviant behavior. T F

THINKING SOCIOLOGY

What type of index crime criminal would be most negatively affected by being labeled a deviant? Why?

◀

tive. Is the taking of another person's life always deviant? What about in times of war?

2. *All people commit deviant acts at some point.* There are no saints among us. If we inadvertently run a stop sign, our first response is to look in our rearview mirror to make certain that a police officer did not spot us. We realize that the police are agents of social control and have the legitimate authority to declare us deviants.

3. *Once the label of deviance is applied, there are consequences for the deviant.* In *Scarlet Letter* by Nathaniel Hawthorne, the label was visible with the letter "A" worn on the clothes, resulting in the rejection and isolation from other people.

🕮 *Quick Glance*

According to Becker, labeling is important for deviant behavior.   T   F

"Criminality" is determined by people's reactions.   T   F

Deviance is absolute.   T   F

Chambliss' Labeling Perspective

Other sociologists and criminologists have expanded on the labeling perspective. Criminologist William J. Chambliss sees a relationship between labeling and social class. This states that the lower the social class, the more likely one is to be labeled as deviant. Conversely, the higher the social class, the less likely one is to be labeled a deviant. The reading for this chapter was written by Jeffery Reiman and was taken from his book, *The Rich Get Richer and the Poor Get Prison*. Once accused of criminal behavior, there is a financial cost to prove one's innocence. For the middle class and the upper class, this may prove possible. However, for members of the lower class, the burden of proving innocence may not be possible. The lower-class person will not be able to afford the retainer fee of lawyers that can amount to five digits or more. The lower-class person is stuck with an appointed lawyer who may not be aware of the specifics of the case until moments before walking into the courtroom.

YOU'RE NOT GOING TO MAKE ME HAVE A BAD DAY. IF THERE'S OXYGEN ON EARTH AND I'M BREATHING, IT'S GOING TO BE A GOOD DAY.

COTTON FITZSIMMONS

Sutherland's Differential Association Theory

Edwin Sutherland devised the theory of differential association. The **differential association theory of deviance** asserts that individuals learn to be deviant. The socialization process with reference groups and significant others may be such that the person is rewarded for being deviant. The differential theory of deviance proposes the following principles of deviance:

1. Criminal behavior is learned through our interactions with others.
2. Criminal behavior is learned within primary groups.
3. We become criminal when definitions favorable to the violation of law outweigh the unfavorable ones.
4. We are most apt to become criminal when our interactions are frequent, long-lasting, intense and happen early in life.

 THINKING SOCIOLOGY

How could Cooley's theory of looking glass self be used in analyzing Becker's explanation of deviance?

Learning TIP

Make concept cards for key concepts and key people. Put the word on the front of the card and the definition in your own words on back. Use these to study.

THEORIES OF DEVIANCE		
Theorist	*Theory*	*Buzz words*
Merton	anomie	gap between goals and means
Cohen	delinquent subculture	blocked opportunities
Becker	labeling	identity
Chambliss	labeling/social class	social class
Sutherland	differential association	deviance is learned

WHAT IS SOCIAL CONTROL?

Social control is essential for the operation of a smooth running society. **Social control** includes all the means and processes used by a society to ensure conformity to the group norms. *One of the most important social control mechanisms is socialization.* In Chapter 4, the socialization agents were listed as family, media, education, peers and religion. These agents of socialization use rewards and punishments, sanctions, to modify behavior. **Informal social control** is based on informal positive and negative sanctions. When I scowl at a student who is trying to look on another's test, I am using an informal negative sanction. I am hoping that my facial expression alone will ensure conformity to the norm of academic honesty and that the student will conform to society's norm. If the student persists in his or her quest for another's knowledge, I shall take the test and the student may face immediate dismissal from school; dismissal is a formal negative sanction. It is hoped that through these methods, the individual will cease his or her deviant behavior and conform to society's expectations. Positive sanctions play an important role in ensuring conformity to society's norms. Knowledge that a pay raise will be awarded for diligent work many times keeps us dedicated to our jobs. When my son does his homework, I use informal positive sanctions to try to encourage him to use the same study methods at a later point in time.

A second division of social control is through social pressure. Conformity occurs when an individual changes his or her behavior in order to be consistent with norms of the group. Most of us have been socialized to like being with other people and being accepted by our families, peers and co-workers. When my daughter drinks "because everyone else is doing it," she is conforming. She is in a group with which she feels social support and feelings of cohesiveness. If these two factors are lacking, rates of conformity go down.

Several important research projects have underlined the importance of conformity. S. E. Asch demonstrated that people will alter an observation that they know to be correct rather than disagree with the group opinion. Each subject in these experiments was placed in a group which included people who were part of the experiment. These conspirators deliberately made wrong factual observations to the person who was being challenged. One-third of the people subjected to incorrect information accepted the wrong observation when opposed by the group opinion which disagreed with them.

Obedience is the most direct form of social control; obedience is obeying someone in authority. When I tell a student to bring me his or her test, I expect the test to be quickly in my hands. When the chairman of the department requests that I come to his office, I go! A very famous study by S. Milgram tested the amount of obedience that people will do. Sixty-five percent of the people in Milgram's research obeyed the experimenter's commands to deliver electric shocks of increasing strength to an innocent victim. Obedience is not always bad, but the effects of total obedience must be considered.

Compliance happens when people alter their behavior based upon direct requests from others; this is not as strong a social control mechanism as obedience. So when I ask, "Would you please not smoke in my home?" I am making a request, but I probably would not do anything at the time if she/he refused my requests.

Formal social control plays an important role for ensuring a functioning society. Formal social control is based on society's authorized agencies such as law enforcement officers and judges. These people have the right to use formal negative (and positive) sanctions to ensure conformity. When a law enforcement officer clocks me driving 65 miles per hour in a 55 mile per hour zone, he has the authorization to issue me a formal negative sanction called a ticket.

🕮 *Quick Glance*

Once a person has been labeled a deviant, they are an outcast to all groups.   T F

William Chambliss is responsible for viewing the relationship between labeling and social class.   T F

Differential association theory is based on inter-action with others.   T F

Criminal behavior is learned in secondary groups.   T F

THINKING SOCIOLOGY
How effective is informal social control?

CRIME IS CONTAGIOUS. IF THE GOVERNMENT BECOMES A LAWBREAKER, IT BREEDS FOR CONTEMPT FOR THE LAW.
JUSTICE LOUIS D. BRANDEIS

🕮 *Quick Glance*

Social control is important for society.   T F

Sanctions are important for social control.   T F

Social pressures cause rather than prevent deviance.   T F

Obedience is a form of social control.   T F

Obedience is the most direct form of social control.   T F

Socialization is important for social control.   T F

The judicial system is an example of formal social control.   T F

WHAT IS A SOCIAL PROBLEM?

◆ THINKING SOCIOLOGY

What is a social problem today that was not a problem 100 years ago? Name a social problem of 100 years ago that is not a social problem today.

◀

When does deviance within the society come to be viewed as a problem by society? What characterizes a social problem? *First, the act has to be recognized as a problem.* At one time tonics contained high amounts of alcohol; cokes contained cocaine. We did not consider this a problem. But now substance abuse is considered a problem that we as a society have to deal with as a social problem. *The condition has to affect a significant number of people (or affect significant people) in ways which are considered undesirable.* Drug abuse was not considered a serious problem until teenagers from middle and upper classes became involved in the activity. Alcoholism received a great deal more attention when Elizabeth Taylor and Betty Ford came forth with their substance abuse problems. AIDS received a great deal more attention when Rock Hudson admitted to having the disease and died of AIDS. In 1991, Magic Johnson came forth with an even greater emphasis of AIDS as a societal problem. It is no longer defined as a gay male disease. *And lastly, people have to believe that something can be done about the problem.* If poverty is viewed as an individual problem, there is nothing that we,

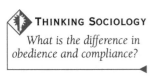

> THE MESSAGE FROM THE MOON . . . IS THAT NO PROBLEM NEED ANY LONGER BE CONSIDERED INSOLVABLE.
>
> NORMAN COUSINS

as a society, can do about it. If we view poverty as a result of the educational or economic system, then we can make changes. We have introduced, for example, Head Start to help children in poverty to have higher achievement in school and to succeed in the job market. In conclusion, a **social problem** is deviance that is recognized by society as a condition needing correction through group effort.

▲ ALCOHOLISM IS A SOCIAL PROBLEM IN THE U.S.A.

IMAGE COPYRIGHT ROMAN SIGAEV, 2008. USED UNDER LICENSE FROM SHUTTERSTOCK, INC.

🐚 *Quick Glance*

A personal problem is always a social problem.   T   F

The finding of a cure for AIDS is a social problem.   T   F

A social problem has to be recognized by society.   T   F

◆ THINKING SOCIOLOGY

What is the difference in obedience and compliance?

◀

▼ CHAPTER SUMMARY

1. Properties of deviant behavior include deviance being neither positive or negative, varying with the historical time period and with the culture or subculture, varying with the situation and involving a labeling process.

2. Two concepts are involved in the process of labeling a person deviant: primary and secondary deviance. Primary deviance involves deviance that is tolerated while secondary deviance results in an individual being labeled as a deviant.

3. People with differences—mental and emotional illness and physical attributes—are often called deviant.

4. Criminal behavior includes index crime, professional crime, white collar crime and victimless crime.

5. Functions of deviance include the following: may help to bring about needed social change, promote a sense of group identity and cooperating, clarify certain norms, allow for diverse forms of expression, help cut the "red tape," act as a safety valve, provides for innovation and creativity, act as a barometer of social strain and provide a source of employment and income.

6. Dysfunctions of deviance include disruption of social order, destruction of the motivation of other people to conform, diversion of resources and destruction of trust.

7. Merton's theory of anomie includes five responses: conformist, innovator, ritualist, retreatist and rebel.
8. Conflict theory analyzes deviant behavior in terms of conflict between different groups, community breakdowns and deviant subcultures.
9. Symbolic interactionism explains deviance through the socialization process and labeling process.
10. The differential perception theory states that deviance is learned in the same way that conformity is learned.
11. Social control may be formal or informal. Society uses both formal means such as laws and informal means such as praise to get conformity from the members of society.
12. A social problem has to be viewed in society as a condition needing solving and as possible to correct.

▼ REFERENCES

Asch, S. E. 1951. "Effects of Group Pressure upon the Modification and Distortion of Judgments," in Heinz Guetzkow (ed.) *Groups, Leadership, and Men*, U.S. Office of Naval Research, Carnegie Institute of Technology, Pittsburgh.

Becker, Howard. 1963. *Outsiders*. New York: The Free Press.

Bernard, T. J. 1992. *The Cycle of Juvenile Justice*. New York: Oxford.

Chambliss, William J., and Robert B. Seidman, 1982. *Law, Order, and Power*. Reading, Mass.: Addison-Wesley.

Cloward, Richard A. and Lloyd E. Ohlin. 1960. *Delinquency and Opportunity*. New York: Free Press.

Cohen, Albert. 1955. *Delinquent Boys: The Culture of the Gang*. Chicago, Illinois: The Free Press.

Merton, Robert. 1957. *Social Theory and Social Structure*. New York: Free Press.

McDonald, D. C., ed. 1990. *Private Prisons and the Public Interests*. New Brunswick, N. J.: Rutgers University Press.

Milgram, Stanley. 1964. "Group pressure and Action Against a Person." *Journal of Abnormal and Social Psychology*, 69, 137–143.

Reasons, C. F. and R. M. Rich, eds. 1978. *The Sociology of Law: A Conflict Perspective*. Toronto: Butterworths.

Rutter, M. and H. Giller. 1984. *Juvenile Delinquency: Trends and Perspectives*. New York: Guilford Press.

Sutherland, Edwin H. 1939. *Principles of Criminology*. Philadelphia: Lippincott.

U.S. Bureau of Census. 1992. *Statistical Abstract of the United States*, 183.

READING

EXCERPT FROM THE RICH GET RICHER AND THE POOR GET PRISON: IDEOLOGY, CLASS AND CRIMINAL JUSTICE, 3/E BY JEFFREY REIMAN*

Think of a crime, any crime. Picture the first "crime" that comes into your mind. What do you see? The odds are you are not imagining a mining company executive sitting at his desk, calculating the costs of proper safety precautions and deciding not to invest in them. Probably what you do see with your mind's eye is one person physically attacking another or robbing something from another on the threat of physical attack. Look more closely. What does the attacker look like? It's a safe bet he (and it is a *he*, of course) is not wearing a suit and tie. In fact, my hunch is that you—like me, like almost anyone in America—picture a young, tough, lower-class male when the thought of crime first pops into your head. You (we) picture some-one like the Typical Criminal described above. The crime itself is one in which the Typical Criminal sets out to attack or rob some specific person.

This last point is important. What it indicates is that we have a mental image not only of the Typical Criminal, but also of the Typical Crime. If the Typical Criminal is a young lower-class male, the Typical Crime is *one-on-one-harm*—where harm means either physical injury or loss of something valuable or both. If you have any doubts that this is the Typical Crime, look at any random sample of police or private eye shows on television. How often do you see Jim Rockford or "The Equalizer" investi-gate consumer fraud or failure to remove occupational hazards? A study of TV crime shows by The Media Institute in Washington, D.C., indicates that, while the fictional criminals portrayed on television are on the average both older and wealthier than the real criminals who figure in the FBI *Uniform Crime Reports*, "TV crimes are almost 12 times as likely to be violent as crimes committed in the real world." In short, TV crime shows broadcast the double-edged message that the "one-on-one" crimes of the poor are the typical crimes of all and thus not uniquely caused by the pressures of poverty; *and* that the criminal justice system happens mainly to pounce on the poor in real life, it is not out of any class bias.

It is important to identify this model of the Typical Crime because it functions like a set of blinders. It keeps us from calling a mine disaster a mass murder even if twenty-six men are killed, even if someone is responsible for the unsafe conditions in which they worked and died. In fact, I argue that this particular piece of mental furniture so blocks our view that it keeps us from using the criminal justice system to protect ourselves from the greatest threats to our persons and possessions.

What keeps a mine disaster from being a mass murder in our eyes is the fact that it is not one-on-one harm. What is important here is not the numbers but the intent to harm someone. An attack by a gang on one or more persons or an attack by one individual on several fits the model of one-on-one harm. That is, for each person harmed there is at least one individual who wanted to harm that person. Once he selects his victim, the rapist, the mugger, the murderer, all want this person they have selected to suffer. A mine executive, on the other hand, does not want his employ-ees to be harmed. He would truly prefer that there be no accident, no injured or dead miners. What he does want is something legitimate. It is what he has been hired to get: maximum profits at minimum costs. If he cuts corners to save a buck, he is just doing his job. If twenty-six men die because he cuts corners on safety, we may think him crude or callous but not a killer. He is, at most, responsible for an indirect harm, not a one-on-one harm. For this, he may even be criminally indictable for violating safety regulations—but not for murder. The twenty-six men are dead as an unwanted consequence of his (perhaps overzealous or undercautious) pursuit of a legitimate goal. So unlike the Typical Criminal, he has not committed the Typical Crime—or so we generally believe. As a result, twenty-six men are dead who might be alive now if cutting corners of the kind that leads to loss of life, whether suffering is specifically intended or not, were treated as murder.

The Defender of the Present Legal Order (I'll call him "the Defender" for short whenever it is necessary to deal with his objections in the future) is neither a foolish nor an evil person. He is not a racist, nor is he oblivious to the need for reform in the criminal justice system to make it more evenhanded and for reform in the larger society to make equal opportunity a reality for all Americans. In general, his view is that—given our limited resources, particularly the resource of human altruism—the political and legal institutions we have are the best that can be. What is necessary is to make them work better and to weed out those who are intent on making them work shoddily. His response to my argument at this point is that the criminal justice system should occupy itself primarily with one-on-one harm. Harms of the sort exemplified in the "mine disaster" are really not murders and are better dealt with through stricter government enforcement of safety regulations. He would admit that this enforcement has been rather lax and recommend that it be improved. Basically, though, he thinks this division of labor is right because it fits our ordinary moral sensibilities.

The Defender maintains that, according to our ordinary moral notions, someone who wants to do another harm and does is really more evil than someone who jeopardizes others while pursuing legitimate goals but wishes no one harm. Being directly harmed by another person, he believes, is terrifying in a way that being harmed impersonally, say, by a safety hazard, is not—even if the resultant injury is the same in both cases. What's more, we should be tolerant of the one responsible for lax safety measures because he is pursuing a legitimate goal, that is, his dangerous action occurs as part of a productive activity, something that ultimately adds to social wealth and thus benefits everyone—whereas the doer of direct harm benefits no one but himself. Thus, the latter is rightfully in the province of the criminal justice system with its drastic weapons, and the former is appropriately dealt with by the milder forms of regulation.

I think that the Defender's argument rests on three errors. First, he overestimates the reality of the "free consent" with which workers enter their jobs. Although no one is forced at gunpoint to accept any particular job, virtually everyone is forced by the requirements of necessity to take some job. Thus, at best, workers can choose among the dangers present at various worksites and not choose to face no danger at all. Moreover, workers can only choose jobs where there are openings, which means they cannot simply pick their place of employment at will. Consequently, for all intents and purposes, most workers must face the dangers of the jobs that are available to them.

Second, the Defender's argument errs by treating our ordinary notions of morality as a single consistent fabric rather than the crazy quilt of conflicting values and ideals it is. In other words, even if it fits some of our ordinary moral notions to believe that one-on-one harm is more evil than indirect harm, other aspects of our ordinary moral sensibilities lead to the opposite conclusion. For instance, it is a feature of both our moral sensibilities and our legal system that we often hold people culpable for harms they have caused through negligence or recklessness, even though they wished to harm no one—thus the kid-glove treatment meted out to those responsible for occupations hazards and the like is no simple reflection of our ordinary

Quick Glance

The perceived typical criminal is middle-aged male.   T F

Television crime shows usually depict property crimes more than personal crime.   T F

If a crime is not one-to-one, we do not perceive the act as criminal.   T F

Quick Glance

The defender justifies mass killings based on intent.   T F

We underestimate the free will in choice of job.   T F

Our standards of cultural morality are consistent.   T F

Legal institutions are fair and just in protecting the welfare of workers.   T F

moral sensibilities, as the Defender claims. Moreover, compare the mine executive who cuts corners to the typical murderer. Most murders, we know, are committed in the heat of some passion like rage or jealousy. Two lovers or neighbors or relatives find themselves in a heated argument. One (usually it is a matter of chance which one) picks up a weapon and strikes the other a fatal blow. Such a person is clearly a murderer and rightly subject to punishment by the criminal justice system. Is this person more evil than the executive who chooses not to pay for safety equipment?

The Defender's argument errs a third time by overlooking the role of legal institutions in shaping our ordinary moral notions. Many who defend the criminal justice system do so precisely because of its function in educating the public about the difference between right and wrong. The great historian of English law, Sir James Fitzjames Stephens, held that a

> great part of the general detestation of crime which happily *prevails amongst the decent part of the community in all civilized countries arises from the fact that the commission of offenses is associated in all such communities with the solemn and deliberate infliction of punishment wherever* crime is proved.

In other words, one cannot simply appeal to ordinary moral notions to defend the criminal law because the criminal law has already had a hand in shaping ordinary moral notions. At least one observer has argued that making narcotics use a crime in the beginning of this century caused a change in the public's ordinary moral notions about drug addiction, which prior to that time had been viewed as a medical problem. It is probably safe to say that in our own time, civil rights legislation has sharpened the public's moral condemnation of racial discrimination. Hence, we might speculate that if the criminal justice system began to prosecute—and if the median began to portray—those who inflict indirect harm as serious criminals, our ordinary moral notions would change on this point as well.

What is the purpose of the criminal justice system? No esoteric answer is required. Norval Morris and Gordon Hawkins write that "the prime function of the criminal law is to protect our persons and our property." *The Challenge of Crime in a Free Society*, the report of the President's Commission on Law Enforcement and Administration of Justice, tells us that "any criminal justice system is an apparatus society uses to enforce the standards of conduct necessary to protect individuals and the community." Whatever else we think a criminal justice system should accomplish, I doubt if anyone would deny that its central purpose is to protect us against the most serious threats to our well-being. I argue that this purpose is seriously undermined by taking one-on-one harm as the model of crime. Excluding harm caused without the intention to harm prevents the criminal justice system from protecting our persons and our property from dangers at least as great as those posed by one-on-one harm. This is so because, as I will show, there are a large number of actions that are not labeled criminal but that lead to loss of life, limb, and possessions on a scale comparable to those actions that are represented in the FBI Crime Index—and a crime by any other name still causes misery and suffering.

◆ THINKING SOCIOLOGY

Do you agree with Reiman? Should acts such as petro-chemical explosions or sugar factory explosions which cause loss of life and health be considered criminal acts and tried and punished as criminal acts? Should intent be part of the criteria for an act to be considered criminal? Support and explain your answer.

Deliberating Social Stratification

CHAPTER OBJECTIVES

1. What is stratification?
2. What are the two basic types of social stratification systems?
3. What is the basis of social inequality?
4. Why is the sociologist interested in social stratification?
5. How does conflict theory explain social stratification?
6. How does structural functional theory explain social stratification?
7. How is social class measured in the United States?
8. How many social classes exist in the United States?
9. What is social mobility?
10. What are the factors that affect mobility rates?
11. How can the individual experience upward social mobility?

caste system: a stratification system based on ascribed status

class consciousness: the awareness of your position in the social class system

closed system: a stratification system which does not allow for a change in strata

conspicuous consumption: the practice of flaunting the symbols of success and wealth

horizontal mobility: the movement from one status to another in which there is little or no difference between the ranks of the two positions

income: the amount of money earned in a given amount of time

intergenerational mobility: the social mobility traced through two or more generations

intragenerational mobility: the mobility occurring within a person's lifetime

life chances: the opportunities in life based on placement in stratification system

open system: a stratification system which allows mobility of an individual in a social stratification system

power: the ability to influence other people to do what we want them to do

social class: the category of people who share approximately the same lifestyle

social class system: the stratification system based on achieved status

social inequality: the condition whereby societal members have unequal amounts of wealth, prestige or power

social mobility: the movement of people between social strata

social stratification: the ranking of individual members of society according to some common accepted basis of evaluation

status: the standing or esteem of people as assessed by other citizens of the society

status inconsistency: the lack of congruence among the components for determining social strata

strata: the people in either a caste or class system sharing similar position in the social stratification continuum

vertical mobility: the movement upward or downward on the stratification system

wealth: an individual's total economic assets including inherited wealth, salary and wages

▼ KEY PEOPLE

Karl Marx, William Ryan, Paul Samuelson, Melvin Tumin, Lloyd Warner, Max Weber

WHAT IS STRATIFICATION?

All societies utilize some form of social stratification for its members. **Social stratification** is the ranking of individual members of a society according to differences in possession of scarce resources such as income, wealth, prestige and power. **Social inequality** is a condition in which societal members have unequal amounts of wealth, prestige or power. Some societies such as the hunters and primitive gardeners called Yanomamo of Brazil and Venezuela do not emphasize differences, but rather are much more egalitarian in their orientation than we are in the United States. The basis of ranking is on such factors as hunting skills and leadership abilities. If I am a successful hunter, for example, I may be deferred to and I shall receive the biggest share of meat or have access to a choice camping spot. Other tribal members may come to me for the informal settlement of disputes. In modern industrial society, this basis of evaluation becomes complex and we shall discuss the basis in a later section of this chapter.

In any society, however, people possessing similar resources are placed into strata. A **strata** consists of those people sharing a similar position in the social stratification continuum. Social stratification can be imagined as a ladder with the top members on the top rung of the ladder and the lowest members on the lowest rung of the ladder.

☙ **Quick Glance**

Social stratification involves ranking.   T   F

A strata is a category of people sharing similar life styles.   T   F

All societies have a stratification system.   T   F

Societal inequality involves money but not prestige.   T   F

A strata is people sharing a position in the social stratification system.   T   F

WHAT ARE THE TWO BASIC TYPES OF SOCIAL STRATIFICATION SYSTEMS?

There are two basic types of social stratification systems: caste and social class. A **caste system** is based on an ascribed status and is considered a closed system. A **closed system** does not allow for a change in strata of individual members of the society. I am born into a caste system and this birth determines what I do for a living, where I live, in whom I associate, and whom I marry. The caste system is supported by either religion and/or law. Since I am born into a caste, I shall die that same caste. A slave system or the feudal system used during the European Middle Ages was primarily a caste system. People were born into royalty and contracts were set up between qualified families to keep titles and land within the privileged positions. People who were serfs, or farmers for the land owners, stayed in these positions as generations rolled by. If I were born a slave in pre-Civil War United States, I would have remained a slave unless my owner gave me freedom. Even with freedom, I still remained limited in my movement. This limited mobility is a characteristic of a caste system. The Hindu caste system of India is the classic example used for a caste system. There are five basic groupings within the system and mobility between castes is not possible. The five groupings are:

1. outcasts (which is not really considered a caste)
2. manual laborers
3. peasants, craftsmen and merchants
4. warriors
5. priests and teachers

Under the onslaught of demands for a more modern economic system, the caste system is breaking down in India.

A social class system, on the other hand, is based on achieved status rather than ascribed status; social class is an open class system. An **open system** allows for social mobility. A **social class** is a category of people who share roughly the same

⚑ **THINKING SOCIOLOGY**

Is the lower-lower class in the U.S.A. a closed system?

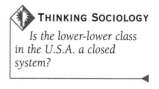

WE KNOW WHAT WE ARE, BUT WE KNOW NOT WHAT WE MAY BE.

WILLIAM SHAKESPEARE

☙ **Quick Glance**

Caste is based on achieved status.   T   F

Social class is based on ascribed status.   T   F

Feudal Europe was a social class system.   T   F

⚑ **THINKING SOCIOLOGY**

Why do the demands of modern economic systems cause the caste system to break down?

lifestyle. People sharing the same social class believe themselves to be social equals. This is the primary type of stratification system that we have in the United States and other technologically advanced societies. I can move into or out of a strata in the society. My social class is not fixed and does not necessarily determine where I live or whom I marry. The hallmark of a social class system is the amount of social mobility tolerated. The upper-upper class in the United States has aspects of a caste or closed system. Members who are considered the upper-upper class in the United States occupy that rung of the social ladder due largely to ascribed status. The upper-upper class have inherited their money and are referred to as "old money." We have an underclass in this country. These are the people born at the bottom of the income/educational hierarchy and, due to family background and lack of opportunities, these people have extreme difficulty leaving their social status behind. These people are bonded into this lower caste. This provides evidence of a closed class system in the United States, although it is not as fixed by religion and law as the caste system in India or the Inca Empire.

THINKING SOCIOLOGY

Is social class based on achieved or ascribed status?

WHAT IS THE BASIS OF SOCIAL INEQUALITY?

Wealth

Max Weber, a German sociologist, identified three components of stratification. The first component recognized by Max Weber was class. Weber was identifying wealth when he referred to class. Wealth is an individual's total assets; it is his or her total economic worth, not necessarily earned money. Economic worth can be stocks, bonds, dividends, rental property and rents, as well as salaries and wages.

Different strata receive their "class" in different ways and the wealth is not distributed evenly through the stratification hierarchy. Those people at the very top of the stratification hierarchy in the United States receive much of their income from dividends and trust funds. Lloyd Warner reported that less than one percent of Americans occupied this social class. This level includes such family names as Rockefeller, Vanderbilt, Mellon and Kennedy. These people command a great deal of the wealth in the United States. The inequality of wealth can be depicted using an analogy constructed by contemporary sociologist, William Ryan. His analogy of the inequality of wealth suggests that if all the personal wealth in the U.S. was piled up and divided equally among all the people in the nation, every one of us, man, woman and child, would own free and clear almost $22,000 worth of goods; $7,500 worth of real estate, $3,500 in cash and about $5,000 worth of stocks and bonds. For a family of four that would add up to almost $90,000 in assets including $30,000 equity in a house, about $14,000 in the bank and about $20,000 worth of stocks and bonds. That much wealth would also bring in an extra $3,000 or $4,000 a year in income.

Quick Glance

A social class shares a feeling of "in-groupness." T F

The highest income is generally earned by managers and professionals. T F

The U.S.'s system contains some aspects of a caste system. T F

THINKING SOCIOLOGY

How much wealth does it take to be upper-middle class? Explain your answer.

MEDIAN WEEKLY EARNINGS, 2006	
All workers	$ 639
Management occupations	968
Computer/mathematical occupations	1,166
Architecture/engineering occupations	1,155
Legal occupations	1,144
Healthcare support occupations	423
Farming/fishing	387

U.S. Census Bureau, Statistical Abstract of the United States, 2006.

▲ FOR MOST AMERICANS, INCOME IS THEIR WEALTH.
IMAGE COPYRIGHT IVANASTAR, 2008. USED UNDER LICENSE FROM SHUTTERSTOCK, INC.

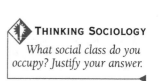

PERSONAL INCOME IN U.S.A.	
2000	$8,422
2002	$8,566
2003	$8,674
2004	$8,970

U.S. BUREAU OF ECONOMIC ANALYSIS, MARCH 2005

For most Americans, their wealth is their income. Income and wealth are different concepts. Wealth is total assets while income is the amount of money a person earns in a given amount of time. Social inequality exists in the distribution of income. The richest fifth of Americans make 47.6% of the total income of the U.S., the fourth richest make 23% of the income, the middle fifth make 15.5% of the income, the next to the last fifth make 9.67% of the income and the poorest fifth make only 4% of the total income in America. Sociologist Paul Samuelson depicted the inequality in income by suggesting that if a pyramid were constructed using children's one-inch building blocks with each level representing $1,000 of income, the pyramid would be higher than the Eiffel Tower, but most Americans would be within a yard of the ground.

Wealth takes different forms in other societies. We look at wealth in terms of money and appraisement in terms of money, but other societies use other criteria. If I am a Masaii warrior in East Africa, it traditionally would have been the number of cattle or other livestock that I owned. If I were a Tiwi from Australia, it might be the number of wives and animals that I possess.

In our society, we are very conscious of wealth and try to gain information on this factor in order to know where people fit on the social stratification (class in our society) hierarchy in our culture. If someone has a new dress, I might exclaim, "Oh, I just love your dress. Where did you buy it?" In essence, I am asking, "Where did you buy it so I can put an approximate price tag on it." We frequently ask people what they do for a living or where they live. By having these pieces of information, I can make estimates on how much money they earn and what they paid for their living quarters. In brief, a determination can be reached concerning the social class of the individual.

🕭 **Quick Glance**

Wealth is an individual's total assets.　　T　F

Income is the amount of money earned.　　T　F

The richest fifth of the population earn about 50% of the income.　T　F

Income and wealth are the same thing.　T　F

Wealth is always money.　　T　F

THINKING SOCIOLOGY
What social class do you occupy? Justify your answer.

Status

The second component of social stratification identified by Max Weber is status. Weber's concept of status is more closely attuned to what we think of as prestige. Prestige or **status** is the standing or esteem of people as assessed by other citizens of the society. Prestige and wealth, in technologically advanced societies, are related phenomena. If one is wealthy, that wealth will probably generate prestige.

In the U.S., we have status symbols such as homes, jewelry and cars. Those who are able to afford those status symbols, receive the reward of prestige. Those in the upper class are economically able to practice conspicuous consumption. **Conspicuous consumption** is the practice of flaunting the symbols of success. James Gordon Bennett, at the turn of the century, once tipped a train porter $14,000. Not a miserly tip even for the 2000s! Mrs. Astor wore diamond necklaces worth $60,000 to $80,000 in public to flaunt her treasures which accounts for the saying, "Don't act like Mrs. Astor." The middle class of the United States has learned the art of practicing conspicuous consumption by using the credit card. It has been said that the middle class of America pays monthly payments on 75% of their personal belongings. Prestige for the middle class is also achieved through their individual occupation or profession.

🕭 **Quick Glance**

Lower-upper class sometimes engages in conspicuous consumption.　T　F

In Weber's terminology, "status" is the same as prestige.　　T　F

Conspicuous consumption is the flaunting of material culture.　　T　F

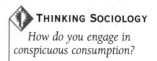

THINKING SOCIOLOGY
How do you engage in conspicuous consumption?

🐦 *Quick Glance*

The credit card facilitates conspicuous consumption.　　T　F

Prestige depends only on wealth.　　T　F

Material possessions such as diamonds never lose status impact.　　T　F

Power is the ability to influence other people's behavior.　　T　F

Where you live is an aspect of social class.　　T　F

◆ **THINKING SOCIOLOGY**

If you could choose only one, would you choose wealth, prestige or power? Why?

> DETERMINE THAT THE THING CAN AND SHALL BE DONE, AND THEN . . . FIND THE WAY.
>
> ABRAHAM LINCOLN

In the United States, we like our material possessions and the status that they imply. Many possessions, however, lose their status impact. Big diamonds are a status symbol but now we ask if it is "real" or a "CZ." Pearls have come out in cultured and artificial forms. Gold can be 10, 12, 14 carat or heavy gold electroplate. We cannot always tell. Furs used to be a status symbol but now the wearing of furs is not politically correct among many groups of people. I can rent a car that belies my status position. I can even have the use of a limousine for an evening. Discount and used clothing stores open up avenues for the purchase of garments. Antiques and original art once were considered status symbols, but now I can buy reproductions and go to the "hungry artists" sales.

Prestige does not totally depend on wealth. Prestige can be based on expert knowledge such as the case for politicians, lawyers and college professors. Mother Teresa had prestige based on known acts of mercy. It is also possible to possess wealth and not have prestige. Organized Crime leaders do not generally possess prestige outside their own circles.

Power

The last component identified by Weber is power. **Power** is the ability to influence other people to do what we want them to do. The possession of wealth generally brings power. The rich have the power to influence tax laws in their favor. Whether I wait in lines or not is an aspect of power. If I am wealthy, I pay someone else to wait in line to buy my groceries and cook my meals. If I live in a more affluent area, the store opens more checkout lines. If I live in a poor area, I buy the day old bread and I wait in line to do it. Airplane riding illustrates differences in social class position. If I fly economy or second class, they load us by row number and I wait in line. If I am first class, they board us first, may have a special door to board or board at our leisure. There may even be special waiting rooms for first class passengers. If I am really at the top end of the class system, I have a plane waiting for me. The plane flies when I want to go! The President of the United States, for example, has a jet at his disposal; so do the Chief administrative officers of such corporations as IBM, Exxon and Shell. Medical care is a factor of power. If I am in the upper class, I have a private room in the hospital and my doctor may even come to my house. If I am in the middle class, I go to my doctor, but I should not have a very long wait. If I am in a lower class, I go to the health clinic and I may spend most of my day there.

▲ THERE IS POWER IN THE RESIDENCY OF THE WHITE HOUSE.

Residence

Wealth, status and power are important dimensions of social stratification, but several other criteria are important in the formation of social stratification. Residence, or one's address, is a criteria for determining social class. If one has the address that is considered upper class, then the person will possess the prestige associated with upper class. The address can be a particular street, section of a city or a suburban area. These particulars associated with residence are usually shared knowledge by the community.

Leisure Activities

The leisure activities in which individuals participate also help in determining social stratification placement. Playing polo is considered upper strata, while bowling is perceived largely as a working class leisure activity. For example, Prince Charles is an avid polo player. Leisure activities such as golf may be more ambiguous. Golf had largely been considered a game for the rich until the middle class acquired the ability to purchase a less costly set of clubs and pay green fees as they go rather than joining a country club. Fishing is another ambiguous leisure activity because all of the classes participate; stratification position depends on where the individual is fishing, the equipment used and why he is fishing. People in the working class take vacations by visiting family; people in the upper class take sightseeing or recreational trips. People in the upper class are more apt to do leisure time activities than those in the lower class.

Another dimension of leisure is having time for leisure activities. Leisure is being able to sit down and not worry about the homework you have to do or the papers we have to grade. People in the upper strata have more leisure time than those in the middle strata. People in the lower strata are usually too worried about lack of money to have what is called "leisure" time. Worry time is not the same as leisure time. The new leisure class in our country is the elderly; never has there been so many people in their age group in better health with the funds to enjoy their retirement.

▲ YACHTS AND SAILBOATS ARE USUALLY PERCEIVED AS UPPER AND MIDDLE LEISURE ACTIVITY.
IMAGE COPYRIGHT SALVADOR GARCIA GIL, 2008. USED UNDER LICENSE FROM SHUTTERSTOCK, INC.

Family Background

Family background is an important criterion for determining social strata. The social strata of the family we are born into largely determines an individual's adult social class. The family we are born into determines our life chances. **Life chances** are opportunities in life. They include not only phenomena such as recreation patterns, opportunities to health care and education, but also the chances of getting a divorce or having a chronic illness. Those at the bottom of the United States class structure are more apt to die younger, suffer from chronic disease and to be victims of violent crime. The life chances available to someone born a Rockefeller are much different from someone born in a lower or middle-class family.

Taste Preferences

Taste preferences are yet another criteria for establishing social strata. At what restaurant do you frequently eat? Does the waiter know you and where you like to sit? What beer do you drink? Where do you purchase your clothing? What car do you drive? Do you like the opera or do you like kicker dancing? Do you eat caviar or fried catfish? Do you value cooperation or independence? These are all taste preferences, and they are all influenced by an individual's social class.

We have discussed some of the various components of social stratification. Where an individual is placed on these various criteria compose where he or she sits on the stratification ladder. When a person sits in the same relative position on all criteria, he/she is said to have status consistency. **Status inconsistency** suggests that there is no congruence among the criteria for determining social strata. There are individuals who have their doctorate degree, but are driving taxi cabs. Generally, the higher the education, the higher the social class. Someone with a doctorate degree would occupy at least upper-middle class based on their education level; however, based on the occupation of a taxi cab driver, the conclusion for the social class of that individual would be upper-lower class. This is status inconsistency; one component denotes one social strata while another criterion indicates another. When there is high consistency among the different elements determining social stratification, sociologists can more easily make accurate predictions on life chances and behavior patterns; the greater the status inconsistency, the less accurate are the predictions. A good example of people with high status inconsistencies are those people who have experienced a dramatic shift in income within a relatively short period of time; the show "Beverly Hillbillies," which is still being shown as television reruns, illustrates status inconsistency.

WHY IS THE SOCIOLOGIST INTERESTED IN SOCIAL STRATIFICATION?

Sociologists are interested in stratification for several reasons:

1. *Social stratification is a very explosive and controversial subject.* Stratification was a critical issue for Karl Marx, for example. He said that there were two strata of people: those who owned the means of production and the workers. He thought that this was unfair and he wanted to see a greater equality of resources. He wrote many articles and books criticizing the economies of Europe.

2. *Social stratification affects all of the institutions of a society.* Where and how much I worship is affected by my placement in the stratification system. What child-rearing techniques I use are partially determined by my position in the stratification system. My stratification position affects how long and where I go to school.

3. *Social stratification position makes a very good prediction tool.* Once I know where you sit in the stratification system, I can predict what kind of furniture you have in your house, where you take a vacation, what kind of recreation you do, what you like to eat and drink. Each of the social classes or strata share a way of life which forms the basis for a subculture.

4. *Social stratification gives us a very good tool for analyzing the society.* Everyone fits somewhere in the system. After I have analyzed the stratification system, I have a very good overview of the total society.

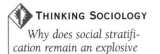
HOW DOES THE CONFLICT THEORY EXPLAIN SOCIAL STRATIFICATION?

Both structural functional theory and conflict theory have an explanation of why stratification systems develop within societies. The conflict theory believes that stratification systems develop because of conquest, competition and conflict. Certain groups within the society control scarce resources within the society. The control of these resources perpetuates itself and these people and their offspring remain in power. Through controlling power and wealth, these people control the life chances of both themselves and other people in the society. The hold that these people in the upper strata have on the economic system keeps other people from gaining control of the means of production. The values of these people, according to the conflict theorist, become the values of the society. The conflict theorist believes that even if stratification systems are universal, they are not inevitable or necessary. They believe that by putting people in strata, we do not maximize the usage of the society's resources. Conflict theorists, such as Marx, advocate doing away with stratification through revolution.

THINKING SOCIOLOGY

Do you agree or disagree with the conflict theorist? Why?

HOW DOES THE STRUCTURAL FUNCTIONAL THEORY EXPLAIN SOCIAL STRATIFICATION?

The structural functional theory looks at what functions or purposes the stratification system serves for the society. They believe that the stratification system emerges in order to ensure that the jobs get done within the society by the most qualified people and that these people continue to do their jobs.

The structural functionalist states that jobs differ along three dimensions. Some jobs are more pleasant than other jobs. I would rather teach in an air conditioned school in the middle of August than gather garbage. Some jobs require more skill and training. For example, it takes more training to be a physician than a garbage collector. Some jobs are viewed as more important to society than other jobs. Garbage collectors are more important for the ongoing urban society than are people who glue on artificial nails or give people permanents.

According to the structural functionalist, we reward people in three ways for competently carrying out their jobs:

1. *Individuals are given wealth.* This allows for the purchase of goods and services that make life easier.
2. *Individuals are allowed to possess power.* Power is the ability to control another person's behavior.
3. *Prestige is awarded to individuals.* Prestige is how valuable society thinks the job is.

Those jobs which are the most unpleasant, require the most ability and talent, and are the most important for society are the jobs which are the more richly rewarded. For example, a physician traditionally has worked very long hours, gets involved in life and death decisions and may be working elbow deep in blood. These are defined as unpleasant working conditions. In order to become a doctor, a person must go through many years of school. And lastly, we consider doctors very essential to the well being of the society. As a consequence, the average doctor earns about $100,000 to $135,000 per year.

On the other hand, those jobs which we consider to have pleasant working conditions, require little ability or talent and are not considered essential to the well being of society, receive little prestige, power or wealth. An example of this would be the shoe-shine person. They work very flexible hours; shined shoes are not considered essential and little talent is needed. As a consequence, shoe-shine people do not receive a great deal of wealth, power or prestige.

Some occupations do not fit this pattern. There are several exceptions. *First, when the job is easily filled, the wealth, power and prestige go down.* Garbage collectors certainly are essential to the well being of society and they do not have pleasant working conditions. Both of these factors should raise the standing of this occupation. But the job is easily filled because it requires little ability or talent. In areas like New York,

I HAVE LEARNED THAT SUCCESS IS TO BE MEASURED NOT SO MUCH BY THE POSITION THAT ONE HAS REACHED IN LIFE AS BY THE OBSTACLES HE HAS OVERCOME WHILE TRYING TO SUCCEED.

BOOKER T. WASHINGTON

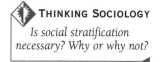

THINKING SOCIOLOGY

Is social stratification necessary? Why or why not?

Quick Glance

Structural functional theory says that certain jobs have to be done. T F

Jobs differ in skill but not importance to society. T F

If a job is easily filled, the prestige decreases. T F

If an occupation is taken over by females, prestige increases. T F

Stratification can inhibit the discovery of talent. T F

Stratification can make some people feel less loyal to their society. T F

The ease of filling a job has no impact on value to society.   T   F

Unionization distorts structural functional analysis of social class placement.   T   F

Fields which women dominate are higher ranked than those dominated by males.   T   F

Stratification placement influences self-image.   T   F

> OTHER LANDS HAVE THEIR VITALITY IN A FEW, A CLASS, BUT WE HAVE IT IN THE BULK OF OUR PEOPLE.
> WALT WHITMAN

An objective measure of stratification is based on income.   T   F

An objective measure of stratification can be years of education.   T   F

Education, income and occupation are always perfectly correlated.   T   F

Wages are based on per year basis.   T   F

The objective measures always form a consistent pattern.   T   F

Those occupations working with their hands have more prestige than those working with their cognitive skills.   T   F

> THOSE WHO HOLD AND THOSE WHO ARE WITHOUT PROPERTY HAVE EVER FORMED DISTINCT INTERESTS IN SOCIETY.
> JAMES MADISON

however, the job is not as easily filled as in Houston, Texas. Therefore, the garbage collectors in New York earn more money than those in Houston do. If an occupation is unionized, this also alters the scope of the structural functional theory. *When women enter a field, the ranking of the field goes down.* Teachers used to be male; it was a very respected field in which to go. As more and more women entered the field, pay and prestige went down in the public schools relative to other occupations. Secretaries used to be males. For example, remember that Auguste Comte was personal secretary to St. Simon. Since this early beginning, secretarial work has been defined as female labor and pay and prestige are relatively low compared to executive assistant or vice president.

Structural functional theory realizes that there are some negative consequences to stratification. Sociologist Melvin Tumin pointed out that stratification systems can be dysfunctional for the society:

1. Stratification inhibits the discovery of talent.
2. Stratification limits the extent to which productive resources can be expanded.
3. Stratification provides those at the top with the power to rationalize and justify their high positions.
4. Stratification weakens the self-images among those at the bottom.
5. Stratification can create hostility and disintegration if it is not fully accepted by all members in society.
6. Stratification may make some people feel that they are not full participants in the society.
7. Stratification may make some people feel less loyal to the society.
8. Stratification may mean less motivation to participate in society.

HOW IS SOCIAL CLASS MEASURED IN THE UNITED STATES?

Social class is commonly measured in three ways: objective, subjective and reputational approach. *Objective measures are based on occupation, income and education.* In some studies, one measure is used, in others, all three. Occupation is what you do to earn the money that you need for food, clothing, housing and luxury items. Studies have been done over a period of years ranking the different occupations. An occupational ranking chart generally will indicate that Americans place more prestige on professions such as physicians, lawyers, dentists and college professors; while bestowing less prestige to those who are janitors, garbage collectors, shoe-shine "boys" or restaurant cooks. In the United States, we make a distinction between people who work with their hands and those who work with their brain. Generally, those occupations dealing with mind work, receive greater prestige. Authority over other people and control over work conditions also contribute to occupational prestige.

Another part of the objective measure is the way we get our money. We addressed this earlier with Max Weber's dimensions of stratification. Wealth involves inherited money and income from trust funds. Salary is contract work; we work for a specified amount of money per year or month. Most college instructors, for example, sign a year contract for a given amount of money. Wages are based on hourly pay. Salary jobs generally have more prestige than those paid by the hour. We are not saying anything about how much money you earn, but about the way you receive the money. Many wage earners receive more than salary people because of the high wages plus overtime. In fact, some people take a cut in pay when they go from wages to salary. Very few salary people bother to calculate what they actually make an hour because they do not punch a clock like hourly employees.

Education is the third objective measure. People have differing amounts of education and, for stratification purposes, how much education you have is the most important. It does not matter how long it took you to get that education, just so you have it. Many students now take more than the traditional four years to graduate with a bachelor degree. Where you received that education also comes into play. Where you get the education does not have as much impact as it did twenty years ago. People, however, are still impressed with diplomas from such schools as Harvard, Stanford or Yale.

These three objective measures do not always correlate. Many college professors, for example, earn less money than many electricians or plumbers. Famous sports figures like baseball players, command tremendous salaries and benefits with a high school diploma. However, there is usually a high correlation between income, occupation and education.

A subjective measure of social class is to ask people to identify their own social class. This is called class consciousness. **Class consciousness** is an awareness of where you are placed in the social class system. Over 80% of people living in the United States say that they are either middle or working class. This is true for several reasons:

1. *There is ego involvement in class ranking.* If I am extremely poor, I do not want to say that I am in the lower class. It is easier to say that I am in the working class. We also find ego involvement at the upper end. It sounds very pretentious to say that I am in the upper-middle class or the lower-upper class. A much safer bet is to say "middle-class."
2. *We do not have the same class consciousness as many European countries.* We do not have the history of royalty and great landed gentry. In our country, people of all classes have to work to achieve or to hang on to their wealth. Even if I am born with a large trust fund, I have to develop some middle-class skills in order to manage and spend my money.
3. *Class consciousness may represent aspiration rather than actual class placement.* I may be a truck driver but I am going to night school and I plan on being a lawyer. I might identify myself with upper-middle class rather than working class. How we identify ourselves has a great impact on our behavior. This truck driver may vote Republican rather than Democratic and enjoy the opera rather than play pool on a Saturday night.

The third measure of social class is called the reputational measure. When we use this measure, we ask one individual to place another individual in a social class strata. What do other people think about you? Do they think you are successful or a total deadbeat? Do they think you are at the middle, bottom or top of the stratification system? In some areas of the country somewhat different criteria are used. In the major urban areas, people focus on house, clothes and car when they judge people. In small rural areas, people might also be interested in your family heritage. In the town where I spent a great deal of my childhood, one of the first questions I frequently get is, "What is your maiden name?" In the community I grew up in, they can assess whether I am an "old timer" (this requires at least two generations) or whether I am "new" (and therefore may be of lesser consequence), and they can also, to a great extent, trace my family lineage. This has overtones of being a caste system. Most reputational studies are limited to small communities or areas because of the difficulties involved in this method.

THINKING SOCIOLOGY

How consistent are you on the objective measures of stratification?

Quick Glance

In a subjective measure, we ask people their class rank.   T   F

Subjective placement includes ego involvement.   T   F

European countries are more class conscious than the U.S.   T   F

Class consciousness represents a realistic assessment of class placement.   T   F

THINKING SOCIOLOGY

What social class do you place O. J. Simpson? Explain.

Quick Glance

The reputational measure is commonly used for large communities.   T   F

The reputational measure is based on other people's judgments.   T   F

The same reputational approach is used in all areas of the U.S.   T   F

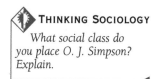

TO ACCOMPLISH GREAT THINGS, WE MUST NOT ONLY ACT BUT ALSO DREAM, NOT ONLY PLAN BUT ALSO BELIEVE.

ANATOLE FRANCE

PERCENT DISTRIBUTION OF INCOME, 2005	
Under $15,000	14.7%
15,000 to 24,999	16.3
25,000 to 34,999	15.2
35,000 to 49,999	17.4
50,000 to 74,999	18.2
75,000 to 99,999	8.9
100,000+	9.3

U.S. Census Bureau, Statistical Abstract of the United States: 2005, Table No. 673.

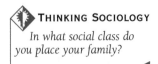

THINKING SOCIOLOGY
In what social class do you place your family?

HOW MANY SOCIAL CLASSES EXIST IN THE UNITED STATES?

How many social classes exist in the United States? The common response is to identify three social classes: upper, middle and lower. Lloyd Warner has identified six social classes in the United States: upper-upper, lower-upper, upper-middle, lower-middle, upper-lower and lower-lower.

The upper-upper class identified by Warner is the blueblood of America. They are born into wealth. They travel in the elite circles and are considered to be the rich. What makes them different from the lower-upper class may not always be the possession of the most wealth. According to Warner, it is rather how long that wealth has been held. The lower-upper class comprise the new rich of the United States. Their families have recently come into money. They have not yet had the opportunity to send their children to the right schools and to travel in the elite circles. The lower-upper might in some cases possess more money than individuals in the upper-upper class. Sam Walton was considered to be the richest man in the United States; he was considered lower-upper class because he was "new rich." Will his children become a part of the upper-upper class of the United States? The Walton family, becoming a part of the upper-upper class, will depend upon their decision in regards to where they will continue to live, what circle of friends they entertain and are entertained by and where they send their children to school. If the Waltons continue to reside in Arkansas, they will remain lower-upper class. If the Waltons do not send their children to private elite schools, they will remain lower-upper class. Will a million dollars today place an individual in the lower-upper class? Assets of a million dollars would mean middle-class because note that $13 billion placed the Sam Walton family in the lower-upper class.

The upper-middle class is comprised of the white-collar professionals in the United States. Physicians, lawyers and bank presidents occupy this social class. White-collar refers to the fact that they wear suits to the jobs and are referred to as professionals. Daniel Rossides has identified that the upper class and the upper-

Quick Glance

Lloyd Warner states that there are three classes in the U.S. T F

The upper-upper class are the blue bloods of America. T F

The upper-upper class has held their money for a long time. T F

THINKING SOCIOLOGY
What social class are politicians?

WRITE IT ON YOUR HEART THAT EVERYDAY IS THE BEST DAY IN THE YEAR.
RALPH WALDO EMERSON

AVERAGE ANNUAL EXPENDITURES				
	1990	2000	2003	2005
Food	$4,296	$5,158	$5,340	$5,931
Apparel	$1,618	$1,856	$1,640	$1,886
Transportation	$5,120	$7,633	$7,781	$8,344
Health Care	$1,480	$2,065	$2,416	$2,664
Entertainment	$1,422	$1,863	$2,060	$2,388

U.S. Bureau of Labor Statistics, Consumer Expenditures, February 2007, Report 998.

middle class together comprise less than 11% of Americans. That puts most Americans at lower-middle and below. The lower-middle class contains the white-collar residue. These are individuals who also wear suits to work, but they are in positions of clerks, department managers and teachers. Also a part of this group are blue-collar skilled workers. This group of the lower-middle would be licensed electricians or plumbers. They wear a uniform to work each morning. They may be able to afford some of the same status symbols of those in the upper-middle class, but because of their occupation, they are viewed as lower-middle class. The determination of the differences between the upper-middle class and the lower-middle class is what one does for a living.

The determining difference between the upper-lower class and the lower-lower class is the possession of a job or not. The upper-lower class comprises the blue-collar residue. These are blue-collar unskilled working for less wages than the blue-collar skilled, and their work is sporadic depending on the job and the weather. The last class, the lower-lower class, are those on welfare, the jobless. This class is sometimes referred to as the underclass or the dependent class. Many of America's single-parented moms fall into this class.

☙ *Quick Glance*

The upper-middle class is made up of professionals.   T F

Upper-upper class and lower-upper class share the same life styles.   T F

The upper-middle and lower-upper classes account for 40% of the population.   T F

◆ **THINKING SOCIOLOGY**

Is there a feminization of poverty? Explain.

WHAT IS SOCIAL MOBILITY?

Social mobility is movement of people between strata of the social class system. I can experience **horizontal mobility**. Horizontal mobility is movement from one status to another when there is little or no difference between the ranks of the two positions. When I am promoted from being a vice president of a large company to president of a small company, I have experienced horizontal mobility. When I lose my job as an electrician and train to be a machinist, I am experiencing horizontal mobility. **Vertical mobility** is movement upward or downward on the stratification system. If I get a promotion from district manager to regional manager, I have been vertically mobile upwards. If I lose my job as a petroleum geologist and take a job at Sears as a sales person, I have experienced vertical mobility downward.

Mobility can also be analyzed in terms of generations. If I look at the amount of mobility in my own lifetime, I am analyzing **intragenerational mobility**. I might analyze my mobility as when I took a job as a secretary, went to school part time, received my teaching certification and became a public school teacher, my further education and my eventual end as college instructor. This is looking at my mobility within my lifetime. If I trace my mobility through two or more generations, I am analyzing **intergenerational mobility**. My daughter has a friend whose father is a doctor. The friend has used every drug in the book, has done very poorly in school and has now dropped out of college. As of this writing, the son has experienced downward mobility from his father.

The vast majority of people in the United States experience social mobility. Most of us will not end up in the same position as our fathers. Most of these moves, however, are very short-range moves. If my father was a blue-collar line worker, I might become a foreman. If my father was an accountant, I shall become a Certified Public Accountant. The line between blue-collar and white-collar jobs is the hardest one to jump. If your father is a blue-collar worker, the chances of you being a blue-collar worker are very strong. The same goes for white-collar workers. Our system is a diamond-shaped system and the line that divides the people who work with their hands from those that work with their brains is a very difficult one to cross.

☙ *Quick Glance*

Vertical mobility is movement down the stratification system.   T F

Intragenerational mobility occurs within a person's lifetime.   T F

The vast majority of people in the U.S. experience social mobility.   T F

TALENTS ARE BEST NURTURED IN SOLITUDE; BUT CHARACTER IS BEST FORMED IN THE STARRY BILLOWS OF THE WORLD.
GOETHE

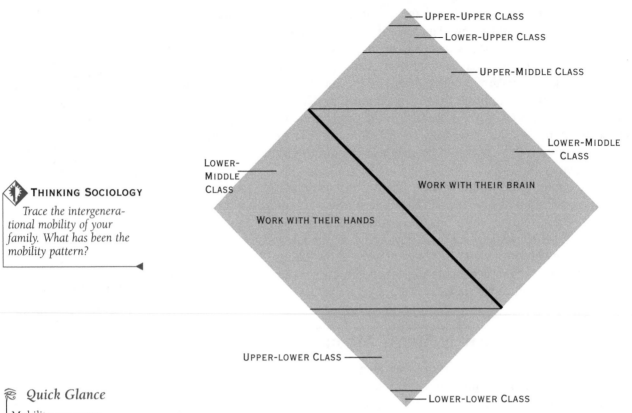

UPPER-UPPER CLASS

LOWER-UPPER CLASS

UPPER-MIDDLE CLASS

LOWER-MIDDLE CLASS

LOWER-MIDDLE CLASS

WORK WITH THEIR BRAIN

WORK WITH THEIR HANDS

UPPER-LOWER CLASS

LOWER-LOWER CLASS

WHAT ARE THE FACTORS THAT AFFECT MOBILITY RATES?

You can be socially mobile with never changing jobs simply because society redefines the importance of a job. A government job, for example, lost status after the Watergate scandal. Doctors have lost some of their prestige because of the greater number of self-tests and books on the market and malpractice suits. Jobs demanding computer literacy did not exist fifty years ago, but now they are extremely important in today's society.

There has been a change in the number of inherited positions in the United States. We have become much more an employee society. When Henry Ford built Ford Motor Company, the family controlled the assets and the wealth. When he died, his children inherited and thus, kept their social class position. Ford has since become a corporation and the family no longer owns all the assets. Many companies which were private have now gone into the public sector through stocks.

There have been changes in legal restrictions concerning trades and professional schools. Guilds and unions were once restricted. Minorities such as women could not join. The unions have now opened up. Many professions used to be male dominated. It was very difficult for women or African Americans to get into medical school or dental school during the 1940s, 1950s and 1960s. There are more women enrolled in law school than there are males and the number of women in medical schools is rapidly increasing.

Immigration impacts social mobility. In the early history of our country, such as during the 1800s, immigration almost guaranteed upper mobility for those already in this country. The immigrants came to this country and filled the bottom rungs and pushed the people already here up the ladder. This is no longer true. Except for political refugees, our country now favors people who already have connections with this country such as spouses or children, and those who have needed skills and edu-

▲ U.S. IMMIGRATION FAVORS SKILLS.
IMAGE COPYRIGHT GELPI, 2008. USED UNDER LICENSE FROM SHUTTERSTOCK, INC.

cation. This country has been accused of being a brain drain because people come over to be educated and then stay. These people are moving into the middle class and upper-middle class positions.

Mechanization has had a tremendous influence on social mobility. Many jobs that used to be lower working class jobs are now skilled labor. Ditches use to be dug with pick and shovel; now a skilled driver runs a back-hoer. Many service jobs have opened up in industries such as healthcare and physical fitness. Computers have opened up jobs for technicians and programmers.

Differential fertility affects social-class mobility. People in farm-related jobs and lower classes tend to have more than two children. People in the upper-upper middle classes have a lower fertility rate than farm workers and lower classes. Therefore, since positions in the upper strata are left vacant, this provides opportunity for those in the lower stratas to experience upward mobility.

Societies that are industrialized, urbanized, ethnically diverse and have an egalitarian social philosophy experience high rates of mobility within the culture. Many countries, such as India, which are just beginning the movement into an industrialized country, will soon experience greater levels of social mobility. We are already seeing this in the People's Republic of China. Farmland has gone back into the private sector, and the farmers have become the wealthy in China. As the economy continues to go back into the private sector, rates of social mobility will increase.

Minority group standing affects social mobility. Gender, race and ethnic factors will be discussed in another Chapter.

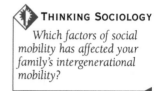

Learning TIP
If you highlight your textbook, highlight what you do not know.

THINKING SOCIOLOGY
Which factors of social mobility has affected your family's intergenerational mobility?

Quick Glance

Occupational improvement can lead to social mobility.	T F
Education is the best way to achieve social mobility.	T F
Cultivation of class behavior is important for social mobility.	T F
A careful marriage can help social mobility.	T F

STATES WITH THE . . .	
Highest Personal Income, 2006	*Lowest Personal Income, 2006*
Connecticut	South Carolina
Maryland	Kentucky
Massachusetts	Utah
New Jersey	Arkansas
New York	West Virginia
	Mississippi

U.S. Census Bureau, 2006, Table No. 659.

HOW CAN THE INDIVIDUAL EXPERIENCE UPWARD SOCIAL MOBILITY?

There are several options for experiencing social mobility:

1. *Occupational improvement creates social mobility.* When you become very good at your job, there is a chance that you will be promoted. A cousin of ours started working at Taco Bell. She is very organized and conscientious and now is a manager.

2. *Economic success breeds social mobility.* Buying stocks and bonds when they are low and selling when they are high, is thought to yield a profit or economic success for the individual or individuals. Investing in land and selling at a profit may bring added riches or economic success.

3. *Educational achievement is the most common and productive method of social mobility.* Education in today's economy is not a sufficient cause of mobility, but it is a necessary one. Getting your college education will pay with greater pay and prestige over your lifetime.

4. *Control of power helps in being socially mobile.* This can be done through running for public office or being a political party boss.

5. *Cultivation of class behavior contributes to social mobility.* You need to know proper English, dress and table manners. People in the middle and upper classes have larger vocabularies, on the whole, than those in the lower classes. When you interview for high-level jobs, they will take you to lunch in order to analyze your table manners and to put you in a more relaxed frame of mind. When you are relaxed, and think you are out of the job-interview situation, you may or may not slip back into normal behavior patterns. Dress is also important in today's job market. There are advisors and books written about how to dress for success.

6. *The last way to be socially mobile is through miscellaneous factors.* These include success in sports, music or movies. It can also include a judicious marriage.

TOP TEN OCCUPATIONS WITH THE HIGHEST MEDIAN EARNINGS

Physicians and Surgeons	Engineering Managers
Dentists	Optometrists
Chief Executives	Petroleum Engineers
Podiatrists	Natural Sciences Managers
Lawyers	Actuaries

U.S. Census Bureau, 2006.

▼ CHAPTER SUMMARY

1. All societies have some form for ranking the members of their society into strata. The social stratification system can be either a caste system or a class system.

2. Max Weber identified class, status and power as components of stratification. Other components include leisure activities, family background, taste preferences and residence. Status inconsistency may exist when different components are applied.

3. The conflict theory does not believe that stratification is necessary or inevitable while the structural functional theory views stratification as being both necessary and inevitable.

4. Social class may be measured using objective, subjective or reputational measures.

5. Lloyd Warner identified six social classes in the United States: upper-upper, lower-upper, upper-middle, lower-middle, upper-lower and lower-lower.

6. Social mobility may be either horizontal or vertical mobility. Mobility can also be analyzed in terms of intergenerational and intragenerational mobility.

7. Factors which contribute to mobility include societal definition of job, changes in inherited positions, changes in legal restrictions, immigration, mechanization and differential fertility.

8. Occupational improvement, economic success, educational achievement, control of power and cultivation of class behavior are options for an individual experiencing upward social mobility.

▼ REFERENCES

Dabbs, J. M. 1992. "Testosterone and occupational achievement." *Social Forces*, 70, 813–824.

Davis, Kingsley, and Wilbert E. Moore. 1945. "Some Principles of Stratification." *American Sociological Review*, 10 (April), 242–249.

Marx, Karl, and Engles, Fredrich. 1965. "The Communist Manifesto." In Arthur Mendel (Ed.), *Essential Works of Marxism*. New York: Bantam Books. (Originally published in 1848)

Peterson, P. 1991. "The urban underclass and the poverty paradox." In C. Jencks & P. Peterson (Eds.), *The urban underclass*. Washington, D.C.: Brookings Institution.

Rossides, Paul. 1976. *The American Class System*. Lanham, Md: University Press of America.

Ryan, William. 1981. *Equality*. New York: Pantheon Books.

Samuelson, Paul A., and William D. Nordhaus. 1985. *Economics* (12th ed.). New York: McGraw Hill.

Schwartz, B. 1973. "Waiting, exchange and power: The distribution of time in social systems." *American Journal of Sociology*, 79, 841–870.

Sennett, R., and Cobb, J. 1972. The hidden injuries of class. NY: Vintage Books. Tumin, Melvin M. 1957. "Some Unapplauded Consequences of Social Mobility." *Social Forces*, 36, 21–37.

Tumin, Melvin M. (Ed.) 1970. *Readings on Social Stratification*. Englewood Cliffs, New Jersey: Prentice-Hall, 380.

Tumin, Melvin M. 1957. "Some Unapplauded Consequences of Social Mobility." *Social Forces*, 36 21–37.

Weber, Max. 1970. "Class, Status, and Party." In H. H. Gerth and C. Wright Mills (trans.), From *Max Weber: Essays in Sociology*. New York: Oxford University Press. (Originally published in 1910)

Zukin, S. 1991. *Landscapes of power: From Detroit to Disney World*. Berkeley: University of Chicago Press.

READING

"WORK-AND-SPEND IS A MIDDLE-CLASS AFFLICTION" BY JULIET B. SCHOR
FROM THE OVERWORKED AMERICAN*

Work-and-spend is not everyone's disease. It is an affliction of affluent, mostly white, Americans. While many middle-class or even upper-middle-class people do not consider themselves affluent or even "well off," in relative terms their economic circumstances are actually quite favorable. A sizable proportion of the U.S. population can reasonably be classified as members of the middle, upper-middle, and upper classes. Furthermore, in the last ten years, the better-off segments of society have done especially well economically. And their ranks have swelled—with the growth in two-earner families and the expansion of professional and managerial jobs. The much-heralded decline of the middle class has occurred not only because blue-collar workers have fallen on hard times, but also because large numbers of people have ascended into the income categories "above" the middle.

How large is the group prone to "work-and-spend?" The answer depends in part on how one chooses to define the middle class and what's above it. A simple procedure is to begin from the top of the income scale and move down to the middle. The top 20 percent, whose average income in 1990 was $105,000, over three times the nation's median, will certainly be included in the ranks of the affluent. The next 20 percent, who receive on average $45,000 a year, should also be counted. Adding 10 percent more, or exactly half the population, would bring us, in income terms, all the way down to about $31,000.

Although $31,000 is in the middle of the distribution, it is no longer sufficient income to put a family into the middle class. Especially for young families, with heavy child-care or housing expenses, it is inadequate. Among the black middle class, responsibility for poorer relatives has put a tremendous strain on earnings, so that even a decent income often can't provide a decent life style. On the other hand, for a single person who owns a house that is paid for, $30,000 or even less may be enough to finance a perfectly comfortable middle-class life. Income is an imperfect measure because individual circumstances—such as family size, age, the price of housing, and where one lives—matter very much. Therefore, to identify the middle class, we may also want to take into account life-style factors—such as the ability to own one's home or finance college education for the children. On these grounds, we get a range—from about two-thirds for home ownership to 37 percent for college education.

Though it is clearly difficult to come up with precise estimates from existing statistics, exact numbers are probably not essential for my purpose. Rough notions will suffice. My own preference is to take 40 percent as a lower bound estimate for "eligibility" in the ranks of the well-off and consider the next 20 percent as questionable. At the other end, we will certainly exclude the poorest quarter of the population—the percent of Americans who in recent years report that they worry "all or most of the time" that they will not be able to meet family expenses and pay the bills.

The worries of the bottom quarter of the population are a reflection of the recent surge in inequality. In earlier decades, the benefits of prosperity were far more evenly distributed, extending even to the least well-off segments of society. In the mid-1970s, a larger proportion of the population could have been identified as "middle class" or above, perhaps as much as two-thirds. At that time, many work-

Quick Glance

Work and spend is an all-American disease.　　T　F

Social class depends on income not life-style factors.　　T　F

Income is the correct measure of social class.　　T　F

---

*From *Overworked American: The Unexpected Decline of Leisure* by Juliet Schor. Copyright © 1992 by Basic Books. Reprinted by permission of Basic Books, a member of Perseus Books, L.L.C.

ing-class families, often by dint of considerable overtime hours, were managing a middle-class life style. They financed their own homes and bought nice cars, sometimes modest vacation places. Many survived on one income. This has now changed as lucrative manufacturing jobs for men have disappeared. The 1980s have also brought a substantial growth in the fraction of the population living in the margins, struggling to get by. According to a 1989 Gallup Poll, 13 percent of those surveyed reported that there were times during the last year when they did not have enough money to buy food. Higher proportions (17 percent and 21 percent) did not have enough income for clothes and medical care. Among people of color, the proportions are far higher, exceeding a third among African-Americans. And because the poll reaches only those with homes (and telephones), these numbers are understated.

Many of these people cannot work long hours even if they want to because their jobs are part-time or intermittent. They may not even have employment, either because they cannot find it or because they cannot afford child care. Among those who do have jobs, hourly pay is very low; long hours or multiple jobs are necessary just to make a subsistence income. They are clearly not working in order to sustain a middle-class lifestyle. Even those with low incomes, however, are not free from pressures to consume. Television, advertising, peer competition, and the ubiquitous example of the economically more fortunate provide continual testaments to the value of high living. The poor are not so much adherents to an alternate (antimaterialist) set of values, as they are unsuccessful at the same game everyone else is playing. Far more than in the past, middle-class culture has insinuated itself throughout the society. If they're not trapped in work-and-spend, it's more because they can't than that they won't.

☞ *Quick Glance*

The benefits from economic growth in the 1990s was evenly distributed throughout the income distribution.   T F

Working class makes it into middle class through salary increases.   T F

Work and spend is aspired to by people who do not have sufficient funds. T F

THINKING SOCIOLOGY

Are you part of what the author calls the work and spend mentality? What determines how you spend your income? How much does the media influence your spending?

Examining Minorities

IMAGE COPYRIGHT YURI ARCURS, 2008. USED UNDER LICENSE FROM SHUTTERSTOCK, INC.

CHAPTER OBJECTIVES

1. What is a minority group?
2. What are the types of minority groups?
3. What is the difference between prejudice and discrimination?
4. What are racism, sexism and ageism?
5. How do minority groups emerge?
6. How does the majority treat the minority?
7. How does the minority react to the majority?
8. How do the theoretical perspectives address minority groups?

acculturation: the adoption by minority group of the majority culture

ageism: a set of beliefs used to justify unequal treatment of older people

amalgamation: the fusion or blending of people from different racial or ethnic groups and biological blending of members of a minority group with the majority group

assimilation: the process by which an individual or group forsakes culture of origin for another culture

attitude: the general evaluation of people, issues or objects

contact hypothesis: states that equal status in a pleasant, noncompetitive atmosphere among groups must exist before prejudice will decrease

cultural pluralism: the condition which permits several cultures within a society to live peacefully side by side

discrimination: the unequal treatment accorded a group in a less powerful position than other members of a society

ethnic group: a social category that shares a common cultural heritage

exclusion: the process of keeping people different from our own out of the country

genocide: the mass killing of a social category believed to be powerless

integration: the condition in society whereby jobs, income, schooling and other life chances are not determined by minority standing

legal protection: special legislation protecting the minority group

majority group: the social category which possesses economic, political and social power

minority group: the social category that is considered subordinate, less powerful to the majority group

population relocation: the transference of a social category to a different environmental location

prejudice: a negative attitude or prejudgment about a social category to which we do not belong

race: the social category of people believed to share common physical characteristics

racism: a set of beliefs used to justify discrimination against less powerful racial categories

scapegoating: blaming societal and personal problems on a social category which is relatively powerless

segregation: a policy enforced by custom or law which excludes a minority from joint participation in the society

self-fulfilling prophecy: reacting to and acting according to a set of characteristics attributed to all members of a social category

sexism: a set of beliefs used to justify discrimination against a gender

social distance: a willingness or unwillingness to have contact with a member of a minority group

stereotype: a set of characteristics or generalizations made about all members of a social category

subjugation: the keeping of a minority group in a powerless position

▼ **KEY PEOPLE**

Gordon Allport, Emory Bogardus, Melvin DeFleur, Franklin Frazier, Richard LaPiere, Robert Merton, Franklin Westie

WHAT IS A MINORITY GROUP?

The term social inequality was used in Chapter 8 to discuss the concept of social stratification. Social inequality is a social condition in which members experience differences in wealth, income, education, prestige and power. This concept will now be applied to minority groups. A **minority group** is a social category that is considered subordinate and members have less control or power over their own lives than members of a dominant or majority group. A **majority group**, on the other hand, is that social category which possesses economic, political and social power.

A minority group has four characteristics:

1. Members share physical, cultural, behavioral or cognitive (belief) traits that identify them as members of a minority.
2. Minorities experience unequal treatment.
3. Membership in a minority is ascribed, not voluntary.
4. Members of a minority develop group solidarity (in-group feelings).

Minority does not always mean that the social category has fewer people than the majority. It is possible to have the majority in population numbers but still be considered a minority group. An example of this is women in the United States; women in the United States outnumber men but women are considered to have less power than men. African Americans are numerically a smaller number than European Americans in the United States and are considered a minority because they do not have as much economic or political power as European Americans. There are, however, many more blacks in South Africa than whites, but since the whites control the political and economic system, the blacks are still considered a minority group.

WHAT ARE THE TYPES OF MINORITY GROUPS?

The classification of minority group can be based on physical characteristics such as race, gender or age.

Racial

In the United States, a person is classified and classifies himself or herself into a race based on some physical characteristic. A **race** is a category of people believed to share common physical characteristics. Each society determines what physical difference is used. In the United States, skin color is frequently used but other criteria are also used such as eye shape. Think back to the forms that you have filled out which asked for race or some such other classification. Invariably, the choices are African American, White, Hispanic, Asian and "other, " or some variation of this selection. This is a cultural definition of race. "African American" contains many subgroups such as Haitians and many "blacks" do not have pure "black" blood. "Hispanic" is not a racial grouping at all. Hispanic Americans are part of the Caucasian or white classification. "Asian" includes very diverse groups such as Japanese, Vietnamese and Chinese. There are also many different groups of Chinese within China itself. And who has heard of the race called "other"? Countries such as Brazil recognize many more races than does the United States and in this country a person can change racial classifications over their lifetime depending on shifts in socioeconomic conditions.

We all belong to some racial category, but not all racial categories are considered to be minorities. People belonging to races that have less power are considered to be minorities. The inferior power of some races leads to racism.

THINKING SOCIOLOGY

Are you a member of a majority group or a minority group? Why?

Quick Glance

A minority group is a social category.	T F
A majority group has the greatest number of people.	T F
A minority group shares unequal treatment.	T F
Membership in a minority is ascribed.	T F
Members of a minority develop feelings of in-groupness.	T F

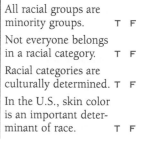

NOBODY HAS EVER GIVEN SATISFACTORY PROOF OF AN INHERENT INEQUALITY OF RACES.

FRANZ BOAS

Quick Glance

All racial groups are minority groups.	T F
Not everyone belongs in a racial category.	T F
Racial categories are culturally determined.	T F
In the U.S., skin color is an important determinant of race.	T F

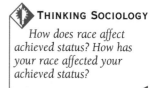

THINKING SOCIOLOGY

How does race affect achieved status? How has your race affected your achieved status?

Gender

A second physical difference leading to minority standing is gender. In our society, and many societies around the world, being female means having less power. Women earn less money than men and are not represented proportionately in higher political offices such as the Senate and Cabinet. Less power for women leads to sexism. Women who are also from a minority racial group face particular problems.

Age

A third physical difference which contributes to minority standing is age. Children are much less powerful than adults but children as a minority have not become an issue except in the cases of children in poverty and abused children. The age group that has become a minority group in the United States is the elderly. There have been laws passed which state that employers cannot deny a person a job because of age; social security benefits are an issue in the United States. A belief that keeps the elderly in a less powerful position is called **ageism**.

Physical Differences

The physically challanged endure the prejudice and discrimination based on physical differences. "Little people" (dwarfs or midgets) remain "children" because of their size. People bound to wheelchairs face problems using restrooms, parking spaces and entrances and exits of buildings.

Ethnic

Minority group standing can be based on cultural differences. An **ethnic group** is a social category that shares a common cultural heritage. These differences can be diverse factors such as language, attitudes towards marriage and food habits. Examples of ethnic minorities include Hispanic Americans (Chicanos, Puerto Ricans and Cubans), Irish Americans, Italian Americans and Polish Americans.

An ethnic group shares some important characteristics:

1. unique cultural traits
2. sense of community and common ancestry
3. ethnocentrism
4. ascribed membership
5. territoriality

Behavioral and Cognitive

The last type of minority to be discussed includes those minorities based on behavioral and cognitive characteristics. A religious minority is an example of a group which receives less power because of beliefs. In the United States, Protestants outnumber members of other religions. People who are Roman Catholic and Greek Orthodox have been classified as minority groups. Other religious minorities include American Jews, Church of the Latter-Day Saints, the Hutterites and the Amish. American Jews are sometimes classified as an ethnic rather than religious grouping. Homosexuals are minorities based on behavioral characteristics. No matter what type of minority in which a person has membership, he or she faces prejudice and discrimination.

Quick Glance

A minority group is based on race but not gender.   T   F

The elderly, but not children, are considered a minority group.   T   F

Hispanics are a minority group.   T   F

Ethnic group membership fosters ethnocentrism.   T   F

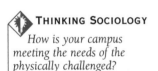

THINKING SOCIOLOGY

How is your campus meeting the needs of the physically challenged?

Quick Glance

An ethnic group shares a cultural heritage.   T   F

An ethnic group has a sense of being an in-group.   T   F

An ethnic group is based on territoriality.   T   F

A minority group can be a religious group.   T   F

If a person is prejudiced, they discriminate.   T   F

WHAT IS THE DIFFERENCE BETWEEN PREJUDICE AND DISCRIMINATION?

Gordon Allport, author of *The Nature of Prejudice*, defined prejudice as "thinking ill of others without sufficient warrant." **Prejudice** is an attitude; a prejudgment about a social category to which we do not belong. An attitude is the general evaluation of people, issues or objects. As individuals, we have attitudes about a number of phenomena. We may hate potato chips. We may love country and western music.

Discrimination is a behavior based on an attitude. **Discrimination** is the unequal treatment given to the objects of our prejudice, the minority group. Discrimination can be of two types: subtle or covert. Subtle discrimination is the unequal treatment of minority members that is visible while covert discrimination is more likely to be hidden and difficult to document. An example of subtle discrimination would be denying African Americans the right to sit in the front of the bus in 1950 or denying a married woman access to an executive position because "her husband would be transferred or she probably will get pregnant." Covert discrimination is more difficult to document. Common types of covert discrimination include tokenism and sabotage. If a male boss "neglected" to give a female employee critical documents, this could be a form of covert discrimination. A female cousin of mine worked for the local law enforcement agency for five years but continued to have problems with the males teasing her about knowing how to use a gun or being able to fight and win. One Saturday morning, she attempted and failed to make an arrest and the following Monday she found that she had been reassigned to a desk job without being consulted about the details of the situation. Her position went to a close buddy of the head of the division.

CORRECTION DOES MUCH, BUT ENCOURAGEMENT DOES MORE.
GOETHE

THINKING SOCIOLOGY
How prejudiced are you? Give an example of discrimination.

IS IT POSSIBLE TO HAVE PREJUDICE AND NOT DISCRIMINATE?

Sociologist, Richard LaPiere tested this question in the 1930s. LaPiere traveled the United States with a Chinese couple. During these trips, LaPiere and the Chinese couple requested service in hundreds of establishments and were refused service only once. Six months after LaPiere visited an establishment with his traveling companions, he would write a letter asking if Chinese guests were welcome in their establishment. Over 90% of the establishments replied that Chinese guests would not be welcome in their hotel and/or restaurant. These establishments had not discriminated or withheld service, but their attitudes suggested prejudice. We can possess the attitude and not commit the overt behavior.

LaPiere, Richard T. 1934. "Attitudes vs. Actions." *Social Forces*, 13 (Oct.), 230–237.

Quick Glance

Prejudice is an attitude.   T F

Discrimination is a behavior.   T F

Covert discrimination is hard to document.   T F

Scapegoating involves blaming personal problems on a minority group.   T F

Prejudice and discrimination involve scapegoating. Scapegoating has a Biblical referent. In Biblical times, people practiced sacrificing a goat to appease for human sins, or the people would put the sins of the tribe onto the goat and chase it out into the desert. We do the same thing with a minority group; **scapegoating** involves blaming social and personal problems on the minority group. I cannot get a job because of all the women competing for jobs, or if those Hispanic Americans would go back across the border, European American males could have a job! In modern society, scapegoating involves blaming rape victims because "they asked for it by wearing lowcut dresses or being out at night," or that the poor would not be poor if they just

BOGARDUS SOCIAL DISTANCE

The scale below will help you gain insight into how prejudice and discrimination are measured using the Bogardus Social Distance Scale. The scale will also give you an idea about how prejudiced you are. Read the headings at the top of the columns on the scale below and then check which column best expresses how you feel about each minority group.

	1 Might marry or have as a close relative	2 Might have as a close friend	3 Would accept as a next door neighbor	4 Would accept in my school church or synagogue	5 Would accept in my community	6 Would accept in my country	7 Would not accept in my country
Hispanic American		✔	✔				
Vietnamese American	✔						
African American					✔		
Jewish American			✔	✔			
Native American			✔	✔			
Japanese American		✔					
Chinese American		✔					
Russian American				✔	✔		
European American		✔	✔				

After you have completed the questionnaire, you will need to make a calculation. In order to do your calculation, refer to the numbers at the top of each column of the Bogardus Social Distance Scale. You will note that the above column category heading (i.e., the top of the second column, "Might have as a close friend," the number "2" appears). These numbers quantify the amount of prejudice indicated in each column. You will also note that the scale is constructed such that if you check "might marry," you would certainly accept this minority as a close friend. The scale, as the numbers go from higher to lower (check the numbers at the top of each column), indicates lesser amount of prejudice; the higher the number, the more prejudiced. In order to calculate how prejudiced you are, add the numbers at the top of columns that you have checked. If you checked more than one column for any given minority group, use the number in the column that indicates the least degree of prejudice. Add these nine numbers and divide by nine. This gives you an average prejudice score.

You will also interpret how prejudiced you are by referring to the numbers at the top of column. For example, if your Social Distance Score is 2.1, you would accept people of minority groups as close friends but would not want to marry or have them as a close friend or relative. If your average score was 4.9, you would accept people of minority groups in your community but would not accept in your school, in religious group, as a neighbor, as a friend or relative. How prejudice are you?

would get their act together and get jobs. Another example of scapegoating is Germany blaming their economic collapse in the 1920s on the Jews.

Prejudice is not an "all or nothing" situation. A very important concept is that of social distance. Social distance is a term generated by a sociologist by the name of Emory Bogardus. **Social distance** is the willingness or unwillingness to have contact with a member of a minority group. One way to measure prejudice is by a set of questions or scale on which a respondent is asked to rate the degree of social closeness or distance he or she is willing to have with a minority group. If a person is very prejudiced, he or she will feel that the minority group should be sent back to their source of origin and locked up away from "decent folk." If a person has a moderate level of prejudice, he or she will accept the person in the community or social clubs. The least degree of prejudice indicates that the person will accept someone from a minority as a close relative or marriage partner. Many times a person is not prejudiced except when it comes to accepting a minority as a close relative.

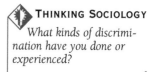
THINKING SOCIOLOGY
What kinds of discrimination have you done or experienced?

IS IT POSSIBLE TO DISCRIMINATE AND NOT HAVE PREJUDICE?

DeFleur and Westie administered a test at Princeton University measuring prejudice. Those students who were less prejudiced were asked to have their picture made with a minority student. The picture would be published in their hometown newspaper along with a writeup. About one-third of the Princeton students would not agree to having their picture made, although they were not perceived as being prejudiced. What happened? When asked, the Princeton students replied that they didn't know how receptive their friends and family would be to the article and picture. We may discriminate if the social pressure encourages us to discriminate.

DeFleur, Melvin, and Franklin R. Westie. 1958. "Verbal Attitudes and Overt Acts." *American Sociological Review*, 23 (Dec.), 667–673.

Quick Glance

Social distance is a measure of prejudice.   T   F

Prejudice is an all or none attitude.   T   F

Prejudice can be based on stereotype.   T   F

Stereotypes are lists of personality characteristics of a minority group.   T   F

An important concept helping to explain the maintenance of prejudice and discrimination is stereotyping. In fact, we use stereotypes to justify prejudice and discrimination. A **stereotype** is a set of characteristics which is attributed to all members of a social group. Whites, for example, are intelligent and self-righteous; Jews are shrewd in business; Chinese are inscrutable; women are naturally dependent; elderly people are senile. Even though these generalizations may be based on inaccurate generalizations, stereotypes aid us in sorting people into fixed categories. They suggest, for example, that if our feeling is that old people suffer from senility, then our conclusion is that if a person is considered old because of chronological birthdays, that person is suffering from senility. If we think that all males who have long hair are drug addicts, then any male who has long hair is viewed by us as being a drug addict.

Stereotypes feed prejudice and impair the ability to perceive others as unique individuals who may, or more often may not, resemble the stereotype. This principle of stereotypes can lead to a self-fulfilling prophecy. The **self-fulfilling prophecy** proposes that members of the minority group are aware of the stereotypes and may respond to the generalizations. This self-fulfilling prophecy is much like the looking-glass self discussed in Chapter 4. The looking-glass theory proposes that the perceptions of who we are is created through feelings about us held by others.

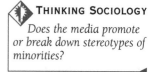
THINKING SOCIOLOGY
Does the media promote or break down stereotypes of minorities?

Quick Glance

A stereotype is categorical thinking.   T   F

Stereotypes can lead to self-fulfilling prophecy.   T   F

A minority may act out the self-fulfilling prophecy.   T   F

Self-fulfilling prophecy can make a stereotype true.   T   F

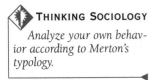

Quick Glance

We learn our prejudices
from significant
others.   T F

Parents can uncon-
sciously teach children
prejudice.   T F

Teachers never teach
children prejudice.   T F

The mass media can
reinforce stereotypes.   T F

When members of a social category experience prejudice and discrimination, they often are at a social disadvantage; the social category, or minority group, does not receive equal education, employment opportunities or political voice. As a result of this disadvantage, it does not fare as well in the social system. Members of the minority group then interpret the lack of success not as the result of earlier prejudice and discrimination but as evidence that the minority group is innately inferior. Then, since the minority group does not achieve success, the cycle repeats itself and prejudice and discrimination continue.

Prejudice and discrimination are learned during the socialization process. Prejudice and discrimination are learned primarily from our significant others. One of the most important significant others is parents. Parents many times do not set out to teach their children prejudice and discrimination; it just slips in. For example, Mom, Dad and Junior are driving down a busy road. A woman makes a left-hand turn in front of Dad. Dad might very easily make some gender comment about "women drivers." There is a good chance that he has a few choice words about a male doing the same behavior, but a gender name will not be among them.

Teachers can instill feelings of prejudice by their actions and words. A woman in my spring semester class told the story of her little girl coming home every day and talking about "Natalie." The mother wanted to meet Natalie and asked the director to introduce her. The director took the mother aside and asked, "Did you know that Natalie is black?" The little girl had not informed her mother of that physical characteristic. I cannot help but believe that the teacher's attitude extended to the classroom in covert discrimination.

Even the very books that we use in schools contribute to prejudice by showing females as nurses and males as doctors; showing African Americans as field hands and European Americans as the bosses. In many textbooks, there is little or no mention of the contributions of minority groups.

The media helps teach children prejudice. Girls learn that they need the Tidy Bowl Man to help clean their toilets and Mr. Brawny to get a really strong paper towel. Other agencies of socialization which contribute to prejudice and discrimination are sit-coms. "All in the Family" and "The Jeffersons," television shows still being shown as reruns, depict very prejudiced people. "The Bill Cosby Show," which stopped production in 1992, was a front runner in breaking the stereotypes of black families.

Prejudice and discrimination are related concepts, but prejudice does not necessarily generate discrimination. Robert Merton devised a typology looking at the relationship between these two concepts:

1. unprejudiced nondiscriminator: all-weather liberal
2. unprejudiced discriminator: reluctant liberal
3. prejudiced nondiscriminator: timid bigot
4. prejudiced discriminator: all-weather bigot

Quick Glance

Robert Merton said that
all prejudiced people
discriminate.   T F

A prejudiced nondiscrim-
inator is a timid bigot.   T F

A prejudiced discrimin-
ator is an all-weather
liberal.   T F

Racism is based on a
set of beliefs.   T F

Sexism is based on a
set of true facts.   T F

A racist belief is that
one race is physically
superior to another.   T F

Older adults are not
as intelligent as younger
adults.   T F

WHAT ARE RACISM, SEXISM AND AGEISM?

Racism, ageism or sexism is a set of beliefs about a social category used to justify discrimination; racism, ageism or sexism is discrimination built into norms and behavior and reinforced by agents of social control. **Racism** is the prejudice and discrimination experienced by an individual based on race. **Sexism** is the prejudice and discrimination experienced by an individual based on gender. **Ageism** is the prejudice and discrimination experienced by an individual based on age. In Chapter 5, the terms ascribed status and achieved status were introduced. The observation was made that ascribed status can affect achieved status. Ascribed status such as race, gender and age may dictate what an individual is able to achieve. Ascribed status can affect life chances. Life chances are those opportunities of individuals to the good life such as an education, housing, job opportunities and health care. There are several important beliefs associated with these "isms."

First, is the belief that some categories are physically superior to others. For example, African Americans have higher rates than European Americans of tuberculosis, infant mortality and sickle cell anemia. Thus, according to racism, African Americans are physically inferior to European Americans. What this belief does not take into account is that European Americans have higher rates of other diseases, including some heart disorders and cancer. Racial interpretations of differences in rates of disease and longevity are suspect because they overlook differences in occupations, education, income, housing, sanitation, nutrition, medical care and group immunities. There is a belief that older people are less physically able than younger people; they will, for example, take more days off sick from work. This is not true; older people have no more days absent from work than do younger employees on the job. The elderly may have more chronic illnesses but these do not affect their daily job performance. In fact, the older adult actually has fewer acute illnesses such as colds than does the younger worker. It is believed, according to sexism, that women are the weaker of the species. Women actually have a higher threshold of pain than men and have greater sustained strength than males.

The second belief is that some social categories are mentally superior to others. After World War I, Native Americans, Hispanic Americans, African Americans and ethnic immigrants from southern and eastern Europe consistently scored lower than people of European ancestry on IQ tests. Many of the group averages later showed miraculous improvement. Since the 1940s, scientific agreement has been strong showing that the tests measure not just learning potential, but also what has been learned, i.e. language, life experiences, schooling. The average scores for subordinate social categories have improved with mastery of standard English and increased education. Females score lower on the math sections of standardized achievement tests, but the number of females enrolled in upper-level math courses decreases with each level. Older people score lower on intelligence tests. For many years, it was thought that as we age we lose intelligence. Research now indicates that if we give an older person a time test, they do score lower. Older people are not used to working under the constraints of time. But if we give an older person a power test, that is, one with no time factor, intelligence does not decrease and problem solving may actually improve with age.

Third, race, gender or age causes behavior. Race, gender and age are traits that are physical, not cultural. Behavior traits are learned, transmitted by the socialization process. A Vietnamese baby adopted by a family in Santa Monica, California, for example, will learn the American culture; the child will speak English. Elderly people do not "naturally" like shuffle board or buttermilk! Women are not naturally prone to liking to clean toilets or be good cooks, not great cooks. The "great cooks" of the world are males according to sexist beliefs. Just watch the "Iron Chef" on television.

Fourth is the belief that category determines temperament. African Americans, according to this belief, are by nature carefree and rhythmic. The Dutch are stubborn. The Irish are gregarious. Old people are short tempered and set in their ways. Females are naturally emotional and prone to crying and suffering from PMS. This type of thinking is based on stereotypes.

Fifth is the belief that racial mixing lowers biological quality. Racial mixing seems dangerous to those who believe that superior and inferior physical, mental and behavioral traits are linked with racial heredity. There is no proof that racial mixing

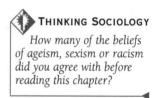

THINKING SOCIOLOGY

How does racism still exist in the U.S.?

Quick Glance

We lose intelligence as we age.   T F

Southern Europeans are less intelligent than Northern Europeans   T F

Sexist belief states that females are less intelligent than males.   T F

THINKING SOCIOLOGY

How many of the beliefs of ageism, sexism or racism did you agree with before reading this chapter?

Quick Glance

Race causes behavior.   T F

Old people always like buttermilk because it is innate.   T F

The mixing of races lowers biological quality.   T F

Ethnic group membership determines temperament.   T F

U.S. Census Bureau, *Statistical Abstract of the United States*, 2005, Table No. 683.

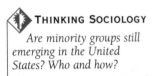

THINKING SOCIOLOGY

Are minority groups still emerging in the United States? Who and how?

Quick Glance

A minority group can emerge through political annexation.   T   F

A minority can emerge through involuntary migration but not voluntary migration.   T   F

Judaic Christian beliefs can create a minority group.   T   F

leads to lower or higher biological quality, although many people through the years have been concerned about "racial purity." Hitler, for example, was fanatical about Aryanism/anti-Semitism. The genetic mixing of human populations has been going on for a very long time. If this were not true, we would have different species unable to interbreed rather than races and ethnic groups with different physical and cultural characteristics.

HOW DO MINORITY GROUPS EMERGE?

There are five basic processes through which minority groups emerge. *First is political annexation.* When one culture "takes over" another culture, the less dominant group may become a minority group. When Russia brought in part of what was once Poland, the Poles formed a minority group. When Turkey annexed a part of what was once Greece, the Greeks became a minority group in Turkey. In Texas and California, several times, the border has dropped south and Native Americans and Hispanic groups have been incorporated into the United States as minority groups. *The second way that minorities emerge within a culture is through the colonial pattern.* This is what happened in South Africa. Europeans went to South Africa and dominated the economy, and through domination of the economy, took control of the government. This has happened in countries such as Kenya and Nigeria. This is what happened to Native Americans. There were many Native American cultures in the New World but Europeans came over and took control of the land, conquered with their advanced technology such as guns and brought in trade goods. The Europeans dominated the economy and thus placed the Native American into minority status. *The third way a minority emerges is through migration.* The Irish migrated to the United States during the 1800s. Stores in New York would advertise that Irish were not welcome. African Americans in the United States were brought over here forcibly to serve as slaves thus relegating them to minority status. *A fourth way that minorities emerge is through economic competition.* The African Americans, after the Civil War, were in competition with European Americans for jobs; European Americans resented this competition. Hispanics come across the California and Texas borders taking jobs at cheaper wages than natives, thus contributing to feelings of resentment and minority status. *The fifth way minorities come about is based on Judaic Christian beliefs, for example, homosexuals and women.* The Judaic Christian Bible states that women are the help mate of men and that God made woman from Adam's rib. This belief is sometimes used to justify women being a minority group. The Christian Bible also states that males should not spill their seed; homosexual behavior is interpreted as the spilling of seed.

HOW DOES THE MAJORITY TREAT THE MINORITY?

The first way the majority treats the minority is through **exclusion**; with this thinking we try to keep the society's population homogeneous by keeping members of a racial or ethnic group different from our own from entering the country in the first place. Orientals were barred from entering the United States from 1924 until the late 1960s.

The second way the majority group behaves towards the minority group is through extermination, physical destruction, annihilation or **genocide**. This involves killing off the minority group. The European population wiped out two-thirds of the Native Americans either directly through warfare or indirectly through diseases. Some of the diseases were deliberately introduced to the Native American because the Native American had low resistance to such diseases as measles and small pox. Whole tribes were eliminated in just weeks. In the nineteenth century, the British decimated the Tasmanians, and Dutch South Africans exterminated the Hottentots. In the effort to establish a "master race," the Nazis murdered six million Jews and thousands of Romany people, known as Gypsies. The AIDS epidemic which started in the 1990s has been said to be a form of genocide against African Americans by extremists groups.

The third manner in which the majority group treats the minority group is through **population relocation**, *transfer or expulsion; the majority group just sends the minority away*. The Nazis put the Jews in concentration camps; the Americans put American Japanese in camps during World War II: North Americans put Native Americans on reservations, frequently, in very different landscapes than their original area. In the 1830s, government officials ordered the Cherokee tribe to travel the thousand mile Trail of Tears from the deep south to Oklahoma. Disease, starvation and the winter cold killed thousands along the way. In 1972, Idi Amin forced about 27,000 people of Indian ancestry to leave Uganda, even though many had never lived in India and considered Uganda to be their homeland.

The fourth way that the majority group treats the minority group is **subjugation**. This keeps the minority group in a position of inequality and can lead to segregation. The dominant group would like to maintain the minority in order to provide a good, cheap labor supply. This is demonstrated in the exploitation of African American, Hispanic and female labor.

Subjugation leads to segregation; **segregation** is a policy which is enforced by custom or law that excludes a social category from joint participation in the society. The effect of segregation is to minimize association between majority and minority groups and to restrict the association that does occur to clearly subordinate/superordinate roles. In the 1950s, the United States continued to segregate African Americans. African Americans had separate schools, rode in the back of buses, and had separate restrooms.

Segregation can be *de jure* or *de facto*. The early segregation in the United States was de jure. This means that the segregation was written into the system of laws. During the period of slavery in the United States, it was unlawful to educate African Americans, for African Americans to attend white schools or for a white to marry an African American. Much of the segregation that occurs now is de facto. The primary de facto segregation is based on residential conditions. Neighborhoods frequently are predominantly one racial or ethnic category. An example of de jure segregation is the apartheid policy in the Republic of South Africa, where a small minority of whites dominates the country and the greatest number of people (persons of mixed race and Asians) have limited freedom of movement and live and work on rural reservations or in selected urban areas. Separate school systems, transportation and public facilities are established by law for the different races.

THINKING SOCIOLOGY

In what U.S. institutions do we see the most segregation? Why?

Quick Glance

Exclusion is never used by the majority group against the minority group.   T F

The importation of disease can cause genocide.   T F

Population relocation never happened in the U.S.   T F

Population relocation is the same as exclusion.   T F

PERCENT BELOW POVERTY LEVEL IN 2005	
ALL RACES	9.9%
WHITE	8.0
BLACK	22.2
ASIAN/PACIFIC ISLANDER	9.0
HISPANIC	19.7

U.S. CENSUS DATA, 2005, TABLE NO. 693.

YOU CAN'T HOLD A MAN DOWN WITHOUT STAYING DOWN WITH HIM.

BOOKER T. WASHINGTON

Quick Glance

Subjugation leads to segregation.   T F

Segregation is part of the legal justice system.   T F

Segregation involves unequal treatment.   T F

Segregation is de facto, based on laws.   T F

De jure segregation is more common in the U.S. than de factor segregation. T F

Fifth, the majority group can promote cultural pluralism. **Cultural pluralism** permits several cultures to live peacefully side by side. Each culture maintains its own language and customs, but each group accommodates itself to the other groups and tolerates cultural diversity. Switzerland is a pluralistic society in which people who speak German, French, Italian and the ancient language of Romanish coexist peacefully. Another pluralistic society is China where 55 ethnic minorities are encouraged to retain their distinct identity while adhering to a vision of harmony in which the Han Chinese, the dominant group, are elder brothers. This official policy of pluralism represents a change from a policy of assimilation only a few years ago. Tanzania provides an example where Africans, Europeans and people from the Middle East share public institutions but retain cultural characteristics in their private lives. In U.S. society, many Americans have retained a strong sense of ethnic identity, and successful politicians often find it necessary to acknowledge and support ethnic interests. In order for cultural pluralism to work, differences must be meaningful, ethnic identities must be supported, group equality must be supported, employment and government practices must maintain equality, and education must be provided for bilingualism. Cultural pluralism preserves ethnicity, but it is also criticized because it can weaken the cohesion of society.

👁 *Quick Glance*

China has a homogenous population.　　　　T　F

Cultural pluralism promotes cultural diversity.　　　　T　F

Minority standing can be supported by the law.　　　　T　F

The sixth reaction of the majority group to the minority group is **legal protection** *of the minority.* In some instances, government officials recognize that to ensure the rights of minorities, they must pass special legislation. The majority group adopts policies that legally protect minority groups from unequal treatment. This can include quotas such as hiring a certain percentage of African Americans, women or Hispanic Americans. There have also been laws protecting women. For example, women in the 1950s and 1960s could not work at jobs where they were required to do heavy lifting or work late hours except in jobs such as nursing. These job restrictions prevented women from competing for heavy construction and high-paying jobs for a good number of years.

THINKING SOCIOLOGY

What is the "Ideal of Americanization?" How has this been a description of the U.S.?

▶

The seventh way that the majority group treats the minority groups is assimilation. **Assimilation** is the process by which an individual or group forsakes their culture of origin for another culture. This policy requires the minority group to abandon its language, traditions and religion for those of the dominant culture. This cultural integration can be encouraged through a system of public education that provides all groups with a common cultural background and common language. In industrial societies, the mass media also plays an important part in acculturating a diversity of racial and ethnic groups. The buzz phrase word here is "The Ideal of Americanization."

There are several dimensions of assimilation:

1. cultural assimilation
   This means that the minority group adopts the language, religion and other cultural norms and traits of the dominant culture. This process is sometimes called **acculturation**. This process can happen either through the minority group accepting the dominant groups' culture or as fusion of the cultural traits and norms of the two groups.

👁 *Quick Glance*

There are two levels of structural assimilation.　　　　T　F

Another word for amalgamation is biological assimilation.　　　　T　F

Assimilation involves redefinition of self.　　　　T　F

2. structural assimilation
   This involves the social interaction between minority and majority group. Members of the minority group are found throughout the society and enter into contact with members of the majority groups. Characteristics such as social class become more important than racial or ethnic identification. There are two levels of structural assimilation: primary or informal and secondary or formal. Primary assimilation occurs within small groups such as family

and peers. This includes minorities entering into clubs, neighborhoods and marriage. Secondary assimilation is equality of power and privileges in the major institutions of society. The minority would have access to equal paying jobs and political position. Secondary assimilation is also called **integration**. Integration means that jobs, income, schooling and other life chances are not determined by minority standing. Integration means that people interact without regarding minority standing. Minority status ceases to exist.

3. biological assimilation
   Another word for this is amalgamation. **Amalgamation** is a biological fusion or blending of people of different minorities and blending of minority with the majority. For example, the marriage of an African American with a Hispanic American would involve amalgamation.

4. psychological assimilation
   Members of minority undergo a redefinition of self. The people now think of themselves as members of the larger society rather than by their minority position. Other people in the society also need to redefine the minority as being a member of society rather than being a member of the minority group.

INTERRACIAL MARRIAGE

1. There is an increase in the number of interracial marriages.
2. There is an increasing proportion of interracial marriages.
3. Blacks have the lowest rates of interracial marriage. American Indians have the highest rate of interracial marriage.
4. Black men are more apt to marry outside their race than black women.
5. Asian women are more apt to marry outside their race than Asian men.

Population Reference Bureau, June 2005.

Several important factors influence the amount and rate of assimilation:

1. *How identifiable the minority group is has a large impact on the rate and amount of assimilation.* If there is a distinct physical difference between the two groups, the rate of assimilation is slowed down. If the difference is based on cultural differences, rates of assimilation can be speeded up.
2. *The concentration of the minority group affects assimilation.* If the category comes in large numbers, rate of assimilation is slowed. The category can maintain its own culture in large concentrations plus the majority group feels more threatened in the face of large concentrations.
3. *The willingness of the two groups to merge into one affects assimilation.* If it is beneficial for the majority group to keep the minority group in a powerless position, assimilation is going to be slowed down. Also, some minority groups wish to maintain their racial and ethnic identity; if this is true, assimilation rates will also be decreased.
4. *Educational and economic opportunities influence the rates of assimilation.* A widespread system of education facilitates assimilation by supplying knowledge of the culture and roads for social mobility. If, however, the economy is suffering from a scarcity of jobs or economic recession, the rates of assimilation are slowed down.

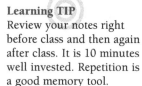

THINKING SOCIOLOGY

After reading about the different ways the majority group treats the minority group, which of the ways increase feelings of prejudice? Why?

☜ Quick Glance

In assimilation, the minority group gives up ethnic identification.   T   F

Structural assimilation is integration.   T   F

Primary assimilation occurs in secondary groups.   T   F

Learning TIP
Review your notes right before class and then again after class. It is 10 minutes well invested. Repetition is a good memory tool.

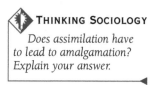

THINKING SOCIOLOGY

Does assimilation have to lead to amalgamation? Explain your answer.

🕮 *Quick Glance*

Rates of assimilation
are affected by num-
bers immigrating into
country.   T F

Rates of assimilation are
not affected by the
economic conditions. T F

Nearness of minority
to country of origin
affects assimilation.   T F

Education positively
impacts assimilation. T F

5. *The degree of contact with or isolation from the dominant group influences rates of assimilation.* If the groups remain isolated from one another, assimilation rates are very slow.

6. *The time of arrival affects assimilation rates.* The more recent the arrival, the less the assimilation.

7. *The nearer the minority is to the country of origin, the lower the assimilation rates.* The nearness can be in physical and in political terms. For example, the Vietnamese who migrated to the United States in the 1960s, were not only physically far removed from their country of origin but they were also politically alienated from the country. Hispanics, on the other hand, who come across the border into Texas and California are very close to their point of origin and travel back and forth between the two countries. It is quite easy for the Hispanic to maintain his or her culture.

HOW DOES THE MINORITY REACT TO THE MAJORITY?

◆ THINKING SOCIOLOGY

*Why do minorities some-
times react to the majority
with acceptance?*

Acceptance is one reaction of the minority member. I will passively accept my status as a powerless member of society. In my case of being a female, I shall accept less pay for the same job or denial of a transfer because of my minority status. This is tied into a concept we talked about earlier in this chapter, self-fulfilling prophecy. When I accept my minority position, I shall act in ways to reinforce the stereotype of the minority group. This sometimes leads to self-hatred; we define ourselves the way the majority group defines us. One of the early studies on racial feelings dealt with children's choice of dolls. It was found in this study that white children preferred white dolls but the African American children also preferred the white dolls. The African American children felt that the white dolls were more attractive than the African American dolls. (These children had developed a negative self-image.) The African American community started a "black is beautiful" movement in the 1960s.

Marginal adaptation is a second response of a minority member. Marginal adaptation means development of skills in what is called "open areas." Open areas include sports, entertainment and crafts. There is less discrimination in these areas, thus more opportunity for upward mobility.

🕮 *Quick Glance*

Avoidance leads to
segregation.   T F

Nativism is not a
reaction of the minority
group.   T F

Auguste Comte wrote
Black Bourgeoisie. T F

A minority member may react using submissive manipulation. If I use this technique, I shall degrade myself according to the stereotype. An example of this is the older African American male who still steps aside for the white man or the African American male who does not make eye contact with a white female. Women who do not play a game to win because of "hurting the male ego" are also using submissive manipulation.

Avoidance is a fourth response. Avoidance leads to segregation. Avoidance can include the Amish's maintenance of their own communities with minimal contact with others, to women who prefer to interact with other women rather than males. The Marcus Garvey Movement among African Americans during the 1920s, urged African Americans to return to Africa. Black Muslims have argued that African Americans should be given land in a few states to form their own nation.

A GREAT MANY PEOPLE
THINK THEY ARE THINKING
WHEN THEY ARE MERELY
REARRANGING THEIR
PREJUDICES.
WILLIAM JAMES

Oppression psychosis may result as a minority reaction. With oppression psychosis, I shall blame all my failures on my minority status rather than on some personal characteristic. The woman who did not get the job for $43,000 a year said it was based on gender rather than not having the qualifications for the job.

Overt aggression or collective action may occur. This can include women burning their bras and going on a sitdown strike or the African American of the 1960s sitting in the front of the bus and at the European American lunch counters.

Overcompensation may result as a consequence of minority status. With overcompensation, a minority member focuses on the external appearances of the majority group.

A very famous black sociologist by the name of Franklin Frazier wrote *Black Bourgeoisie*. He said that the African American middle class focused on the correct car, dress or games such as poker or bridge rather than the internal feelings of the middle class. Many women today swear more than they did a generation ago and smoke more than they did a generation ago. These are both traditionally masculine behavior. Also, to dress for success a female is to dress in a very tailored suit, like a man!

Nativism is a minority reaction to the majority group. Nativism is the dedication to minority group pattern. The Black Muslims promoted black art, styles of dress and haircuts. Women who dedicate their lives to the traditional roles of housewife and mother are personifying this type of adaptation pattern.

Passing is the last minority reaction to be discussed. Individual members of a minority group try to pass as members of the dominant group. The person passing abandons traditional mode of dress, converts to a different religion, or changes their name. A very light skinned African American, for example, might move into the white community as a white person. A Native American could move off a reservation and merge with the Anglo community.

🔱 *Quick Glance*

Acceptance is the conforming to minority status.   T   F

Marginal adaptation occurs in open areas. T   F

Submissive manipulation frequently involves self-degradation.   T   F

Sit-ins are overt aggression.   T   F

How Do the Theoretical Perspectives Address Minority Groups?

Structural Functional Theory

Structural functional theory looks at the parts of the society and how these parts interrelate and function for the good of the society. Thus, we must ask the question, "What functions do minority groups serve for the society?" Prejudiced beliefs provide moral justification for depriving another group rights and privileges given to the dominant group. Prejudiced beliefs also discourage the subordinate group from challenging the system. And, prejudiced beliefs encourage support for the existing order by introducing the argument that if there is any major societal change, the minority group would experience greater poverty and the majority might see a lowered standard of living.

There are also dysfunctions with prejudice, discrimination and concomitant segregation. *First, they involve a wasteful duplication of facilities.* In Southern areas during the 1940s and 1950s, there were two high schools, one for African Americans and one for European Americans. *Second, human resources remain inadequately trained and wasted.* How many great musical compositions have we missed because of segregation of women and African Americans? How many great scientists have been excluded because of women being discouraged from going into medical school in the 1950s and 1960s? *Third, some of the dominant manpower must be used to maintain dominance.* Police force has to be used to make sure each group stays in their own area. *Fourth, cohesion and consensus of the society are impaired.* If we are prejudiced, the bonds that hold the society together are ripped apart. Look what happened during the 1960s and 1970s in the United States. Consider what happened during the 1980s and 1990s in South Africa. *Fifth, segregation retards the blending of the minority group into the majority group.* Hispanic Americans who attend all Spanish-speaking schools and live in Hispanic American areas are handicapped with learning English, thus experiencing difficulties achieving social mobility. *Sixth, segregation increases social problems such as crime and poverty.* Young, unmarried African American females contribute disproportionately to poverty; young African American males have a very high unemployment rate and are overrepresented in the criminal justice system. *Seventh, segregation can impair international relationships.* How can we as a nation discuss human rights when we still have discrimination and segregation?

🔱 **Thinking Sociology**
What would be the advantages of avoidance for a minority member? Disadvantages?

> YOU NEVER REALLY UNDERSTAND A PERSON UNTIL YOU CONSIDER THINGS FROM HIS POINT OF VIEW.
> HARPER LEE
> TO KILL A MOCKINGBIRD
> (HARPER/COLLINS)

🔱 *Quick Glance*

Prejudiced beliefs encourage the subordinate group to challenge the system.   T   F

Segregation retards the blending of the minority group into the majority group.   T   F

Structural functional theory sees only good about prejudice.   T   F

Prejudice causes part of the population to be underutilized.   T   F

Segregation retards assimilation.   T   F

Conflict Theory

The conflict theory focuses on differential power. The majority group has more power and uses this power to keep the minority in a subservient position for economic and political gain. Activist groups such as the Gray Panthers, National Organization for the Advancement of Colored People, National Organization for Women and American Associates of Retired Persons are trying to shift the power structure such that minorities have a greater role in the political and economic arena of the United States.

Symbolic Interaction Theory

Quick Glance

Conflict theory states that the majority group has more power.   T F

Gordon Allport stated that a child learns prejudice in stages.   T F

Labeling minority is a symbolic interactionist interest.   T F

Children innately are prejudiced.   T F

The symbolic interaction theory looks at how prejudice is learned. Gordon Allport has described two stages in the learning of prejudice. In the first stage, the pregeneralized learning period, children have not yet learned to categorize people into general groupings. When a child hears a parent object to people of some specific group moving into the neighborhood, he or she is introduced to the second state of learning prejudice, that of total rejection. When a child reaches the second stage, all members of the minority group are rejected, on all accounts, in all situations.

Symbolic interactionist theory would also look at the labeling process involved in stereotypes and self-fulfilling prophecy. This was discussed when prejudice was explained.

Finally, the symbolic interactionist would explain the **contact hypothesis** to people. The contact hypothesis states that if contact between minority group and majority group is on an equal status in a pleasant, noncompetitive atmosphere, chances are prejudice feelings will decrease for both the majority and minority member.

THINKING SOCIOLOGY

Does forced integration of schools and workplace ensure that the contact hypothesis will happen? Why or why not?

▲ PREJUDICE SHOULD GO DOWN IN THIS SCHOOL.
IMAGE COPYRIGHT PATRICIA MARKS, 2008. USED UNDER LICENSE FROM SHUTTERSTOCK, INC.

CONTACT HYPOTHESIS			
Prejudice decreases		*Prejudice increases*	
Condition	*Example*	*Condition*	*Example*
Equal status	Subdivision civic club	Different strata	Different area high schools
Common goal	Decrease crime rate in area	Winner	Football game
Cooperation	Form a neighborhood watch	Competition	Each team wants the trophy

▼ CHAPTER SUMMARY

1. A minority group is distinguished from a majority group because of the disparity of economic, political and social power experienced by members of the minority group.

2. Members of a minority group have the following characteristics: possess shared physical, cultural, behavioral or cognitive traits; experience unequal treatment based on their traits; do not have voluntary membership; develop group solidarity.

3. Types of minority groups include racial groups, ethnic groups, women, elderly, some religious groups and homosexuals.

4. Members of minority groups experience both prejudice and discrimination. Prejudice is an attitude often based on stereotyping while discrimination is unequal treatment against the members of minority groups. Prejudice and discrimination are learned during the socialization process.

5. The "isms" (racism, sexism and ageism) share an ideology: some categories are physically superior to others, some groups are mentally superior to others, race, gender or age causes behavior, race, gender or age determines temperament and racial mixing lowers biological quality.

6. Minority groups emerge through five basic processes: political annexation, colonial pattern, migration, economic competition and Judaic Christian beliefs.

7. Treatment of the minority group by the majority group includes exclusion, extermination, relocation, subjugation, cultural pluralism, legal protection and assimilation.

8. The minority groups reactions to the majority group include acceptance, marginal adaptation, submissive manipulation, avoidance, oppression psychosis, overt aggression, overcompensation, nativism and passing as a member of the dominant group.

9. The theoretical perspectives address minority groups in the following way: structural functional looks at the functions and dysfunctions of minority groups; conflict theory focuses on the differential power possessed by members of a minority group; and the symbolic interactionist theory looks at how treatment of minority groups is learned.

▼ REFERENCES

Allport, Gordon. 1979. *The Nature of Prejudice, 25th Anniversary Edition*. Reading, MA: Addison-Wesley.

Banton, Michael. 1970. "The Concept of Racism." pp. 17–34 in Sami Zubaida (Ed.). *Race and Racialism*. London: Tavistock.

Benedict, Ruth. 1959. *Race: Science and Politics*. New York: Viking.

Bogardus, Emory. 1959. *Social Distance*. Yellow Springs, OH: Antioch Press.

Frazier, Franklin E. 1957. *The Black Bourgeoisie: The Rise of a New Middle Class*. New York: Free Press.

Gordon, Milton M. 1964. *Assimilation in American Life: The Role of Race, Religion and National Origins*. New York: Oxford University Press.

Marger, Martin N. 1991. *Race and Ethnic Relations: American and Global Perspectives: Second Edition*. Belmont, CA.: Wadsworth.

Merton, Robert. 1949. "Discrimination and the American Creed." In R. H. MacIver (Ed.), *Discrimination and National Welfare*. New York: Harper & Row, 99–126.

Montagu, Ashley. 1972. *Statement on Race: Third Edition*. New York: Oxford University Press.

Nash, Manning. 1962. "Race and the Ideology of Race." *Current Anthropology*, 3 (June), 258–288.

Shibutani and Kwan. 1965. *Ethnic Stratification: A Comparative Approach*. New York: Macmillan.

Tuman, Melvin. 1964. "Ethnic Group." p. 243 in Julius Gould and William L. Kob (Eds.), *Dictionary of the Social Sciences*. New York: Free Press.

Wagley, Charles and Marvin Harris. 1958. *Minorities in the New World: Six Case Studies*. New York: Columbia University Press.

Yinger, Milton. 1981. "Toward a Theory of Assimilation and Dissimilation." *Ethnic and Racial Studies*, 4: 249–264.

READING

To be a woman in America at the close of the 20th century—what good fortune. That's what we keep hearing, anyway. The barricades have fallen, politicians assure us. Women have "made it," Madison Avenue cheers. Women's fight for equality has "largely been won," Time magazine announces. Enroll at any university, join any law firm, apply for credit at any bank. Women have so many opportunities now, corporate leaders say, that we don't really need equal opportunity policies. Women are so equal now, lawmakers say, that we no longer need an Equal Rights Amendment. Women have "so much," former President Ronald Reagan says, that the White House no longer needs to appoint them to higher office. Even American Express ads are saluting a woman's freedom to charge it. At least, women have received their full citizenship papers.

But what "equality" are all these authorities talking about?

If American women are so equal, why do they represent two-thirds of all poor adults? Why are nearly 75 percent of full-time working women making less than $20,000 a year, nearly double the male rate? Why are they still far more likely than men to live in poor housing and receive no health insurance and twice as likely to draw no pension? Why does the average working woman's salary still lag as far behind the average man's as it did twenty years ago? Why does the average female college graduate today earn less than a man with no more than a high school diploma (just as she did in the 1950s)—and why does the average female high school graduate today earn less than a male high school dropout? Why do American women, in fact, face one of the worst gender-based pay gaps in the developed world?

If women have "made it," then why are nearly 80 percent of working women still stuck in traditional "female" jobs—as secretaries, administrative "support" workers and salesclerks? And, conversely, why are they less than eight percent of all federal and state judges, less than six percent of all law partners, and less than one half of one percent of top corporate managers? Why are there only three female state governors, two female United States senators, and two Fortune 500 chief executives? Why are only 19 of the 4,000 corporate officers and directors women—and why do more than half the boards of Fortune companies still lack even one female member?

If women "have it all," then why don't they have the most basic requirements to achieve equality in the working force? Unlike virtually all other industrialized nations, the United States government still has no family-leave and child care programs—and more than 99 percent of American private employers do not offer child care either. Though business leaders say they are aware of and deplore sex discrimination, corporate America has yet to make an honest effort toward eradicating it. In a 1990 national poll of chief executives at Fortune 1000 companies, more than 80 percent acknowledged that discrimination impedes female employees' progress—yet, less than one percent of these same companies regarded remedying sex discrimination as a goal that their personnel departments should pursue. In fact, when the companies' human resource officers were asked to rate their department's priorities, women's advancement was ranked last.

If women are so "free," why are their reproductive freedoms in greater jeopardy today than a decade earlier? Why do women who want to postpone childbearing now have fewer options than ten years ago? The availability of different forms of contraception has declined, research for new birth control has virtually halted, new laws

*From *Backlash* by Susan Faludi, copyright © 1991 by Susan Faludi. Used by permission of Crown Publishers, a division of Random House, Inc.

Quick Glance

Women and men are equally represented among the poorest in the U.S.A.　　T　F

Women now earn as much as men.　　T　F

Women are well represented in all major job arenas.　　T　F

restricting abortion—or even information about abortion—for young and poor women have been passed, and the United States Supreme Court has shown little ardor in defending the right it granted in 1973.

Nor is women's struggle for equal education over; as a 1989 study found, three-fourths of all high schools still violate the federal law banning sex discrimination in education. In colleges, undergraduate women receive only 70 percent of the aid undergraduate men get in grants and work-study jobs—and women's sports programs receive a pittance compared with men's. A review of state equal-education laws in the late 1980s found that only 13 states had adopted the minimum provisions required by the federal Title IX law—and only seven states had anti-discrimination regulations that covered all education levels.

Nor do women enjoy equality in their own homes, where they still shoulder 70 percent of the household duties—and the only major change in the last fifteen years is that now middle-class men think they do more around the house. (In fact, a national poll finds the ranks of women saying their husbands share equally in child care shrunk to 31 percent in 1987 from 40 percent three years earlier.) Furthermore, in thirty states, it is still generally legal for husbands to rape their wives; and only ten states have laws mandating arrest for domestic violence—even though battering was the leading cause of injury of women in the 1980s. Women who have no other option but to flee find that is not much of an alternative either. Federal funding for battered women's shelters has been withheld and one third of the one million battered women who seek emergency shelter each year can find none. Blows from men contributed far more to the rising numbers of "bag ladies" than the ill effects of feminism. In the 1980s, almost half of all homeless women (the fastest growing segment of the homeless) were refugees of domestic violence.

The word may be that women have been "liberated," but women themselves seem to feel otherwise. Repeatedly in national surveys, majorities of women say they are still far from equality. Nearly 70 percent of women polled by the New York Times in 1989 said the movement of women's rights had only just begun. Most women in the 1990 Virginia Slims opinion poll agreed with the statement that conditions for their sex in American society had improved "a little, not a lot." In poll after poll in the decade, overwhelming majorities of women said they needed equal pay and equal job opportunities, they needed an Equal Rights Amendment, they needed the right to an abortion without government interference, they needed a federal law guaranteeing maternity leave, they needed decent child care services. They have none of these. So how exactly have we "won" the war for women's rights?

Seen against this background, the much ballyhooed claim that feminism is responsible for making women miserable becomes absurd—and irrelevant . . . the afflictions ascribed to feminism are all myths. From "the man shortage" to "the infertility epidemic" to "female burnout" to "toxic day care," these so-called female crises have had their origins not in the actual conditions of women's lives but rather in a closed system that starts and ends in the media, popular culture, and advertising—an endless feedback loop that perpetuates and exaggerates its own false images of womanhood.

Women themselves don't single out the women's movement as the source of their misery. To the contrary, in national surveys 75 to 95 percent of women credit the feminist campaign with improving their lives, and a similar proportion say that the woman's movement should keep pushing for change. Less than eight percent think the woman's movement might have actually made their lot worse.

⚜ *Quick Glance*

Corporate America has programs in place to help women advance.   T F

Women receive fewer grants to attend college.   T F

Men share equally with women in the chores around the home.   T F

⚜ *Quick Glance*

Twenty-five percent of women are homeless due to domestic violence.   T F

The women's movement has been successful in getting more rights for women.   T F

The media has played a role in perpetuating the myths of feminism.   T F

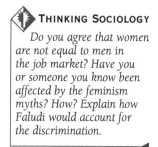

THINKING SOCIOLOGY

Do you agree that women are not equal to men in the job market? Have you or someone you know been affected by the feminism myths? How? Explain how Faludi would account for the discrimination.

Peering at Population and Ecology

10

IMAGE COPYRIGHT ILJA MAŠIK, 2008. USED UNDER LICENSE FROM SHUTTERSTOCK, INC.

CHAPTER OBJECTIVES

1. What is demography?
2. What did Thomas Malthus say about population growth?
3. What do the Neo-Malthusians believe?
4. What are pronatalist and antinatalist policies?
5. What is the theory of demographic transition?
6. What are the consequences of rapid population growth and overpopulation?
7. What are the solutions to the population problem?
8. What factors do demographers study?
9. What is a city and an urban environment?
10. What are the theories of urban growth?
11. What is the urban way of life?
12. What are the suburbs?
13. What are the major urban ecological processes?

age-specific death rate: the death rate measured in terms of deaths per 1,000 people in a specific age group

antinatalist: the policies to limit family size

CBD: central business district

city: a large number of people who are densely concentrated into a small area and who are dependent on others for food

compositional theory: a theory which states cities do not destroy intimate relationships or a sense of purpose

concentric zone theory: a theory which states cities grow and develop in circular zones spreading out from a downtown center

crude birthrate: the annual number of live births per 1,000 members of a population

demographic transition theory: the theory which demonstrates changes from high fertility and mortality rates to low fertility and mortality rates

demography: the systematic study of population

dependency ratio: the proportion of people in productive years relative to number of people in nonproductive years

determinist theory: the theory which states that impersonality and diversity of city life undermines the sense of affiliation and community

emigration: the migration from an area

fecundity: the potential number of births for a female

fertility: the birth rate of a society

fertility rate: the annual number of live births per 1,000 women ages 15 to 44

fertility ratio: the number of children produced by women of childbearing age

gentrification: the renovation of central city areas

immigration: the migration into a geographical area

infant mortality rate: the number of deaths among infants under one year of age per 1,000 live births

life expectancy: the number of years an individual can expect to live by being a member of a particular society

life span: the number of years a person can expect to live, species determined

megalopolis: the densely populated areas containing two or more cities and their surrounding suburbs

metropolitan statistical area: the urbanized area which has a city of 50,000 inhabitants or more and includes adjacent country side and other populated areas

migration: the movement of people from one geographical location to another

morbidity: the occurrence of disease within a population

mortality: the occurrence of death within a population

multiple nuclei theory: the theory which explains why cities grow around several business districts

population: the number of people living within a given space or area

population pyramid: a diagram showing age and sex distribution of a population

pronatalist: the policies in favor of a large number of births for each woman of childbearing age

rurban: the movement of urban people to rural areas in nonfarming capacity

sector theory: the theory which states that industrial, commercial, and residential sectors form wedge-shaped sectors around a central business district

sex ratio: the proportion of males to females within a given population

subcultural theory: the theory which maintains that the very size of a city's population promotes the development of a variety of subcultures

suburbanization: the movement of people from central cities to smaller communities in the surrounding areas

urbanization: the process by which large numbers of people gather in a relatively small geographical area and are interdependent on each other for goods and services

ZPG: Zero Population Growth

▼ KEY PEOPLE

Ernest Burgess, Kingsley Davis, Claude Fischer, Herbert Gans, Chauncey Harris, Homer Hoyt, Thomas Malthus, Edward Ullman, Louis Wirth

What Is Demography?

The study of population has received much attention in recent years. The systematic study of population is called demography. **Demography** studies birth and death rates, migratory patterns, minority and ethnic distributions and characteristics such as age, sex, marital status, race, religion and occupation of a population. **Population**, to the sociologist, is people living within a given space or area; in other words, population is generally determined by residence within stated political boundaries. Information gained from demographic studies is important for economic planning and governmental intervention into such areas as health care, housing and education.

What Did Thomas Malthus Say about Population Growth?

One of the most famous population theorists was Thomas Malthus. He lived during the sixteenth and seventeenth centuries and wrote what has become a very famous essay on population entitled *An Essay on the Principle of Population as it Affects the Future Improvement of Society*. Malthus theorized that it was human nature that caused population problems because sexual urges would lead to reproduction, thus causing people to produce more rapidly than food production. He said that population increased in geometric ratio (2, 4, 8, 16, 32, 64, 128), while the food supply increased in arithmetic ratio (1, 2, 3, 4, 5, 6, 7). Thus, population would outstrip food production; people would continue to reproduce until they were at the very brink of extinction. According to Malthus, positive checks on population would stop the growth rate. The positive checks identified by Malthus included poverty, misery, disease and deterioration of morality. He said that there were also preventive checks or limits on population, but he did not put much faith in these. Preventive checks included celibacy, deferment of marriage and moral restraint, thus leading to the reduction of the number of births. Malthus did not believe that any devices of political or economic organizations or of emigration would stop the positive checks from operating.

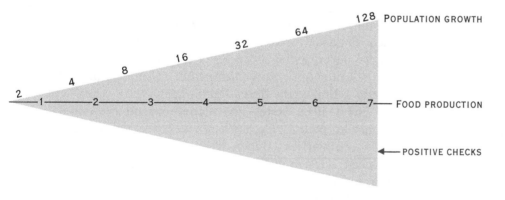

What Do the Neo-Malthusians Believe?

Could Malthus be correct for the 2000s in the United States? Followers of Malthus, referred to as Neo-Malthusians, caution that the success of the United States in meeting the needs of the population with an ample food supply could be short-lived. The Neo-Malthusians believe that the United States, as well as other countries, need active intervention in order to curtail what they regard as out-of-control population growth. They believe that it is imperative to educate the masses to advantages of

☞ *Quick Glance*

Sociologists are not concerned with the study of population. T F

Demography is the systematic study of population. T F

Population is generally defined by numbers of people in a geographical area. T F

Thomas Malthus was a modern theorist. T F

Thomas Malthus maintained that there are no checks on population. T F

Thomas Malthus stated that food production grew geometrically. T F

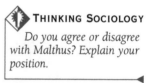 **Thinking Sociology**

Do you agree or disagree with Malthus? Explain your position.

☞ *Quick Glance*

Neo-Malthusians do not adhere to the same moral restraints for limiting population that Thomas Malthus did in his lifetime. T F

Kingsley Davis is a well-known Neo-Malthusian. T F

Cutting tax advantages of children could cut the birth rate. T F

smaller families and the use of birth control in order to consciously cut down the number of births. Worldwide, population doubled in the last forty years.

Kingsley Davis, a Neo-Malthusian, makes seven suggestions for population control:

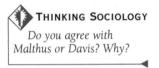

THINKING SOCIOLOGY

Do you agree with Malthus or Davis? Why?

1. Make it more practical for people to postpone or avoid marriage.
2. Reward nonfamilial life styles by removing the penalties for being single, divorced or widowed.
3. Restrict tax exemptions for dependent children, paid maternity leave and family allowances.
4. Abolish public housing grants tied to family size and fellowships for married students.
5. Remove penalties for engaging in nonprocreative sexual relations.
6. Designate population a problem for ministries of economics and education, rather than ministries of health.
7. Redefine traditional family, particularly for women, and allow everyone the right to education and gainful employment.

▲ THIS FAMILY SUPPORTS ZPG.
IMAGE COPYRIGHT LOSEVSKY PAVEL, 2008. USED UNDER LICENSE FROM SHUTTERSTOCK, INC.

🐚 *Quick Glance*

Antinatalist promote use of birth control.　T　F

Zero population growth is a pronatalist position.　T　F

Religious norms promote ZPG programs.　T　F

WHAT ARE PRONATALIST AND ANTINATALIST POLICIES?

Pronatalist policies are programs and values in favor of a large number of births for each woman of childbearing age. Pronatalism does not have to be stated as a public policy, but rather can operate as a norm within a society. Some countries, such as France, the Soviet Union, Italy and Germany during WWII, encouraged pronatalist ideas by offering monetary rewards for births.

Antinatalist policies try to limit family size. The antinatalist policies may be either through laws or campaigns of persuasion. The People's Republic of China has adopted a government antinatalist national policy by establishing the Family Planning Association of China. This program has adopted a one-child family contract featuring the *Glorious One-Child Certificate*. Married couples sign an agreement to limit their family size to one child in an exchange for economic and educational benefits. This official policy has been issued by the Communist party chairman in an effort to hold the population to 1.2 billion by the end of the century.

The United States has a combination of pronatalist and antinatalist policies. On one hand, we have a tax deduction for each child and married couples frequently pay less taxes than single people; this is a pronatalist policy. Custom in the United States, however, is largely an antinatalist policy. The average family is smaller than it was in the 1950s and more people are reporting that they want 0, 1, 2 or 3 children. Large families are frequently looked upon as being an economic burden. Antinatalist policies in the United Sates are not based on public policy, but more on a public awareness of population issues.

Proponents of antinatalist policy desire what is called ZPG (Zero Population Growth). **Zero Population Growth** is the antinatalist policy that desires to keep the population at the current level. ZPG programs have been difficult to instigate in many areas of the world for several reasons:

1. *Religious norms can make ZPG programs difficult to achieve.* The world's two main religions, Islamic and Roman Catholic, influence a large portion of the world's population and both prohibit birth control and abortion.

2. *Individual needs contradict the needs of the country.* In developing countries, children are a vital source of labor and an insurance policy ensuring care during old age. High infant mortality rate influences the thinking of people to have large families in order to raise several to adulthood.

3. *Military protection, especially if the country does not have a nuclear arsenal, depends upon a large standing army.*

4. *Traditional values influence ZPG programs.* In many cultures, virility and sexual attractiveness are linked to the ability to father and bear children. A woman gets her identity and meaning in life through her role of being a mother. These beliefs encourage high birth rates.

5. *Ignorance contributes to the failure of ZPG programs.* In the United States and other technologically advanced societies, we are used to taking pills and undergoing medical procedures. But in many countries, a pill is not the answer to headaches and sore throats. Even in our own country, misconceptions about birth control abound. It is widely believed, for example, that a vasectomy causes impotence.

Several factors contribute to the success of ZPG programs:

1. Conspicuous consumption contributes significantly to people desiring smaller families.

2. Improved contraception has contributed to successful ZPG programs.

3. Urbanization has increased the success of ZPG programs. Within the city, space is expensive and children take up room.

4. The value of labor has changed; child labor is no more productive than before, but child care does take time and money.

5. Extended education has caused a decrease in the birth rate because education is expensive.

WHAT IS THE THEORY OF DEMOGRAPHIC TRANSITION?

One of the most important theories of population growth is the theory of demographic transition. The **demographic transition** theory analyzes changes in birth and death rates. This is a four stage model:

Stage 1: High Birth Rates and High Death Rates

Scientific control of disease is not present at this stage of a society's development; families must bear several children to be assured that three or four will survive infancy. Since both birth and death rates are about the same, the population growth rate is close to 0 and population is stable in size. This stage includes the very early history of humankind. Hunters and gatherers are included in Stage 1.

Stage 2: High Birth Rates and Low Death Rates

During this stage, there are very high birth rates and rapidly failing death rates which cause a rapid growth in population size. This is the stage that is characteristic of many third-world countries such as Ethiopia, Somalia and Guatemala. Modern medical practices have been brought to these countries resulting in a dramatic drop in death rates, particularly in maternal and infant death. Family values toward the number of

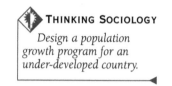

CITY LIFE: MILLIONS OF PEOPLE BEING LONESOME TOGETHER.

H. D. THOREAU

THINKING SOCIOLOGY

Design a population growth program for an under-developed country.

U.S. FERTILITY RATES 2004	
HISPANIC	2.82
BLACK/NON-HISPANIC	2.01
ASIAN/PACIFIC ISLANDER	1.90
WHITE/NON-HISPANIC	1.85
AMERICAN INDIAN	1.74

POPULATION BULLETIN VOL. 60, No. 4, 2005.

Quick Glance

Ignorance frequently supports pronatalists. T F

Conspicuous consumption raises birth rates. T F

Stage 2 of the demographic transition theory is the stage that is characteristic of many third-world countries today. T F

Hunting and gathering societies are in Stage 1 of demographic growth. T F

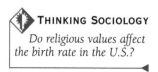

THINKING SOCIOLOGY

Do religious values affect the birth rate in the U.S.?

Population Growth Rates for Selected Countries and Population Per Square Km (2006)

Country	Growth Rate (%)	Population Per Square Km
Afghanistan	2.7	48
Australia	.85	2.7
Bangladesh	2.08	1100.5
Brazil	1.04	22.2
Cambodia	1.78	78.6
Canada	.88	3.6
Chad	2.92	7.9
China	.59	140.9
Ecuador	1.50	48.9
Ethiopia	2.31	66.8
France	.35	111.6
Ghana	2.07	97.4
Greece	.18	81.7
Greenland	−0.03	0.2
India	1.38	368.4
Iraq	2.66	61.7
Japan	.02	322.9
Kenya	2.57	61.00
Mexico	1.16	55.9
Nigeria	2.38	144.8
Pakistan	2.09	212.9
Philippines	1.80	300.1
Russia	−0.37	8.4
Singapore	1.42	7,199.0
South Africa	−0.40	36.2
Switzerland	.43	189.2
Thailand	.68	126.3
United Kingdom	.28	250.9
United States	.91	32.6
Vietnam	1.02	259.4

From U.S. Census Bureau, "International Database" 2006.

children have not changed as quickly; therefore, these countries have continued to experience tremendous population growth rates. Industrialized countries such as the United States and Great Britain were not as affected by this stage of demographic transition. In the industrialized nations, the industrialization of a country and improvement in medical practice go hand in hand resulting in a reduction in the death rate. The Industrial Revolution acted to increase the production of manufactured goods and their transportation and distribution. Moreover, these changes in the eco-

DEATH RATE AND BIRTH RATE PER 1,000 PEOPLE			
	Death Rate	Birth Rate	
Country	2006	2001	2006
Afghanistan	20.3	41.42	46.6
Argentina	7.5	18.41	16.7
Australia	7.5	12.86	12.1
Bangladesh	8.3	25.3	29.8
Cambodia	9.1	33.16	26.9
Canada	7.8	11.21	10.8
China	7.0	15.95	13.2
Congo	12.9	46.02	42.6
El Salvador	5.8	28.67	26.6
Ghana	9.7	28.95	30.5
India	8.2	24.28	22.0
Japan	9.2	10.04	9.4
Kenya	14.0	28.5	39.7
Mexico	4.7	22.77	20.7
Russia	14.7	9.35	9.9
United Kingdom	10.1	11.54	10.7
United States	8.3	14.2	14.1

From U.S. Census Bureau, "International Database" 2001, 2006.

Learning TIP
Use mnemonic devices when you study. For example, make up a word for a list of characteristics or walk through a room and put each item in a place.

DEATHS IN THE U.S.	
	DEATHS/ 1,000 POP.
1900	17.2
1950	9.6
2000	8.7
2003	8.3
2006	8.1

U.S. NATIONAL CENTER FOR HEALTH STATISTICS, VITAL STATISTICS OF THE UNITED STATES.

nomic patterns of cultures provided jobs for an increasing number of people. All this, in turn, made for a higher standard of living. New outlets in the Americas and elsewhere provided an outlet for the expanding population of Europe and Asia. Also, the Americas furnished foodstuffs and raw materials to keep the industrial system going and provided a market for goods manufactured in Europe. There was also gradually improved medical care which reduced infectious and contagious diseases, improved maternal and infant care and enhanced public sanitation.

Stage 3: Declining Birth Rate and Declining Death Rate

In this stage, the birth rate begins to fall at a rate that is faster than the decline of the death rate. The industrialization of a country has typically been followed by a reduction in the birth rate. Population size is still growing, but not as quickly as in Stage 2. Puerto Rico, Taiwan and South Korea are in this stage.

Stage 4: Low Birth Rates and Low Death Rates

The population reaches ZPG, as is found in Stage 1, but the birth rates and death rates are much lower than before. Population growth is stable, but at a much greater number of people than in Stage 1 because death and birth rates are balanced. People are having fewer children because children are economic liabilities, more women are in the work force, people have higher living standards and better health care has controlled infant mortality. Countries of Europe, the United States and Japan are in this stage.

THINKING SOCIOLOGY
Do you think that the U.S. will ever enter the fifth stage? What is your opinion on euthanasia? Support your answer.

INFANT MORTALITY RATES/1000			
	Male & Female	*Male*	*Female*
1996	7.3	8.0	6.6
2000	7.0	7.7	6.2
2006	6.4	7.1	5.7

U.S. Census Bureau, "International Database" 2006.

Learning TIP
Turn off your cell phones and ipods. Don't wear headphones in class.

There is the possibility that a fifth stage could occur either with or without planning. In the fifth stage, there would be low fertility and high mortality rates. Conditions would exist in the society such that the populace would see a need to lower their population and would come to view their older people as an economic drain on limited resources. These resources could be related to economics, space or energy. The society would begin to set standards for those eligible for health care and the older and disadvantaged people would be denied medical needs or access to certain medical attention. For example, an individual aged 75 who might need a heart transplant to live a few more years might be denied that transplant because of the individual's age and the cost of the procedure. Euthanasia would then be practiced, and stage five of the demographic transition theory would become a reality for that society.

THIS COUNTRY WAS BUILT UP BY IMMIGRANTS WHO, IN THE VAST MAJORITY OF CASES, CAME HERE TO ESCAPE POVERTY, OPPRESSION AND LACK OF OPPORTUNITY AT HOME.

ALFRED E. SMITH

WHAT ARE THE CONSEQUENCES OF RAPID POPULATION GROWTH AND OVERPOPULATION?

Rapid population growth has negative consequences for both underdeveloped and developing nations. We shall first focus on the underdeveloped nations:

Quick Glance

Bangladesh has a higher birth rate than Ghana. T F

Rapid population growth has negative consequences only for underdeveloped nations. T F

Political upheaval may reflect the frustrations of a low quality of life. T F

Overurbanization is a result of rapid population growth. T F

1. Economic advances that are made in the society as a whole are canceled by the addition of people.
2. Unemployment and underemployment for large numbers of people are created when the rate of population growth exceeds the economy's rate of growth.
3. Political instability increases with rapid population growth. Under the conditions of low per capita income, unemployment and urban concentration, the potential for political instability and upheaval is a very real threat. Political upheaval may reflect the frustrations generated by a low quality of life.
4. A significantly younger population creates problems for the developing country. Greater proportions of children lead to specific problems with education, health care and provision of jobs. Moreover, in agricultural societies (which most third-world nations are), there are intergenerational stresses when children must wait longer to inherit the family's holdings and intragenerational problems because there is more competition between siblings because there are more siblings.

THINKING SOCIOLOGY

Do developed countries face some of the same problems with rapid population growth as developing countries?

5. Overurbanization is a result of rapid population growth. In many of these underdeveloped countries, the agricultural areas can no longer support the growing population, so people go to the city to find help and jobs. At the edges of virtually every large city in Latin America, there are people living in the shack towns that have been established. These people seek advantage in the urban environment, but are forced to live near the starvation level in unsanitary, disease-ridden conditions.

Large populations also create problems for developed countries. The enormous size of the current population makes it more difficult to accomplish the many complex tasks necessary to maintain a highly urbanized, technological society. The widespread emphasis on the autonomy of local political units and the persistent reluctance to undertake regional planning is difficult with large numbers of people. The desire for private rather than social needs must be met. The human need for space, recreation, transportation, and respite from the intensity of urban life has to be addressed. Affluence frequently leads to the ravaging of the environment. The heterogeneity of the urban environment in technologically advanced societies make consensus more difficult.

Another problem whether in first- or third-world nations is unequal population growth. In Lebanon, for example, the average Moslem family has over 6 children, but the average Christian family has 3. The Christians are rapidly finding themselves losing their majority status and becoming a minority in numbers. This creates the potential for friction between groups within the society.

Finally, every country in the world is facing some critical issues concerning diminishing minerals and fossil fuels and pollution of the air, water and land.

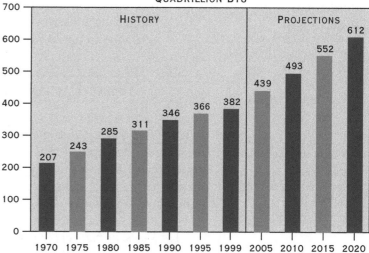

WORLD ENERGY CONSUMPTION, 1970–2020
QUADRILLION BTU

HISTORY — 1970: 207, 1975: 243, 1980: 285, 1985: 311, 1990: 346, 1995: 366, 1999: 382

PROJECTIONS — 2005: 439, 2010: 493, 2015: 552, 2020: 612

SOURCES: **HISTORY:** ENERGY INFORMATION ADMINISTRATION (EIA), OFFICE OF ENERGY MARKETS AND END USE, INTERNATIONAL STATISTICS DATABASE AND "INTERNATIONAL ENERGY ANNUAL 1999," DOE/EIA-0219(99) (WASHINGTON, DC, FEBRUARY 2001). **PROJECTIONS:** EIA, WORLD ENERGY PROJECTION SYSTEM (2002).

WHAT ARE THE SOLUTIONS TO THE POPULATION PROBLEM?

The first solution to the problem is to increase the death rate. Some people say this is what the high abortion rate has done. Other cultures increase the death rate at the other end of the life cycle. Among some Eskimo groups and American Indian groups, when a senior citizen feels like she or he is a burden and threatens the survival of fellow tribe members, she or he can choose to go off and die, thus decreasing the burden on the rest of the group.

The second solution is migration from an overpopulated area to an underpopulated area. If the values of the incoming group are changed, and if the environment is compatible, this just might work; historically, this solution has not.

The third solution that has been advocated in most technologically advanced societies is a decrease in the birth rate. A large number of people in the United States use birth control and one of the favorite birth control of educated people over the age of 30 is sterilization.

The fourth solution is to have a rise in food production. With more food being produced, a larger population could be supported. More land could be used for food production. Or the land that is in production could be made more efficient. This increase in efficiency is part of the Green Revolution. The Green Revolution has worked quite well in industrialized nations, but faces major difficulties in undeveloped countries for several reasons:

1. *The Green Revolution is based on the use of hybrid seed.* Hybrid seed is geared towards narrow soil and climatic conditions. Any shift in either factor causes a decrease in production. Hybrid seed has to be purchased each year unlike

 THINKING SOCIOLOGY

Which solution do you think would be most effective? Why?

the use of other types of seed where the best can be saved and planted the next year.

2. *The Green Revolution is based on the heavy use of fertilizer, insecticides and herbicides.* These are petrochemical products and are very expensive.

3. *The Green Revolution is also based on the use of machinery.* The people must have the money to buy, operate and maintain the machinery in order to make it profitable. They also need to have the education to operate and fix the machinery.

▲ THE GREEN REVOLUTION AT WORK.
IMAGE COPYRIGHT REGIEN PAASSEN, 2008. USED UNDER LICENSE FROM SHUTTERSTOCK, INC.

🔯 *Quick Glance*

The crop from hybrid seed can be planted the following year.   T F

Fertilizer is a petrochemical product.   T F

Machinery is not necessary for the Green Revolution.   T F

WHAT FACTORS DO DEMOGRAPHERS STUDY?

The first factor we shall discuss is the sex ratio. The **sex ratio** is the proportion of males to females and is stated as the number of males per 100 females. A sex ratio of 100 means that the population is evenly divided between males and females; a figure greater than 100 means that there are more males than females; a figure less than 100 means that there are more females than males. A sex ratio that deviates markedly in either direction is said to be biased. The sex ratio is affected by several factors:

1. *Males are more apt to migrate into an area than females* (**immigration**). This is one reason why for so many years the western United States had more males than females. The east coast, on the other hand, has more women. The area that the males move out of (**emigration**), has a raised sex ratio.

2. *Most societies are more apt to put young males at jeopardy in war.* Countries such as France and the Soviet Union lost many young men during WWII and, as a consequence, are experiencing a low sex ratio.

3. *In general, a young population tends to have high sex ratios; older populations tend to have low sex ratios.* The sex ratio for whites at birth in the United States is about 106, but at successively older ages the proportion of males diminishes; that is, the sex ratio declines with increasing age. Right now the sex ratio is about 95. In 1910, it was 106 for all ages. States on the eastern seaboard tend to have a lower sex ratio while western states have a higher sex ratio. Rural areas have a higher sex ratio than urban areas.

🔯 *Quick Glance*

Immigration and emigration are defined the same.   T F

Rural areas have higher sex ratios than urban areas.   T F

Younger populations have a greater number of females.   T F

Men are more apt to emigrate than women. T F

Age composition is an important demographic variable. The median age in the United States is about 36 and by 2080 it will be 42.6. We are an aging country. In large part the industrial and military potentials of a nation depend on its age composition. A population with heavy concentrations in the productive years has a larger labor force and a greater potential for mobilization in time of emergency. A population with smaller proportions in the productive years is less able to respond to threats against its security and is probably less adaptable to technological change.

A diagram of both age and sex ratio of a population is called a **population pyramid**. The diagram shows the distribution of genders in each of the major age groups.

▲ THE DEPENDENCY RATIO OCCURS AT BOTH EXTREMES OF THE AGE SPAN.

IMAGE COPYRIGHT LOSEVSKY PAVEL, 2008. USED UNDER LICENSE FROM SHUTTERSTOCK, INC.

In societies such as the United States, the population pyramid is nearly rectangular, but in societies with extremely high birth rates, such as Guatemala or Iran, the population pyramid is a triangle shape showing the high rate of younger children in the population. The population pyramid of the Yanomamo Indians of Venezuela and Brazil show not only a very young population, but also a larger number of male infants.

A population concentrated at either extreme of the age distribution has a heavy dependency ratio. The **dependency ratio** is the population of people under 15 and over 65 divided by the number of people from 15 to 65. If the dependency ratio is high, there is a large number of nonproductive individuals relative to productive individuals, and this burdens the productive population. This ratio enables us to compare the dependency load for different nations. The dependency ratio of the United States is 54.2; that is, it takes 100 working people to support themselves plus 54.2 dependents. Canada, like ourselves, has a relatively low dependency ration, 51.5. Developing nations have much higher dependency nations: Iran, 92.0 and Mexico, 98.2.

Fertility and fecundity are important demographic variables. **Fecundity** is potential reproduction; it is the biological capacity to bear children. Technically, between 12 and 49 every woman has the potential to have about 44 children, assuming single births and an interval of 10 months between children. The highest median number of children per woman at the end of her reproductive years is the 10.9 reported among the Hutterites. The most children produced by a mother was in an independently attested study in the Moscow Jurisdiction of Russia. The first wife of Fyodor Vassilet (1816–72), a peasant, had in 27 confinements 69 children; she produced 16 pairs of twins, seven sets of triplets and four sets of quadruplets.

Fertility is the actual rate of childbearing. The fertility of populations in modern urbanized and industrialized nations is only a small part of their fecundity, and even in the agrarian countries of Asia, where fertility is very high, it does not reach the biological maximum. There are two measures used to determine fertility:

1. **Crude birthrate** which is the annual number of live births per 1,000 members of a population. This is a very easy measure to calculate but does not take into account the women who give birth to the children and ignores the age structure of the population. A younger population, for example, will have more children than an older population.

2. **Fertility rate** is the annual number of live births per 1,000 women ages 15 to 44.

We, as a nation, are averaging about 1.9 children per family. Rural areas tend to have a higher birth rate than urban areas and in general, the larger the city, the lower the fertility. In general, manual workers' wives have more children than do wives of white-collar workers; Catholic fertility tends to be higher than Protestant fertility, while Baptists have the highest fertility. Older Catholic women are more fertile than younger Catholic women. The lowest birth rate is among Jewish and Presbyterian women. Differential birth rates among denominations reflect age, color, residential and occupational variations, but there are also religious differences.

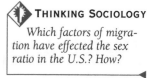
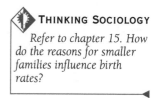

THINKING SOCIOLOGY

What were the causes of your grandparents' and great grandparents' death? What do you anticipate will be the cause of your death? Why?

Mortality is the fourth demographic variable. **Mortality** means <u>death rates</u>. Mortality is measured by crude death rate and age-specific death rates:

1. **Crude death rate** is the annual number of deaths per 1,000 members of a population. In developed countries, such as the United States, the death rate is about 9 per 1,000 people; in lesser developed countries the death rate is about 10 per 1,000 people.
2. **Age-specific death rates** are measured in terms of deaths per 1,000 people in a specific age group. Demographers are interested in studying the impact of age, sex, race, stratification position, standard of living and health care on the rate of death.

Two concepts are important for this discussion, life expectancy and life span. **Life expectancy** is the number of years an individual can expect to live by being a member of a particular society. The life expectancy in the United States will rise from 73.7 in 1980 to an estimated 77 by the year 2000. Life expectancy is dependent upon maternal and infant death rates. **Infant mortality rate** is the number of deaths

LEADING CAUSES OF DEATH BY AGE GROUP	
LESS THAN 1	CONGENITAL ANOMALIES
1–34	UNINTENTIONAL INJURY
35–64	MALIGNANT NEOPLASMS
65+	HEART DISEASE

FROM CENTERS FOR DISEASE CONTROL AND PREVENTION, FEB., 2002

among infants under one year of age per 1,000 live births. In 1850, only three-fourths of the newborn in the United States reached the age of 5; in 1901, the same proportion reached age 24; and in 1959, the same proportion survived more than 60 years.

Infant mortality has no affect on life span. **Life span** is the number of years I can expect to live by being a member of a species. My rabbit, for example, can live to be about 20 years old;

▲ HEART DISEASE AND CANCER AFFECT LIFE EXPECTANCY IN THE U.S.A.
IMAGE COPYRIGHT NAGIB, 2008. USED UNDER LICENSE FROM SHUTTERSTOCK, INC.

that is the average life span of a rabbit. Right now our life span is about 115 to 120 years. Over 30,000 people have celebrated their 100th birthday. One of the two oldest people in the United States was Charlie Smith who died in 1978 at 137. He was born in Liberia, Africa in 1842. The second oldest person in the United States was Jesus Coronado. He died in 1981 at 129. A woman living in Ecuador holds the 2006 record as being the oldest living person. As of this writing she is 116 years old. The second oldest is from the United States, she is 115. Until we get a breakthrough in either cardiovascular disease and/or cancer, we are not going to take another step towards reaching our life span of over 100 years.

BURN DOWN YOUR CITIES AND LEAVE YOUR FARMS, AND YOUR CITIES WILL SPRING UP AGAIN AS IF BY MAGIC; BUT DESTROY OUR FARMS AND THE GRASS WILL GROW IN THE STREETS OF EVERY CITY IN THE COUNTRY.

W. J. BRYAN

THINKING SOCIOLOGY

How does an increased life expectancy affect the U.S.?

LIFE EXPECTANCY FOR U.S.A.			
	1929	1998	2005
All Americans	57.1	76.7	77.7
All Males	55.8	73.8	74.5
All Females	58.7	79.5	79.9
White Males	57.2	74.5	79.1
White Females	60.3	80.0	80.3
Black Males	45.7	67.6	68.8
Black Females	47.8	74.8	75.6

From National Vital Statistics Report, 2/18/01 and 2/28/05.

Morbidity is the occurrence of disease and illness in a population. In the 1800s, influenza, pneumonia and tuberculosis were at the top of the list for killing; these three diseases accounted for almost 25% of the deaths. These diseases have been much more closely brought under control with vaccines and antibiotics. Now chronic degenerative diseases such as heart disease, stroke and cancer take increasing numbers of the population. Such lifestyle diseases as emphysema, diabetes, suicide, accidents and homicides were not even on the top 10 list of killers in the 1800s; now they are among the top reasons for death in the United States.

Learning TIP
In a multiple choice exam, if you do not know the answer, make each choice into a True/False question. You can often eliminate responses this way.

TEN TOP CAUSES OF DEATH IN U.S.A.

Heart disease
Cancer
Stroke and cerebrovascular disease
Chronic obstructive pulmonary disease
Accidents and adverse effects
Pneumonia and influenza
Diabetes
Suicide
Kidney disease
Chronic liver disease and cirrhosis

From National Vital Statistics Report, Vol. 48, No. 11.

Quick Glance

Life expectancy is decreasing in the U.S.   T   F

Infant mortality has no influence on life span.   T   F

Morbidity is a measure of disease.   T   F

Migration is movement across political boundaries.   T   F

The desire for economic improvement is recognized as a push and pull for migration.   T   F

Political oppression is a push factor but not a pull factor in migration.   T   F

Migration is movement across political boundaries. Migration is analyzed in terms of pushes and pulls:

1. Desire for economic improvement
2. Desire to be free from political oppression
3. Individual maladjustment to family or community life
4. Desire to secure freedom of belief and worship
5. Pressure associated with military/national considerations

WHAT IS A CITY AND AN URBAN ENVIRONMENT?

A **city** consists of a large number of people who are densely concentrated into a small area and who are dependent on others for food. There were cities early in the history of humans such as Troy and Athens. These cities are called preindustrial cities. Preindustrial cities were characterized by a closed-class system, rudimentary division of labor, prevalence of religious structures and communication through information means. This type of city still exists in many parts of Africa, Asia and Latin America because of lack of industrialization. With the advancements in agricultural and the Industrial Revolution, cities took on an entirely different character. The population density now made it possible to have a specialized division of labor, large-scale enterprises, an open-class system with elaborate divisions of labor and sophisticated communications techniques. Secularization became prevalent and standardized education important. The industrialized city depended and still depends on an agricultural base to support its people who are engaged in manufacturing and service industry.

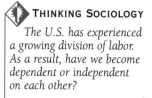

THINKING SOCIOLOGY

The U.S. has experienced a growing division of labor. As a result, have we become dependent or independent on each other?

Since 1960, the government has recognized what is now called a **Metropolitan Statistical Area (MSA)**. This is an urbanized area which has a city of at least 50,000 inhabitants and its adjacent country side including other populated areas. The MSA encompasses both urban and suburban areas within a region. The Greater Houston Metropolitan area is an example of a MSA.

Some metropolitan areas have spread so far that they are now called **megalopolis**. These are densely populated areas containing two or more cities and their surrounding suburbs. The coastal area between Los Angeles and San Diego is classified as a megalopolis. In fact, each of the four coastal areas—the Pacific coast, the Atlantic coast, the Great lakes and the Gulf area—are lined with megalopolis.

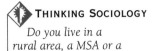
WHAT ARE THE THEORIES OF URBAN GROWTH?

Concentric Zone Theory

The concentric zone theory was developed by Ernest Burgess in 1924. His model for this theory was Chicago. According to the **concentric zone theory,** cities grow and develop in circular zones spreading out from a downtown center. The downtown is the central business district which has the major stores, theaters and office buildings. As the city grows, the business district spreads outward into old residential sections. This becomes the zone in transition and contains deteriorating homes and warehouses. The third zone is working-class housing; the next zone is middle-class housing and the outer zones are the upper-class suburbs.

Sector Theory

The sector theory was designed by Homer Hoyt when he did a study for the Federal Housing Administration. His theory stated that land use is strongly influenced by transportation routes rather than by distance from the central city. According to the **sector theory,** the industrial, commercial and residential sectors are not circular, but rather form wedge-shaped sectors around the central business district. Residential areas tend to push out from the center of the city along existing routes such as railroads and highways. Factories and businesses dominate other sectors because of their nearness to docks and highways. Both Los Angeles and Minneapolis could be analyzed using this theory.

Multiple Nuclei Theory

The multiple nuclei theory was devised by Chauncey Harris and Edward Ullman. The **multiple nuclei theory** states that local economic or social reasons explain why cities grow the way they do. Certain economic activities need special facilities; retail stores need to be where the customers are and manufacturing plants need large spaces and transportation services. People want quiet areas in which to live. According to this theory, there may be several business districts scattered throughout the city.

What Is the Urban Way of Life?

Determinist Theory

Louis Wirth believed that emotional stress and social isolation weakened social controls over individuals' behavior. Cities were busy, crowded places where people got lost in the shuffle, lost their individualism and no one knew or cared what they did. The **determinist theory** believes that impersonality and diversity of city life undermines the sense of affiliation and community.

THINKING SOCIOLOGY

Which pattern of urban growth best characterizes your city?

Compositional Theory

Herbert Gans did not agree with Wirth. According to Gan's **compositional theory**, cities do not destroy intimate relationships or a sense of common purpose. City dwellers congregate in homogeneous neighborhoods, such as Chinatown, and work in occupational districts. The local units mitigate against the anonymous urban conditions. Who, according to Gans, lives in the city?

1. *The trapped*, largely consists of old people, usually live on pensions or public assistance and cannot afford to leave the city.
2. *The deprived* includes the poor minorities, the aged, divorced mothers and others. To the deprived, city life offers cheap housing, higher welfare payments than the rural poor enjoy and increased opportunities for employment.
3. *The ethnic villagers* are usually recent immigrants; the ethnic villager lives in a closed, almost independent community within the city. Kinship ties remain strong and there is suspicion of those things beyond the boundaries of the ethnic community.
4. *The unmarried or childless* live in the city by choice but experience little commitment to it. They find the city an advantageous place for meeting people. They tend to change residence frequently and often leave the city entirely when they marry or have children.
5. *The cosmopolitan* are well educated and enjoy a high income. These people are concentrated in the professions and the executive positions of industry and the arts. Members of this group choose to live in the city largely because of its cultural offerings, but rarely have strong ties to a neighborhood.

> THE ONLY BIRD THAT GIVES THE POOR A REAL TUMBLE IS THE STORK.
> WILSON MITZNER

Quick Glance

Determinist theory states informal social control remains strong in the city.   T   F

Gans says that cities destroy in-groups.   T   F

Ethnic villagers live in the city because of high welfare payments.   T   F

Subcultural Theory

The subcultural theory was proposed by Claude Fischer and forms an intermediary position between the two preceding theories. The **subcultural theory** maintains that the very size of a city's population promotes the development of a variety of subcultures. People of similar interest are able to band together by sheer numbers because people of similar characteristics are in relatively close proximity. There are close, personal relationships within the subculture.

THINKING SOCIOLOGY

Why do people choose to live in the city? In the suburbs?

What Are the Suburbs?

Suburbanization may be defined as the movement of people from central cities to smaller communities in the surrounding area. Although suburbanization has taken place to some degree in many developed nations, it has been more extensive in North America than elsewhere. Approximately 39% of all Americans now live in the suburbs.

Why has suburbia become common in the United States?

 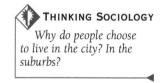

Quick Glance

Fischer combines Gans'
and Wirth's theory.   T F

Suburbanization is the
movement of people from
central cities to smaller
communities in the
surrounding area.   T F

As the population of the
U.S.A. has desired larger
homes, suburbia has
become a phenomena. T F

The suburbs are predomi-
nately a middle-class
phenomena.   T F

The U.S.A. Government
has contributed to
suburbanization.   T F

1. *Residential use of land had to compete with other land uses.* Increasingly, the land near central business districts has been taken over by parking lots and commercial uses. As a result, less land is available for residential use.

2. *Production has shifted to tertiary industry, law firms, hotels, health spas, accounting firms, etc.* The spreading out of jobs reinforces the spreading out of residences.

3. *The population is richer and can afford cars and homes.*

4. *The improved automobile, highways, public transportation and communication systems* have made it practical to move away from the central city.

5. *People want larger homes.* They can afford them now. Many families are willing to commute to work in order to obtain more room in their housing.

6. *The government has helped people afford home ownership.* The federal government allows tax write-offs for interest payments. Moreover, both the United States and Canadian governments have made it possible for the average family to afford a mortgage.

▲ DUE TO DESIRE FOR LARGER HOMES, THE SUBURBS HAVE GROWN.
IMAGE COPYRIGHT ANNE KITZMAN, 2008. USED UNDER LICENSE FROM SHUTTERSTOCK, INC.

One of the interesting suburban movements occurring now is called the rurban movement. The **rurban** movement is the shifting of urban people into rural areas in nonfarming capacity. Many small towns around major cities have experienced growth, and farm areas along major highways have been stripped by rows of houses with septic tanks and water wells.

THINKING SOCIOLOGY

What problems do you see with living in the suburbs? Are they different from urban problems? How?

Quick Glance

CBD stands for College
Better Degree.   T F

Urban living means
that the number of
people per square mile
increases.   T F

Services tend to concentrate in the CBD. T F

Cities grow along the path
of least resistance.   T F

People segregate into
natural areas.   T F

WHAT ARE THE MAJOR URBAN ECOLOGICAL PROCESSES?

The first major ecological process is that cities tend to grow up on trade routes, and trade tends to follow the topography of least resistance. Wherever there is a break in the trade route, a city tends to arise. Houston, Chicago, New York, Galveston, Los Angeles are all examples of cities that have developed from travel shifting from sea to land. Atlanta is a hub for a major airline. This is an artificially developed break in trade route.

The second ecological process is the concentration of people into a limited area. Urban living means that the number of people per square mile increases. Areas like Hong Kong and Singapore have very high concentrations of people. Earlier in this chapter is a table showing population per square mile.

The third ecological process is the concentration of services. Services tend to concentrate in what is called the Central Business District, or **CBD**. I can remember as a little girl my grandmother going downtown and having her hair and nails done; seeing a lawyer; seeing the dentist or doctor; buying a new dress, gloves and shoes; buying groceries; and hopping on a bus to come back home. Downtown areas used to be the heart of a community where products and services were readily available. Many cities now, such as Houston, have become business centers due to the availability of transportation and communication services.

The fourth ecological process is decentralization. After conditions become congested, services and products start to leave the centralized area and become decentralized. Shopping and industry move to the suburban fringe. Medical care and other professional services, such as accountants, move to the suburban fringe.

The fifth ecological process is the segregation into natural areas. People do this in order to provide continuity with the old culture, to see new country and culture through eyes of our own culture, in order for fellow countrymen to soften the blow of change and help assimilation. Subdivisions also form natural areas. Many suburbs have housing that shares similar life styles and incomes. Suburbs become income ghettos.

The sixth ecological process is invasion and succession. Inner city areas which used to be upper class become lower class. Areas in Boston and New York which originally were ritzy areas became slum areas. In some cities, middle-class people are now moving back into these areas and refurbishing the houses into middle-class, single dwellings once again.

Gentrification is the settlement and renovation of rundown inner-city neighborhoods by affluent newcomers. These people tend to be young, white, highly educated professionals who are already residents of the city. In most cases, the renovators have replaced poor and often minority tenants for whom rising property values mean higher rents, taxes and prices. The gentrification of central cities is due to the maturing of the "baby boom" generation, a shortage of urban housing, the higher cost of suburban houses, the inconvenience of commuting, an appreciation of historic neighborhoods and advantages of city life.

The seventh ecological process is migration. Migration means mobility in space. We each experience three types of mobility. First is migration to the city. People are still leaving the rural areas and moving into the city. Second is changes in residence. The third type of migration is daily movement of people. Most of us start out in our automobile early in the morning as we drive to work and school; we drive to grocery stores and other shopping areas. The automobile has become a way of life in the United States, and our ratio of cars to people is the highest in the world.

THINKING SOCIOLOGY
Would you rather live in the city or in a rural area?

Quick Glance

Gentrification benefits everyone.	T F
People continue to migrate to the city.	T F
The U.S. has the highest ratio of cars to people in the industrialized world.	T F
Gentrification has partially come about because of maturing "baby boomers."	T F

THINKING SOCIOLOGY
What area in your city has experienced gentrification?

▼ CHAPTER SUMMARY

1. The world population has reached the five billion mark. Demography studies the growth of population.

2. Thomas Malthus wrote the first essay on population. Malthus observed that population increased geometrically while food production increased arithmetically. He identified both positive checks and preventive checks on population. Modern-day followers of Malthus are referred to as Neo-Malthusians.

3. Both pronatalist and antinatalist views exist in the United States. The pronatalist policies are in favor of large birth rates while antinatalist policies are in favor of limiting the number of births.

4. Zero Population Growth (ZPG) has been difficult to achieve because of religious norms, individual needs contradicting the needs of the country, military protection, traditional values and ignorance.

5. The demographic transition theory analyzes changes in birth and death rates. Birth and death rates are considered in the four stages included in the theory.

6. Rapid population growth has negative consequences for both underdeveloped and developing nations.

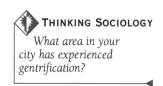

Learning TIP
Stop procrastinating. Do work when assigned rather than right before it is to be submitted.

7. Solutions to the population problem include increasing the death rate, migrating from an overpopulated area to a less populated area, using birth control and increasing food production.

8. Although "The Green Revolution" has worked well in the United States, it faces difficulties because it is based on the use of hybrid seed, heavy use of fertilizer and use of machinery.

9. The proportion of males to females (sex ratio) is affected by immigration and emigration, war casualties and age of population.

10. Fertility is measured by the crude birthrate and the annual number of live births per 1,000 women ages 15 to 44.

11. The concentric zone theory, the sector theory and the multiple nuclei theory analyze patterns of urban growth.

12. The urban way of life has been identified by the determinist theory, the compositional theory and the subcultural theory.

13. Suburbanization has become a phenomenon in the United States. Many reasons account for this phenomenon.

14. The major urban ecological processes include the following: cities tend to grow up on trade routes, concentration of people into a limited area, invasion and succession, concentration of services, decentralization, segregation into natural areas and migration.

▼ REFERENCES

Burgess, Ernest. 1924. The Growth of The City. *Publications of the American Sociological Society*, 18, 85–97.

Davis, Kingsley and Wilbert E. Moore. 1945. "Some Principles of Stratification." *American Sociological Review*, 10 (April): 242–249.

Ehrlich, Paul. 1968. *The Population Bomb*. New York: Ballantine Books.

Fischer, Claude. 1975. "Toward a Subcultural Theory of Urbanism." *American Journal of Sociology*. 80 (May): 1319–1341.

Fischer, Claude. 1984. *The Urban Experience*, 2nd ed. San Diego: Harcourt Brace Jovanovich.

Gans, Herbert. 1962. *The Urban Villagers*. New York: Free Press.

Gans, Herbert. 1968. *People and Plans: Essays on Urban Problems and Solutions*. New York: Basic Books, 36–38.

Gottman. 1964. *Megalopolis: The Urbanized Northeastern Seaboard of the United States*. Cambridge, Mass.: M.I.T. Press.

Jencks, Christopher, Marshall Smith, Henry Acland, Mary Jo Bae, David Cohen, Herbert Gintis, Barbara Heynes, and Stephan Michelson. 1972. *Inequalty: A Reassessment of the Effect of Family and Schooling in America*. New York: Basic Books, 209–211.

Harris, Chauncey and Edward Ullman. 1945. "The Nature of Cities." *Annals of the American Academy of Political and Social Science*, 242, 7–17.

Hoyt, Homer. 1939. *The Structure and Growth of Residential Neighborhoods in American Cities*. Washington, D.C.: U.S. Government Printing Office.

Laska, Shirley B. and Daphne Spain. 1980. *Back to the City: Issues in Neighborhood Renovation*. Elmsford, NY: Pergamon Press.

Malthus, Thomas. 1978. *An Essay on the Principle of Population as it Affects the Future Improvement of Society*. London: Reeves and Turner.

Palen, J. John and Bruce London (Eds.). 1984. *Gentrification, Displacement, and Neighborhood Revitalization*. Albany, NY: Albany State University of New York Press.

Wirth, Louis, 1938. "Urbanism as a Way of Life." *American Journal of Sociology*, 44 (July): 3–24.

READING

THE NATIONS OF THE WESTERN COMMUNITY BY BEN WATTENBERG
AND KARL ZINSMEISTER*

The history of development is a history of declining birth rates. In 1780, U.S. women bore an average of about six children each. In 1880, it was down to between four and five. By 1980, the total fertility rate (TFR) stood at just 1.8 children per woman. Although the time frames are not identical, similar sorts of fertility reductions have been taking place in the rest of what is now the modern industrial world: in Canada, Western Europe, Japan, Australia, and New Zealand.

This long decline has been marked by major fluctuations, usually corresponding to wars or economic conditions. Our century has seen two such oscillations. During the worldwide depression of the 1930s, total fertility rates in many modern nations fell dramatically, implying population loss for many of them if the rates held. By 1939, however, before actual declines could set in, most nations had returned to above-replacement fertility, although barely so.

The other noteworthy recent aberration in the long line of Western fertility decline was the post-World War II "Baby Boom." With the demobilization of armies following peace in 1945, G. I. Joe and Rosie the Riverter—along with their counterparts in both Axis and Alliance nations—did some notable catching up. The total fertility rate reached about 3.0 in both France and the United Kingdom. In the United States, fertility rose sharply and stayed up, peaking at 3.8 children per woman in 1957. The result was a tidal wave of baby boom babies born from 1945 to 1965.

But once the baby boom ended, birth rates resumed their decline throughout the modern world. In the United States, the total fertility rate tumbled from a high of 3.8 children per woman in 1957 to 1.7 just nineteen years later. That is well below the crucial "population replacement" threshold of 2.1 children per woman. (If, on average, each couple doesn't produce at least two children plus an increment for child mortality, in the long run the population will fall, absent immigration.) The successor generation is on a track that would produce children at half the rate of their parents! The baby boom has turned into a Birth Dearth.

As of 1983, West Germany and Denmark have the lowest national fertility rates in the world. West German and Danish women are bearing a lifetime average of 1.3 children; Italy and the Netherlands are at 1.5; Japan averages 1.7; France, the United States, and the United Kingdom today stand at 1.8. Overall, the Western community of nations averages 1.76. That is 15 percent below replacement, and probably still falling in many nations. It is not a brand new phenomenon: most Western nations have been at below-replacement rates for a decade or more.

In the West, below-replacement fertility is near-universal: it obtains in both Catholic and Protestant nations in Europe, among Asians in Japan, and for both blacks and whites in the United States. It is a phenomenon which cuts across racial, ethnic, and religious lines. It is probably best described as a product of modernism.

The United States, Canada, and Australia accept significant numbers of immigrants, but not nearly enough to keep a 1.8 fertility rate from ultimately leading to substantial population loss in years to come.

Under the current pattern, total population of the industrial democracies will have moved from the high growth rates of the recent past, to current low growth rates, to stability during the next few decades, and then—unless present rates are dramatically changed—to decline.

🐦 *Quick Glance*

Fertility rate has remained stable in the U.S.A. since 1945.   T   F

Italy and Denmark have higher fertility rates than the United States.   T   F

Low fertility rate is a result of modernism.   T   F

---

*Reprinted with the permission of The American Enterprise Institute for Public Policy Research, Washington, D.C.

Such growth, as is expected, is only a demographic echo of the earlier baby boom; many mothers, even with small families, still tend to increase population—but only for a while. World Bank projections reveal that from a level of 732 million today, Western community population will likely increase by a further 8 to 9 percent over thirty-five years, peaking at about 795 million around the year 2020. By 2065, when today's babies will be approaching the end of their life span, the current industrial democracies as a group will have shrunk to 683 million. If one were to carry out these projections in a straight line for one more lifetime—to 2150—Western population would be down to 484 million, just two-thirds of the current total. (If the current fertility freefall goes even lower before stabilizing—as some demographers expect—the future drop would be even sharper.)

And loss of numbers will not be the only problem. The age structure of the population will shift in important ways as fertility stays low. In the next decade, the number of young adults will drop sharply. (Think of armed forces levels.) Within fifty years the fraction of the Western population that is sixty-five or older will double, from 12 percent to 24 percent. (Think of pensions and health care.)

Does Population Matter?

It is quite possible that modern nations and cultures can remain strong for a long while even in the face of the sharp absolute—and even sharper relative—population declines. World history is full of examples of small populations preserving or extending their influence through superior organization, technology, or spirit. As early as 500 B.C., the Greek city states were able to dominate societies many times larger than their own, thanks to innovative military techniques. Rome's superb roads allowed Rome to project power all along a 7,000-mile frontier in Europe and North Africa while its army was never any larger than 500,000 (and usually closer to a third of that).

But to acknowledge that there can be compensations for smaller populations is not to say that population doesn't matter. While it is not at all clear where the tipping point lies today, it has generally been true that no amount of technical superiority could balance a gross population disadvantage over an extended period of time.

For big powers and dominant cultures, the critical relationship seems to be this: a large population is no guarantee of great-power status, but it is one necessary precondition. Virtually every great power in history has either had a relatively large population itself, or has held sway over the economic production and manpower of large populations influenced by the mother state or mother culture.

This remains true even in an age of missiles and submarines. The advantages of a large labor force, big military establishments, and the economies of scale and production are simply too important to lasting global influence.

Larger populations produce larger GNPs, and brute economic production is one critical aspect of national strength and security. Moreover, within limits, population growth can break down institutional rigidities, and sharply quicken the pace of economic change and innovation, with favorable results for national power. Economist Alvin Hansen suggested that perhaps two-thirds of the growth of U.S. economic output from its founding up to the time of World War I was caused by population growth. This occurred both directly, via increases in the labor supply, and indirectly, through the productivity enhancements of such things as longer production runs.

Larger and denser populations—again, within reasonable limits—can also more easily build the infrastructure of industry, transport, and communications that support national defense. Power is in some way related to the number of railroad cars, cyclotrons, hospitals, electric plants, and universities a nation possesses. Further, attaining technological leadership requires a large body of scientists. And only a substantial consumer market can support broad industrial innovation and a major research and development sector. In none of these areas is a large population enough to produce success in and of itself. But in each instance, a big nation is likely to have a strategic advantage.

One of the lessons of the U.S. Civil War was that a larger population and economic base can contribute a great deal to overpowering superior military prowess. Likewise, America's logistical advantage over the Japanese, which was calculated by the Japanese themselves at ten to one, ultimately outweighed disadvantages of surprise and preparation in the Pacific during World War II. Even in an atomic age, it is sometimes forgotten, only large populations have tax bases broad enough to support the defense systems that are the basis of national power and security.

Perhaps the clearest example of a national security system that could not possibly be built by other than large nations is the Strategic Defense Initiative, popularly known as "Star Wars." At an estimated cost of approximately $300 billion, it could be put together only by amortizing it over a large population.

The national security benefits of a substantial population accrue most clearly to nations that are already developed. But even when very poor or disorganized, large nations must be taken seriously in global calculations of power. China and India, for instance, both have per capita GNPs of under $300. But because of the aggregate size of their economic production, their masses of soldiers and the near-impossibility of an occupier subduing such large populations, they are accorded national power out of all proportion to their level of development. One of the clearest indications of this is the Soviets' positioning over fifty of their troop divisions on or near the Chinese border. (Not unrelated to population resources, both China and India are also nuclear powers.)

Compensations

Clearly, modern military technology can go a long way in helping to compensate for an inferior population level, as the Israelis—a nation of 4 million surrounded by more than 100 million hostile or potentially hostile neighbors—have amply demonstrated. But several things must be remembered. First, Israel had its own population explosion. If Israel's Jewish population had remained at the 600,000 figure that was the level when the state was founded in 1948, there would likely be no Israel today. More to the point, if not for the special nature of its relationship with the United States, a nation as small as Israel would find it extremely difficult and perhaps impossible to afford the sophisticated weapons that are necessary to its survival. The United States provides Israel with credits and subsidies of several billion dollars per year—nearly $1,000 per Israeli citizen—and even so the Israelis must devote 30 percent of their GNP to defense, require military service up to age forty-nine, and operate on a permanently militarized footing. The Israeli example, therefore, can hardly be taken as a general model for overcoming the national security disadvantages of a low population base.

Besides, most nations, in most circumstances, cannot assume they will have a continuing technological advantage over their rivals. And when opposing societies maintain an approximately equal level of scientific, material, and industrial advancement, population level can become a vital differentiator of national power. That is why—as history has demonstrated—it can be extremely destabilizing when traditional competitors suddenly take divergent demographic paths.

Politics and Culture

If population plays a heavy role in both the military and military-related economic spheres, it should be clear that it is also potent in the political realm, where wealth

Quick Glance

Large populations are a necessary but not sufficient basis for super-power status.   T F

Population size affects GWP and the pace of economic change.   T F

Large populations can overpower military power.   T F

Quick Glance

Factors such as technology can never fully compensate for shrinking population size.　　　　T　F

Housing market will face difficulties with shrinking population.　　　　T　F

Wealthy nations influence other cultures due to monies and other mass media.　　　　T　F

and power are the chips in the games that nations play. For example, in a world increasingly interdependent in economic matters, the sheer sizes of domestic markets and labor forces are critical variables in international competitiveness. America's wealthy continental market of 240 million people gives it geopolitical influence and leverage that smaller populations do not have. How many Hondas can you sell to Holland? Conversely, it is no accident that Holland does not produce 747s.

The linkages continue: the influence of population on power, economics, and politics relates, in turn, to culture and values. Weak nations tend to emulate strong ones. Wealthy nations export goods and services—like movies and television programs—that indirectly transmit values and culture. There is an economy of scale in many aspects of culture just as there is in military weaponry. Nations that are populous and wealthy enough to build aircraft carriers can also amortize the cost of a multitude of high-quality (and thus influential) films, sitcoms, and traveling art exhibits.

Economic Turmoil

THINKING SOCIOLOGY

Do you agree or disagree with the authors of this article? What impact, if any, do you see on the military and economy of the U.S.A. in facing shrinking population?

Before beginning our speculations on the geopolitical future, it is worth noting in passing that the mechanics of low fertility are such that the West may be headed for a difficult time economically in the intermediate to long-range future. Europe, North America, Japan, and Australia will likely be aging, with fewer and fewer young workers and fresh ideas fueling the bottom of the social pyramid. Many important economic markets will be disrupted at least temporarily. (What happens in the housing industry when and if vacancies due to death exceed the number of new entrants into the market?) There will likely be massive social welfare financing problems. Society will move from growth, to stasis, and then to absolute decline. It is uncharted water—a process that has not been experienced since the advent of the Industrial Revolution. At the very same time, then, that the Western community is declining demographically relative to its actual and potential competitors, it may also be losing some of the magic touch at home, or at least be enduring a bumpy transition.

Grilling the Government

11

IMAGE COPYRIGHT TAD DENSON, 2008. USED UNDER LICENSE FROM SHUTTERSTOCK, INC.

CHAPTER OBJECTIVES

1. What is government?
2. What is power?
3. What are types of authority?
4. What are the forms of government?
5. What are the functions of government?
6. What are the trends in the government of the United States?
7. What are the models of power structure in the United States?
8. What influences voter participation in the United States?
9. How do the theories differ in assessing the government?

▼ KEY TERMS

authoritarian government: a political system whereby the leader is not elected by the people of the society

authority: a power identified as legitimate

charismatic authority: the authority that is based on the leader's ability to appeal to the emotions of people

democracy: rule by the people

dictatorship: rule by one person

elitism: the belief in the existence of an elite few who actually make key decisions that affect the masses of people

expert power: the power based upon the person possessing information and being sought for guidance

force: the use of coercion to get what is desired

government: the social institution that has the power and authority to decide and distribute the resources of the social structure and is formally organized

ideal type: a model that is used as a measuring stick for the evaluation of actual cases

influence: the technique of coaxing others to do what we want them to do

informational power: the power based on knowledge of the facts and control of information

legitimacy: given the right to do something

monarchy: a government based on an inherited position of power

oligarchy: a rule by a few or small group of people

pluralism: the belief that many powerful groups exist in the United States and compete with one another to influence decisions

political alienation: the belief that a person cannot change the decision-making process through political participation such as voting

political institution: an institution dealing with means and processes by which a society maintains order

political socialization: the acquisition of political attitudes and behavior

power: the ability to cause others to do what we want them to do

rational-legal authority: the authority based on laws

referent power: the power based on people identifying strongly with a leader and wanting to follow and emulate that person

reward power: the power based on return of money or power from the leader if allegiance is given

state: a political body with broad jurisdiction for decision making found in technologically advanced societies

totalitarian state: a government where total control is exerted over the people in the society

traditional authority: a legitimate power given by custom or common practice

▼ KEY PEOPLE

William Greider, William Kornhauser, Seymour M. Lipset, C. Wright Mills, P. J. O'Rourke, David Riesman, Max Weber

WHAT IS GOVERNMENT?

We are now going to shift our attention to presenting a chapter on each of the five institutions which make up a society. In primitive or preliterate societies, the five institutions are blended into the family unit, but in technologically advanced societies, each institution takes on importance in its own right. The first institution we are going to discuss is the government.

Like the social institution of the family, religion, economics and education, the political institution is a cultural universal. All societies have a political institution. The **political institution** consists of those means and processes by which a society maintains order; the political institution is the larger, overall regulation dealing with the general welfare of the tribe, community or state. For many centuries, and in many cultures, kinship and local communities were the centers of political organization. In societies in which the extended family was the central unit, the emphasis of the political institution was on the primary group. The Masaii of Kenya, for example, was a society centered around a clan and age-grade system. The focus of the Masaii at the local level was the clan; older males and heads-of-household made decisions for the smaller family units which consisted of three to five closely related families. On larger issues, the older warriors made decisions. After a male became a warrior at about age 16 and had served his society through war and long-distance herding of cattle, he then graduated to being an older warrior who acted as a statesman. These men informally met and discussed issues for the clans and served as judges and juries for disagreements that went beyond the extended family unit. This, however, was not a formalized system; the system was supported by tradition rather than written law.

When a society develops a definition of national boundaries, a breaking down of local barriers to trade and communication, political integration under a central agency and a uniform system of education transmitting an official and unifying language, a formalized political institution develops. A society that has these characteristics generally has developed an agricultural system based on irrigation and use of tools and/or an industrial base. When we discuss these types of societies, we have the development of a state or nation state. With the development of the state, the political institution becomes formalized into what is called a government. A **government** is the social and cultural system establishing formal methods for acquiring and exercising power within a given jurisdiction through agencies believed to have legitimate authority. The government has the power and authority to decide and distribute the resources within the state and to use physical coercion to ensure conformity to the cultural norms institutionalized into laws. We have been using two words that need further clarification, power and authority.

Quick Glance

Government is a cultural universal.　　T F

Some political systems are based on kinship.　　T F

All political organizations are governments.　　T F

A government is a formalized system of political organization.　T F

THINKING SOCIOLOGY

What types of power do you have? Explain.

WHAT IS POWER?

Power is the ability to force others to do what is wanted. The government of the United States has been granted the power to make broad decisions that affect the citizens of our nation state. According to P. J. O'Rourke, this power ranges from taking between a fifth and a quarter of all my money every year to analyzing the amount of tropical oils in my snack foods and coffee creamer. Furthermore, the government tells me what kind of gasoline I can buy for my car and how fast I can drive. The government tells me, the business manager, whether the door to my office or shop should have a wheelchair ramp. The government tells me what and where I can smoke. The government, in essence, exercises power.

There are three primary sources of power within the political systems. *Force or coercion is the use of physical or psychological duress to get what is desired.* By sheer physi-

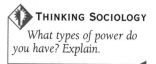

cal strength, compliance is gained. Airplane hijackers use coercion to convince others to do what they want. The force is normally in the form of demands that are to be met or people will lose their lives. When a person comes to trial for murder, it is the "state" versus Smith. If Smith is convicted of capital murder, it is the state that either imprisons the person or puts the person to death.

Influence is not as strong as force and refers to techniques of coaxing others to do what we want them to do. There are several ways that we can coax others:

1. **Reward power** is based on return of money or power from the leader if allegiance is given. If, for example, I support a political candidate with large donations, I might hope to gain an appointed governmental position. This was one of the concerns with the very large donations given to Bill Clinton for his inauguration celebration during 1992. President George Bush came under fire in 2002 because of contributions by Enron to his campaign. In January 2006, Jack Abramoff, a lobbyist, is causing several elected officials anxiety due to some questionable donations.

2. **Informational power** is concerned with who knows the facts and controls the information. People who know and control information control those people around them. When spouses let their significant other maintain all the financial records and do not keep abreast of these matters, those spouses gain informational power.

3. **Expert power** is closely akin to informational power. When someone is an expert in an area, it is logical to turn to that person for guidance. If my personal computer fails to work properly, I seek an expert in the field to make the repairs.

4. **Referent power** happens when people identify strongly with a leader and want to follow and emulate that person. Martin Luther King possessed influence with his public speeches, such as his speech that we have come to think of as "I Have a Dream. . . ."

🦅 Quick Glance

Power is the ability to make others do what we want.   T   F

Government possesses power.   T   F

Force means influence.   T   F

Coercion is the use of physical power.   T   F

Influence is the same as force.   T   F

Authority is never legitimate.   T   F

Ideal type is an actually occurring situation.   T   F

Max Weber designed an ideal type of authority.   T   F

▲ JUDGES HAVE INFLUENCE AND AUTHORITY.

🔦 THINKING SOCIOLOGY

What is the difference between charismatic leader and referent power?
◀

The third form of power is called legitimacy. **Legitimacy** is based on the use of power as authorized by the society. A group judges that the leader has sanctioned use of power. As employees we often accept the demands of our bosses because that power is legitimate. Parents also feel that they have power based on legitimacy and children feel like they have to obey because guidance of children is part of the parental role.

WHAT ARE TYPES OF AUTHORITY?

When we speak of legitimate power, we speak of authority. **Authority** is power that is identified as legitimate. There are three types of authority: traditional, charismatic and rational-legal. These three types of authority are ideal types. The term ideal type was used by sociologist Max Weber. An ideal type is a model that is used as a measuring stick for the evaluation of actual cases.

Traditional authority is given by custom or common practice. It is based on "what was done in the past." An example of traditional authority is a monarchy; the Royal family of England possesses traditional authority. Family and clergy have this kind of authority. There are some families who have dominated politics in the U.S. and can be said to have traditional authority, for example, members of the Roosevelt and Kennedy family.

Chapter 11: Grilling the Government
Essay Questions

Complete the following 6 questions on Chapter 11: Grilling the Government and turn in by Monday, April 7th. I will give you 5 extra credit points for having it in class and completed.

1. Compare and contrast political institution and government.
2. Discuss the three types of authority. Which one is the U.S.? *p. 212*
3. Know and understand the difference between the 5 forms of authoritarian government *p. 213*
4. Compare and contrast the characteristics and features of an authoritarian government and democracy. *p. 213*
5. The textbook gives you the manifest functions of government: use critical thinking and give examples of possible latent functions of the U.S. government (refer to Chapter 1).
6. Discuss the four reasons people vote. Discuss the reasons people do not vote. *p. 222*

Charismatic authority is based on the ability of the individual leader to appeal to the emotions of people; it is based on "who said it." Charismatic authority depends on personal magnetism. People who had charismatic authority include Jesus Christ, Martin Luther King, John F. Kennedy, Ronald Reagan, Adolph Hitler of Germany, Fidel Castro of Cuba, Ayatollah Khomeini of Iran and Mahatma Gandhi of India. These people had the ability to make others believe in their personal missions and thus were obeyed.

The government of the United States is thought to utilize the third type of authority characterized by Max Weber, rational-legal authority. *Rational-legal authority is based on laws.* The leaders derive their authority from the written rules and regulations established by the society. This authority is based on "what the rules say." The government of the U.S. is based on rational-legal authority as established by the United States Constitution. The Prime Minister in Great Britain has rational-legal authority.

Even when a government is based on rational-legal authority, charismatic authority still remains important. Such people as Winston Churchill and Margaret Thatcher of Britain had rational-legal authority, but they also were very charismatic. In order to be elected president of the United States, a person usually must be a charismatic leader in order to draw votes. Ronald Reagan, John F. Kennedy and Bill Clinton are well-known for their charm. Leaders such as John F. Kennedy had all three forms of authority; rational-legal, traditional and charismatic.

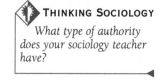

THE FUNCTION OF GOVERNMENT MUST BE TO FAVOR NO SMALL GROUP AT THE EXPENSE OF ITS DUTY TO PROTECT THE RIGHTS OF PERSONAL FREEDOM AND OF PRIVATE PROPERTY OF ALL ITS CITIZENS.

F. D. ROOSEVELT

THINKING SOCIOLOGY
What type of authority does your sociology teacher have?

WHAT ARE THE FORMS OF GOVERNMENT?

Authoritarian systems of government have been very common throughout human history and in many cultures. In an **authoritarian government**, the leadership does not necessarily reflect the will of the people and the people cannot legally change the leadership. There are several types of authoritarian governments which include a **monarchy** (hereditary leadership), **dictatorship** (rule by one person), **oligarchy** (rule by small group of people), **military junta** (rule by military leaders) and **colonial democracy** (small group of colonizers rule native populations). An authoritarian can also be called a **totalitarian government** (rule by dictatorship or oligarchy but control is total).

Quick Glance

Traditional power is based on inheritance. T F

The U.S.A. government is based on charismatic authority. T F

A monarchy is a form of charismatic authority. T F

A Supreme Court justice has rational-legal authority. T F

Authoritarian Government

Authoritarian governments share several or all of the following characteristics:

1. *An authoritarian government involves large-scale use of ideology.* Authoritarian societies offer explanations of every part of life. Social goals, valued behaviors, even enemies, are conveyed in simple, sometimes distorted, terms. The People's Republic of China, Cuba and the U.S.S.R. were based on the communistic ideology as spelled out by Karl Marx in Communist Manifesto. Louis the XIV said that "I am the state" and expected his subjects to accept him at that evaluation. The pharohs of Egypt were directly descended from the God.

2. *An authoritarian government has a one-party system.* Authoritarian states are one-party systems led by dictators or a collective leadership. The one party is the only legal party in the state and monopolizes the offices of government. The U.S.S.R. had elections every year, for example, during the 1960s, but only one party was listed; therefore, the choice was quite easy for all the citizens who were required by law to vote.

THINKING SOCIOLOGY
What type of power, influence and/or authority does Laura Bush have?

Quick Glance

An authoritarian government is always a democracy. T F

An authoritarian government can be a monarchy. T F

An oligarchy is rule by the masses. T F

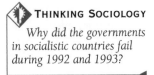
THERE ARE NO EVIL THOUGHTS EXCEPT ONE: THE REFUSAL TO THINK.

AYN RAND

3. *An authoritarian government is frequently based on the use of terror.* Terror is used to maintain control. Torture and interrogation may be used both against internal and external enemies of the regime. Dictators in several South American countries have been accused of using torture in questioning political dissidents. Fidel Castro imprisoned journalists who contradicted his economic plans.

4. *An authoritarian government monopolizes the media.* The media communicates "official" interpretations of events and reinforces behaviors that the regime wants or expects. Russia is currently rewriting its history from what was presented during the reign of the dictatorship (i.e. Stalin and Lenin).

5. *An authoritarian government controls weapons.* This is one of the arguments against having arms control in our own country because totalitarian governments control arms.

6. *An authoritarian government directs the economy or major portions of the economy.* Each industrial and agricultural sector may have specified goals to meet. It may also dissolve private ownership of either industry or farms. The People's Republic of China has put much of the farmlands back into private control and production.

7. *An authoritarian government controls the other institutions.* In the People's Republic of China, for example, the government has influenced the family by its "single-child" policy. The government controls education and, in many authoritarian states, rids the country of religious organizations. By controlling or destroying the independence of most institutions and groups, the authoritarian government is like the "Big Brother" society that George Orwell portrayed in the book *1984.* During the Middle Ages, the Vatican (the Catholic Church) took control over the educational system and controlled great areas of wealth within the European continent.

Democracy

The second form of government is called a **democracy**. This form of government means control by the people. Within a democracy, there are opportunities for a change in leadership according to what the citizens want. A good example of a democracy is among hunters and gatherers. The adult members gather together to make the decisions that affect the whole group. The democracy among hunters and gatherers is called a direct democracy. The other type of democracy is called a representative democracy. We have a representative democracy because the geographical area and population size is too great for a direct democracy. There are three types of representative democracies. The first is called a democratic republic. In this system, the chief executive (i.e. the president of the United

▲ VOTING IS NECESSARY IN A DEMOCRACY.
IMAGE COPYRIGHT KENNETH SUMMERS, 2008. USED UNDER LICENSE FROM SHUTTERSTOCK, INC.

States) is elected by popular vote. The second is called a constitutional monarchy. The monarch serves as a popular head but is not considered the chief executive. Great Britain is an example. The third type of democracy is called the parliamentary system. The chief executive is elected from the popularly elected parliament or legislature rather than by popular vote. Many constitutional monarchies also have a parliamentary system, i.e. Great Britain. Israel is an example of a country with a parliamentary system but no monarch.

A representative democracy shares several common features:

THINKING SOCIOLOGY

Do party coalitions exist in the U.S.A.? Explain.

1. *A democracy is based on individualism.* This is the belief in the importance of the individual rather than the group. Individual rights must be protected.

2. *A democracy is a constitutional government* because it is based on bodies of law and legal traditions, both written and unwritten, that stand above the individual, the government and the society. These traditions form the basic law of the land and serve to define the distribution and limits of political power. Several examples include the Magna Carta, Rights of Man and the United States Constitution.

3. *A democracy is based on loyal opposition.* After a very bitter election during the fall of 1992, President Bush lost the election to Governor Clinton. In his speech after the election, President Bush said, in essence, "let's all pull together and work for a greater society; drop the bad that happened in the election and realize that we are all citizens of the United States." Whether the political processes incorporate a two-party system or a multiple-party system, the democratic values stress that dissent is distinct from disloyalty and that differing points of view should have a means of expression. Whether in groups or in parties, citizens should have the right to voice opinions.

4. *A democracy is culturally diverse and open.* There are many organizations, voluntary associations and single-issue movements, as well as, secondary groups to represent religious, ethnic, racial, regional and economic interests.

5. *A democracy is based on a party system.* The United States is characterized by a two-party system. All democracies have at least two parties.

Quick Glance

The U.S.A. has a two-party system unlike many European countries.   T F

The Democratic party appeals only to those of the working class.   T F

There are factions within each of the two major parties in the U.S.A.   T F

Candidates never switch party affiliations.   T F

The "independent" voting coalition is gaining strength.   T F

A labor party has developed in the U.S.A. because of the belief in equality.   T F

A labor party has not developed in the U.S.A. because of the influence of labor unions.   T F

Some democracies, such as Sweden or Italy, have many parties that form coalitions when votes come up. We traditionally have had two strong parties in recent history; these are the Democrats and the Republicans. The Democrats have traditionally been supported by the poor and working class. Since the Democrats attract the poor and working class, the party tends to attract minority groups. Highly educated liberals are sometimes attracted to this party. This party is sometimes called a leftist-party (or left-wing). The Republicans however, have traditionally been supported by business people. The party is considered more conservative (right-wing) and is associated with the middle and upper classes. But even within each of the parties, there are two basic factions: liberal Democrats versus conservative Democrats and liberal Republicans versus conservative Republicans. President Clinton, for example, campaigned as a moderate Democrat trying to draw from the Republican vote. The Republican Primary of 1992 had come out with an extremely conservative platform which alienated some Republican voters. The two-party system, however, remains strong because each party has only one candidate for each office and the candidate with the most votes wins the election.

Minority parties have tended to not become powerful in the United States because they have almost no chance of gaining a majority of the votes in a win-lose situation. Independent voters have almost become a third party because so many people identify themselves as being "independent" in this age of politics. This independent sector has grown because people are voting outside of their party line and because voters are more dissatisfied with the performance of elected officials from both parties. Some elected officials have even switched parties through the course of their lifetime in order to get elected to public office.

Learning TIP
Remember there are no "stupid" questions. The unasked question is the "stupid" question.

THINKING SOCIOLOGY

Explain "government" in your family in terms of a democracy or an authoritarian government.

Worker parties have not developed as a strong party or even a minority party in the United States as they have in other democracies such as Italy and Spain. The formation of a worker party has not happened in the United States for several reasons:

1. The Democrats say they are the party of the working man.
2. Labor unions form strong interest groups within the political system.
3. Workers are alienated or complacent.
4. We believe that "everyone can make it" in our country due to our egalitarian social philosophy.

We have an ethnocentric bias towards a democracy in our country; but in order for a modern democracy to work, certain conditions have to be met in a complex society.

1. advanced economic development
2. low inequality in income
3. urbanized, literate population
4. some restraints on government power such as laws limiting a presidency to two terms and impeachment procedures
5. free criticism by the press and other media
6. general consensus on basic values
7. tolerance of dissent
8. diffusion of power

If one group can monopolize power, a democracy will turn into a dictatorship. The United States Constitution, for example, separates the powers of the executive, legislative and judicial branches. There are also separate centers of power such as competing interest groups. This includes such organizations as labor unions, corporations, churches, etc.

WHAT ARE THE FUNCTIONS OF GOVERNMENT?

There are eight important functions of the government:

1. *The government institutionalizes the laws.* It is the government that says we drive on the right side of the road, pay income taxes and send our children to school.
2. *The government enforces norms of behavior considered important to the survival of the society.* Police, who represent the government, may give us tickets when we drive over the speed limit or arrest us for being abusive to another person.
3. *The government settles disputes and resolves conflicts.* This is the purpose of our criminal and civil courts. We have popularized this function with shows on television such as "Judge Judy" or "Divorce Court."
4. *The government is responsible for planning and coordinating activities that are necessary for the total society.* This may be organizing a giraffe hunt, planning a new road system or organizing an army to defend an ally. In his campaign of 2000, George Bush took on the task of improving education and reducing tax loads. Due to the suicide bombing of the Twin Towers, in his second campaign he focused on the War on Terrorism.
5. *The government is in charge of administration of the state.* The government of the United States runs the Social Security system and delegates task force committees to see to the issues.

Quick Glance

We are ethnocentric about democracy in the U.S.A.   T F

In order for a democracy to work, there must be a free press.   T F

A culture has to have economic development for a democracy to work.   T F

THINKING SOCIOLOGY

Which function of the government do you think is most important? Why?

A MIND STRETCHED TO A NEW IDEA NEVER GOES BACK TO ITS ORIGINAL DIMENSION.
OLIVER WENDELL HOLMES

Quick Glance

A government writes laws for the people.   T F

A government is responsible for planning societal activities.   T F

A government does not declare war.   T F

A government sometimes solves interpersonal conflict.   T F

THINKING SOCIOLOGY

What happens in a society where individuals can form armies and declare war?

6. *The government provides protection against enemies.* The President of the United States is also commander in chief of the armed services. It is up to the President and Congress to declare war on another country; as an individual, I cannot decide to form an army and fight in the name of the United States. Vietnam was never a "war" but a police action; Operation Desert Storm was a resolution to action decreed by our House of Representatives and Senate. The government is also responsible for protecting citizens against internal enemies such as terrorists.

7. *The government establishes societal goals such as full employment or education.* President Bush continues to push to get the economy going at a stronger pace, improving and standardizing education in kindergarten through high school and cutting taxes.

8. *The government allocates goods and services.* The government controls fire protection, police, water districts, telephone and telegraph and radio and television waves and collects social security taxes and income taxes in order to build roads, run schools, etc.

Quick Glance

Interest groups wield a great deal of power in the U.S.A.   T F

Interest groups have power because of having money.   T F

Interest groups have power because of organizational alliances.   T F

Greider states that legislation is influenced by public relations firms.   T F

WHAT ARE THE TRENDS IN THE GOVERNMENT OF THE UNITED STATES?

The first trend in our government is the tremendous power wielded by interest or lobby groups. Who gets what and how much is tremendously influenced by these groups. These groups are economic groups such as Chamber of Commerce, agricultural groups such as the American Dairy Association, professional groups such as the American Medical Association, special interest groups such as Greenpeace and American Association of Retired Persons, labor groups such as the American Federation of Teachers, veterans groups such as Veterans of Foreign Wars and ethnic or racial groups such as National Association for the Advancement of Colored Persons. Organized interest groups propose most of the statues passed by state legislatures and originate much legislation in Congress. Organizational power derives from several sources:

> GOVERNMENT, EVEN IN ITS BEST STATE, IS BUT A NECESSARY EVIL; IN ITS WORST STATE, AN INTOLERABLE ONE.
> THOMAS PAINE

1. yearly or monthly dues to provide money to campaigns
2. large membership to send money and write letters to influence the elected officials
3. bureaucratic structure designed to get a task completed
4. power orientation
5. organizational alliances used to combine influence

THINKING SOCIOLOGY
How has your political behavior been altered by media?

William Greider in his book *Who Will Tell the People: The Betrayal of American Democracy* looks at modern methodologies of persuasion, often originating in the public relations firms, direct mail companies and opinion-polling firms that are located in the Capitol. He believes that these modern methodologies have created a new hierarchy of influence over government decisions. He shows us today's Capitol Hill, where a lone congressman who tries to represent the public interest can find himself aligned against an army of well-paid "authorities." Where are the institutions designed to represent the people? Where are the unions? The political parties? The press? Gone, Greider writes, or transformed so radically that it no longer speaks for the United State's citizen.

▲ FREEDOM OF SPEECH IS NECESSARY IN A DEMOCRACY.
IMAGE COPYRIGHT ALEX HINDS, 2008. USED UNDER LICENSE FROM SHUTTERSTOCK, INC.

Quick Glance

The American election system has experienced reform.   T F

PACs are Peace Always Costs Something.   T F

There has been a reform in financing campaigns in the U.S.A.   T F

The government has been decreasing in size in the U.S.A.   T F

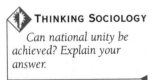

THINKING SOCIOLOGY

What form of election should be done if the electoral college is eliminated? How would the system be implemented?

Quick Glance

Government is becoming less involved in social issues.   T F

There has been an increase in the power of the Supreme Court.   T F

Supreme Court justices serve 4-year terms.   T F

THINKING SOCIOLOGY

Can national unity be achieved? Explain your answer.

The second trend has been the reformation of the election system. Since the 1970s, the American election system has seen reform. Two areas were at issue: nomination of candidates and raising of campaign monies. The corruption of party bosses caused great concern about the way public officials were nominated and financed. Local and state nominations are now decided by primaries open to all voters and national nominations are also filled in a primary system. After the primary election for president, representatives go to the national convention and the final choices are made, along with a party platform. Fund raising has also come under increasing scrutiny. Now, campaign money is given to the candidates through the state or federal government or by political action committees (PAC) representing private interest groups and individuals. PAC contributions include National Association of Realtors, International Brotherhood of Teamsters, American Medical Association, National Education Association, United Auto Workers and American Federation of State, County and Municipal Employees.

The third major trend is the growing size of government. Government is involved in areas it never used to be. For example, it controls what I can hunt and where I can hunt. And in many areas if I want to hunt or fish I must get a license from a governmental agency. The government is getting very involved in medical care due to Medicare and Medicaid. Due to technological change, government has become involved in regulating the mass media in order to control the number and placement of radio waves and television stations. Selfish interests such as subsidies to different groups have caused an increase in the size of government. This statement has been made against the tobacco industry because of government subsidies. The federal government also pays farmers not to put land into production to grow corn, wheat and soy beans or subsidizes farmers when crop prices are low.

There has been an increase in the power of the Supreme Court. We do not know if a law is law until it is passed upon by the Supreme Court. There has been discussion on limiting the terms of the Supreme Court justices because they do not have to retire and may serve beyond the time that they are physically and mentally able. A president also has the power to pack the court by members that agree with him during his term when there are available vacancies. The Supreme Court is now a judicial counterpart of the legislature. President Bush has appointed two Supreme Court justices during his second term in office. John Roberts and Samuel Alito were placed on the court in 2005 and 2006.

The electoral college has come under scrutiny. The electoral college was designed by our founding fathers who did not feel that a direct popular vote for the president was good. Now, much thought is given to popular election rather than to electoral vote. Presidents Nixon and Carter both tried to eliminate the electoral college, but the Senate has traditionally blocked this change. In the sense that the electoral college has and still could potentially elect a president other than that supported by popular vote, it is not democratic. For example, it is possible to have a very close popular vote, but the electoral college vote gives the illusion of being a landslide victory. For example, in the 1988 election, Dukakis received 45.6% of the popular vote and 111 electoral votes and Bush received 53.4% of the popular vote but received 426 of the electoral votes. The election of President Bush hinged on Florida's electoral votes. Then Governor Bush and Vice President Gore both needed the votes to win the election and it was settled in the courts.

The advantages and disadvantages of line-by-line veto by the president and state governors continue to be discussed. Without line-by-line, if a president wants a piece of legislation, he has to sign the whole package, including items he does not want. These are called "riders to bills" and frequently involve special interests. With line-by-line veto, the president or governor could exclude these and thus cut the cost of many pieces of legislation.

The government has shown great support and regulation of industry. There are anti-trust laws to prevent large companies from gaining a monopoly, but there is also support of industry. A good example of these is the governmental buyout and takeover of many savings and loans between 1990 and 1992. The U.S. Government also stepped in with financial support to the airlines such as Continental after September 11, 2001.

There has been a greater emphasis on national unity. The trip to the moon, the Olympics, the shuttle explosion, Operation Desert Storm and the War on Terrorism have increased national unity.

Relations with other nations have become more significant. Former President Nixon made inroads with the People's Republic of China and former President Bush had much interaction with the U.S.S.R. from the years 1988 to 1992 and faced issues dealing with Saddam Hussein during his term of office. After September 11, one of the first tasks President Bush did was to contact leaders of other countries to gain their support for a War on Terrorism. Colin Powell went to Palestine and Israel in April 2002 trying to establish peace.

Since the 1930s, more and more professionally trained persons, including lawyers, doctors, academicians, social workers and scientists, have become employees of the municipal, state and federal governments. This is largely a reflection of the increasing number and complexity of governmental functions and responsibilities and the resulting need for trained specialists in many fields, including economics, sociology, psychology and the natural sciences. Partly, but by no means entirely, because of the development of modern weaponry, scientists have come to play an important role in governmental activities, including the role of policy-making itself.

There have been changing characteristics in the composition of government personnel. More minorities such as Hispanics, African American, younger people and women are becoming involved in the political process. According to USA Today, February 17, 1999, 94% of people polled in a General Social Survey would vote for a woman for president if she were qualified for the job. Government is no longer the domain of white Anglo-Saxon Protestant males.

Many ethnic and religious groups have shifted their political affiliation. The election in 1992, saw many Republicans voting for the new moderate Democrats because of their promise to cut down the deficit and to promote job growth.

Quick Glance

The electoral college is a democratic system.   T   F

Line-by-line veto is accepted by the federal government.   T   F

Government is anti-industry.   T   F

National unity is important for the operation of government.   T   F

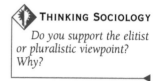

THINKING SOCIOLOGY

Do you support the elitist or pluralistic viewpoint? Why?

Learning TIP
Listen actively. Think about what the teacher is saying and take notes.

WHAT ARE THE MODELS OF POWER STRUCTURE IN THE UNITED STATES?

Who rules America? Two classic books have addressed this question: *The Power Elite* and *The Lonely Crowd.* C. Wright Mills, a political sociologist, wrote *The Power Elite.* Mills is credited with being the pioneer in identifying the elitist model of power. **Elitism** is the belief in the existence of an elite few who actually make key decisions that influence the masses of people. The elite is made up of the elite of the military, business and government. The elitist believes that there is a unified power elite drawn primarily from upper classes, that there is a diversified and balanced plurality of interest groups which wield no power because they are diversified, and a mass of unorganized people who have no power over the elite. This elitist group determines all major policies and manipulates people at the bottom. This is a monomorphic power structure.

David Riesman with Nathan Glazer and Reuel Denny wrote *The Lonely Crowd* and identified numerous observations concerning the United States culture. Riesman, Glazer and Denny agreed with the model of power structure known as pluralism. **Pluralism** is the belief that many powerful groups exist in the U.S. and compete with

Quick Glance

C. Wright Mills believed in pluralism.   T   F

Elitism believes that a small group of people control the government.   T   F

Pluralism takes into account interest groups in the government.   T   F

The elite form the basis of a polymorphic system.   T   F

TWO PORTRAITS OF THE AMERICAN POWER STRUCTURE

	Mills	Riesman
Levels	a. Unified power elite b. Diversified and balanced plurality of interest groups c. Mass of unorganized people who have no power over elite	a. No dominant power elite b. Diversified and balanced plurality of interest groups c. Mass of unorganized people who have some power over interest groups
Changes	a. Increasing concentration of power	a. Increasing dispersion of power
Operation	a. One group determines all major policies b. Manipulation of people at the bottom by group at the top	a. Who determines policy shifts with the issue b. Monopolistic competition among organized groups
Bases	a. Coincidence of interests among major institutions	a. Diversity of interests among major organized groups b. Sense of weakness and dependence among those in higher as well as lower status
Consequences	a. Enhancement of interests of corporations, armed forces, and executive branch of government b. Decline of politics as public debate c. Decline of responsible and accountable power-loss of democracy	a. No one group or class is favored significantly over others b. Decline of politics as duty and self-interest c. Decline of capacity for effective leadership

Source: Kornhauser, 1961.

Quick Glance

Kornhauser determined Mills to be correct in his book, *The Power Elite*. T F

Riesman is considered an elitist. T F

Kornhauser compared two books written about the Power Structure in the U.S.A. T F

> THE FINAL TEST OF A LEADER IS THAT HE LEAVES BEHIND HIM IN OTHER MEN THE CONVICTION AND THE WILL TO CARRY ON.
> WALTER LIPMANN

one another to influence decisions. With the pluralistic viewpoint, there is no dominant power elite but there is a diversified and balanced plurality of interest groups which do control decisions of government. The masses of unorganized people have some power over interest groups. These interest groups can be reformulated or new ones can be formed in order to gain access to the political system. Those groups which exercise power in one kind of decision do not necessarily exercise power in others.

William Kornhauser wrote an article entitled "'Power Elite' or 'Veto Groups'" which compared the books written by Mills and Riesman.

> *It would appear that* The Power Elite *has been most favorably received by radical intellectuals, and* The Lonely Crowd *has found its main response among liberals. Mills and Riesman have not been oblivious to their differences. Mills is quite explicit on the matter: Riesman is a "romantic pluralist" who refuses to see the forest of American power inequalities for the trees of short-run and discrete balances of power among diverse groups (Mills 244). Riesman has been less explicitly polemical, but he might have had Mills in mind when he spoke of those intellectuals "who feel themselves very much out of power and who are frightened of those who they think have the power," and who "prefer to be scared by the power structures they conjure up than to face the possibility that the power structure they believe exists has largely evaporated" (257–258).*

WHAT INFLUENCES VOTER PARTICIPATION IN THE UNITED STATES?

Political socialization is the acquisition of political attitudes and behavior. This is the process by which you acquire your political knowledge, beliefs, attitudes and behavior. One aspect of political socialization is voting behavior. What influences your vote?

 **THINKING SOCIOLOGY**

Why do you have your current party affiliation? Why did you vote the way you did in the last election?

1. Party affiliation and social class identification still influence voting behavior.
2. With party affiliation, there is a tendency to vote all, if not a large proportion, of a ballot as a straight ticket. The advent of voting machines makes this type of behavior easier since it involves the pulling or punching of one switch rather than a series of marks.
3. Most people tend to vote, at least at first, for the party that their parents' support.
4. Older and middle-aged people are more apt to register and vote than younger people. In fact, up until the golden years, the older the person, the more apt they were to vote. In the United States, only about half of those between 18 and 30 are registered to vote.
5. Better-educated people are more apt to vote than lesser educated.
6. European Americans are more likely to register and vote than African Americans or Hispanic Americans.
7. Males are more apt to vote than females.

> NURTURE YOUR MINDS WITH GREAT THOUGHTS. TO BELIEVE IN THE HEROIC MAKES HEROES.
> BENJAMIN DISRAELI

🕮 Quick Glance

Political socialization influences voting behavior. T F

Party affiliation is not influenced by parents. T F

Most first-time voters vote against the beliefs of parents. T F

People don't vote because they trust the government. T F

VOTER PARTICIPATION AND VOTER REGISTRATION BASED ON DATA FROM 2004 PRESIDENT ELECTION		
Characteristic	Percent Registered	Percent Voted
Race		
European American	67.9	60.3
African American	64.4	56.3
Hispanic American	34.3	28.0
Gender		
Male	64.0	56.3
Female	67.6	60.1
Age		
18 to 20	50.7	41.0
21 to 24 years	52.1	42.5
25 to 34 years	55.6	46.9
35 to 44 years	64.2	56.9
45 to 64 years	72.7	66.6
65+ years	76.9	68.9
Education		
Elementary 0 to 8 years	32.5	23.6
Less than High School Graduation	45.8	34.6
High School Graduation/GED	61.5	52.4
College 1 to 3 years	73.7	66.1
4 or more years	78.1	74.2

U.S. Census Bureau, Statistical Abstract of the United States: 2005, Table #404.

> TO UNDERSTAND A MAN, YOU MUST KNOW HIS MEMORIES. THE SAME IS TRUE OF A NATION.
> ANTHONY QUALE

Learning TIP
Start studying for the next exam immediately after finishing an exam.

In analyzing the characteristics of those people who register to vote, we can make the conclusion that those people who feel they have a vested interest in the system and who feel they can make a difference by voting, are those people who are most apt to vote. Seymour Martin Lipset in the 1950s, identified four major reasons why people vote:

1. People are more likely to vote if they see governmental policies as affecting them personally.
2. People are more likely to vote if they have access to information about the effects that governmental policies may have on them personally.
3. People who are subject to pressure from groups to vote or participate are more likely to vote.
4. People are more likely to vote if they are not subjected to pressures from diverse groups who have divergent views.

A very large percentage of people do not register to vote and of those who register to vote, many people choose not to exercise that right. This is particularly true in many local elections such as school board elections. Lack of interest comes from several sources:

1. People are happy with the system and see no reason to vote.
2. Nonvoters feel like they cannot change conditions by voting. This is called **political alienation**.
3. There is a high degree of distrust of politicians and public officials.

Television and polling has had an increasing impact on people's political behavior. The reelection of President Reagan in 1984 was the first election in which television played a critical role in presidential politics. His media advisors had to plan not only for stump speeches and whistlestop tours but advertising spots, staged news events and photo opportunities. We now have television debates between presidential and vice presidential candidates as a matter of course. It is not so much the "if" as the "how" and "when." I, like many other people, tuned into the 2000 presidential and vice presidential debates even though I basically thought I knew for whom I was going to vote. These debates had been arranged by the League of Women Voters. A great deal of money is spent on this media airing.

Types of behavior not traditionally shared by Americans are revolution and terrorism. Revolution is the overthrowing of an existing government. Terrorism occurs when a subgroup tries to destroy or undermine an existing government. Revolutions occur when people feel like they have less economically and politically than other members of the society or other societies, the ruling elite is weak and divided, and the existing regime is called into question.

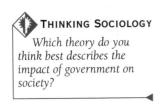

> BETTER TO LOSE A BATTLE THAN TO LOSE THE ADVANTAGE OF THE FREE PRESS.
> WILLIAM E. BORAH

🕮 Quick Glance

People vote more for National elections than local elections.   T F

Voters feel political alienation.   T F

Media has little impact on voting behavior.   T F

HOW DO THE THEORIES DIFFER IN ASSESSING THE GOVERNMENT?

When we discussed the functions of government, we were taking a structural functional viewpoint. The structural functionalist believes that government serves a necessary function for the operation of a society. Conflict theorists such as Karl Marx take a very different view of government. Marx said that the nature of a society is determined by the relationships between bourgeoisie (property owners and rulers) and the proletariat (workers and ruled). The bourgeoisie controlled the resources and used the government to serve their own needs. The government provides the means by which the bourgeoisie could control the workers. It is only through revolution that the proletariat can overthrow this "unfair system" and take control of the means of production, thus taking control of power and their own lives. Other conflict theorists basically agree with Marx that there is a basic division in power because of ownership of resources and control of government agencies of power such as executive branches, military and police. The power elite model discussed in an earlier section is another example of the conflict view of government. The symbolic interactionist model would be interested in such factors as changing people's voting behavior, getting people to vote and interaction within a political campaign and between rulers and subjects.

🐾 *Quick Glance*

Structural functionalist theory looks at the good that government does for a society.　T　F

Conflict theory sees government in terms of a struggle for power.　T　F

Symbolic interactionist theory looks at changing voting behavior.　T　F

▼ CHAPTER SUMMARY

1. The government is a formalized political institution. The government possesses power, influence and authority. The government of the United States utilizes rational-legal authority. Other types of authority are traditional and charismatic.
2. Two types of governments are authoritarian and democratic. A democracy is based on individualism, constitutional law, loyal opposition, cultural diversity and a party system.
3. The functions of the government include making laws, enforcing norms considered important to the survival of the society, settling disputes, planning and coordinating activities that are necessary for the society, administering the state, providing protection against outside enemies, establishing societal goals and allocating goods and services.
4. Several trends in our government are the tremendous power wielded by interest groups, reformation of the election system, growing size of government, increase in power of the Supreme Court, line-by-line veto by the president, greater support and regulation of industry, greater emphasis on national unity, relations with other nations becoming more significant, more professionally trained persons, changing characteristics in the composition of government personnel and changes in political affiliation of ethnic and religious groups.
5. Elitism and pluralism are two models of the power structure in the United States.
6. Political socialization, television, and polling affect people's political behavior.

▼ REFERENCES

Alderman, Ellen and Caroline Kennedy. 1991. *In Our Defense: The Bill of Rights in Action.* New York: William Morrow and Company Inc.

Dahl, Robert. 1956. *A Preface to Democratic Theory.* Chicago: University of Chicago Press.

Domhoff, G. William. 1974. *The Bohemian Grove and Other Retreats.* New York: Harper TorchBooks.

Domhoff, G. William. 1970. *The Higher Circles: Governing Class in America.* New York: Vintage Books.

Greider, William. 1992. *Who Will Tell the People: The Betrayal of American Democracy.* New York: Simon and Schuster.

Kornhauser, William. 1961. "Power Elite or Veto Groups?" In Seymour Martin Lipset and Leo Lowenthall (Eds.) *Culture and Social Character.* New York: Free Press, 252–267.

Lasswell, Harold D. 1936. *Politics: Who Gets What, When, How.* New York: McGraw-Hill.

Lipset, Seymour M. 1960. *Political Man.* New York: Doubleday.

Mills, C. Wright. 1961. *The Power Elite.* New York: Oxford University Press.

O'Rourke, P. J. 1991. *Parliament of Whores.* New York: The Atlantic Monthly Press.

Piven, Frances Fox and Richard A. Cloward. 1988. *Why Americans Don't Vote.* New York: Pantheon.

Riesman, David, with Nathan Glazer and Reuel Denny. 1961. *The Lonely Crowd*. New Haven, Conn.: Yale University Press.

Stern, Philip. 1988. *The Best Congress Money Can Buy*. New York: Pantheon.

Weber, Max. 1946. *From Max Weber*. Edited by H. H. Gerth and C. Wright Mills. New York: Oxford University Press.

Welch, Susan, John Gruhl, Michael Steinman, and John Comer. 1990. *Introduction to American Government*, 3rd Ed., St. Paul: West.

Wolf, Richard. 1999. (2/17). Women's Political Gains in past 3 decades level off. *USA Today*. 7A.

READING

Hundreds of miles from the ambitions and deceits of Washington there is a little town in New Hampshire where I live. Let's call it Blatherboro . . . The government of Blatherboro is as homey and reasonable as Blatherboro itself. There is a traditional New England town meeting held once a year. Here the business of democracy is disposed of in one sitting. And here I go to do my civic duty and help dispose of it.

Despite the minimal nature of Blatherboro town government and, indeed, the minimal nature of Blatherboro, and despite the goodwill, good sense and good New England parsimony of Blatherboro's residents, the result of the annual town meeting is always a stupid and expensive mess.

Much of the stupidity is common to all government. There are certain subjects about which people are incurable boneheads. Humans apparently cannot rationally consider what constitutes a danger to humanity or how likely any given danger is to occur. Thus, Blatherboro has fifteen police officers—the same ratio of police to population as New York City. The annual Blatherboro police budget is $425,000. This is a town that, in 1989, had 520 crimes, of which 155 were incidents of teenage vandalism. The cost of police protection against the remaining 365 more or less serious malefactions was $1,164 each—more than the damage caused by any of them.

On the other hand, almost everything in Blatherboro is built out of wood. Half the town is too rural to have fire hydrants, and a lot of the town is too cheap to have smoke detectors. Every home has a fireplace, most have wood stoves and quite a few have wood-burning furnaces, so that in March 1989, for example, there were three chimney fires in four days. But, the Blatherboro Fire Department is a completely volunteer organization with an annual budget of less than $50,000.

People also are very stupid about what makes people smart. The local school system, which serves Blatherboro and the nearby town of Quaintford, isn't very bad. But it isn't any good either. The Blatherboro-Quaintford School District Annual Report expounds at length on "competency-based programs," "whole-language instruction" and "curriculum coordination" and devotes a dozen pages to discussing "budget objectives" and listing the various administrators, speech pathologists, special-education consultants and so forth, that are thought necessary to modern education. But, nowhere does the annual report remark on the fact that the high school's ninth grade has 124 students, while the high school's tenth grade—whose denizens are of legal age to leave school—has 79. This is a 36-percent drop-out rate, about the same as the drop-out rate in most inner-city slums.

The Blatherboro-Quaintford schools have only a total of 1,488 students, kindergarten through twelfth grade, yet there is a complete school-district office with a staff of fifteen people, including a superintendent of schools, an assistant superintendent and a business administrator. And, there are an additional twenty-eight principals, assistant principals, counselors, aids and other people who don't actually teach anything on the school-system payroll.

Blatherboro's annual per-student spending is over $5,000—almost three times the national average for state college tuitions. If Blatherboro's parents and taxpayers were as serious about education as they—and every other parent and taxpayer in America—always say they are, they could gather the youngsters into miniature acad-

Quick Glance

Blatherboro represents the U.S.A. government.　T F

The annual town meeting is organized and meaningful.　T F

Government, according to O'Rourke, realistically calculates danger.　T F

emies of perhaps fifteen students each and hire $75,000 private tutors to teach them. In the academic-infested groves of New England, $75,000 would hire a fine tutor. Alternatively, Blatherboro students could be packed off to the local Catholic schools, where they'd get a better education—and a good, sharp rap on the knuckles if they showed a need for counseling—for less than half the price.

City planning is also beyond Blatherboro's ken. The town has a Planning Board, a Board of Adjustment, a building inspector, a Conservation Commission, and the place still looks like hell. Of course, there are patches of trees and precious prerevolutionary beauty, as there are in all old New England towns. Sections of Blatherboro are so overrun with white clapboard and green shutters that if a man were to unzip his fly in these parts of town, the Historic District Commission would probably make him put green shutters on either side of that, too. But the rest of the place looks like every other piece of overpaved, cheap-jack, fake-front highway sprawl in the nation. I don't happen to mind this sprawl myself, at least not in theory, because in theory I'm a private-property strict constructionist. But I do mind all the boards and commissions and employees of the town wasting my money failing to prevent it.

It really is impossible to overstate the tedium of government. As boring as civics classes were back in high school, they were a bacchanal compared with civics itself. The next six hours of the Blatherboro Town Meeting were devoted to bickering about whether the Department of Public Works should have exclusive authority to approve sewer-line hookups. Of course, I have used the words quarrel, fight and even bicker in a strictly poetic sense. I doubt that in the course of the evening's long and brutal fray so much as one voice was raised. A town meeting is tedious with that amazing and inexplicable tedium of a large number of people behaving themselves in public. It is the opposite of a mob or a riot, the flip side of human collective behavior. Taking part in a New England town meeting is like being a cell in a plant.

Nevertheless, there were very strong feelings about effluvian matters in Blatherboro. An article was proposed that, if passed, would require that a special town meeting be convened to approve any expansion of the town sewer system costing more than $50,000. The idea was not to save money on sewers. User fees and hookup charges already reimburse the town for all sewer costs. The purpose of the proposal was, instead, to control growth. Every commercial, industrial or housing development of any size would need to be approved by the town as a whole or wind up swimming in its own waste. Specifically, this article was aimed at stopping a golf course and condominium complex already under construction on the west side of town. The golf-course developer had been punctilious in meeting the town's Planning Board, Board of Adjustment, Conservation Commission and Historic District Commission requirements and in obeying all applicable state and federal laws. The golf-course and condo-complex owner had needed to obtain forty-seven permits from eleven different government agencies in order to start building his golf course and condo complex. But he had done so. An all-sewage special town meeting was the last possible way to stop the guys in plaid pants and elite shoes.

As I mentioned before, I hold private-property rights to be sacred—in theory. Which is like saying I'm rich—in Bulgaria. In theory, we're all lots of things: good, kind, and above all, consistent. I hold private-property rights to be sacred in theory, but in practice I had thrown in with the anti-golf-course faction.

To be fair, we weren't opposed to the golf course for any Pals-of-the-Animals, Eco-Stalinist reasons. Most of us play golf. We didn't have any cutesy-artsy objections to seeing trees cut down. It's a lot easier to shoot a deer on a 350-yard par-four fairway than it is in the deep woods. And we weren't opposed to growth itself—in theory. But the sad truth of local governments, like the sad truth of national government, is that people are no longer an asset. Humans do not benefit the modern state. Total 1989 Blatherboro town expenditure—including the town's share of county government and school-system costs—was $9.5 million, or about $1,860 per person. Almost all this money was raised through property taxes and automobile registration fees. A typical new family moving to Blatherboro, with a mom, dad and two kids (for families still come in that configuration in New Hampshire) would be buying a town-house condominium with a tax-assessed value of $100,000. The current property tax rate on that condominium is $2,860 a year. If the new family owns two late-model cars, registration fees (which are based on the blue-book value of the automobile) would be about $340. Add in a few miscellaneous levies and charges, and the new family ends up contributing approximately $3,500 per annum to the Blatherboro town coffers. But that is almost $4,000 less than what the town will spend on these people. A family of four must own at least a quarter of a million dollars worth of property to carry its own weight in the Blatherboro town budget.

It was at this moment, in the middle of the Blatherboro sewer debate, that I achieved enlightenment about government. I had a dominion epiphany. I reached regime satori. The whole town meeting was suddenly illuminated by the pure, strong radiance of truth.

It wasn't mere disillusionment that I experienced. Government isn't a good way to solve problems; I already knew that. And I'd been to Washington and seen for myself that government is concerned mostly with self-perpetuation and is subject to fantastic ideas about its own capabilities. I understood that government is wasteful of the nation's resources, immune to common sense and subject to pressure from every half-organized bouquet of assholes. I had observed in person, government solemnity in debate of ridiculous issues and frivolity in execution of serious duties. I was fully aware that government is distrustful of and disrespectful toward average Americans while being easily gulled by Americans with money, influence or fame. What I hadn't realized was *government is morally wrong*.

The whole idea of our government is this: If enough people get together and act in concert, they can take something and not pay for it. And here, in small-town New Hampshire, in this veritable world's capital of probity, we were about to commit just such a theft. If we could collect sufficient votes in favor of special town meetings about sewers, we could make a golf course and condominium complex disappear for free. We were going to use our suffrage to steal a fellow citizen's property rights. We weren't even going to take the manly risk of holding him up at gunpoint.

Not that there's anything wrong with our limiting growth. If we Blatherboro residents don't want a golf course and condominium complex, we can go buy that land and not build them. Of course, to buy the land, we'd have to borrow money from the bank, and to pay the bank loan, we'd have to do something profitable with the land, something like … build a golf course and condominium complex. Well, at least that would be constructive. We would be adding something—if only golf—to the use of civilization's accomplishments. Better to build a golf course right through the middle of Redwood National Park and condominiums on top of the Lincoln Memorial than to sit in council *gorging on the liberties of others, gobbling their material substance, eating freedom*.

What we were trying to do with our legislation in the Blatherboro Town Meeting was wanton, cheap and greedy—a sluttish thing. This should come as no surprise. *Authority has always attracted the lowest elements in the human race*. All through history mankind has been bullied by scum. Those who lord it over their fellows and toss commands in every direction and would boss the grass in the meadow about which way to bend in the wind are the most depraved kind of prostitutes. They will

Quick Glance

A high education budget has contributed to Blatherboro's low school dropout rate.   T F

Boards and commissions successfully control urban sprawl.   T F

The town wanted a golf course.   T F

Quick Glance

Government is all about improving life for the community.   T F

O'Rourke believes in the freedom of private property.   T F

Government according to O'Rourke, limits the individual's rights.   T F

submit to any indignity, perform any vile act, do anything to achieve power. The worst off-sloughings of the planet are the ingredients of sovereignty. Every government is a parliament of whores.

The trouble is, in a democracy the whores are us.

Excerpted from O'Rourke, P. J. Parliament of Whores. New York: A MorganEntrekin Book, 1991, pp. 223–233.

Examining the Economy

IMAGE COPYRIGHT JEFF GYNANE, 2008. USED UNDER LICENSE FROM SHUTTERSTOCK, INC.

CHAPTER OBJECTIVES

1. What is the economy?
2. What are the different types of production?
3. What are the economic systems in preindustrial societies?
4. What are the economic systems in industrial societies?
5. What is the economic system in postindustrial societies?
6. What are the manifest functions of the economic institution?
7. What are some of the latent functions of the economic institution?
8. What are the trends in the economic insitution in the United States?
9. How do the different theoretical perspectives explain the economic institution?

absolute poverty: the economic standard set which people cannot fall below or they will be considered in poverty

agrarian system: the economic structure based on farming using tools, irrigation and fertilization

burnout: a lack of meaning in work

capital: the investment of a culture in the economic system

capitalism: an economic system with an ideology of private ownership and benefit of profit

communism: an economic system in which all property is owned communally

consumption: the usage of goods and services

corporation: an economic organization in which individuals act under a common name in order to own, hold and manage property or an enterprise

democratic socialism: an economic system by which the major industry is under governmental control, but other industry is in the private sector

economy: a social institution organized around the production, distribution and consumption of goods and services

extrinsic factor: a condition within the workplace contributing to worker satisfaction such as pay and health benefits

horticultural system: an economic system based on farming using simple technology

hunters and gatherers: an economic system based on foraging for plants and animals in the environment

individual proprietorship: an individual owns and operates his or her own business

intrinsic factor: a condition of personal satisfaction in the work place

laissez faire: a free market with a minimum amount of government intervention in the economy

market economy: a redistribution system based on money exchange

mixed economy: the combination of socialism and capitalism systems

monopoly: one business controls the market

partnership: an agreement drawn between individuals according to a set of regulations

pastoral system: an economic system which depends on the domestication of cattle, sheep, camels, reindeer and other animals for meat, milk and skins

postindustrial society: a society which focuses on tertiary production

preindustrial society: a society characterized by small production units and human and animal power as sources of energy

primary industry: the part of the economy concerned with the direct extraction of natural resources from the environment

production: based on physical environment, natural resources, labor and capital

reciprocity: a balanced exchange of goods and services

redistribution: a centralized agency collects the surplus and distributes to other sources

relative poverty: a poverty judged by comparing self with others

secondary industry: consists of manufacturing raw materials into a finished consumer product

socialism: exists when the production and distribution of goods are collectively owned

soft culture: the nonmaterial culture including movies, music and television shows

tertiary industry: a part of the economic system involved in the production of services and information

use-value: the value of goods based on supply and demand and translated into money value

---

▼ KEY PEOPLE

Milton Friedman, John Keynes, Karl Marx, Paul A. Samuelson, Adam Smith, Max Weber

WHAT IS THE ECONOMY?

All societies have an economic system; an economic institution is a cultural universal. The **economy** is that socially sanctioned system involved in producing, distributing and consuming scarce goods and services according to well-defined rules.

The economic system of any society is comprised of three components: production, distribution and consumption of goods and services. The way that each of these three variables is addressed within a culture determines the structure of the economic institution. Before we discuss the different types of economic structures on a historical and crosscultural basis, we would like to discuss production of goods and services.

WHAT ARE THE DIFFERENT TYPES OF PRODUCTION?

Production is based on physical environment, natural resources, labor and capital. The type of physical environment in which a culture exists determines to a large extent the type of resources which are available. If the land is arid, for example, without technology, farming is very difficult, if not impossible. If a land is rich in mineral deposits, such as South Africa, the natural resources underpin a potentially prosperous economy. Labor and capital are necessary for a culture to be capable of extracting and utilizing the natural resources. Labor refers to the physical and mental power needed to produce goods and services. In our society, the workers are predominantly those people age 18 to 65. In other cultures, people begin in the labor force at a much younger age. Traditionally, the breakdown in industrialized societies has been blue-collar versus white-collar worker, but in other cultures the division of labor may be based on age and gender.

Capital is the investment of a culture in the economic system. In the United States, we think of capital in terms of a factory or a store. In other cultures, such as the Tiwi, capital can take the form of pigs or a supply of flint.

Based on the technology, territory and natural resources, there are three types of production. *The first is called primary industry.* **Primary industry** is the extraction of natural resources. This includes activities such as mining, farming and fishing. When the man that farms my mother's land harvests the corn and soybeans, he is engaged in primary industry.

Secondary industry is the manufacture of raw materials into a finished consumer product. Grinding grain or canning of the vegetables is a secondary industry. Producing automobiles, airplanes, computers, golf clubs, tennis rackets, baseball bats and hockey sticks are all a part of the secondary industry. The growth of the secondary industry is responsible for the industrialization of the U.S. as well as all other industrialized countries.

The third type of industry is called tertiary. **Tertiary industry** is the production of services and information in the economic system. When I visit my doctor or go to the health spa, I am dealing in the tertiary industry. Service jobs involve some type of direct, interpersonal contact such as face-to-face, or at the very least, voice-to-voice. As we enter the computer age, it may be modem-to-modem. In the tertiary industry, we are concerned with people's emotional states as well as task definition.

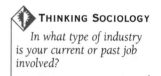

WHAT ARE THE ECONOMIC SYSTEMS IN PREINDUSTRIAL SOCIETIES?

Learning TIP
Try and try again. Accept the challenge to learn and master a course in order to reach your goals.

THINKING SOCIOLOGY

Which type of economic system would have the least involved role complex?

Quick Glance

Hunters and gatherers grow crops to eat.   T   F

Reciprocity is the same as barter.   T   F

Horticulture depends on sophisticated technology.   T   F

Pastoral people live exclusively by eating meat.   T   F

THINKING SOCIOLOGY

How could the value of goods be judged other than money? What type of distribution is associated with use-value? Explain your answer.

Preindustrial societies are characterized by small production units which use human and animal power as sources of energy. These small production units lead to an integration between economic activities and other aspects of life such as family, economy and education. The vast majority of people in a preindustrial system are involved in primary production, that is, extracting raw materials from the environment.

The first type of preindustrial structure is **hunters and gatherers**. These societies depend upon foraging the land for food to eat. Traditionally, men do the hunting and women do the gathering. This, on the whole, is a secure economic system because they eat a wide variety of different kinds of food. Distribution is based on reciprocity. In **reciprocity**, there is an exchange of goods and services. In generalized reciprocity, little or no consideration is given for ability, but the focus is on need. When parents provide for the needs of their children, they are engaged in generalized reciprocity.

The second type of preindustrial economic system is a **horticultural society**. These societies depend upon simple agricultural techniques such as digging sticks and self-fertilization of the land. The Yanomamo Indians of Venezuela and Brazil are horticultural. They use a technique called slash and burn. The Indians clear small segments of land to grow their crops. They use digging sticks for both planting and harvesting. After several years, when the ground is no longer fertile, they move their planting to another area. The distribution among horticultural societies is primarily based on reciprocity, but redistribution can occur. Redistribution calls for a centralized agency to collect the surplus and distribute the goods to other sources. When the government collects taxes and social security payments, they are engaged in redistribution. There is a story in the Christian Bible that tells of Joseph collecting grain in order to redistribute it during the years of famine; this is redistribution.

The third type of preindustrial economic system is the **agrarian system**. With this system, there is widespread use of plows, irrigation systems and fertilizer. The economic system of the colonial United States was an agrarian society.

The fourth type of preindustrial system is a pastoral system. The **pastoral system** *depends on the domestication of cattle, sheep, camels, reindeer and other animals for meat, milk and skins.* The people are nomadic, shifting from pasture to pasture searching for food for the animals. Many pastoral people do not eat the meat of the animal, but rather utilize products such as milk, yogurt, cheese and blood. Many of the pastoral societies also weave rugs which they use themselves and sell to others. Leather is frequently an important trading product too. The pastoralist often trades these products for fruits, vegetables and other necessities not provided by their animals. The Kurds, who have caused so much controversy in Iraq, Iran and the Soviet Union, were traditionally a pastoral people. The Masaii of Kenya and Tanzania rely on large herds of cattle. The Warriors herd the cattle when grazing is far from the home camp. In both the agrarian and pastoral societies, the types of distribution occurring are redistribution and market exchange.

WHAT ARE THE ECONOMIC SYSTEMS IN INDUSTRIAL SOCIETIES?

Under the feudalistic system in Europe, villages and people were virtually self-sufficient. During this period, the society was agrarian. Economic positions were broad categories like farmers, supervisors, soldiers or artisans such as blacksmiths and carpenters. To a large extent, as discussed in Chapter 8, positions of freeman or serf were inherited. People who were free men were bound to the land by tradition and law. Once the feudal system collapsed, workers were free to find their own place in the economic structure. Status now was much more achieved than ascribed. This set the framework for the Industrial Revolution. With the Industrial Revolution came economic systems based on a bureaucracy, new sources of energy such as petroleum products, and secondary and tertiary production. The market economy became the means of redistribution. The **market economy** is based on supply and demand of goods and services and use-value. **Use-value** is translated into a price for a consumer product which is stated in terms of some form of money.

▲ A PASTORAL SOCIETY.
IMAGE COPYRIGHT MMMM, 2008. USED UNDER LICENSE FROM SHUTTERSTOCK, INC.

Industrial economic systems can be viewed from Max Weber's idea of ideal types of capitalism, socialism and communism. Many economic systems, however, do not fit into one of the three ideal types. There may be a blurring of the distinct characteristics. Societies may experience what is called a **mixed economy**, or a combination of types of economic systems. Democratic socialism is considered a mixed economy.

We will briefly discuss the existing industrial economic systems.

Capitalism is based on an ideology of private ownership. In 1776, British economist Adam Smith proposed the main principles of the capitalistic economy in his book *Inquiry into the Nature and Causes of the Wealth of Nations*. Smith believed in laissez faire for the marketplace. **Laissez faire** is a free market with a minimum amount of government intervention in the economy. Prices are left to fluctuate according to the market and businesses are free to compete with one another. In captialism, there is the deliberate pursuit of personal profit, and there is free competition among buyers and sellers of goods and services.

In order for a capitalistic system to work, four conditions must be present:

1. acceptance of routines and time schedules
2. traditional norms dealing with ascribed status must not be allowed to jeopardize the workplace
3. free geographical movement of workers
4. little absenteeism or quitting from the labor market

Critics of Adam Smith suggest that pure capitalism results in the building of monopolies; therefore, government intervention is needed to restrict the formation of monopolies. A **monopoly** occurs when one business firm controls the market. Monopolies eliminate competition and make it possible for these firms to fix prices.

We, in the United States, say that we have a capitalistic system, but the marketplace of America today has experienced government intervention resulting in the loss of pure capitalism. Although government interferes, it does not completely control the marketplace but rather monitors the marketplace.

A second ideal type of economy is socialism. Karl Marx believed that socialism would be the answer to what he viewed as problems with capitalism. Socialism was believed to take competition and inequality from the marketplace. In **socialism**, the means of production belong to the state which is the representative of the people. The government acts for the benefit of the people by determining the amount of production, the type of industry engaged in production and the regulation of prices.

☙ *Quick Glance*

Use-value is the same as price.   T F

The Industrial Revolution caused the breakdown of the Feudal System.   T F

Capitalism is based on private ownership.   T F

THE EFFICIENCY OF MOST WORKERS IS BEYOND THE CONTROL OF THE MANAGEMENT AND DEPENDS MORE THAN HAS BEEN SUPPOSED UPON THE WILLINGNESS OF MEN TO DO THEIR BEST.

S. H. SLICHTER

☙ *Quick Glance*

During the seventeenth century, Europe was agrarian.   T F

Capitalism is based on laissez faire.   T F

A market economy is based on a money exchange.   T F

In order for a capitalistic system to work, workers have to be free to change geographical locations. T F

Monopolies restrict capitalism.   T F

Production and distribution should not be for private profit, and competition between different firms producing similar products is a waste of resources. It is not productive, for example, to have many factories producing shoes when just one or two factories would do. Just as in capitalistic America, most societies espousing socialism actually have a mixed economy.

In **democratic socialism** or **mixed economy**, the state takes strategic industries and services into public ownership. Strategic industries include railways, airlines, banks, radio, televisions, telephones, etc. Private ownership of other means of production is permitted or even encouraged, but the economy is closely regulated in accordance with national priorities. Very high tax rates are used to prevent excessive profits or an undue concentration of wealth. A measure of equality is achieved by the high tax rate and governmentally supported health insurance and retirement programs. This system is practiced in nearly all the countries of western Europe.

Communism is an economic system in which all property is owned communally. Karl Marx's view was that socialism would evolve naturally into communism. Communism advocates a classless society or a state of equality. In a communistic system, the government has shrunk and the means of production are owned by the people as a whole. There is an abundance of goods and services. People would no longer regard property as private, wealth and power would be shared in harmony by the community as a whole, and each would contribute according to their abilities and receive according to their needs. The U.S.S.R. and the People's Republic of China were not communistic; they were socialistic. Pure communism does not exist in any technologically advanced society.

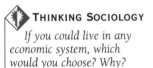

THINKING SOCIOLOGY

If you could live in any economic system, which would you choose? Why?

WHAT IS THE ECONOMIC SYSTEM IN POSTINDUSTRIAL SOCIETIES?

The **postindustrial society** focuses on tertiary production. The workplace for the postindustrial society consists of jobs such as teacher, waitress, insurance agent, financial planner and advisor, cab driver or computer programmer and operator. This system is not directly involved in production but is directed towards service; more specifically, the production and distribution of information.

One important aspect of the postindustrial economic structure is called soft-culture. **Soft-culture** is nonmaterial culture such as movies, television and music. Soft-culture has become one of the United States' most important exports. When I was wandering down some of the back streets in Shanghai, I heard Madonna's voice wafting from several of the stores. The dance that I attended in the People's Republic of China played more American music than Chinese music and the cassette tape of Chinese popular music that I purchased in China sounds like an American tape. I watched a John Wayne movie dubbed in Chinese and saw advertisements for Sylvester Stallone movies. When I visited Kenya, I had very much the same experience. CNN news is one of the most widely broadcast shows in the world today; it is an export of the United States. Our sitcoms are also very popular in other countries. My daughter's French pen pal's favorite show is an American show. The mass production and distribution of American media has had an influence on the behavior and thoughts of many people throughout the world.

WHAT ARE THE MANIFEST FUNCTIONS OF THE ECONOMIC INSTITUTION?

Production and Distribution of Goods and Services

Production and distribution of goods and services are based on division of labor and physical needs of food, shelter and clothing. Nature's resources are unusable in their natural state. The steer in the pasture that I observe on my way to work does me no good. I have no idea how to butcher it nor do I have the legal right to butcher it. I need to go to the grocery store in order to get the butchered and divided steer.

Distribution of Power

Power, to a large extent, comes through the position that people occupy on the economic hierarchy; people who have control of money also have power. Additionally, there is a division of power within a company or factory system. The most obvious division is between workers and managers. Managers make decisions that workers carry out; the board of directors makes decisions that managers obey. Among the workers, there are gradations in skill and pay which gives certain people or groups more power than other people or groups. In urban industrial societies, the economy requires so many specialists and provides so many different roles that the economy has become a major criterion for social stratification. A small agricultural community is more likely to rank its members on the basis of their family lineage; an industrialized society is more likely to place its members according to their occupational roles and income.

The economic institution also influences the distribution of political power. For example, in the United States, workers and managers traditionally support different parties: labor and labor unions have traditionally affiliated with the Democratic party, and business interests have traditionally affiliated with the Republican party. There is, for example, much concern during presidential elections about party platforms and their influence on the economy.

Welfare or Noneconomic Function

We give, for example, money to charitable organizations such as United Way, Red Cross or the American Cancer Association. We also value our career intrinsically. From our major workplace, we gain a great deal of our self-esteem and sense of identity. If I asked, "Who are you?" a very frequent response is to tell me what your primary job is. The daily work regime gives structure to our lives. For example, I am at the office at 8:00 a.m., but on most days I am home at about 4:30 p.m. After people retire from their jobs, they frequently enjoy several months of catching up on chores around the house and traveling, but if they have not formed any long-term commitments, time hangs heavy on their hands and they begin to wonder about what to do with their time. When a person is fired or loses a job, rates of spouse abuse, child abuse, substance abuse and suicide go up; these people lose a sense of identity when their jobs are lost. Interestingly enough, approximately 70% of working people who were asked if they would work, if they did not have to say that they would continue to work. We gain income, keep busy, receive approval of others, feel useful to society and intrinsically enjoy our work. We do not want to do dull jobs, but rather look for satisfaction and self-fulfillment in work. This is a noneconomic function of the economic institution.

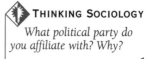

THINKING SOCIOLOGY

What political party do you affiliate with? Why?

Quick Glance

The economy is needed for the distribution of goods and services.   T   F

A preindustrial society judges people according to income.   T   F

Business people are generally democratic.   T   F

Political power is associated with economic power.   T   F

THE ILLITERATE OF THE 21ST CENTURY WILL NOT BE THOSE WHO CANNOT READ AND WRITE, BUT THOSE WHO CANNOT LEARN, UNLEARN, AND RELEARN.
ALVIN TOFFLER

Quick Glance

We gain a sense of self from our work.   T   F

People do not value their work, they value leisure time activities.   T   F

Self concept is associated with economic position.   T   F

THINKING SOCIOLOGY

What do you plan on doing when you retire? Why? How?

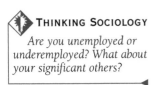

FAMILIES BELOW POVERTY LEVEL, 2006	
MARRIED COUPLE	5.1%
FEMALE HEADED	28.7%
MALE HEADED	13%

U.S. CENSUS BUREAU, 2006, TABLE NO. 694.

Consumption

Many of us are experts at the last function of the economic institution, consumption. **Consumption** is the usage of goods and services. Consumption includes use of utilities such as electricity, long-distance phone calls, food from the grocery, clothes from department stores and gasoline from the service station.

Some interesting shifts have resulted in consumption patterns during the last 100 years due to mass production of goods. *First, goods are now rarely done to individual specifications.* For example, if I were a colonial woman, I would have gone to the local shoemaker, and he would have designed and made a pair of shoes for me at my specifications. I still have that luxury if I am wealthy enough, but probably I shall go to the local mall or shoe store in order to buy a pair of shoes. *Second, there is no standardization in the pricing of goods.* I can buy a pair of tennis shoes, for example, at a specialty store and pay a great deal more for them than had I gone to the local discount mall. The service may not be as good nor will the discount store honor a money back guarantee, but the price would be cheaper. *Third, there is no standardization in quality and durability of goods.* I bought a pair of tennis shoes at a local "we sell for less" shoe store. The first time I wore them, I ended up walking home in the rain. My shoes were ruined! The insoles came out and the bottom of the sole became unglued from the top. Several weeks later I purchased an international brand running shoe at an outlet mall, paying about the same price, and, two years later, I am still wearing the same shoes.

Advertising has profoundly altered buying habits. Industrial and service concerns create a demand for new goods through advertising. We used to buy cassette tapes; now I am trying to replace all my tapes with CDs! And video tapes are becoming cheaper as DVDs are becoming more common.

Another change that has occurred concerning consumption is market segmentation. Products and advertising no longer are geared towards the general audience but marked for a particular aggregate of people. Saturday morning television leans to advertising on games and presweetened breakfast cereal, while primetime shows focus on eating establishments, beer and automobiles. Catalogs, such as Victoria's Secret and Lane Bryant, are focused to particular audiences.

Product diversification has happened at an ever expanding rate. Look at what has happened to frozen foods in just the last ten years! Frozen food used to be a limited selection of frozen evening meals. Now we have a choice of hearty meals, lean meals or gourmet meals in the frozen section. Bread used to be a fairly straight forward decision, but now there is a wide choice of white, dark, novelty grains, low fat or high-fiber breads from which to choose.

WHAT ARE SOME OF THE LATENT FUNCTIONS OF THE ECONOMIC INSTITUTION?

People in Poverty

There are large numbers of people in poverty. Two concepts are used to discuss types of poverty: absolute or relative. **Absolute poverty** is a standard, usually set by the government, below which people cannot fall or they will be considered living in poverty. This figure is frequently half the national median income. Median income means that half the people earn above this dollar amount and half earn below the dollar amount. The median income is approximately $42,000 for a family of four, so poverty would be those families earning around $21,000. I can very well get rid of this type of poverty by lowering the dollar amount that is used to define poverty. I can say that anyone earning two or more dollars a year is not in poverty; there goes

MEDIAN ANNUAL INCOME BY RACE AND SEX IN 2005		
Race/Gender	*Earnings*	*Wages as % of White Men*
White men	$32,179	100.0%
Black men	$22,653	70%
Hispanic men	$22,089	68%
White women	$18,669	58%
Black women	$17,631	54%
Hispanic women	$15,036	46%

U.S. Census Bureau, Table No. 679.

☙ **Quick Glance**

There is no discrimination towards women in the economic system.　T　F

Unemployment indicates people actively looking for work.　T　F

The unemployment rate has remained the same in the U.S.A.　T　F

the poverty problem, at least by absolute standards. **Relative poverty** is comparing yourself to others around you. If you drool when the black shiny Rolls Royce passes you on the freeway as you are driving your 1980 Cadillac, you experience relative poverty. There is no way that we can rid a society of relative poverty.

Unequal Treatment of Minorities

Minority groups are not receiving equal wages to that of European American males. On the average, women earn $.76 for every dollar that a white male earns. Companies may call women by different titles or do not give them the same position on the job ladder and, thus, pay them less.

Unemployment and Underemployment

The unemployment rate in the United States is about 7%; it has been higher and it has been lower. This rate reflects those people actively looking for jobs; those people that have given up the job search are not included in those figures.

Underemployment is less obvious. A man who would like to work sixty hours a week in order to earn overtime may only be working forty hours. He feels like he is underemployed. The person with a master's degree who is working as a taxi driver is underemployed for his educational level. We had a taxi driver in New Orleans who claimed he had a masters in psychology as well as an engineering degree; he definitely felt like he was underemployed for his education level. Another phenomena that is happening in our culture is the increase in the number of part-time workers. This benefits the company because if a worker is hired as a part-time employee, the company does not have to pay benefits such as health and disability insurance. One of the growing trends in many colleges is the increase of adjunct faculty. We also find many hospitals being staffed by part-time nurses. These people are frequently holding down two or more jobs, but they are not receiving any benefits.

Meaning in Work

We are having more difficulty in finding meaning in work. If we practice a very narrow range of skills or do very repetitive work, we may find ourselves dreading going to work. We receive no sense of accomplishment or mental stimulation. A job revolution seems to be developing as a result of two significant factors: a failing economy and growing workers' demand for greater work satisfaction. Industrial leaders are becoming aware that the United States' working people are often no longer satisfied with such traditional remedies as more pay, four day weeks and better health benefits. Satisfaction or dissatisfaction depends on several factors:

1. *A satisfied worker believes that he/she is paid well for his/her efforts.* Besides wages or salary, such fringe benefits as medical care, retirement and paid vacation time are important considerations.

UNEMPLOYMENT RATES FOR DECEMBER, 2007	
ALL WORKERS	5%
ADULT MEN	4.4%
ADULT WOMEN	4.4%
TEENAGERS	17.1%
WHITE	4.4%
AFRICAN AMERICAN	9.0%
HISPANIC	6.3%
BUREAU OF LABOR STATISTICS	

◆ **THINKING SOCIOLOGY**

Do you find meaning in your work? Why or why not?

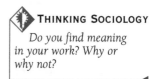

FEW THINGS HELP AN INDIVIDUAL MORE THAN TO PLACE RESPONSIBILITY UPON HIM, AND TO LET HIM KNOW THAT YOU TRUST HIM.

BOOKER T. WASHINGTON

☙ **Quick Glance**

Unemployment and underemployment are the same thing.　T　F

There has been a decrease in the number of part-time workers.　T　F

Extrinsic factors involve psychological satisfaction.　T　F

People need only good pay and benefits to be satisfied with their work.　T　F

▲ INTRINSIC AND EXTRINSIC FACTORS ARE IMPORTANT IN OUR JOBS.
IMAGE COPYRIGHT PETER BLOTTMAN, 2008. USED UNDER LICENSE FROM SHUTTERSTOCK, INC.

2. *People generally are happier in jobs that offer high autonomy.* This gives them some chance for control, especially over their own schedules.
3. *Workers are more satisfied in a place which is pleasant in a physical sense:* not too hot or too cold, not too dirty, not too noisy or dangerous.
4. *Workers like facilities such as cafeterias, lounges, gyms and such advantages as training programs or promotion-from-within policies. The factors mentioned above are called* **extrinsic factors**.
5. *Employees are pleased when they have a chance to learn on the job, when the work relates to their particular abilities and preferences and when it provides a sense of accomplishment. These are* **intrinsic factors**.

THINKING SOCIOLOGY

Many people have their first job in a fast food establishment. How do these jobs fulfill or not fulfill the factors of worker satisfaction?

Some of the programs suggested to increase worker satisfaction include flexible time, job sharing, team production systems, workplace democracy and employee stock ownership plans (ESOPs). Through these programs, management hopes to alleviate worker alienation; managers want both intrinsic and extrinsic satisfaction to be high among workers.

Part of the dissatisfaction with work comes with the phenomenon called **burnout**. People stop finding meaning in their work, start watching the clock, dread going to work each morning and withdraw from personal contact with clients. This happens particularly in those occupations dealing with people. On the average, a good teacher faces burnout after about seven years of public school teaching. Other occupations with high burnout rates include nurses, social workers and peace officers.

THE LIFE AND SPIRIT OF THE AMERICAN ECONOMY IS PROGRESS AND EXPANSION.
H. S. TRUMAN

Omnipotent Bureaucracies

In the United States, we are getting omnipotent (very powerful) corporations which dominate the economy. Large corporations such as Exxon, Pepsi Cola and Alcoa have tremendous financial control over other companies. Many companies have what is called subsidiaries. Pepsi Cola, for example, also own Taco Bell and KFC. As a consequence, companies such as these wield financial power. They have power because:

Quick Glance

Large corporations have political, as well as, financial power.   T   F

Little money is devoted to war-production during our peaceful times.   T   F

There is little overlap between government and business.   T   F

1. an overlap exists between corporate heads and governmental officials
2. wealth commanded by large corporations can be used to hire public relations firms and to directly influence governmental decisions
3. interlocking directorates and conglomerates further extends the large scope and power of the corporation.

Permanent War Economy

THINKING SOCIOLOGY

Would you be willing to cut your standard of living in order to share the world's resources?

Much of the wealth in the United States is expanded for what can be labeled a permanent war economy. When the government stops or cuts back on defense contracts, many industries in the economy suffer. The economy of Houston is heavily influenced by NASA, as are the economies on the west coast. However, now that the Cold War appears to have ended, there may need to be a shift in our thinking. It was interesting that in December of 1992, the armed forces did a peace mission to Somalia and that the U.S. and their allies continue to try to maintain a presence in Iraq.

Meeting People

The workplace is a good location to meet people. After completion of our school years, many of our friends and acquaintances come from the workplace. As we marry at older ages, the workplace is also becoming a good place to meet prospective spouses.

Depletion of World Resources

Americans are exploiting a disproportionate and large share of the world's economic resources. We use more gasoline per person than any other country. We are heavy electricity users because of our air conditioned and heated electric homes. We also own large refrigerators and microwaves, use aluminum soft drink cans and buy many objects and foods wrapped in plastics. These types of material goods use up a great deal of the world's available resources. As more and more countries become economically advanced, we may have to share these resources to a greater extent.

▲ ENERGY USE IS INCREASING AROUND THE WORLD.
IMAGE COPYRIGHT JOHANNES COMPAAN, 2008. USED UNDER LICENSE FROM SHUTTERSTOCK, INC.

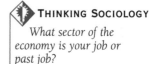

WEALTH, IF YOU USE IT, COMES TO AN END; LEARNING, IF YOU USE IT, INCREASES.
SWAHILI SAYING

▶ **THINKING SOCIOLOGY**
What sector of the economy is your job or past job?

WHAT ARE THE TRENDS IN THE ECONOMIC INSTITUTION IN THE UNITED STATES?

Several trends in the economic institution in the United States can be identified.

First, a radical change has occurred in the composition of the labor force. The most spectacular change has been the increase of women in the workplace. Women now comprise almost one half (46%) of the work force. During the 1950s and '60s, it was preferable, if at all possible, for the woman to stay home and be a housewife and mother, but more and more women are entering the workplace. The fastest growing segment of women returning to work are those women with preschool children. Many of these jobs are in low-paying clerical, service or blue-collar jobs. Often these

FACTS ABOUT WOMEN IN THE WORKFORCE IN THE U.S.

1. Women make up 46% of the workforce.
2. Women make up 14% of the boards of Fortune 500 companies.
3. Women make up 16% of corporate offices.
4. Women make up 50% of law school students.
5. Women make up 50% of medical students.
6. Women make up 15% of the Army.
7. Women make up 15% of the Navy.
8. Women make up 6% of the Marine Corps.
9. Women make up 14% of the Air Force.

Newsweek, October 24, 2005, p. 66.

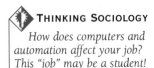
jobs have no career lines, so women cannot advance to higher positions. More women, however, are working in supervisory and higher level jobs. There has been a decrease in the proportion of farm workers. Many migrant workers have been replaced by machinery and the small, family farm is falling to large corporation farming. There has been an increase in service workers. These are the occupations that fall into what is called the tertiary industry. Health spas, health clinics, hair salons and restaurants all fall under this category. There has been a spectacular increase in white-collar workers. As jobs require more education and experience, the number of white-collar jobs has increased. In 1950, 65% of working Americans were in the industrial sector and 17% in information occupations (jobs that involve creating, processing and distributing information such as banks, the stock market, insurance companies, education and government). By 1981, a dramatic shift had taken place. Thirty percent of the work force was in the industrial sector and over 55% in the information realm.

Second, there has been an increase in automation and computerization of the jobs. The travel agent used to have to look up in a large book with very fine print the number and destinations of airplane flights. Now they use a computer to book a flight, confirm reservations, issue tickets and even give boarding passes. The grocery checker scans the grocery items and an automatic listing is given to the customer. Much of the grocery store's inventory is done through the same computer system used for checking the groceries. Some grocery stores do not even price individual items now because the computer reads the code on the item and registers it on the computer. One argument for computer technology is that computers eliminate boring jobs, but other people maintain that the computer creates boring jobs. If you have to input data for several hours on a computer, you might agree with the latter statement!

The disparity in income distribution has been a third change in the economy of the United States. The labor force has increasingly been divided into two broad segments: one highly paid, relatively secure with the possibility of mobility and one lower paid with little chance for advancement. The core jobs have security, benefits, good pay and stability. The periphery jobs are the last hired, first fired, carry few, if any benefits and have little chance for advancement.

Fourth, government regulation is steadily increasing. The government has anti-trust laws; the government has bailed out failing car and steel industries. During the 1990s, the government bailed out many failing savings and loan associations at a cost of millions of dollars to the taxpayer. There is, however, beginning to be a backlash on this issue. In 2001 the government provided aid to the airlines. In Congress, Democrats have started to unite with Republicans to oppose regulations.

▲ **FLEX-TIME INCREASES LEISURE TIME.**
IMAGE COPYRIGHT FOTUM, 2008. USED UNDER LICENSE FROM SHUTTERSTOCK, INC.

Fifth, in the United States, we have had an increase in leisure time available and a redefinition of leisure. We used to work a six- or seven-day work week, but now most jobs consider 40 hours of work to be a work week. Some industries are experimenting with a four-day work week and other companies are doing flex time. People control, with certain limitations in this program, when they start work and when they quit for the day. The lower strata people will be working about 40 hours a week; people in the upper levels will be working about 50 hours a week.

Sixth, we have also redefined the meaning of leisure. The Greeks and Romans viewed leisure as good, and they avoided work if at all possible. During the early Christian eras, idle hands were considered opportunities for the devil. During the 1950s and 1960s, leisure was viewed as a restorative for work, but more and more we are viewing leisure as good in and of itself.

Seventh, the United States is increasingly becoming an employee society. We generally ask people, "Whom do you work for?" Most people work for a large or small corporation; they work for someone else.

Eighth, unions, management and government are becoming increasingly interrelated. Corporations and unions maintain lobbies in Washington and they get together for meetings and conferences. In fact, it is not uncommon for labor leaders and corporation leaders to talk about their alma mater's before the meeting starts. The stereotype of the union leader emerging from the ranks is now a phenomenon of the past.

Ninth, labor has been effectively organized in blue-collar occupations since the enactment of the National Relations Act of the 1930s. This movement peaked in 1955. Since that time, some work areas have decreased in unionization. Unions have lost power because of loss of jobs in highly unionized industries such as auto manufacturing and steel production, lack of interest in organizing service industries, success of employer-sponsored programs such as health insurance and the relocating or threat of relocation to nonunionized areas. Other occupations such as public school teachers and nurses have, however, become more unionized. Unions promote job control, ensure protection of job against potential competitors and against unfair treatment by the company and provide a continuous effort through collective bargaining to improve wages and working conditions. Unions maintain discipline among members and see that members do not engage in wild strikes and slow downs.

Tenth, many occupations have become professionalized. The traditional professions have been doctors, lawyers and dentists. Now such occupations as nurse, hair stylist and real estate agent consider themselves professionals. These groups have developed a body of knowledge, licensing, peer control, have a code of ethics and professional associations.

Eleventh, corporations, especially those that are large and visible to the public, are redefining their goals and ethics. The chemical companies advertise what good things they are doing for us, the major oil companies are more concerned about environmental issues; hospitals advertise about the humane treatment of patients.

Twelfth, multinational corporations are becoming increasingly important. What is developing is a true global economy because information can be instantaneously shared. As a result of the global economy, the production capacities of different countries are now widely understood. The United States and other developed nations have been decreasing their output in a variety of industries, including steel, automobiles, machinery, apparel, shoes, textiles and appliances. Additionally, they are becoming involved in such enterprises as electronics, bio-industry, alternative sources of energy and mining of seabeds. This is viewed by some as another form of colonialism and control of the local economy. Neocolonialism may be a consequence of this. Underdeveloped countries are contracted to be the sites of a modern factory. Then technical people come into the country, along with money, to build the industry. Through controlling the economy, there is a risk of the industrial country also controlling the government and influencing the educational system.

Thirteenth, we, in the United States, have a growing underground economy. This includes unreported income and employment. More and more of the middle-class people who do not think of themselves as criminals, are engaging in the illegal activity of tax evasion by participating in the underground economy. The first type of tax evasion is work occurring in properly registered, legal activities and purposely under reporting incomes or over reporting deductions when tax returns are filed. The second type involves the failure to report income or even to file income tax forms by individuals who run or work for businesses that are not registered and licensed

THINKING SOCIOLOGY

What do you think will be the status of unions in the year 2050?

Quick Glance

We are an employee society.	T	F
Fewer occupations are professions than 50 years ago.	T	F
Corporations are more concerned about ethics.	T	F

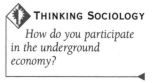

THE FUNDAMENTAL IDEA OF MODERN CAPITALISM IS NOT THE RIGHT OF THE INDIVIDUAL TO POSSESS AND ENJOY WHAT HE HAS EARNED, BUT THE THESIS THAT THE EXERCISE OF THIS RIGHT REDOUNDS TO THE GENERAL GOOD.

R. B. PERRY

THINKING SOCIOLOGY

How do you participate in the underground economy?

Quick Glance

Government regulation of the economy is declining.	T	F
Multinational corporations can lead to neocolonialism.	T	F
The U.S.A. does not have an underground economy.	T	F

as required by law and that do not file the required governmental forms. Illegal aliens are foreigners who are in our country illegally. We estimate that 30% of the illegally working population found employment in "off-the-books" economic activity. Stolen goods and fencing are part of the underground economy. Arson is a way some individuals make a bad business pay for itself. Illegal drugs are part of the underground economy. Many of the designer drugs can be made right in a kitchen or with very little chemical equipment for a quick, if unlawful, profit. Gambling is still not legal in many states, but it is widely practiced in bingo halls, pool halls and in sports betting. Prostitution is unlawful. There have been some suggestions to make both drugs and prostitution legal so that the government could tax the income.

Fourteenth, we face continued problems with recessions and inflation, but inflation seems to be the more serious of the problems. Inflation comes about because of the additional government spending in the areas of health care and other welfare functions. Government regulations of the economy encourage borrowing because of no fear of a bust cycle; thus, prices are sheltered by monopolistic tendencies.

HOW DO THE DIFFERENT THEORETICAL PERSPECTIVES EXPLAIN THE ECONOMIC INSTITUTION?

Theories of the economy help us understand the institution of the economy better. Two theories used to explain the institution of the economy are the classical economic theory and Keynesian economic theory. The first is a structural functional theory and the second is a conflict theory.

The classical economic theory has its roots with British economist, Adam Smith. Smith's view of economics is now considered to be conservative economics. In his theory, free trade produced the growth of the economy. Smith said that people would produce goods and trade those goods with others in a way that both would profit. Competition would motivate each producer to develop a high-quality product in order to compete in the marketplace. Milton Friedman is a modern classical economic theorist. Friedman's views are that the government should not intervene to minimize monopolies. His view is that government does not need to interfere in the economy.

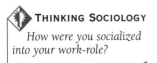

THINKING SOCIOLOGY

How were you socialized into your work-role?

The Keynesian economic theory is based on the economic views of John Maynard Keynes. This theory is at odds with the classical economic theory. Keynes believed that government intervention would be inevitable to control the cycles of the economy. He believed that the government should intervene in the economy to be certain that the economy was stable and experienced growth and the government should regulate interest rates and the supply of money. Paul A. Samuelson is a contemporary Keynesian economic theorist.

The symbolic interactionist theory addresses such issues as buying behavior, changing behavior patterns and socialization into work roles.

▼ CHAPTER SUMMARY

1. Production, distribution and the consumption of goods and services are the three components of the economic institution of any society.
2. There are three types of production: primary industry, secondary industry and tertiary industry.

3. Hunters and gatherers, horticultural societies, agrarian system and pastoral systems are the four types of preindustrial economic systems. Capitalism, socialism and communism are the three major types of industrial economic systems.
4. The postindustrial economic system is primarily based on tertiary production.
5. The five functions of the economic institution include: production and distribution of goods and services, distribution of power, distribution of political power, welfare and consumption. Latent functions of the economic institution include: people in poverty, unequal treatment of minorities, unemployment/underemployment, meaning in work, burnout, omnipotent bureaucracies, a permanent war economy, meeting people and the depletion of the world's natural resources.
6. Trends in the United States economic system include changes in composition of labor force, technology and regulation.
7. Two major theories explaining the economic institution are the classical economic theory and the Keynesian economic theory.

▼ REFERENCES

Adams, Frank and David Ellerman. 1989. "The Many Roads to Worker Ownership in America." *Social Policy*, Winter, 1989, 12–18.

Dahrendorf, Ralf. 1959. *Class and Class Conflict in Industrial Society*. Palo Alto, CA: Stanford University Press.

Druker, Peter F. 1974. *Concept of the Corporation*. New York: John Day.

Druker, Peter F. 1974. *Management Tasks—Responsibilities—Practices*. New York: Harper and Row.

Dulbeare, Kenneth M. 1984. *Democracy at Risk: The Politics of Economic Renewal*. Chatham, NJ: Catham House.

Erikson, K. and S. P. Vallas. 1990. *The Nature of Work: Sociological Perspectives*. New Haven: Yale University Press.

Friedman, Milton and Rose Friedman. 1980. *Free to Choose*. New York: Harcourt Brace Jovanovich.

Jaffe, David. 1986. "The Political Economy of Job Loss in the United States, 1970–1980." *Social Problems*, 11, 297–315.

Kalleberg, Arne and Ivar Berg. 1987. *Work and Industry: Structures, Markets, Processes*. New York: Plenum.

Kohn, Melvin I. and Carmi Schooler. 1983. *Work and Personality*. Newwood, NJ: Ablex.

Peters, Thomas J. and Robert H. Waterman. 1982. *In Search of Excellence: Lessons from America's Best-Run Companies*. New York: Harper & Row.

Rothchild, Joyce and Raymond Russell. 1986. "Alternative to Bureaucracy: Democratic ParSchor, J. B. 1992. *The Overworked American*. New York: Basic Books.

Smith, Adam. 1937. *An Inquiry into the Nature and Causes of the Wealth of Nations*. New York: Modern Library.

Weber, Max. 1958. *The Protestant Ethnic and the Spirit of Capitalism*. New York: Scribner's.

READING

"WHAT TO DO ABOUT CHOICE" EXCERPTED FROM THE PARADOX OF CHOICE: WHY MORE IS LESS BY BARRY SCHWARTZ, NEW YORK: HARPER PERENNIAL. 2004, PP. 221–236.

The news I've reported is not good. Here we are living at the pinnacle of human possibility, awash in material abundance. As a society, we have achieved what our ancestors could, at most, only dream about, but it has come at a great price. We get what we say we want, only to discover that what we want doesn't satisfy us to the degree that we expect. We are surrounded by modern, time-saving devices, but we never seem to have enough time. We are free to be the authors of our own lives, but we don't know exactly what kind of lives we want to "write."

The "success" of modernity turns out to be bittersweet, and everywhere we look it appears that a significant contributing factor is the overabundance of choice. Having too many choices produces psychological distress, especially when combined with regret, concern about status, adaptation, social comparison, and perhaps most important, the desire to have everything—to maximize.

I believe there are steps we can take to mitigate—even eliminate—many of these sources of distress, but they aren't easy. They require practice, discipline, and perhaps a new way of thinking. On the other hand, each of these steps will bring its own reward.

1. Choose When to Choose

Having the opportunity to choose is essential for well-being, but choice has negative features, and the negative features escalate as the number of choices increases. It isn't this or that particular choice that creates the problem: it's all the choices taken together. The key thing to appreciate, though, is that what is most important to us, most of the time, is not the objective results of decisions, but the subjective results. If the ability to choose enables you to get a better car, house, job, vacation, or coffeemaker, but the process of choice makes you feel worse about what you've chosen, you really haven't gained anything from the opportunity to choose. And much of the time, better objective results and worse subjective results are exactly what our overabundance of options provides. To manage the problem of excessive choice, we must decide which choices in our lives really matter and focus our time and energy there, letting many other opportunities pass us by.

2. Be a Chooser, Not a Picker

Choosers are people who are able to reflect on what makes a decision important, on whether, perhaps, none of the options should be chosen, on whether a new option should be created, and on what a particular choice says about the chooser as an individual. It is choosers who create new opportunities for themselves and everyone else. But when faced with overwhelming choice, we are forced to become "pickers," which is to say, relatively passive selectors from whatever is available. Being a chooser is better, but to have the time to choose more and pick less, we must be willing to rely on habits, customs, norms, and rules to make some decisions automatic.

🕮 *Quick Glance*

Having all the choices we do in society has made our lives easier.   T F

Some choices should not be a matter of importance in our lives.   T F

Never make a decision automatic; always carefully choose.   T F

3. Satisfice More and Maximize Less

It is maximizers who suffer most in a culture that provides too many choices. It is maximizers who have expectations that can't be met. It is maximizers who worry most about regret, about missed opportunities, and social comparisons, and it is maximizers who are most disappointed when the results of decisions are not as good as they expected.

Learning to accept "good enough" will simplify decision making and increase satisfaction. Though satisficers may often do less well than maximizers according to certain objective standards, nonetheless, by settling for "good enough" even when the "best" could be just around the corner, satisficers will usually feel better about the decisions they make.

To become a satisficer requires that you think carefully about your goals and aspirations, and that you develop well-defined standards for what is "good enough" whenever you face a decision. Knowing what's good enough requires knowing yourself and what you care about.

4. Think About the Opportunity Costs of Opportunity Costs

When making a decision, it's usually a good idea to think about the alternatives we will pass up when choosing our most-preferred option. Ignoring these "opportunity costs" can lead us to overestimate how good the best option is. On the other hand, the more we think about opportunity costs, the less satisfaction we'll derive from whatever we choose. So we should make an effort to limit how much we think about the attractive features of options we reject.

5. Make Your Decisions Nonreversible

Almost everybody would rather buy in a store that permits returns than in one that does not. What we don't realize is that the very option of being allowed to change our minds seems to increase the chances that we will change our minds. When we can change our minds about decisions, we are less satisfied with them. When a decision is final, we engage in a variety of psychological processes that enhance our feelings about the choice we made relative to the alternatives. If a decision is reversible, we don't engage these processes to the same degree.

❧ *Quick Glance*

"Good enough" is not a good choice.   T F

Do not dwell on a choice after the choice is made.   T F

When we can change our minds we are more satisfied with our choice.   T F

6. Practice an "Attitude of Gratitude"

Our evaluation of our choices is profoundly affected by what we compare them with, including comparisons with alternatives that exist only in our imaginations. The same experience can have both delightful and disappointing aspects. Which of these we focus on may determine whether we judge the experience to be satisfactory or not. When we imagine better alternatives, the one we chose can seem worse. When we imagine worse alternatives, the one we chose can seem better.

We can vastly improve our subjective experience by consciously striving to be grateful more often for what is good about a choice or an experience, and to be disappointed less by what is bad about it.

7. Regret Less

The sting of regret (either actual or potential) colors many decisions, and sometimes influences us to avoid making decisions at all. Although regret is often appropriate and instructive, when it becomes so pronounced that it poisons or even prevents decisions, we should make an effort to minimize it.

8. Anticipate Adaptations

We adapt to almost everything we experience with any regularity. When life is hard, adaptation enables us to avoid the full brunt of the hardship. But when life is good, adaptation puts us on a "hedonic treadmill," robbing us of the full measure of satisfaction we expect from each positive experience. We can't prevent adaptation. What we can do is develop realistic expectations about how experiences change with time. Our challenge is to remember that the high-quality sound system, the luxury car, and the ten-thousand-square-foot house won't keep providing the pleasure they give when we first experience them. Learning to be satisfied as pleasure turn into mere comforts will ease disappointment with adaptation when it occurs. We can also reduce disappointment from adaptation by following the satisficer's strategy of spending less time and energy researching and agonizing over decisions.

9. Control Expectations

Our evaluation of experience is substantially influenced by how it compares with our expectations. So what may be the easiest route to increasing satisfaction with the results of decisions is to remove excessively high expectations about them. This is easier said than done, especially in a world that encourages high expectations and offers so many choices that it seems only reasonable to believe that some options out there will be perfect. To make the task of lowering expectations easier, reduce the number of options you consider, be a satisficer rather than a maximizer and allow for serendipity.

10. Curtail Social Comparisons

We evaluate the quality of our experiences by comparing ourselves to others. Though social comparison can provide useful information, it often reduces our satisfaction. So by comparing ourselves to others less, we will be satisfied with more. "Stop paying so much attention to how others around you are doing" is easy advice to give, but hard advice to follow, because the evidence of how others are doing is pervasive, because most of us seem to care a great deal about status, and finally, because access to some of the most important things in life (for example, the best colleges, the best jobs, the best houses in the best neighborhoods) is granted only to those who do better than their peers. Nonetheless, social comparison seems sufficiently destructive to our sense of well-being that it is worthwhile to remind ourselves to do it less. Because it is easier for a satisficer to avoid social comparisons than a maximizer, learning that "good enough" is good enough may automatically reduce concern with how others are doing.

11. Learn to Love Constraints

As the number of choices we face increases, freedom of choice eventually becomes a tyranny of choice. Routine decisions take so much time and attention that it becomes difficult to get through the day. In circumstances like this, we should learn to view limits on the possibilities we face as liberating not constraining. Society provides rules, standards, and norms for making choices, and individual experience creates habits. By deciding to follow a rule (for example, always wear a seat belt; never drink more than two glasses of wine in one evening), we avoid having to make a deliberate decision again and again. This kind of rule-following frees up time and attention that can be devoted to thinking about choices and decisions to which rules don't apply.

In the short run, thinking about these second-order decisions—decisions about when in life we will deliberate and when we will follow predetermined paths—adds a layer of complexity to life. But in the long run, many of the daily hassles will vanish, and we will find ourselves with time, energy, and attention for the decisions we have chosen to retain.

Our parents tell us "you can be anything you want to be—no limits." But living in the constrained, protective world enables us to experiment, to explore, to create, to write our life story without worrying about starving. Without constraints, there truly would be no limits. But we would have to spend all of our time just struggling to stay alive. Choice within constraints, freedom within limits, is what enables us to imagine a host of marvelous possibilities.

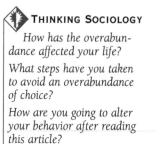

THINKING SOCIOLOGY

How has the overabundance affected your life?

What steps have you taken to avoid an overabundance of choice?

How are you going to alter your behavior after reading this article?

Perusing Religion

CHAPTER OBJECTIVES

1. What is religion?
2. What are the manifest functions of religion?
3. What are the elements of religious behavior?
4. How are religions formally organized?
5. What is secular religion or civil religion?
6. What are the trends of religion in the United States?
7. How do the three major theories view religion?

agnostic: a religion with no opinion about the existence of God

animatism: the belief that supernatural quality is attributed to an act or object

animism: the belief in spirits that are capable of helping or harming people

atheist: a person who claims no religious beliefs

civil religion: the set of beliefs that fulfills functions and has elements of religion but does not contain a supernatural entity

cosmology: a story or belief of the origin of the earth, people and supernatural deities

cult: a smaller, newly formed and more secretive religious organization with a charismatic leader

denomination: a large and organized religious organization, not officially associated with the state

Doctrine of Predestination: the theory that states the destination to heaven or hell is predetermined for the individual

ecclesia: a state religious organization

ethicalism: a religion that emphasizes moral principles for living a religious life

magic: a practice designed to manipulate or control the supernatural

monotheism: the belief in one supernatural being

polytheism: the belief in many supernatural beings of equal or similar power

profane: those things considered ordinary

Protestant Work Ethic: the beliefs based on the Protestant Reformation and behavior patterns that make people economically successful

religion: the unified system of beliefs and practices relative to sacred things

religious belief: the statement of doctrine which members of a particular religion adhere to

religious experience or affective element: a feeling gained from perception of being in contact with a higher being

religious object: a material culture used for carrying out religious rituals and for symbolizing the religion

religious ritual: the formalized actions expected of believers of a religious organization

sacred: those things considered holy

sect: a religious organization based on strict interpretation of scriptures

secularization: the process through which religion loses influence over society

theism: the belief in a supernatural being

▼ KEY PEOPLE

Emile Durkheim, Marvin Harris, Saul Levine, John Lofland, Bronislaw Malinowski, Karl Marx, Bryan Wilson, Max Weber

WHAT IS RELIGION?

Religion is a cultural universal because all societies, whether primitive or modern, have some form of religion. Religion provides a meaning for human existence. How religion is practiced, however, varies considerably from culture to culture. Some religions have a strong central deity such as Christians and Muslims, while other religions are agnostic. **Agnostic** means that the religion has no opinion about the existence of God. Some people claim to have no religious beliefs. The term for this is **atheism**. According to Erik Strand in the January/February 2004 *Psychology Today*, there is a movement for people who call themselves atheist, humanist or free-thinkers to call themselves Brights. They feel that name carries a positive connotation while the term atheist or heathen has a negative sound.

Emile Durkheim (see Chapter 1) analyzed religion from the sociological perspective, and his definition of religion is still in current usage. Durkheim defined **religion** as a unified system of beliefs and practices relative to sacred things which unites into a single moral community all those who adhere to that system of beliefs and practices. In his definition of religion, Durkheim states that all religions have those things which are considered sacred in contrast to those things which are considered profane. By **sacred**, Durkheim meant:

1. It is recognized as a power or force.
2. It is ambiguous; both physical and moral, both human and cosmic, both positive and negative, both attractive and repulsive, both helpful and dangerous.
3. It cannot be controlled for practical purposes.
4. It cannot be studied by observation or experimentation.
5. It goes beyond logic and reasoning.
6. It strengthens and supports the worshipers.
7. It makes moral demands on the worshiper.

In Christianity, the sacred are such objects as the cross and the *King James Bible*. The **profane**, according to Durkheim, are those things that are considered ordinary and include objects such as the desk at which we sit, the pen with which we write or the car we drive. According to Marvin Harris, there are two major conditions that specify whether an object is considered to be sacred or profane:

1. What is considered to be sacred and what is considered to be profane will depend on the culture. To most Americans, a cow would fall into the realm of the profane, along with goats, chickens and dogs. But to the Hindu, the cow is sacred because it is connected with the god, Vishnu.
2. What is considered to be sacred and what is considered to be profane will depend on the situation. For Christians, the practice of Communion is considered to be sacred. The wine or grape juice and the broken bread take on sacred meanings and their partaking is done with awe and reverence. However, if I drink Welch's grape juice with my lunch, it is considered profane or if I have crackers with my soup, it is considered profane.

Magic shares in the belief that humans can make contact with the sacred; but while religion helps to relate to the supernatural, magic tries to manipulate or control the supernatural; magic is goal oriented. A magic ritual, for example, would try to prevent death in childbirth while a religious ritual would celebrate the birth of a child. Malinowski believes that humans turn to magic when they feel like they cannot control the environment.

THINKING SOCIOLOGY

Give an example of something in your life that is considered sacred and another example of something you consider profane.

Quick Glance

Religion is not found in every society.	T F
Every religion has a strong central deity.	T F
Primitive societies have primitive religions.	T F
Max Weber defined "religion" as the term is used in this text.	T F
What is considered sacred is the same in all societies.	T F
Profane means sacred.	T F
What is sacred in one context will be sacred in another.	T F

THINKING SOCIOLOGY

In what types of magic have you engaged? Explain your answer.

Quick Glance

Magic and religion are the same.   T F

Imitative magic is based on the use of signs to tell the future.   T F

Magic is goal oriented. T F

Divination is negative magic.   T F

Sociology is interested in theological truths.   T F

Taboo is the same as divination.   T F

Religion serves no functions for a society. T F

There are five basic types of magic:

1. *Imitative magic* operates under the assumption that like produces like. A witch doctor makes an image of a living person and then puts a hat pin through the heart in the anticipation that the person will die.
2. *Contagious magic* is based on the belief that things which have once been together must always have a magical connection. The Nandi (living in East Africa) believe that it is dangerous for other people to get hold of such personal items as pieces of hair.
3. *Repetitive magic* believes that events which are observed to occur at the same time or in a given sequence will continue to follow the same pattern. Athletes, for example, may use the same warmup every time in order to ensure success.
4. *Taboo* or negative magic is a set of practices which forbids certain acts such as touching a forbidden religious symbol. We have a form of this type of magic in hospital ritual. Most hospitals have strict rules about sterilizing equipment and coming into and out of patient rooms. But books travel freely with no sterilization procedure. Money also regularly changes hands with no thought of sterilization.
5. *Divination* involves the use of signs to see into the future. This can be based on eclipses, comets or tea leaves. The Northwest Indians have a myth that states if you hear an owl call your name, you have been chosen to die.

In a course in sociology, we are not interested in magic and religion from a theological point of view but rather in the differences between cultures about religious beliefs and practices.

WHAT ARE THE MANIFEST FUNCTIONS OF RELIGION?

Support and Consolation

We are faced with uncertainties or disappointments in life and religion provides a means of coming to terms with these unknowns. Religion provides an explanation of things that cannot be directly verified or explained otherwise. My mother died in 1992 at a relatively young age; religion could answer the question of why she had to die at that particular time, as well as offering comfort to the bereaved in dealing with the death. The belief of a higher being who has control of the universe calms the anxiety that humans may feel when confronting their world.

Religion helps us cope with the transitional states of life. Transitional stages usually mean stress for us as we cope with making changes in our lives. Changes such as marriage, giving birth and death of loved ones are all stressful events in our life. Religion gives instruction on dealing with each of these events and most religions have rituals that deal with each transitional stage. Weddings, baptism, and funerals give a spiritual meaning to each stage helping us to cope with that transitional stage of our life.

Identification and Enhancement of Self-Importance

Religion provides us with a sense of identity. Religion helps us answer the question, "Who am I?" In Christianity, the answer becomes "I am one with God" or "I am created in the image of God." That sense of identity also may come from the religious affiliation that we may have. We identify with the particular religious organization to which we belong. Religion enhances self-importance by allowing us to relate to a

THINKING SOCIOLOGY

Which function of religion do you think is the most important? For you? For society? Why?

Quick Glance

Religion helps people understand unhappy events.   T F

Religion plays a role in rites of passage.   T F

Religion provides a sense of identity.   T F

Religion helps provide humans with a purpose in life.   T F

cosmic design. We can be reincarnated in many religions or go to a better place after we die such as heaven or a happy hunting ground.

Meaning to Life and Understanding of Spiritual Realm

Religion gives meaning to life. The belief in a supernatural being helps people to believe that there is a purpose in life. There is a belief that life has an origin and religion helps us to feel that we fit into a plan of life.

Religion helps us to understand how our culture defines what is considered to be holy. Religion tells me what is considered to be "godly." It may be fasting, praying, meditating, chanting, frenzied dancing or taking drugs such as peyote.

Social Control

Religious beliefs form the foundation for the basic mores within the society. For example, our primary felony laws are based on the Ten Commandments of the Christian faith. Fear of reprisals can keep us conforming to the expectations of society. Religion adds divine sanction to human values.

Societal Cohesiveness

Religion knits into a unity all those that support a particular belief. Moses, for example, led the Jews out of Egypt into the Promised Land. The cohesive role of religion is reflected in the survival of the Jews for almost 3,000 years even though they are geographically dispersed and do not live under a uniform government.

Prophetic Function

Many religious organizations are involved in trying to improve the conditions of contemporary life. Religious leaders often criticize some of the basic societal conditions of the established order. Moses led his people into the Promised Land and Martin Luther King was a founding force of the Civil Rights Movement.

WHAT ARE THE ELEMENTS OF RELIGIOUS BEHAVIOR?

Religious Beliefs

Religious beliefs are statements of doctrine to which members of a particular religion adhere. Religious beliefs can be divided into values and cosmology.

Religious values are shared conceptions of what is good and proper. What is good and proper is delineated in religious books, folklore, myths and legends. The *Bible*, the *Koran* and Christian Science's *Science and Health* give the basic tenants for their followers. Among primitive or preliterate cultures, the religious beliefs are more apt to be taught through the use of the spoken word. A good example of a norm that pervades many religions of the world is that of the *Golden Rule*. This rule states something to the extent that we should act towards other people as we would wish them to act towards us.

The belief or nonbelief in a supernatural entity is part of religious beliefs. Reality is that some religions, such as Christianity, believe in God, but others, such as Buddhism, do not. The great religions around the world can be divided into major "isms:" theism, ethicalism, animatism and animism. **Theism** is the belief in a supernatural being. Two forms of theism are monotheism and polytheism. **Monotheism** is the belief in one supernatural being. For Christianity, Judaism, and Islam the supernatural being is God. **Polytheism** is the belief in many supernatural beings of

THINKING SOCIOLOGY

How has religion influenced felony laws?

I SAY THE REAL AND PERMANENT GRANDEUR OF THESE STATES MUST BE THEIR RELIGION.
WALT WHITMAN

Quick Glance

Religious beliefs support the social control mechanisms.　T　F

Religion forms a unifying agent for a society.　T　F

Religion has become interested in the prophetic function.　T　F

THINKING SOCIOLOGY

How does religion help bond the people of the U.S. together? Or has it?

Quick Glance

Religious beliefs are statements of doctrine.　T　F

Legends can contain religious beliefs.　T　F

All religions believe in a god or many gods.　T　F

Polytheism believes in one deity.　T　F

Buddhism is polytheistic.　T　F

Animatism plays no role in U.S.A. life.　T　F

equal or similar power. The most widely known of the polytheists would be Hinduism. The Ancient Greeks and Romans also had pantheons of gods and goddesses in their belief system. **Ethicalism** is a religion that emphasizes moral principles for living a religious life rather than a supernatural being. Buddhism is the largest ethical religion. There is emphasis on meditation and freeing one's mind from worldly matters. It emphasizes the right thinking, right speech, right action and the right kind of living. In **animatism**, a supernatural quality is attributed to an object or an act. For example, some Native American tribes believe in an all pervasive force called "Mana." Examples of animatism in our own culture include a lucky rabbit's foot or a good luck pencil for exams. Some cultures believe that souls exist in animals and plants. These people support a belief system called **animism**. These spirits are capable of residing in humans, animals, plants, rivers or even the wind.

Numbers also have interesting meanings for different religions. For the Sioux, there is the belief in the significance of the number four. The religion of the Sioux supports the belief in the Great Spirit and the creation of the four winds, four seasons and four things above the earth (sun, moon, stars and planets). For Christians, there is the significance of the number three; God the Father, God the Son, and God the Holy Spirit.

Cosmology is a general theory of the origin of the universe. Not only does the cosmology account for the beginning of time, but it also might describe the origins of the deities and such concepts as heaven and hell. Among the Papago Indians (Southwestern United States), the world was formed by a spider web anchoring the earth to the sky. Part of the cosmology of Christianity is based on the story of creation found in Genesis, the first book of the *Old Testament*.

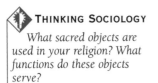
THINKING SOCIOLOGY

What "lucky" objects do you have? What is the significance of these objects?

Religious Rituals

Religious rituals are practices or actions that are expected of the believers of a religious organization. A ritual is a standardized, rhythmic action, or series of actions, directed toward some specific end. Most often rituals are collective practices which provide a form of intrastimulation that supports and renews religious beliefs. When an emotional response is associated with a ritual, the repetition of the ritual arouses the same emotion. In the U.S. culture, many of the religious organizations share communal prayer, a ritual. Rituals such as dancing, feasting or fasting might be performed to please the spirits so that crops can be planted or for rain to come. Other rituals include sacrifices, offerings, feasts, fasts, processionals, chants, dances, marriage and death rites, kneeling, immersing, abstaining from tabooed acts such as the eating of human flesh and taking of communion.

Religious Experience and Objects

A **religious experience or affective element** is the feeling gained from the perception of having contact with a higher being. Religion generally stimulates strong emotions such as awe, reverence, respect, love, fear, ecstasy or zeal. The religious experience can range from a feeling of having experienced being "born again" to a feeling of a higher being as we survey the beauty of earth.

▲ **RELIGION GENERATES STRONG EMOTIONS.**

THINKING SOCIOLOGY

What sacred objects are used in your religion? What functions do these objects serve?

AN ANALYSIS OF SOME OF THE WORLD'S MAJOR RELIGIONS

Hinduism (Vishnu, Shiva, Brahmanism):
1. belief in karma (fate) and transmigration
2. multiple gods within one greater power
3. belief in reincarnation
4. belief that good life will lead to reincarnation into a better life

Buddhism:
1. emerged from a purification of Hinduism
2. evil is a result of unrealistic desires
3. the world is guided by Buddhas which are Enlightened Ones
4. by following a "Noble Eightfold Path" people can escape reincarnation

Confucianism:
1. a social ethic with toleration for popular magic
2. vague gods and multiple gods
3. Tao is the harmony that is in all things unless disturbed by dysfunctional conduct
4. people achieve happiness by following ethics of Confucius
5. ancestor worship

Judaism:
1. one supreme deity
2. world is passing through a history that eventually ends
3. the Messiah will come at the end of the world
4. stress on ethics and rituals

Catholicism:
1. one God with a trinity which consists of Father, Son, and Holy Spirit
2. salvation through the Spirit and crucifixion of Christ
3. use of seven sacraments of the church
4. largest Christian church and claims to be the one true church

Protestantism:
1. great variation in belief
2. single God
3. trinity common
4. grew out of Catholicism
5. emphasis on love of God and saving power of faith

Islam (Mohammedanism):
1. partly grew out of Judaism and Christianity
2. one god called Allah
3. Mohammed is a prophet
4. a day of judgment will come
5. by following Mohammed and taking a pilgrimage to Mecca (if possible), people can go to Paradise after death

Johnson, Harry M. 1960. *Sociology: A Systematic Introduction.* New York: Harcourt, Brace and World, 402–403.

Religion generally relies on sacred objects to make the unseen world seem real. **Religious objects** also provide material equipment for carrying out the rituals and symbolize the religion. Objects can include shrines, cathedrals, altars, robes, magic stones and images.

Sacred objects have five characteristics:

1. Sacred objects have ambiguous meaning which is physical and moral, human and superhuman, positive and negative.
2. Sacred objects are not to be used for ordinary or utilitarian purposes.
3. Sacred objects cannot be reduced to objective criteria.
4. Sacred objects do not involve knowledge gained through the senses.
5. The sacred object can give strength to worshipers.

How Are Religions Formally Organized?

There are four ideal types of religious group structures: ecclesia, denomination, cult and sect. Each of the formal organizations involve a body of devotees, organization for religious ritual, a hierarchy of leaders and a body of doctrine. We shall analyze the four major types of religious organizations using these as the basis for discussion.

*An **ecclesia** is a state religion.* Since the ecclesia is a state religion, it takes on governmental and educational functions. Every member born into the society is a part of the religious structure. Membership is automatic and inclusive. Essentially two ways of life are provided: one for the clergy and another for the people. The head of the church is frequently called a "priest" and he/she wields tremendous power. Doctrine and ritual are determined by the leadership, and personification of belief or ritual is not acceptable; what the religious organization says is the proper belief and ritual is what is followed. The ecclesia has accommodated to the secular world and in most cases it holds a vested interest in the secular world. For this reason, the ecclesia supports the status quo and existing nonreligious organizations. Some examples are the Roman Catholic church during the Middle Ages and the Catholic church in Spain. The United States has never had nor do they now have, an ecclesia. One of the factors in the founding of the colonies was religious freedom.

The Catholic church in the United States is viewed as a denomination. *A **denomination** is a large, structured religious organization which is not officially associated with the state or government.* Members choose to become a part of a denomination rather than gaining membership by being born in that culture and is accomplished by rites or social prerequisites. Many parents, however, influence their children through the socialization process into becoming members of the denomination. Membership is composed chiefly of the affluent and property owners. The membership of a denomination has some control of the daily running of the religious organization, but there is also a formally trained leader. These leaders are usually called ministers or pastors. The ministers are specialized, educated and hold full-time jobs running the church.

A denomination has adjusted to the secular society and to other religious groups, particularly other denominations. The denomination supports the current world order and emphasizes a rational understanding of biblical and denominational teaching. There is a liberal interpretation of scripture with an emphasis on religious education, liturgy and ritualistic incantations. Services occur at regular intervals and are based on restraint, passive listening to sermons and a fixed, highly traditional order of worship. Some examples are the Presbyterian and Lutheran churches.

*A **sect** is a smaller religious organization than a denomination or an ecclesia, and generally develops out of opposition to an established church or ecclesia.* People drawn to sects are usually the poor and those without property. Some examples of sects include Black Muslims among African Americans, Jehovah's Witnesses and other pentecostal churches.

Membership in a sect is frequently based on an emotional individual experience. After undergoing this emotional experience, a person, through a confession, can then become a member of the church. This conversion experience usually occurs among

🕮 Quick Glance

All religions will conform to one of the 4 ideal types of religious structure.   T F

An ecclesia is a religion of the whole society.   T F

The American Colonies started out as an ecclesia.   T F

MAJOR RELIGIONS OF THE WORLD RANKED BY NUMBER OF BELIEVERS	
CHRISTIANITY	33%
ISLAM	21%
NONRELIGIOUS	16%
HINDUISM	14%
INDIGENOUS	6%
CHINESE TRADITION	6%
BUDDHISM	6%
SIKHISM	.36%
JUDAISM	.22%
ADHERENTS	

◆ THINKING SOCIOLOGY

What type of religious organization do you or have you belonged to? Why do you categorize the organization the way you do?

🕮 Quick Glance

The U.S. has an ecclesia.   T F

Both the ecclesia and the denomination have adjusted to secular society.   T F

A sect frequently has an emotional conversion experience.   T F

Leadership in a sect and cult is democratic.   T F

ALL RELIGIONS, ARTS AND SCIENCES ARE BRANCHES OF THE SAME TREE.
ALBERT EINSTEIN

adults or near adults. Unlike the ecclesia and denomination, both of which are very interested in children, the sect is principally concerned with adults. Most Christian sects in the United States, for example, believe in adult baptism rather than infant baptism found in Church of England or the Catholic church.

Leadership within a sect is very democratic. The congregation takes an active role in both running the church and conducting services. There is generally no definite clergy and no training for the clergy but, rather, the church is organized and run by an unspecialized, unprofessional part-time ministry who are often lay minsters.

Rituals within the sect are generally emotional and enthusiastic with active audience participation. Services tend to be spontaneous and emotional. Within the church, there is emphasis on evangelism, conversion and effective experiences.

Religious doctrine is strict and structured. There is an uncompromising view on religious doctrine with adherence to strict biblical standards, such as tithing, nonresistance, brotherly love and peace, and the group feels like they alone have the truth. With their strict interpretations of their Holy Books, the sect is typically out of step with the demands of secular society and tend to be isolationists. These groups usually refuse to cooperate with other religious or secular groups, i.e. Jehovah's Witnesses will not salute the flag.

B. Wilson developed four types of sects:

1. *The conversionist sect* is one whose teaching and activity centers on evangelism.
2. *The adventist or revolutionist sect* focuses attention on the coming overturn of the present world order, and participation in the new kingdom will be limited and only those who have maintained doctrinal and moral rectitude will be eligible.
3. *The introversionist or pietist sect* directs the attention of its followers away from the world and to the sect community.
4. *The gnostic sect* emphasizes some special body of teaching of an esoteric kind.

Sects are usually short-lived in duration, but not always. An example of a long-term sect is the Old Order Amish which you will read about in Chapter 15. A sect, however, may also grow and become widely accepted, thus becoming a denomination. Mormons or The Church of Jesus Christ of Latter Day Saints (which started out as a cult) would be an example of a sect that progressed from a smaller religious organization to a denomination. The Jehovah's Witnesses are considered to now be a denomination, or well along the way to being a denomination, according to some sociologists.

Cults are smaller, newly formed and more secretive religious organizations. Saul V. Levine refers to cults as "radical departures." Levine reports that the cults he studied were controlled by a charismatic leader and their followers might be encouraged to give up their financial means, not communicate with their families or old friends and live within the confines of the cult. Some experts estimate that there are 300,000 cult members in the United States. The People's Temple is considered a cult. In 1978, 912 people died following the orders of Jim Jones whom they considered to be "priest" and father. Other examples include snake worshipers, urban store-front churches, UFO cults, ESP cults and self-awareness cults. A highly publicized cult was the Branch Davidians lead by David Koresh. This group isolated themselves for two months at their farm in Waco, beginning March of 1993.

In a cult, members do not join in the sense of a public ceremony such as occurs in a sect or a denomination but rather accept the view of the cult leader. Members often characterize their conversion experience into a cult as a sudden, dramatic change, sometimes termed "snapping." People who join cults frequently come from

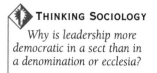

THINKING SOCIOLOGY

Why is leadership more democratic in a sect than in a denomination or ecclesia?

Quick Glance

Religious doctrine within a sect is unstructured. T F

A conversionist sect emphasizes a special body of teaching. T F

The Old Order Amish is a cult. T F

Cults are centered around a charismatic leader. T F

An ecclesia has a strict interpretation of the scriptures. T F

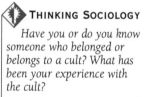

THINKING SOCIOLOGY

Have you or do you know someone who belonged or belongs to a cult? What has been your experience with the cult?

Learning TIP
Do not forget to read boxed material and charts.

MY RELIGION IS VERY SIMPLE. MY RELIGION IS KINDNESS.
DALAI LAMA

urban centers and feel like they have few if any connections to the community, or they feel like they are out of step with the expectations of society.

Rituals in a cult are often exotic and shrouded in an aura of secrecy and mystery. For example, among the Snake Handlers of West Virginia, believers handle rattlesnakes as an act of indicating their faith and their salvation.

Leadership is extremely important in a cult. A cult is characterized by being started and led by a charismatic leader; a charismatic leader has great personal magnetism which draws people to his or her beliefs and rituals. The cohesiveness of the group depends on this leader and members swear devotion to this person. The leader determines the rules for daily life and proclaims doctrines or truths, but generally the leader and his or her inner circle are exempt from the rules or prohibitions. These rules, doctrines or truths, however, cannot be questioned by cult members. Cult members commonly believe that they are an elite vanguard who have been chosen to help the charismatic leader spread the religious beliefs. Several examples of charismatic leaders are Christ, Mohammed, Jim Jones and David Koresh.

The leaders of the cults interpret or compose sacred writings to support their beliefs. Joseph Smith, founder of the Mormons, for example, went back to the Old Testament and adopted the practice of multiple wives. David Koresh's followers believed that he was the "lamb of God" and that the end of the world was approaching. Rev. Sun Yung Moon, founder of the Moonies, believed that he was Jesus, reborn.

In order to get members, some cults use very deceptive recruitment techniques. *First, a potential follower may not be told what he or she is getting into and what will be required of him or her.* The Unification Church, for example, often does not mention its name or that of Reverend Moon for perhaps several weeks. By then, the person is indoctrinated into the movement. Most cult members probably would not join if they knew ahead of time what was involved.

Second, after an initial interest is expressed, resocialization starts. This frequently begins with a retreat to some isolated area, quite often pastoral. Resocialization techniques (refer to Chapter 4) used by some cults include such activities as isolation, forced confession and sensory deprivation. Through isolation, indoctrinators remove outside influence in order to ensure that "the message" is heard. In addition to presenting a single message, some cults have the person participate in long hours of prayer and discussion without sleep and minimum calories. Even after a person becomes a member of a cult, this type of behavior can become quite common and continue to undercut rational thinking.

Third, after indoctrination, these cult members turn to the group for their every physical and psychological need or problem. And by maximizing activity, a person is not allowed much time for rational thought; in fact, many cults do not want their members to engage in rational thought. If the follower shows signs of doubting, he is made to feel that the fault lies within himself, not with the ideas, and he feels intensely guilty about this doubt. Inner doubts about doctrine are attributed to one's own evil, the influence of the devil, or the spiritual pollution of the society outside. Cult leaders assure the follower that faithful following of the cult's teachings will in time eliminate these doubts. Cults offer total, unconditional love but demand total submission to the group.

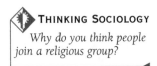
WHAT IS A SECULAR RELIGION OR CIVIL RELIGION?

Even if a culture does not have a supernatural deity or presence at the center of their religious beliefs, a secular or civil religion fulfills the functions of a religion. A civil religion can even exist side-by-side with other religions. A **civil religion** is the set of institutionalized religious features sacred to a nation. They do not emphasize super-

Characteristic	Ecclesia	Denomination	Sect	Cult
Size	Entire citizenry	Large	Generally small but may become large	Generally small but may become large
Expected duration Membership	Long time State religion so membership is automatic	Long time Primarily middle class and above	Many short time Working class and lower middle class	Brief time People disenchanted with current religions
Joining	Automatic	Little emotion required	Emotional conversion experience	Emotional conversion experience
Leadership	Formal/educated/ full time	Formal/educated/ full time	May be part time and lay leadership	Charismatic leader
Interpretation of scriptures	Liberal	Liberal	Literal	New and different
Services	Formal	Formal	Emotional	May include esoteric practices
Relationship to society	Accommodated	Accommodated	Segregationist	Segregationist
Relationship with other religions organizations	Not an issue	Accommodated	Segregationist	Segregationist

naturalism, but they do possess most of the other characteristics of religion such as beliefs, rituals and symbolism. These civil religions provide a source of integration for the population. Some examples of civil religions are American patriotism, communism, fascism and humanism.

> ◢ **THINKING SOCIOLOGY**
> *What beliefs, rituals and sacred objects are part of American patriotism?*

WHAT ARE THE TRENDS IN RELIGION IN THE UNITED STATES?

Church membership has been increasing faster than population. About 60% of the population are members of some church; in 1920 membership stood at about 43%. Membership has increased because:

1. *Joining a church is not much different than joining any other organization.* Many religious organizations require a series of classes and a verbal commitment but this is true in many other organizations, too. I can remember joining a Protestant church in California; all we had to do was walk to the front of the church, sign a form and put a pledge on the altar. The religious organization required no classes, no discussion, no questioning of commitment or belief.

2. *Joining a church is a response to anonymity and loneliness of urbanized mass society.* Church is a good place to meet people. In fact, leaders in the major company for which my husband works, recommend joining a church for meeting people when transferred to a new community.

▲ **PATRIOTISM AS A CIVIL RELIGION IS GROWING.**
IMAGE COPYRIGHT JASON STITT, 2008. USED UNDER LICENSE FROM SHUTTERSTOCK, INC.

3. *Joining a church is a "correct" behavior pattern.* Many forms have a space for religious affiliation. Joining the military, entering a hospital and registration forms in some universities ask for religious affiliation or preference.
4. *Sending children to church provides an ethical instruction and basic knowledge of our Judaic-Christian heritage.* Several churches in our area send school buses around to pick up worshipers; this means both old and young, but the age composition on the bus is almost always in the much younger age groups.

The three main religions in the United States have a Judaic-Christian heritage; these religions are Jewish, Catholic and Protestant. This is in reverse order of numbers belonging to each faith. We are, however, a nation with many different religions represented.

People do not participate equally in the religious structures. People in lower classes participate less in church activities than do those of the middle class. The lower classes are also more orthodox in their beliefs than the middle classes. For example, the lower classes are more apt to believe in hell, the devil and life after death than middle-class Americans. When people are socially deprived and join churches, we find that they are more intense in their religious participation than middle classes. Women, the aged and poorly educated people participate more than men, youths and highly educated people. People with children participate more than those without children.

Secularization has been an ongoing trend in the United States. There has been an ascendancy of nonreligious institutions over the religious institution. **Secularization** is the process through which religion loses influence over society as a whole. Religion itself becomes a specialized, isolated institution. American clergy are increasingly involved in the community and public affairs; they were heavily involved, for example, in the civil rights movement and the Vietnam War protests of the 1960s. Our holy days have become holidays. Christmas is associated with presents and Santa Claus, while Easter is new clothes. Halloween has completely lost its religious beginnings of All Saints' Eve.

Even in the face of secularization, we are a very religious country. We do not necessarily believe that people have to attend church, but there is a prevalent belief that we should believe in God. Compared to other technologically advanced countries, we are a religious nation. After the September 11, 2001 terrorist attacks, interest in religion took a dramatic upswing but religious fervor and interest are returning to the pre-September 11 level.

Churches have taken on many new functions in today's society. Religious organizations now offer sports such as basketball and baseball teams. Many churches run card games and bingo to earn money. Senior citizens groups and singles groups are sponsored by religious groups. Many churches are getting involved in child care, day care centers and primary grade education.

There has been more interaction across religious lines. More people are marrying outside of their faith. Communities have interdenominational councils to share common problems. This used to be across Protestant lines, but now religious groups such as Catholics and Jewish groups, are also joining the counsels to discuss common problems.

The social gospel movement has gained strength. There is an increasing emphasis on social action. Personal sins such as murder used to be emphasized, but now emphasis is also on economic exploitation, racial injustice and fraudulent business practices.

There has been a decline of established religions. For several years now, there has been evidence of a significant decline in commitment to the Roman Catholic Church, to the established Protestant denominations and to mainstream Judaism. The decline

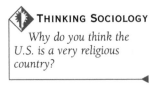

THINKING SOCIOLOGY

Why do you think the U.S. is a very religious country?

of established Protestant denominations is likewise reflected in lay participation; their membership has either leveled off or decreased.

Along with the decline in established religions, there has been an increase in the fundamentalist revival. These are the "born again Christians." Fundamentalist religious organizations have grown rapidly in recent years with the most marked increases in membership occurring among the Seventh-day Adventists, the Southern Baptist Convention and Church of the Jesus Christ of Latter Day Saints (Mormons). Fundamentalist religions attract members who see the sacrifice demanded as meaningful, in comparison to the prevalence of indulgence in society today. Fundamentalist religions may simply reflect a continuing fundamental strain of beliefs in the American culture. Some youths, especially middle-class whites, appear to search for strong, clear norms, which fundamentalist groups offer to them.

There also has been the emergence of new religions in the United States. New sects and cults have appeared in the United States since the 1960s, some with beliefs and names that seem alien or exotic to most Americans. These new religions frequently turn to eastern religions. Eastern religions such as Hinduism, Buddhism, Confucianism and Shintoism appeal because of the emphasis on self-discipline, a belief in the unity of humans with nature and the higher value placed on experience rather than intellect. One new religion founded in eastern faith is the Unification church founded by Sun Mung Moon, a Korean industrialist. Those turning to eastern religions tend to be white, educated, middle and upper-middle class. Scientology is an interesting new religion. It was founded by science fiction writer Ron Hubbard who came up with the therapy and techniques of Dianetics. This is based on metaphysical speculation, doctrine of reincarnation and the performance of mental and physical healing. There is very little formal religious ritual in this religion.

An emerging pattern in religion is the New Age Movement. The basis of this religion is support of many kinds of occult forces such as psychic healing, reincarnation, talking to the dead through mediums, regressions into past lives and telling current and future events via astrology and tarot cards. There are many shops opening centered around the New Age Movement. One shop I am familiar with, called the Balance Beam, deals in many different kinds of readings plus offers a selection of dancing and meditation methods based on Native Americans.

There has been a growth in the electronic church. Jim Baker, Jimmy Swaggart, Oral Roberts and Joel Osteen are examples of this type of religious growth. Many people watch these television shows, sometimes on a daily basis, and contribute large sums of money to the organization. In fact, in many cases, the people who are hard pressed to support themselves are sending significant percentages of their income to support these groups.

▲ YOGA IS PERCEIVED AS PART OF THE NEW AGE MOVEMENT.
IMAGE COPYRIGHT DENIS PEPIN, 2008. USED UNDER LICENSE FROM SHUTTERSTOCK, INC.

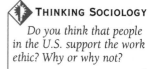

THINKING SOCIOLOGY

Why has the social gospel become increasingly important in U.S. religion?

◀

🕮 *Quick Glance*

There has been a decreasing interest in Eastern religions.　　T F

The New Age Movement deals with the occult.　T F

Television has played an increasingly important role in religion.　　T F

THINKING SOCIOLOGY

Do you think that people in the U.S. support the work ethic? Why or why not?

◀

HOW DO THE THREE MAJOR THEORIES VIEW RELIGION?

The structural functional theory is interested in what functions religion serves for the society; when we discussed the functions of religion, we were analyzing religion through this theory.

Learning TIP
Make sure all of your work
is high quality and neat
in appearance. Use only
blue or black ink unless
specified.

🦉 *Quick Glance*

Max Weber believed that
the Protestant Reformation
contributed to the growth
of capitalism.   T F

The work ethic stresses
self-discipline and
individualism.   T F

The Doctrine of Predes-
tination was part of the
Catholic faith.   T F

The Protestant Reformation
came before the Industrial
Revolution.   T F

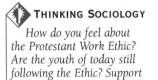
THERE ARE NO ATHEISTS IN
FOXHOLES.
WILLIAM T. CUMMINGS

⚡ **THINKING SOCIOLOGY**

*How do you feel about
the Protestant Work Ethic?
Are the youth of today still
following the Ethic? Support
your answer with three
examples.*

Max Weber wrote about the importance of Protestant thinking on the development of capitalism in the western world. He noted that a majority of business leaders were Protestant and that the Protestant Reformation preceded the Industrial Revolution. Based on his analysis, he developed the ideas of the Protestant Ethic and the
Spirit of Capitalism. These ideas lead to beliefs and behavior patterns which made
people successful in business. This is commonly called the **Protestant Work Ethic**.

In the Catholic church, the Catholic participant could, through mediation to the
deity by the saints and clergy, secure forgiveness for sins and thus be assured salvation. Protestantism, however, did not believe that any person could mediate between
the deity, and that each person faced his deity alone; he could not turn to others for
absolution. This led to the growth of individualism.

Furthermore, Protestant groups developed the Doctrine of Predestination. In the
Doctrine of Predestination, it was determined at some point, either at birth or conception, of whether we would go to heaven or hell; and not knowing was a very
uncomfortable position to be. We wanted knowledge of which direction so this created an interest in the search for signs of grace. Since the Protestant's command was
to establish the kingdom of God in this world, and since the command gradually
came to be identified with one's calling, further transition was made to the acceptance
of worldly individual success as a sign of grace, i.e. predestination into everlasting
life.

According to Weber, the Protestant ethic stimulated the rise of modern bureaucratic capitalism with its emphasis on individual responsibility, self-discipline, impersonal devotion to one's task, hard work as an end in itself and saving instead of self-
indulgent spending.

Weber contended:

1. That Protestantism emphasized individual responsibility, self-discipline, impersonal devotion to work and hard work. Work became a moral obligation.
2. That the pursuit of money was an end in itself, rather than a necessary evil
   or a means to other more important ends.
3. That we could pursue money without limit. Weber opposed this attitude to
   one he believed was much more common, namely, "traditionalism," or the
   pursuit of money to a level where it can support some traditionally defined
   standard of living.
4. That Protestantism had an "ends-justify-the-means" attitude toward the
   methods of acquiring money, that is, the capitalist spirit is not hampered by
   traditional ways.
5. That in his dealings with others, the capitalist is not bound by traditional
   obligations. For the capitalist, the breaking of traditional obligations results
   in an individualistic philosophy of "every man for himself."
6. That since a person is not bound by traditional beliefs and obligations he
   could charge interest on loans. The Catholic Church had forbidden Christians to lend money at interest, this rule made capitalism impossible and
   Jews took over the function of money lenders during the Middle Ages. Some
   time after Calvin's day, Protestantism began to allow the taking of interest,
   and this freed Christians to invest their capital.
7. That worldly success could not be flaunted in self-indulgence or ostentatious
   spending, for we worked not for ourselves but for the greater glory of God.
   Our success meant saving and capital accumulation.

These behavior patterns and attitudes laid the foundation for the operation of the
bureaucratic structure and the development and growth of modern capitalism. Some
writers say that the Protestant Work Ethic has become an attitude of the past, while

others say that we still are a nation that supports the Protestant Work Ethic but people now seek more than just money, they also want enjoyment and meaning from their life's work.

Conflict theory takes a different look at the place of religion in society than Weber. Karl Marx disagreed with Weber and believed that religion was dysfunctional for people in the lower classes. Marx believed that the upper classes used religion to support their own life styles and to keep workers in a complacent frame of mind with the upper classes. The elite, according to Marx, hoped to keep attention focused on the next world or heaven, therefore, not noticing how bad conditions were in the present world.

The conflict theorist states that different religions within a society can tear the society apart. Ireland has had many fights over the last 200 years between Catholics and Protestant. In the sixteenth century, Mary Queen of Scots and Queen Elizabeth I tore the country apart with their Catholicism versus Protestantism.

Religion can be in conflict with other institutions in society. The Catholic belief on birth control is viewed by some as out of step with the demands of rapidly growing populations in many South American countries. The Hindu caste system is out of step with the demands of modern industrializing society. The caste system has been outlawed but still plays an important role within the Indian system. If I am in an upper caste, I technically cannot, for example, come in direct physical contact with an untouchable, and if I do, I have to go through a purification ritual. I am in serious trouble in today's society if I am a manager, an upper caste, and the computer expert is an untouchable!

Religion can be a force of prejudice between individuals, groups or nations. Some of the great wars of history have been fought in the name of religion. The Crusades were religious wars, the Spanish Inquisition caused the loss of many lives.

The symbolic interactionists, among other interests, study why people join cults. Some professionals state that those who join cults are individuals who have a low self-esteem, are easily led by others and have difficulties making decisions. However, John Lofland in *Doomsday Cult* maintains that there is not a psychological profile of those who join cults. Lofland identifies a series of seven stages for joining a cult. John Lofland studied a group of Moonies or those who had become total converts. Lofland concluded that:

1. Some form of *tension* was mentioned by the converts. The stress was not the same for every convert; some converts mentioned stress related to family or education.
2. The type of *problem-solving perspective* utilized by those who became total converts was a religious problem-solving perspective. Lofland suggests that there are at least three different types of problem-solving perspectives that most individuals use to deal with stress. A psychiatric problem-solving perspective suggests that we might talk to someone else about our problem or even talk to ourselves. We might seek therapeutic help. A second perspective is political problem-solving. We look at what is going on around us to better understand the stress that we are experiencing. We are able to say, for example, that things will get better once we complete this semester. The last perspective identified is religious problem-solving. The stress is viewed as God trying to teach us something or punish us for something.
3. Those who became total converts experienced a religious *seekership*. They had failed to find satisfaction in mainstream religious organizations. These converts believed that mainstream religion talked about love, joy and happiness but failed to find that the followers practiced love, joy and happiness.

🕮 *Quick Glance*

Marx believed that religion supported the beliefs of the elite.   T F

Two or more religions within a society can weaken social cohesion.   T F

The symbolic interactionist is interested in why people join cults.   T F

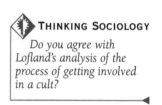
THINKING SOCIOLOGY

Do you agree with Lofland's analysis of the process of getting involved in a cult?

🕮 *Quick Glance*

Cult members experience a religious seekership.   T F

Cult converts redefine "self."   T F

Lofland wrote about Jim Jones.   T F

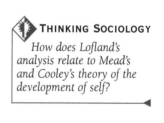
THINKING SOCIOLOGY

How does Lofland's analysis relate to Mead's and Cooley's theory of the development of self?

🕮 *Quick Glance*

Joining a cult is a marker event.   T F

Joining a cult usually means cutting ties with significant others.   T F

Cults are out of step with mainstream religion.   T F

THINKING SOCIOLOGY

Do you think that college students are more suscep-tible to joining a cult than a young working person? Why or why not?

4. A *turning point* occurred in the converts' lives. Each of the converts experi-enced a worsening of the stress in their lives. For some it was a spouse ver-balizing their desire for a divorce, for others it was receiving a rejection let-ter for graduate school.

These four conditions are viewed as predisposing conditions. When these con-ditions are present and the person meets with a cult member, they are well on their way to becoming a total convert. After a person is converted and becomes a part of the cult, he frequently quits his life in the "outside world" and moves into the cult. Cult converts undergo a changing definition of self, a change in who their significant others are and, frequently, a loss of sense of self.

▼ CHAPTER SUMMARY

1. Durkheim defined religion as a unified system of beliefs and practices related to sacred things. He distinguished between the sacred and the profane.
2. Magic shares in the belief that humans can make contact with the sacred. There are five types of magic: imitative, contagious, repetitive, taboo and divination.
3. The manifest functions of religion include support and consolation, identifica-tion and enhancement of self-importance, meaning to life and understanding of spiritual realm, social control, societal cohesiveness and prophetic function.
4. The elements of religious behavior include religious beliefs, religious rituals, re-ligious experiences and religious objects.
5. There are four types of religious group structures: ecclesia, denomination, sect and cult.
6. A civil religion is the set of institutionalized religious features sacred to a nation.
7. Church membership, secularization, social gospel movement, growth in funda-mentalism, emergence of new religions and a growth in the electronic church are current trends in religion.
8. The structural functional theory is interested in what functions religion serves for the society. The conflict theory posts that different religions within a society can tear the society apart. The symbolic interactionist theory focuses on the social interaction between members of religious organizations.

▼ REFERENCES

Berger, Peter. 1961. *The Noise of Solemn Assemblies.* Garden City, NY: Doubleday.

Durkheim, Emile. 1915. *The Elementary Forms of the Religious Life.* Glencoe, IL: Free Press.

Harris, Marvin. 1974. *Cows, Pigs, Wars and Witches.* New York: Vintage Books.

Howells, William. 1948. *The Heathens.* Garden City, NY: Doubleday, 50–53.

Levin, Saul V. 1984. *Radical Departures: Desperate Detours to Growing Up.* Harcourt, Brace, Jovanovich.

Lindenthal, Jacob, Jerome K. Myers, Max P. Pepper, and Maxine S. Stern. 1970. "Mental Sta-tus and Religious Behavior." *Journal for the Scientific Study of Religion,* 9 (summer), 143–149.

Lofland, John. 1977. *Doomsday Cult.* New York: Irvington Publishers, Inc.

Malinowski, Bronislaw. 1954. *Magic, Science, and Religion.* Glencoe, IL: Free Press, pp. 39–40.

McGaa, Ed. 1990. *Mother Earth Spirituality.* New York: Harper Collins.

Weber, Max. 1930. *The Protestant Ethic and the Spirit of Capitalism,* trans. Talcott Parsons. New York: Scribner's.

Weber, Max. 1964. *The Sociology of Religion,* trans. E. Fishchoff. Boston: Beacon Press.

Wilson, Bryan. 1959. "An Analysis of Sect Development." *American Sociological Review,* 24 (Feb), 3–15.

READING

I LOST MY DAUGHTERS TO A CULT BY KAYLAN PICKFORD
AS TOLD TO CLAIRE SAFRAN

It's 1981 and I'm in a shabby neighborhood in New York, sitting in an almost barren room, facing a middle-aged stranger dressed in a saffron-colored robe. Although I don't know it yet, I will spend the next ten years fighting this man for the souls of my two daughters.

He knows my face. I'm 51 at the time and no longer a suburban homemaker in Connecticut—I've begun a new career as a model, one of the first "older" faces. But I am finding it hard to smile.

My firstborn Susan, has wanted me to meet him. "Mom, he is the best teacher. He knows everything," she said. I'd seen her glow this way before, when she was embarking on a new romance. "Are you in love?" I asked. "Not in the way you think," she answered.

My daughters—Susan, 28, and Anne, 25—call him Babaji, an affectionate Indian term for a guru or leader. He and his inner circle of some 12 women, including Susan, live together here: unbeknownst to me, Anne has just begun to visit him, and soon she'll be moving in too.

Indian-born and now calling himself Patel R Patel[1], he leads a temple, one of 3,500 small cults now operating in this country. In a singsong voice, Patel tells me about his direct line to God and about the day he revealed what Patel was "destined" to do: enlighten not the poor and hungry but the educated and privileged.

Suddenly he stands and places both hands on my head and says, "I am going to give you the most precious thing I have." Then he chants the word ram until it vibrates inside my head. I begin to understand the magnetism that has drawn my daughters to him.

Still, I'm uneasy. I know that Susan is somewhere in the apartment, and I'm tempted to find her and drag her home with me. "She's a grown-up," I tell myself. "You can't do that." I also knew that no matter what I did, she wouldn't leave.

That seems like lifetimes ago. In the intervening years I've talked with psychiatrists, deprogrammers, cult investigators, attorneys, and former members, trying to understand cults and why my children would be in one. Small cults like this one count their members by the dozen; large ones—the Unification Church, Scientology—have tens, even hundreds of thousands of followers. All told, cults now have 5 to 10 million members, and although their leaders teach different beliefs, all seem to use the same manuals for mind control. The experts say these groups attract people who are "alienated," or going through a difficult transition, or feeling wobbly in their self-esteem—descriptions that didn't seem to fit my bright and shining daughters.

It was true that the girls had had losses. They were 8 and 5 when their father's drinking problem led to our divorce. Three years later I married again—but just after our honeymoon, Bill, whom the girls adored, was diagnosed with cancer. He died four years after that, and Anne and Susan lost another beloved father.

Yet, as they had after the divorce, they seemed to cope well. I remember them as lively, good-natured children, quick with funny duets and dances. And they were bright, winning scholarships to prestigious private schools. Susan went to Yale, Anne to Harvard.

[1]Name changed

*Reprinted from *Redbook*, March 1995. Copyright © 1995 by Clair Safran.

Quick Glance

The daughters want their mother to meet the cult leader.   T F

The mother supports the decision of her daughter to join the cult.   T F

The cult leader is from China.   T F

Quick Glance

Cults have a small
membership in the
U.S.A.   T F

Cults attract people
who are alienated.   T F

The mother disapproved
of New Age thinking. T F

Over the years, as the three of us adjusted to the tragedies in our lives, we forayed into New Age territory. I explored reincarnation, astrology, taro cards, and metaphysics. At 14, Anne spent a summer studying transcendental meditation, later she took a course in deep meditation and visited an ashram (spiritual retreat) for two weeks. Susan spent eight months living communally in Washington, D.C. Recently I was told that many cult members have dabbled in these areas. At the time it all seemed harmless, though now I'm not so sure.

Anne became a traveler and a promising artist. Susan was a commercial artist who, at 28, had contracts to create humorous greeting cards and a cartoon strip for a national syndicate. It was another artist, whom Susan met on a train in 1981, who told her about a "wonderful guru" and urged her to attend her first meeting.

At the time, both girls had active social lives and circulated in an elite group. Susan had a live-in boyfriend (they broke up shortly after she met Patel). Anne was sharing an apartment, with Caroline Kennedy, a former classmate, and two male friends.

But Susan and Anne were confronting still more tragedy: the death of their father, also by cancer, and then the death of my mother, whom they adored. If my daughters had turned to drugs, I might have spotted the warning signs. But I wasn't at all sure how to interpret their changes in behavior. Were they due to grief, or something else?

The first signs were subtle—the girls were uncharacteristically rude, cranky, and critical. They told me that I was "insincere" and "lazy." Their phone calls, once so frequent, grew rare, and there was always an excuse—"too busy," "too tired"—for why we couldn't get together.

It took only three months, in the spring and summer of 1981, for them to be hooked. (It was around this time that I heard of Patel and was invited to meet him.) By September, both girls had moved in with Patel. Cults usually begin by bombarding a newcomer with love and information: Susan told me how special and honored she felt to be chosen as one of Patel's students. With Patel she and other cult members worked their way through fat volumes of obscure Eastern writings. In group confessions they were learning to feel humble and "unworthy."

Like most cult leaders, Patel controlled the flow of information. He "interpreted" the television news for the group and explained the "true" meaning of my conversations with Susan and Anne. At the same time, their minds were being numbed by sessions of meditation and chanting. They were following a strict vegetarian diet and living in a crowded apartment, where their sleep was irregular and broken. They were awakened at dawn for the day's first meditations.

In short, they were being brainwashed and isolated, and were turned against family and friends. Early on, Anne was urged to invite Caroline to meet Patel. When Caroline declined, Anne pressed her repeatedly, ultimately fracturing a friendship of more than ten years.

Naturally their travel was sharply curtailed too. At the end of that first summer, Anne was allowed to spend a vacation weekend with me in Maine. She seemed thin, pale, edgy, and she avoided being alone with me. When she suddenly announced she was going to leave, I insisted that we take a walk. We'd gone only a few steps when she turned and attacked me.

"There is no truth here," she began, "none in this family."

Suddenly, she was blaming me for the divorce and accusing me of profiting from Bill's death, even though she knew I'd used the money he'd left me to pay both girls' college tuitions. For the first time ever, I wanted to slap her. I raised my hand. "Hypocrite," she screamed. "Liar!"

Quick Glance

Both girls had successful
careers.   T F

Losses pushed the
daughters toward the
cult.   T F

It took over a year for
the girls to be resocialized
into the cult.   T F

I dropped my hand and turned away. "Aren't you going to do anything?" she yelled after me.

Anne left for New York the next morning. Frantic, I called Susan the next day. "What is happening?" I asked her. "I don't understand what's going on."

Back from Maine, I called Patel, whom I'd already met by now. He began calmly, explaining that my daughters were with him because he told them the truth. When I told him Anne and Susan wouldn't keep living there, his voice turned cold and hard, and he said, "You will find out that I always win."

Win? Is that how a man of God talks?

Panicked, I began to search for help. I hired a private detective and cult investigator to learn more about Patel, and I called the Cult Awareness Network and the American Family Foundation. I tracked down the document incorporating Patel's group as a nonprofit organization, and saw its tax return, which listed few expenses but showed tax-free assets of more than $2 million. As the private investigator discovered, Patel had other members, beyond the "inner circle," who lived with him: most worked and then turned over all or most of their paychecks to the temple.

Meanwhile, under Patel's guidance, Susan was disengaging herself from her career, helping with the cult's housework and seldom leaving the apartment. Anne, told that her own dreams of becoming an artist were a mistake, was doing clerical work in an office with two other cult members, all of who traveled together, watching each other constantly and dutifully reporting any "deviant" word or act to Patel.

Finally, I located some former members of this cult, and my worst suspicions were confirmed. They claimed Patel was having sex with all the women who lived with him. And he threatened those who dared to defy him. I listened to a tape that another member, a young man trying to leave the cult, had made of a phone conversation with Patel. The guru cursed him, called him a piece of excrement, and threatened him, saying, "I will deal with you."

I contacted a psychiatrist who specialized in cult awareness and asked him, "What would you do if it were your child?"

"I'd get her out of there as fast as possible, any way I could," he said. A year after my meeting with Patel, I was planning to have my daughters kidnapped.

Cult experts referred me to deprogrammers. The one I chose explained that Susan and Anne would have to be picked up at the same time; leaving one of them behind with an angry Patel would be dangerous. The rescuers, two six-person teams, would be flying to New York from various locations in the United States. To pay for their plane fares, housing, food, and expertise, a total of more than $30,000, I emptied my bank account and then borrowed the rest from friends and family. Now the deprogrammers needed to work out logistics: once kidnapped, where could my daughters safely be hidden from the cult? Where could the kidnapping be staged without too many people seeing and perhaps interfering? And how would I get Anne and Susan there—together?

Although Patel permitted them to meet me only rarely, they were allowed to meet my father more often. A churchgoing Episcopalian, he was intrigued by religious esoterica and had established a friendly connection to Patel. So the team leader told me, "Your father is the key."

Explaining the plan, I asked my father, "Will you invite the girls for lunch or for tea? That's all you have to do." My father and I have frequently been at odds; somehow whatever I said or did was wrong. "They're grown women," he answered, "entitled to lead their own lives." But he agreed to think about it.

A week later his answer came in a letter: He refused, declining to be "the Judas goat."

᭣ *Quick Glance*

The cult leader was open to free flow of information.   T F

The daughters were thankful to their mother under the guidance of the cult leader.   T F

The mother hired a team of deprogrammers.   T F

"We'll find another way," the team leader reassured me. Two weeks later I met my "contact," a young woman who'd been rescued from another cult and who would help plan the kidnapping. I walked back to my apartment feeling scared but hopeful.

It didn't last. Soon after I got home, Susan telephoned. "I'm calling to tell you that I'm leaving for California." My last hope had backfired. "When?" I asked. "Tomorrow or the next day," she said. There would be no time to meet and say good-bye.

The plan was blown, and I was finding it hard to breathe. How could this happen? Seven years later, my daughters confirmed what I suspected even then: Their grandfather had found a way to warn them.

In 1984, two and a half years after Anne and Susan joined the cult, the entire group moved West, and Anne joined her sister at its headquarters in Los Angeles. I shuddered as I watched the cult shoot-out in Waco, Texas, in February, 1993 and heard of the mass deaths last fall in Switzerland. Would my daughters be vulnerable to such hideous self-destruction?

As the years passed and the girls moved into their thirties, I kept trying to reach them. Now and then they'd answer a letter or return a phone call. But in the past 13 years, my daughters and I have met face-to-face maybe ten times, usually in public places, always with my promise not to try another kidnapping. I have begged them again to rethink their lives, to leave the cult, if only temporarily. But they no longer trust me. "Babaji says you're going to kidnap us," they told me. "He says that you're going to put us into a mental institution and leave us there to rot and die." We can only be "at peace" with each other if I accept, honor, and respect Patel, they said. First, I must apologize to him and beg forgiveness for my rude words and unkind thoughts. That I couldn't do.

Cult experts advise parents like me to maintain as much contact with our children as possible, and I tried hard to do that. But finally it became too painful. Three years ago I wrote my daughters that if they ever decided to leave the cult, my door would be open. Then I stopped calling and writing, and there has been silence between us ever since. As I write this, part of a book I'm preparing, they are 41 and 38, and I ache for what they have lost to this cult. Promising careers. Marriage. Motherhood.

Like so many mothers, I wonder if I'm to blame for what has gone wrong in my children's lives. What could I have done differently? Wanting to be strong for them after the divorce and after Bill's death, I hid much of my own grief and loneliness. Was that a mistake? Did they, too, have hurts and needs they had buried?

Some days I search for cause and effect. On others I think of my daughters as targets of random violence, like the victims of drive-by shootings or runaway trains. They were unlikely prey, two young women looking for truth, and tragically, finding their version of it in the wrong place.

◆ THINKING SOCIOLOGY

Do you think the mother was correct in her actions?

If your daughter were in a cult, what would you do?

How did the girls' experience illustrate the characteristics of resocialization as discussed in Chapter 4?

Investigating Education

IMAGE COPYRIGHT JOHANNA GOODYEAR, 2008. USED UNDER LICENSE FROM SHUTTERSTOCK, INC.

CHAPTER OBJECTIVES

1. What is education?
2. What are the structures within the educational system?
3. What are the manifest functions of education?
4. What are the latent functions of education?
5. Are academic standards declining?
6. What changes can be made in the educational system?
7. What are the trends of education in the United States?
8. How do the three major theories view the educational system?

certification function: the diplomas and certificates earned through education which are important in today's job market

core of knowledge: the basic information on English, Math and Science shared nationwide by students

credentialism: the belief that education confers greater ability in accomplishing a task regardless of the educational needs of the job and ability of the person

de facto segregation: a segregation based on residential pattern

de jure segregation: a segregation based on law

education: an institution dealing with the formal transmission of culture and knowledge

educational achievement: the amount of educational success based on standardized testing

formalism: the practice of establishing rules to govern the educational system

gerrymandering: the process where a school district can either maintain segregated schools or divide school boundaries to promote integration

hidden curriculum: the attitudes and practices exhibited by the student that are not part of the academic curriculum but are deemed to be important for success in the educational process

informal structure: the customs and interest subcultures that exist in the educational system; high school and college subcultures

mainstreaming: use of mixed ability groups

multiple-track system: the educational system based on career selection after primary grade years

multiculturalism: the educational philosophy stressing the importance of and knowledge about different racial, ethnic and religious categories

single-track system: the educational system that is used in the United States based on primary, intermediary and secondary school with no formal occupational placement until after secondary school

teacher expectancy: the effect that a teacher's expectation of each student influences the learning for that child

tracking: the placing of students in different groups according to the abilities of the students

---

▼ **KEY PEOPLE**

James Coleman, Robert Fulghum, E. D. Hirsch, Jonathan Kozol, Robert Rosenthal

What Is Education?

Education is that institution which transmits knowledge, skills and mental abilities to the members of the society. Education is considered to be an agency of socialization and is a cultural universal. Some societies teach through informal methods; children living in primitive or preliterate societies, such as the Yanomamo, learn through watching and imitating adult role models and listening to legends and folklore. Within a horticultural or agrarian society, small-scale farming utilizes unskilled workers who do not need much formal education. In the early industrial system, society depended on semi-skilled and skilled workers; therefore, education for the common man was not considered of vital importance. Education was reserved for the upper classes. As cultures moved on into an industrial and a postindustrial system, education became critical because of changes in the labor force. We increasingly employed technicians, managers and other professional personnel. Parents began demanding education for their children in order to improve upward mobility, and law enforcement agencies realized that education served as a means of social control. There has been a steady rise in the amount of formal education required in industrial and postindustrial societies. The institution of education no longer depends solely on informal training, but is now a formalized system.

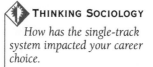

Quick Glance

The institution of education is found only in industrialized societies.　T F

Education has become less important in today's economy than 100 years ago.　T F

Education complements law enforcement agencies.　T F

Education is an agency of socialization.　T F

What Are the Structures Within the Educational System?

Multiple- or Single-Track System

In the **multiple-track system**, a child begins his educational career in a primary school; at approximately age 9, a child is tested and put into a specialized secondary school such as vocational education, teacher's college, university or terminal degree. The decision for the person's career is made during the ages of about 9 to 12. This system exists in many societies in Europe and eastern countries.

The second system is called the **single-track system**. Within the single-track system, a child attends a primary school, an intermediary school and then a secondary school. (Some children start before kindergarten in preschools or prekindergarten.) From secondary school, the child goes to the job market, teacher's college, university or a vocational education program. The decision for future plans is made at a much later date than that of the multiple-track system. If a child opts for further education, this is called post-secondary education. A child can change his/her mind about career choice at any point in the secondary and post-secondary system. This is the strength of the single-track system: people are given the opportunity to change their educational plans at many points in the life cycle. We use this system in the United States.

Formalism

Another characteristic of the educational system is formalism:

1. *Age is strictly regulated.* A child, for example, has to be 5 years old on or before September 1 in Texas in order to enter kindergarten.
2. *Educational attainment is determined by the state.* A student cannot drop out of high school until 16 or earning a diploma.
3. *Amount of time in school session is state determined.* For example, the state determines the number of days in the school year, the number of contact hours that is required per student and the times the school days start and end. We,

Thinking Sociology

How has the single-track system impacted your career choice.

Quick Glance

A single-track system gives students more flexibility in job placement.　T F

The single-track system exists in many societies in Europe.　T F

Formalism is a characteristic of the educational system.　T F

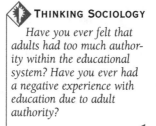

Thinking Sociology

Have you ever felt that adults had too much authority within the educational system? Have you ever had a negative experience with education due to adult authority?

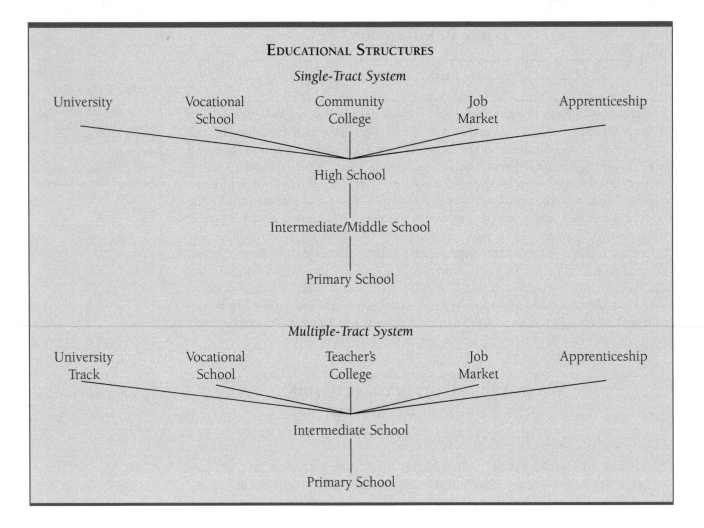

EDUCATIONAL STRUCTURES

Single-Tract System

| University | Vocational School | Community College | Job Market | Apprenticeship |

High School

Intermediate/Middle School

Primary School

Multiple-Tract System

| University Track | Vocational School | Teacher's College | Job Market | Apprenticeship |

Intermediate School

Primary School

as instructors, know when it is time to end a class because books close, jackets go on and one foot is in the aisle as students ready themselves to take off!

4. *Adults carry considerable authority*. Think back when you were in grade school. If you had to go to the restroom, you had to ask permission. If you wanted to ask a question or answer a question, you had to raise your hand.

5. *The educational system is based on a bureaucratic structure*. At the top of the pyramid are the trustees; they make basic policy for the school district. Next in line are district administrators and then school administrators. There are more administrators and support administrative positions than there are teachers in the classroom in many school districts. Next in line are teachers. At the bottom of the pyramid are students. Students technically are the teachers' employers, but, in reality, employers are administrators and boards.

 **THINKING SOCIOLOGY**

What subculture were you in during high school? What college or university subculture were/are you in?

Informal Structure

Informal structures develop among high school and college students. These subcultures form reference groups for students thus influencing behavior and attitudes toward school.

1. *There are three subcultures in high school*. Students in the fun subculture are interested in sociability, clothes, cars, dates and good personality. The academic subculture are those students which are defined as the "good" students. These students are interested in grades and the ideas of the classroom.

The delinquent subculture consists of those students who stress rebellion, contempt, ridicule and defiance of the system.

2. *In college, there are four subcultures.* Students in the collegiate orientation are interested in money and having a good time in college. They take courses in which they know they can achieve passing grades and are on the lookout for good parties. Star athletes sometimes fall into this category. Students with the vocational orientation view college in terms of future jobs. They take curriculums which they know should lead to a good paying job. They frequently do not have a strong sense of college or university loyalty, but rather look to their future profession. The third subculture is the academic orientation. These students work very hard to earn good grades and are very involved in the ideas and interests of the faculty and frequently go into graduate work or professional training. Students in the fourth subculture, nonconformist orientation, are critical of the establishment and even though they are interested in new ideas, they do not necessarily identify with or relate to the faculty and are frequently hostile to administrators and feel detached from the system. These students often adopt distinctive styles of dress and speech. As the job market has shifted, more and more students are viewing college and university as a way to a better job; little time is left over for the nonconformist orientation of the 1960s, when the job market was open and jobs were plentiful.

Informal structures also exist among teachers based on scholastic reputation, length of teaching service and, among colleges and universities, presentations of papers and publications.

WHAT ARE THE MANIFEST FUNCTIONS OF EDUCATION?

Transmission of Culture

It is up to the educational system to complete the socialization of the young into the basic values, norms and practices of society. As a society, we want the educational system to make up any deficiencies that occur in the home training. Right along with finishing up the socialization of the young, is the teaching of immigrants in the ways of the culture. In fact, this was one of the initial functions of the mass educational system developed in the United States. Through a mass education system, immigrants could learn the American way of life and mainstream into the rest of society. The public schools have been relatively successful in acculturating immigrant populations.

Achievement of Literacy Skills

Students learn to read, write and do arithmetic. **Educational achievement** refers to how much the student does learn and is frequently measured by standardized tests that determine mastery of the subject. Information becomes more specialized as we

THINKING SOCIOLOGY

What did you learn in kindergarten? What norms were part of the hidden curriculum?

🦅 **Quick Glance**

The hidden curriculum is a latent function.　　T　F

"Play Fair" is learned in kindergarten.　　T　F

We learn about keeping clean and healthy in school.　　T　F

THINKING SOCIOLOGY

What credentials do you need for your chosen occupation? Do you feel these credentials are really necessary?

advance through the educational system. For example, I learned how to subtract and multiply before I learned calculus.

Development of Social Skills

The educational system tries to make its students well-adjusted individuals who function adequately in interpersonal relations. Social skills include getting along with classmates in the classroom and on the playgrounds and showing respect to teachers. Students should learn how to follow orders, give orders, and to work in a neat and timely manner.

This objective addresses ideas that are considered to be a part of the hidden curriculum. The **hidden curriculum** are those attitudes and practices exhibited by the student that are not a part of the academic curriculum but are thought to be important for success in the educational process. The hidden curriculum includes the ability of the student to be on time for school, to raise his hand to ask for permission to get a drink of water, to sit "Pretzel style" when instructed in a reading class and to line up for a fire drill. Robert Fulghum's book *All I Really Need to Know I Learned in Kindergarten* suggests that the important social skills are actually learned in kindergarten. (Refer to Insert Box for a summary of what you needed to learn in kindergarten.) A child's inability to adhere to the hidden curriculum may be viewed as concern for the child's ability to be successful in school, and this concern may be voiced to the child's parents.

Dispensing Information Concerning Physical and Psychological Well-Being

Emphasis is placed on health education classes in order to teach information concerning personal hygiene, sex education, proper diet and dental hygiene. Efforts are made to improve personal adjustment through personal counseling and through offering developmental courses in career placement. The curriculum to transmit knowledge for well-being varies depending on the age level.

WHAT YOU NEEDED TO LEARN IN KINDERGARTEN

Robert Fulghum gives the following skills that are learned in kindergarten:

Share everything.
Play fair.
Don't hit people.
Put things back where you found them.
Clean up your own mess.
Don't take things that aren't yours.
Say you're sorry when you hurt somebody.
Wash your hands before you eat.
Flush.
Warm cookies and cold milk are good for you.
Live a balanced life—learn some and think some and draw and paint and sing and dance and play and work everyday some.
Take a nap every afternoon.
When you go out into the world, watch out for traffic, hold hands and stick together.
Be aware of wonder.

Fulghum, Robert. 1989. *All I Really Need to Know I Learned in Kindergarten.* New York: Villard Books.

Preparation for Higher Education and Occupational Role

Some students may choose the curriculum that will prepare them for higher education while other students will take cosmetology or auto mechanics and seek employment immediately after high school. Because the diplomas and certificates earned through education are so important in today's job market, these are called the certification functions. The certification function has led to what is called credentialism. **Credentialism** assumes that a diploma or a degree makes an individual more qualified for an occupation or job.

Promotion of Technological Change and Preservation of Status Quo

It is within major universities that much of the medical and business research occurs. In some of these colleges and universities, faculty members must do research and publish findings or they are in danger of losing their position. The educational system also tries to preserve the culture. Within the educational system, we teach such basic values as patriotism, achievement and work ethic.

WHAT ARE THE LATENT FUNCTIONS OF EDUCATION?

Sorting and Sifting Agency

Success in the school system contributes to upward mobility. Those students who do well in school, if they cannot afford upper education, can get scholarship and work-study money in order to help them attend college. Ambitious children can climb the social class ladder. Education is not a sufficient condition for success, but it is usually a necessary one. The amount of education that a person has is a good indicator of social status.

Establishment of Social Relationships

As children, we meet our friends in school; we get into our cliques in high school; at college and the university, we make future business contacts.

Marriage Market

Many people meet their future spouses in school. For example, both of us met our husbands at school.

Future Professional and Business Contacts

During your days at school, you will meet people who you will depend on for advice and reference when you enter into the work force. My family doctor, for example, referred me to an orthopedic surgeon who graduated from the same medical school that he did.

MEAN ANNUAL EARNINGS OF LEVEL OF EDUCATION, 2005		
Not a HS Grad $16,321	HS graduate only $30,134	Some college, no degree $36,930
Associates $41,903	Bachelors $51,700	Masters $64,498
Professional $90,878	Doctorate $76,937	

Census Bureau, Current Population Reports. From Statistical Abstract of the United States, 2006, Table No. 680.

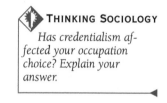

Sizable and Predictable Proportion of People Remain Out of the Labor Market

Market analyzers know how many people are now graduating every spring from high schools, universities and colleges around the country. Based on these figures, they know the number of jobs that need to be available to accommodate these new workers. Advisers also make predictions, based on the labor market, of what occupations would be good choices for people currently in school.

Status Confirmation

To a large extent, social class standing is contingent on the amount of education you have.

Custodial Services

Many parents rely on the educational system for a babysitting service. Preschools advertise not only child care but child education; many parents enroll their children in child care agencies not only for custodial care but for a head start advantage at school. During the grade school and high school years, the schools provide planned activities for young people.

Prolonged Adolescence

Due to changes in our age of mandatory school attendance, we have extended adolescence in our culture. Students today have to remain in school longer than they once did; the age has been raised from 12 to 14 to 16. Another factor that has increased the number of years students spend in school is that many jobs require a high school or college diploma. Students stay in school longer when unemployment rates are high and jobs are not available, and parents have to continue to support and assume responsibility for their children during this extended period of education. As a result, childhood and adolescence sometimes continues for almost two decades in the United States and maybe even longer for upper-middle-class children.

Age Segregation

We divide our children into age groups within the educational system. Children in school spend their time with children of the same age, their peers. Peer groups sometimes develop into distinct subcultures whose members dress alike, listen to the same music, eat the same foods, adopt similar hairstyles and develop code words and slang.

Are Academic Standards Declining?

There has been a great deal of concern about declining academic standards in the United States. Jonathan Kozol wrote in his book *Illiterate America* that 25 million American adults cannot read the poison warnings on a can of pesticide, a letter from their child's teacher, or the front page of a daily paper. He believes that about one-third of the entire adult population cannot read well enough to meet survival needs of our culture. Why are these academic standards declining?

Decline has been laid at the feet of modern childrearing practices. This argument states that our current practices are comparatively permissive, and this, some people believe, may have left the young without the self-discipline necessary for academic success. Right in line with modern child-rearing practices is the issue given to the breakdown of the traditional family structure due to such factors as easy divorces and a high rate of illegitimacy. Many young people, therefore lack the stable home back-

THINKING SOCIOLOGY

How long did you anticipate your adolescence as lasting? How has age segregation affected this prolonged adolescence?

Quick Glance

People frequently meet their mates in school. T F

Parents use the school system as a babysitting service. T F

The educational system has prolonged adolescence. T F

We divide children into age grades in the educational system. T F

THINKING SOCIOLOGY

What impact has television had on your academic performance? Family structure?

Quick Glance

Breakdown of the traditional family causes decline in academic standards. T F

Television raises academic achievement. T F

Schools have increased their number of functions. T F

ground that would otherwise help and support the efforts of the school. Single parents do not have the time and money, frequently, to help the child with school work.

Television has been accused of contributing to lower academic standards. The average child spends more time in front of a TV set than in school. Television encourages a passive orientation; viewers expect to be entertained and can switch channels as soon as unwelcome demands are made on their powers of concentration.

Conflicting demands have been placed on the school system. We request that the schools teach children about drugs and sex, how to drive a car, how to maintain physical fitness, how to do artistic things and how to be good citizens. These new functions may interfere with the school's traditional tasks of teaching children reading, writing and arithmetic.

The quality of teaching is poor in many schools. The average high school teacher earns less than the average plumber and the profession does not attract the most able people. High school graduates who intend to go into teaching score far lower on SAT measures than the average college-bound student; people majoring in education traditionally score 34 points lower on verbal tests and 43 points lower on math tests.

The authority structure is breaking down in many urban schools and teachers are often less concerned with teaching than with merely maintaining order. Over 100,000 teachers are assaulted by their pupils each year, and disciplinary problems undermine the educational effort in many classrooms.

New and inadequately tested teaching fads have disrupted the learning process. The introduction of the much-vaunted new math, for example, was followed by a sharp decline in math skills. The open classroom with its various learning centers easily degenerates into chaotic shambles.

Frequently, there is a low level of community support for learning and education. Dedication to sports may take precedence over school work. Factors such as reduction of homework, lowered quality of textbooks, tolerance of absenteeism and automatic grade promotion are cited as example of changes which had occurred without community objections.

Traditionally, the United States' school systems have not been geared to test taking like some other cultures. The strength of our system in the past has been critical thinking skills and creativity. We, also, are now teaching the tests. And tests generally measure a narrow range of cognitive skills. The Japanese are worried about their school system not putting out creative people; is this what we want our educational system to worry about?

WHAT CHANGES CAN BE MADE IN THE EDUCATIONAL SYSTEM?

The following recommendations have been made to improve the educational system:

1. *Create smaller schools such that any given school would have a student body of several hundred rather than thousands.* This would allow a feeling of community to develop among the teachers and students.
2. *Assign each student to an adult who has the time* to talk with the student in order to provide an adult mentor to serve as a significant other and role model.
3. *Encourage small groups of students to work together to solve problems.* Students would help one another as equals rather than slower students being placed in a separate group. This means that tracking would be abolished.
4. *Organize teachers into teams with authority to revise schedules and curriculum;* place control of curriculum back into the local schools' hands.

THINKING SOCIOLOGY

Should the school be responsible for such learning as the dangers of drugs, sexual behavior and driving?

THINKING SOCIOLOGY

What do you think of home schooling? How does home schooling affect how the functions of education are accomplished?

Quick Glance

Conflicting demands on the school system do not affect quality of education.   T F

There is a high level of community support for education.   T F

Childrearing practices contribute to the decline in academic standards. T F

New teaching techniques always improve the quality of education.   T F

Authority has increased in schools.   T F

THINKING SOCIOLOGY

What one change would you most like to see within the educational system?

🪬 *Quick Glance*

Parents need to be involved in children's education.　　T　F

An adult mentor is unnecessary in today's school system.　　T　F

Core curriculum is important to improve education.　　T　F

Smaller schools and smaller classes would be of no benefit.　　T　F

5. *Support student volunteer work in the community.* Research findings suggest that students benefit academically and socially when they participate in efforts such as keeping highways picked up and serving Thanksgiving dinner to the homeless.

6. *Involve parents in their children's schooling.* Research findings suggest that parental involvement would be beneficial to the student.

7. *Have a strong basic core emphasizing reading, writing, arithmetic and science for all students.* A **core of knowledge** in basic information on English, math and science which would be shared nationwide by students. According to Hirsch, a core of knowledge would provide a shared background knowledge which could make schooling more fair and democratic and allow any child entering a new school to be on equal footing with their classmates, which is better than in the system that we have now.

8. *Instigate a system of discipline and order that is perceived as fair.*

9. *Create a smaller class size which would allow the teacher to give more attention to each student,* spot students that were experiencing difficulties in a subject area and get them help to master the particular concept in order to build on that one and then go on to the next level of learning.

10. *Have committed teachers who like what they are doing* and dedicate their time, energy and knowledge to the education of students.

> BE CURIOUS ALWAYS! FOR KNOWLEDGE WILL NOT ACQUIRE YOU, YOU MUST ACQUIRE IT.
>
> SUDIE BACK

WHAT ARE THE TRENDS IN EDUCATION IN THE UNITED STATES?

There has been an increased proportion of people enrolled in school at every level. The largest advances have been among high school and college-age people. There is also a growing trend for people beyond the traditional college age to return to college either for further education or career shift. This is true because of the increase in demand for the professional, technical and managerial skills that are needed in today's economy. There is a growing belief that youth should secure a high school and even a college education. Education has become a lifetime activity, and most of us attend classes and training programs throughout our working career.

The fastest growing segment in the educational field is the growth and expansion of the two-year school. These schools usually offer very good value for the dollar because the tuition is less expensive than state or private four-year colleges and universities; classes are traditionally smaller so the student receives more personalized attention; professional teachers teach the classes rather than graduate assistants; schools are located close to the home; class scheduling is very flexible; and there is an open enrollment policy.

Parents are implementing a grass roots movement in order to select the schools that their children attend or for parents to receive tax credits for sending their children to private schools. If a parent currently sends their child to a private school, the parent pays twice for education, with tax money and tuition. Some parents feel that their child will receive a better education in a private or parochial school. University of Chicago sociologist, *James Coleman* has found that Catholic high school students do better in reading, vocabulary, mathematics and writing than their public education counterparts. Eighty-three percent of high school graduates of Catholic schools attend college compared to 52% of public school students. Coleman believes that the success of Catholic schools is due to practicing and preaching old-fashioned values, discipline and parental accountability and involvement. Parochial schools also have higher expectations which are manifested in more homework, emphasized study habits and stricter discipline. There are less administrators in Catholic schools than in public education.

🪬 *Quick Glance*

De facto segregation is based on residence patterns.　　T　F

Gerrymandering no longer exists.　　T　F

De jure segregation is based on law.　　T　F

Busing has successfully integrated schools.　　T　F

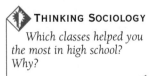

THINKING SOCIOLOGY

Which classes helped you the most in high school? Why?

Gerrymandering for segregation and integration continues. With gerrymandering a school district can either maintain segregated schools or divide school boundaries to promote integration. School desegregation is still an issue in many areas. This has been going on since 1959 when desegregation was as issue in the border states of Delaware, Kentucky, Maryland, Missouri, Oklahoma, West Virginia and District of Columbia. There are two types of segregation. The first is **de jure segregation**. This means that schools are segregated based on law. This is now unlawful, but our school system still gets segregated based on de facto segregation. **De facto segregation** is based on residential areas. School districts are politically drawn lines based on residential patterns. Many school districts now use creative school districting in order to desegregate schools. Many school districts have tried busing as a solution to the problem of segregation. Children from racially and ethnically segregated schools are bused to a school in another area. The weaknesses of busing include the problems of wealthier students not wanting to attend schools in less affluent areas, time and money expended on the busing process and teachers not wanting to teach in schools located far from their homes. Busing has met mixed results.

Fundamental changes have occurred in curriculum. There has been a shift from curriculum oriented around subject matter to a curriculum that is also interested in the child as a person with the additional emphasis on self and social development. There has also been a shift towards making education more useful or practical. Latin, for example, was taught during the 1950s and 1960s, but during the 1970s and 1980s, its popularity decreased because it was a dead language. During the late 1980s and early 1990s, there has been an increase in the popularity of Latin because educators are newly aware of the benefits of Latin in learning English grammar, romance languages and as a tool to improve verbal SAT and ACT scores.

Secondary school has been extended to include the last two years of high school and the first two years of college. Many high schools now offer honors courses and second year courses which include college material and use college textbooks. High schools offer courses in advanced placement in English and mathematics. Some colleges offer classes within the high school in order for high school students to receive college credit, and some colleges offer early enrollment for high school students into college. Many colleges, particularly community colleges, offer programs to help students either learn or brush up on basic math and English skills that they have not learned or that they have forgotten. High schools and colleges offer mentoring programs to help individual students achieve success in the educational system.

Another change in curriculum has been increasing importance to multiculturalism. **Multiculturalism** is the educational philosophy which stresses the importance of and knowledge about different racial, ethnic and religious categories. Many colleges and universities now require non-western literature and art courses. For example, my daughter is taking a course in African Art to fulfill a non-western humanities requirement. Principles of Sociology courses, many times, now incorporate cross-cultural examples. In this textbook we mention the Masaii and the Yanomamo Indians. Students in high school and grade school include units in each area as Black History and gender issues.

Considerable research has been conducted on learning styles and brain activity during the learning process. The college system has traditionally been geared to the auditory learner, listening to lectures. Some people, however, are not auditory learners. Your two authors are a case in point. We both are visual learners and prefer learning, and do better at learning, when we can read the material for ourselves. Brain research also has been conducted on what vitamins and minerals, for example, extend learning. The buzz word is "smart pills."

Not only has there been extensive research on learning styles, there has also been research on different teaching methods or strategies. The teaching of English in the

Quick Glance

The college system has been geared to the auditory learner.   T   F

There has been little change in curriculum over the past 40 years. T   F

Two-year colleges are an important component of the educational system.   T   F

Quick Glance

The cost of higher education is rising.   T   F

Book censorship does not occur in schools.   T   F

Diet may influence learning.   T   F

IF A MAN EMPTIES HIS PURSE INTO HIS HEAD, NO MAN CAN TAKE IT AWAY FROM HIM. AN INVESTMENT IN KNOWLEDGE ALWAYS PAYS THE BEST INTEREST.
B. FRANKLIN

grade schools and high schools has been subject to different teaching methods. One method is called the *whole English* approach. Using this method, students read and study works of literature. For example, in high school students might read *A Tale of Two Cities* by Charles Dickens. Through these readings students will learn sentence construction, paragraph structure and expand vocabulary and spelling. Another method being used is *balanced literacy*. This came on the scene in 1996 and is a combination of language and phonics instruction. For example, children are read to, children are read with (such as shared reading of a poem), and children read both by themselves and by teacher help. Writing is the other side of the coin. Works written for children are read, a teacher writes with the student and the child does independent writing. For example, my kindergarten grandchild keeps a daily journal at school. Through these methods the student will develop English skills needed in future education and life.

Computers have had a big impact on instruction in all levels of education. Even kindergarten classes have computer stations. College students can earn college credit and even degrees from internet classes and never have to step foot on a college campus. Teachers can integrate or teach classes through computers. PowerPoint presentations are used by some instructors.

One important topic for brain activity is developing classroom settings for special needs children. Horizon, Vanguard or Gifted Programs focus on high achievers and high mental ability children. Teaching strategies and special classrooms have been developed for children with Attention Deficit Disorder and Attention Deficit Hyperactive Disorder. These children have shortened attention spans which require specialized teaching strategies.

The controversy between religion and the school still continues. Some of the issues here are the differences concerning evolution versus creationism and which one of the theories, or both of the theories, should be taught in the school system. Book censorship remains an issue. Such books as *Uncle Tom's Cabin* and *Lord of the Flies* have been banned in some schools. The controversy continues about some books either being literature or racist or too violent.

The cost of higher education is rising dramatically. Four years at Notre Dame is over $153,000. This figure covers tuition, room and board. Tuition continues to rise yearly at state-supported schools.

Homeschooling has become more common. Parents choose to homeschool their children for several reasons. Some parents prefer that their children receive a religious-based education. Other parents feel that the public schools their children would attend expose their children to negative experiences such as gangs, drugs, bad language and peer pressure to engage in sexual activity. Some parents feel that their children receive a higher quality of education by homeschooling or that the school system does not adequately challenge their child.

Learning TIP
Always read the choices from the last choice to the first choice on a multiple choice exam. That alerts you for choices such as "all of the above are correct."

THINKING SOCIOLOGY

Do you think teaching multiculturalism is important or should education be focusing on "Melting Pot Theory"? Support your answer.

☞ *Quick Glance*

Social class and gender do not impact education. T F

The conflict theory looks at the manifest and latent functions of education. T F

The structural functionalist does not analyze education. T F

PERCENTAGE OF RACIAL/ETHNIC GROUPS COMPLETING FOUR OR MORE YEARS OF COLLEGE				
	1980	*1990*	*2000*	*2004*
White	18.4%	23.1%	28.1%	30.6%
Black	7.9%	11.3%	16.6%	17.6%
Hispanic	7.6%	9.2%	10.6%	12.1%
Males	20.9%	24.4%	27.8%	29.4%
Females	13.6%	18.4%	24.3%	26.1%

National Center for Educational Statistics, Digest of Education Statistics 2003 and U.S. Census Bureau, Current Population Survey, March 2005.

Many programs have developed to help parents homeschool their children. There are pre-planned, package curriculums for parents to follow. Organizations have formed to help parents homeschool children. Organization of homeschooled children provide opportunities for team spirit such as baseball and basketball. There has been a movement in some areas to devise program utilizing a combination of home-schooling and class attendance.

HOW DO THE THREE MAJOR THEORIES VIEW THE EDUCATIONAL SYSTEM?

Structural Functional Theory

When we listed the manifest and latent functions of education, we viewed the educational system through the eyes of the structural functional theorist.

Conflict Theory

Conflict theory views education as some people being winners in the educational system and others being losers. This theory states that:

1. Students are sorted into winners and losers based on nonacademic variables such as race, gender and social class.
2. Education is set up to reproduce inequality in support of the existing economic system.
3. The approved culture is reflected in curriculum and textbooks such as to delegitimize other ways of perceiving the world. There has been, however, a recent trend into multiculturalism.
4. Middle- and upper-class parents and above get more privileges for their children in contrast to the relative powerlessness of lower-class parents with children in the same school.

Social class and gender impact education in several ways. We, in theory, have a free public education system. Many schools, however, require that students buy school supplies, gym clothes and rent lockers for physical education classes. Teachers frequently require special notebooks, folders or poster board for projects. Many of the electives offered in junior high and high school can quickly become expensive. Band, for example, requires renting or purchasing an instrument, unless it is a large or unusual instrument like a tuba where it is required to buy a mouthpiece. There is the cost of music, entrance fees into contests and music lessons. Choir, orchestra and art programs frequently have added expenses not stated up front. Honors programs require special projects such as science fair, history fair or special projects in English; these cost money. The access to a computer is discriminatory against the child who cannot afford or does not have access to a computer. For example, one of my daughter's grade school English teachers added five points to an essay if it was typed. My child "earned" five points because her mother could type! English teachers count off for spelling errors and grammatical errors. A computer can check both spelling and grammar. Is this fair to the child who does not have access to a computer? Extra curricular activities also cost money. Drill teams, flag squads and cheerleading all cost hundreds of dollars each year. However, these activities help a student get scholarships. Cost factors discriminate against students who cannot afford to spend the money.

Family expectations influence how well a child performs in school. Middle- and upper-class families are inclined to take it for granted that their children will do well

🕮 Quick Glance

Family expectations influence how well a child performs in school.　T　F

Childhood nutrition does not influence how well a child performs in the classroom.　T　F

The conflict theory states that all students do not have equal opportunity within the educational system.　T　F

The free public educational system costs money in Texas.　T　F

Family expectations have little influence on student performance.　T　F

Minority students sometimes have difficulties with language in school.　T　F

THINKING SOCIOLOGY

How has your socioeconomic/ethnic background influenced your educational achievement? What factors most affected your choice of college?

Learning TIP
As you study your textbook, make up test questions. Know the answer!

🕮 *Quick Glance*

Middle class parents have skills which are needed to work with school personnel.   T   F

Democratic child-rearing facilitates school success.   T   F

Lower class parents gradually give independence from parental control.   T   F

▲ DIVERSITY OFTEN INCREASES PROBLEMS IN THE CLASSROOM.
IMAGE COPYRIGHT JOSEPH, 2008. USED UNDER LICENSE FROM SHUTTERSTOCK, INC.

academically. A very common scenario is that middle-class parents keep upping the rewards for improving performance. You come home with an 80, they ask why you did not get a 90. You come home with a 90, parents ask why you did not come home with a 100. Come home with a 100, and they ask why you did not get the bonus points! The basic middle-class orientation is that an individual can accomplish anything they set out to do, if they just work hard enough and put the shoulder to the grindstone.

Middle- and upper-class children have the cultural background which maximizes their chances of doing well in school. They are reared in such a way as to be conducive to achievement. Families are smaller so there is more time and money to devote to child-oriented activities. Homes are more likely stocked with books and magazines. Children who see parents read are more likely to read themselves. Parents are very conscious of the toys that they provide for their children. Parents tend to pick out educational toys. Two of the major toy manufacturers and designers advertise the educational value of their toys. Children are encouraged to defer immediate gratification in favor of long-term goals such as saving money for college or staying home to study rather than going out and partying. Middle and higher social classes give children freedom within consistent limits to explore and experiment with their environment. Lower-class children are more apt to have limited freedom for exploration because of crowded and dangerous aspects of environment. Middle-class students are more apt to have a wide range of parent-guided experiences, offering visual, auditory, kinesthetic and tactile stimulation while lower-class students lead constricted lives led by parents, and are reared to fear and distrust the unknown. Middle-class parents have gradual training and value for independence while lower classes have a tendency for abrupt transition to independence and parents tend to "lose control" of children at early ages. The occupational success of parents makes a good role model for children in the middle classes. This advantage is not given to children in the lower classes. Verbal communication used in middle classes gives children a boost in the educational system. Right along with verbal communication, middle-class parents are more apt to use democratic child-rearing practices which also increase the ability of the child to benefit from the educational system. Middle-class parents have a cooperative attitude towards the school system. If my child has difficulties in the school, I have no fear or hesitation to talk with the teacher, principal, or higher administrator, if need be. Many lower-class parents feel threatened by the formal educational system.

Childhood nutrition influences how well a child performs in the classroom. If a child is hungry, it is very difficult to concentrate. Subsidized breakfast and lunch programs have tried to alleviate some of these problems.

Language problems create difficulties for children from different cultural backgrounds and lower socioeconomic classes. This is true because teachers generally teach in standard middle-class English, and if a child learns a language different from this, she/he experiences problems. For example, some students from minority groups enter school scarcely able to speak any English. These students frequently suffer an initial setback from which they have great difficulty recovering. The issue of bilingual education has become an issue in many predominantly Hispanic areas in states such as Texas and California. The issue of black English has been addressed in northern states.

Unequal school resources influence the quality of education. Because public schools are financed largely by local tax revenues, some school systems have more than ample economic support while others are in financial ruin. More than one-half the funds supporting public education are from local revenues with more than 80% of this money coming from property taxes. From state to state, the amount of money spent varies widely. Many school districts allocate substantially more money to schools in rich neighborhoods than in poorer neighborhoods. Results are that the average child from a poor family receives four fewer years of education than a youngster from a wealthy family, and a disproportionate number of children from poor families are enrolled in vocational, rather than in educational, courses. Many industrialized societies have unequal school resources; Japan has mandated equal funding of schools, but students still attend private schools to help study for standardized tests needed to get into the best colleges in Japan.

Symbolic Interactionist Theory

Symbolic interactionist theory is interested in studying the smaller units of society and includes the analysis of role playing and scripts.

Teacher attitude affects how well students perform in the classroom. Most teachers have middle-class values and attitudes and may unintentionally penalize students who fail to display them. Teachers tend to appreciate students who are punctual, clean, moral, neat, hardworking, obedient and ambitious. Pupils who do not behave according to middle-class norms risk being considered bad students, regardless of intelligence or ability. As early as kindergarten, teachers start making an assessment of children's abilities based on physical appearance alone. Studies have shown that students who are physically more attractive are deemed to have higher intelligence than their less attractive counterparts. Based on these assessments, teachers begin tracking students. **Tracking** is placing students in different ability groups. In kindergarten, the teacher determines the knowledge that her students possess and the students are placed in groups according to those abilities. If the students cannot recognize their letters, then they may be in the "yellow birds." If the children know their letters, but do not know the sounds of the letters, then they may be in the "blue birds." For the children who know letter recognition and the sounds of the consonants and vowels, they will be in the "red birds." For the "red birds," "blue birds," and "yellow birds," they are moving at a pace in the educational system based on their abilities. However, for the "yellow birds," they may be finishing kindergarten before they are at a level that the "red birds" were at during the beginning of the school year, which means that "yellow birds" will still be the slower group in first grade and throughout their academic careers. For students who excel, there is a feeling of "I can" and, thus, a higher self-esteem than for those who are in the slower group. A criticism of tracking is that it benefits those who are in the higher groups of the tracking process. Students in the slower tracked group can experience a labeling process. The labeling theory and the self-fulfilling prophecy suggests that if people are treated in a specific manner, they may actually fulfill those expectations. A child who is aware that there are differences in the type of work that is being done by the "yellow birds" and the "red birds" comes to view the "yellow birds" as the slow group. Parents may become concerned with the lack of ability of their children and their children may come to view themselves as "slow." The labeling perspective suggests that the children come to view what is expected of them and exhibit slower behavior in learning. Rosenthal and Jacobson studied teacher-expectancy in what has come to be referred to as "Pygmalion in the classroom." **Teacher-expectancy** refers to the effect that a teacher's expectation of each student influences the learning for that child.

Rosenthal divided students randomly into two groups. He told teachers that students in one group were expected to show progress this year and those in the other

THINKING SOCIOLOGY

How has funding of your school influenced your education?

TRAINING IS EVERYTHING. THE PEACH WAS ONCE A BITTER ALMOND; CAULIFLOWER IS BUT CABBAGE WITH A COLLEGE EDUCATION.

MARK TWAIN

🕮 *Quick Glance*

All Americans speak the same English.   T F

Since schools are paid for by tax revenues, all are supported equally.   T F

Teacher attitude affects student performance.   T F

Tracking is placing students in equal-ability groups.   T F

THINKING SOCIOLOGY

What experiences have you had with teacher expectations?

🕮 *Quick Glance*

There are no criticisms of the tracking process. T F

Rosenthal and Jacobson studied teacher-expectancy.   T F

Students in the slower tracking group can experience a labeling process.   T F

Labeling can lead to self-fulfilling prophecy.   T F

group were expected to make normal growth. The group which the teachers were told were going to do significantly better showed dramatic improvement in scores. This is true for several reasons:

1. Teachers created a warmer, social-emotional atmosphere for them.
2. Teachers gave them more feedback concerning their performance.
3. Teachers presented "better" students with more supplementary materials in order to stimulate their intellectual blooming.
4. Teachers gave these special students greater opportunity to pose questions or to respond in other ways.

In later years of school, around third grade in most areas, the judging of students shifts from the subjective to objective measures. Once standardized testing formally enters the educational process, formalized labeling becomes a common phenomenon. The basic tool is the use of I.Q. scores. The use of scores for pupil placement legitimizes the stratification system rather than generating it. Higher scores and economic success tend to go together, but a higher score is not a predictor of economic success. Based on these standardized test scores, the educational establishment labels students. The school systems use labels based on standardized achievement tests in order to track students formally. The stated purpose of tracking is to keep uninterested students in school by permitting them to study subjects that are suitable to their skills and interests. Most research indicates that the student stays in school no longer than if he had not been put in special courses. Performance is not improved with tracking either. Another reason for tracking is to let children compete on their own ability level. However, the student is then never exposed to anything else. Tracking does make it easier on the teacher.

The opposite of tracking is **mainstreaming**. This involves the use of mixed ability groups. Two benefits occur in this situation. First, the brighter children help the slower students and, thus, learn the material better themselves. Through the process of teaching, retention of material increases. Second, the questions asked by the students, other than the very brightest, clarified material for those who just accepted the information by rote.

There are also male-female differences in the classroom. Boys were found to be naturally more assertive in the classroom. If a boy calls out in class, he gets teacher attention, especially intellectual attention; if a girl calls out in class, she is told to raise her hand before speaking. Teachers praise boys more than girls, give boys more academic help and are more likely to accept boys' comments during classroom discussions. Through these advantages, boys increase their chances for better education and possibly higher pay and quicker promotions.

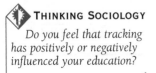

THINKING SOCIOLOGY

Do you feel that tracking has positively or negatively influenced your education?

Quick Glance

Males and females are treated the same in the classroom.   T   F

In mixed ability groups, students help one another.   T   F

Tracked students are less apt to drop out of school.   T   F

Formalized labeling is frequently based on I.Q. scores.   T   F

▼ CHAPTER SUMMARY

1. Education is a formalized system in industrialized societies but an informal system in preindustrialized societies.
2. The educational system in the United States is based on a single-track system, formalism and informal structures.
3. The institution of education is responsible for transmission of culture, achievement of literacy skills, development of social skills, dispensing information concerning physical and psychological well-being, preparation for higher education and occupational role, promotion of technological change and preservation of status quo.

4. The latent functions of education include sorting and sifting agency, establishment of social relationships, marriage market, future business and professional contacts, sizable and predictable proportion of people entering the labor market, confirmation of status, custodial service, prolonged adolescence and age segregation.

5. It has been suggested that academic standards are declining due to the influence of television, modern childrearing practices, conflicting demands on the school system, teaching quality, disintegration of authority structure, teaching fads, lack of community support and nonstandardized test taking orientation.

6. Changes in school size, curriculum, teacher organization and community support need to be completed for improvement in the educational system.

7. Trends in education include changes in school enrollment, parental involvement and curriculum.

8. The conflict theory views education supporting the existing upper economic classes while the structural functional theory establishes the benefits to society of education.

9. The symbolic interaction theory is concerned with tracking and teacher-expectancy.

▼ REFERENCES

Apple, Michael W. 1986. *Teachers and Texts: A Political Economy of Class and Gender Relations in Education*. New York: Routledge & Kegan Paul.

Bourdieu, Pierre and Jean-Claude Passeron. 1984. *A Social Critique of the Judgment of Taste*. Cambridge, MA: Harvard University Press.

Carnegie Corporation of New York. 1989. *A Nation Prepared: Teachers for the 21st Century*. New York: Carnegie Corporation.

Coleman, James and Thomas Hoffer. 1987. *Public and Private High Schools: The Impact of Communities*. New York: Basic Books.

D'Souza, Dinesh. 1991. *Illiberal Education: The Politics of Race and Sex on Campus*. New York: The Free Press.

Elkind, David. 1981. *The Hurried Child Growing Up Too Fast Too Soon*. Reading, Massachusetts: Addison-Wesley Publishing Company.,

Elkind, David. 1984. *All Grown Up and No Place to Go*. Reading, Massachusetts: Addison-Wesley Publishing Company.

Freire, Paulo. 1985. *The Politics of Education: Culture, Power, and Liberation*. Translated by Donald Macedo. South Hadley, MA: Bergin & Garvey.

Fulghum, Robert. 1989. *All I Really Need to Know I Learned in Kindergarten*. New York: Villard Books.

Gamoran, Adam and Robert D. Mare. 1989. "Secondary School Tracking and Educational Inequality: Compensation, Reinforcement, or Neutrality?" *American Journal of Sociology*, 94, 1146–1183.

Hirsch, E. D. 1991. *What Your First Grader Needs To Know: Fundamentals of a Good First-Grade Education*. New York: Doubleday.

Kozol, Jonathan. 1986. *Illiterate Americans*. New York: Anchor Press/Doubleday.

Kozol, Jonathan. 1991. *Savage Inequalities*. New York: Crown Publishers, Inc.

Rosenthal, Robert. 1973. "The Pygmalion Effect Lives." *Psychology Today* (Sept.), 56–63.

READING

EXCERPT FROM "WHAT YOUR 1ST GRADER NEEDS TO KNOW"
BY E.D. HIRSCH, JR. NEW YORK: DOUBLEDAY, 1991, PP. 2–5.

A core of shared knowledge in elementary grades is necessary for excellence and fairness in schooling. Before I outline the reasons for making this blunt assertion, I shall briefly mention a striking piece of evidence which supports it. All of the best—i.e., highest-achieving and most egalitarian—elementary school systems in the world, such as those in Sweden, France, and Japan, teach their children a specific core of knowledge in each of the first six grades, thus enabling all children to enter each new grade with a secure foundation for further learning. By contrast, those educational systems that have recently declined in educational achievement, England, Australia, and the United States, did not give children a specific core of shared knowledge in early grades. Research could have predicted that result for reasons that are apparent to common sense. Here they are, briefly.

Quick Glance

A core of knowledge would improve U.S. education.   T   F

The best elementary education systems have a core of knowledge.   T   F

Shared knowledge lets each student learn from their own unique base.   T   F

(1) Shared background knowledge makes schooling more effective. The one-on-one tutorial is the most effective form of schooling, in part because a parent or teacher is able to provide tailor-made instruction for the individual child. The tutor knows what the child already knows, and can build upon that already-acquired knowledge to teach something new. In a nontutorial situation, say, in a classroom of twenty-five students, one cannot share the background knowledge for all students unless they all share the background knowledge that is being built upon. When all the students in a classroom do share that relevant background knowledge, a classroom can begin to approach the effectiveness of a tutorial.

(2) Shared background knowledge makes schooling more fair and democratic. When all the children who enter a grade can be assumed to share some of the same building blocks of knowledge, and when the teacher knows exactly what those building blocks are, then all students are empowered to learn. Even when some children in a class don't have elements of the core knowledge they were supposed to acquire in previous grades, the possibility of identifying exactly what the knowledge gaps are enables the teacher or parent greatly to speed up the process of making up for lost time, giving all students a chance to fulfill their potentials in later grades. Under a core-of-knowledge system, by the same token, students who have to move from school to school are treated more fairly. When they enter a new school they are on a more equal footing with their classmates than are students in a system like ours. For these reasons, school systems that use core standards have proved to be more democratic and fair than systems like ours which do not.

Quick Glance

Shared knowledge makes schooling authoritarian.   T   F

Shared knowledge makes it easier to establish attainable standards.   T   F

Attainable goals has a positive impact on self-esteem.   T   F

(3) Defining a specific core of knowledge for each grade motivates everyone through definite, attainable standards. This is not the place to discuss the great political issue of making schools accountable for their outcomes by defining more concretely the goals that are to be achieved. On the other hand, accountability in education is important and motivational for children themselves. When children are made aware of clearly defined, achievable learning goals can monitor and take pleasure in their progress. Attainment of those defined goals should be expected, demanded, and when achieved, praised. The self-esteem of children, so important for their alter confidence and ambition, arises from earned self-esteem, not from praise that is automatically handed out on a regular basis regardless of accomplishment.

(4) Shared background knowledge helps create cooperation and solidarity in school and in the nation. The shared background knowledge that makes for communication and learning in academic work also makes for cooperation and toleration among students within the classroom community. In our diverse nation, students within the classroom usually come from varied home cultures, and those different cultures should be honored and understood by all students as part of the common core. Schooling should create a school-based culture that is common to all and welcoming to all because it includes knowledge of many cultures. Such shared, multicultural knowledge gives all our students, no matter what their background, a common ground for understanding our uncommon diversity.

The schools of a modern nation are the institutions through which children become members of the wider national community. They will grow to adults who will live cooperatively and sustain one another only if they feel that they truly belong to the larger society. Such universal belonging has always been the hope and promise of the United States. As the great American writer Herman Melville said in 1849: "We are not a narrow tribe.—No: our blood is the flood of the Amazon, made up of a thousand noble currents all pouring into one. We are not a nation so much as a world." Here, above all, shared, school-based knowledge, which alone can lead to educational and social fairness, should be encouraged as part of our best traditions.

The evidence of educational decline and widening social unfairness has become ever more obvious and undeniable since my book was published in 1987. Verbal aptitude scores have dropped further. These declines are commonly explained by claiming that they arise from our democratic progress in bringing minorities into the school system. Alas, it is not true; the greatest decline has been in the numbers of students who make high scores. Worst of all, our fall from our own achievements seems even steeper when we compare our current situation with the educational advances made by other developed countries. They have moved forward as we have retreated. In 1970, American elementary students ranked seventh in science achievement among the seventeen countries measured. By 1980, we ranked fifteenth—third from the bottom, just above the Philippines. That decline can be reversed. But no modern nation has achieved both excellence and fairness in education without defining core knowledge for the elementary school. It is reasonable to predict that we will fail to reverse our educational decline unless we do the same.

🕮 Quick Glance

Shared knowledge helps connect students and schools.   T F

Shared knowledge supports the Melting Pot Theory held by Americans.   T F

A core of knowledge will benefit students and schools.   T F

◆ THINKING SOCIOLOGY

Do you think you learned a core of knowledge when you were in grade school?

What do you think should be required information in the core of knowledge?

How can we support multiculturalism and core of knowledge?

Beholding the Family

CHAPTER OBJECTIVES

1. What is the family?
2. What are the types of families?
3. What is marriage?
4. What determines whom we marry?
5. What authority structures exist within families?
6. How is family residence determined?
7. How are kinship patterns determined?
8. What are the functions of the family?
9. What are the trends of the family in the United States?
10. How do the theories look at the family?

bigamy: unlawfully having more than one spouse at a time

bilateral descent: a descent system in which both the mother's and father's family of orientation are viewed as important in determining kinship

blended, binuclear, step or reconstructed family: a family composed of previously married people along with his, hers and their children

boomerang kids: children who officially establish their own homes, then return to live at the parental home

cenogamy or group marriage: two or more men married to two or more women

composite family: two or more nuclear families that share a common spouse

consensual family: unmarried man and woman with children living together in one household

dysfunctional families: families who do not meet the needs of the members in that family

egalitarian family: a family in which there is sharing of decision making between the spouses

endogamy: rules governing marriage within a specified group

exogamy: rules governing marriage outside of a certain group

extended or consanguine family: nuclear family members plus other relatives living in the same household

family: people related by marriage, birth, adoption or by mutual definition

family of orientation: the family we are born into

family of procreation: the family we establish

incest taboo: prohibition against marrying members considered to be relatives

joint family: brothers plus wives and children living together

kinship: state of being related

marriage: the legal or social contract between two people for sexual, economic and procreation purposes

matriarchy: family authority structure in which mother's family possesses the authority to make decisions that affect the family

matricentric or matrifocal family: the family structure in which formal control is with male (and his family), but female makes day-to-day decisions

matrilineal descent: the descent system placing importance on the mother's family of orientation for determining kinship

matrilocal pattern of residence: bride and groom set up residence with bride's family of orientation

modified extended family: several nuclear families who live in their separate households, but maintain a sharing of a network of family belonging

monogamy: a form of marriage that allows for a man and a woman to be married only to each other

neolocal pattern of residence: the residence pattern in which newly formed couple set up separate household from families of orientation

no-fault divorce: a divorce which is not an adversary proceeding

nuclear or conjugal family: the mother, father and their dependent children

patriarchy: a family authority structure in which father dominates with the authority to make decisions that affect the family

patrilineal descent: a descent system placing importance on the father's family of orientation for determining kinship

patrilocal pattern of residence: the bride and groom set up residence with groom's family of orientation

ping-pong kids: a cycle established by children alternating living at home and then at another domicile

polygamy: the form of marriage allowing for multiple spouses at one time

polyandry: the form of polygamy that allows for the female to have multiple spouses at one time

polygyny: the form of polygamy that allows for the male to have multiple spouses at one time

post-rearing family: a husband and wife who have already reared their children

serial monogamy: the practice of having one spouse at a time, but having several spouses in a lifetime

single-parented family: one parent and children

single-person household: a family of one person

traditional family: a husband and wife and their children living in one household with the dad being the economic provider and the mom providing the nurturing of the children

tribal family: several nuclear families living together as a clan or tribe

▼ KEY PEOPLE

Paul Bohannan, George Murdock, William Ogburn, Nick Stinnett, Judith Wallerstein

WHAT IS THE FAMILY?

The last institution to be discussed is the family. George Murdock identified the family as a cultural universal. Most primates (we are classified as primates) live in family units. This is true because we rely on the group for survival. Between women's gathering and men's hunting in hunting-gathering societies, humans achieve the balanced diet they need to survive. We rely on the group effort for protection. We cannot run very fast, we do not have sharp teeth, nor do we have unusually good vision or smell. As a consequence, like chimpanzees, we rely on the group effort for defense. Humans have a long period of infant dependency in which the little ones need to be nurtured and protected. It is the family unit which helps ensure that babies grow up to be adults.

We have been using the concept of family, but have not yet defined just exactly what a family is. The institution of the **family** has several characteristics:

1. Two or more members are united by blood, marriage or adoption.
2. Members typically live together.
3. Members interact according to norms and roles established by the large society.

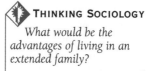

FAMILIES WITH BABIES AND FAMILIES WITHOUT BABIES ARE SORRY FOR EACH OTHER.
E. W. HOWE

WHAT ARE THE TYPES OF FAMILIES?

Most of us would define a family as husband and wife, who are also a mother and father, and 2.1 children. Maybe you would include grandparents and aunts and uncles within the family unit. This is a culture-bound definition of the family rather than the sociological definition; this is an ethnocentric definition of family because there are many different forms of families in other cultures.

The **nuclear or conjugal family** consists of mother and father and dependent children. This type of family allows for easy geographical and social mobility. Eskimos and other people living in other very harsh environmental conditions frequently have this type of family as a cultural norm because they need to move readily to new food sources. Most of the industrialized countries in the western world, as does the United States, emphasize the nuclear family. This is the type of family system that we consider "normal."

The **extended or consanguine family** stresses blood or kin ties and is made up of two or more nuclear families plus other relatives. The household consists of grandparents, married children and grandchildren. The family in the television show "The Waltons" would be an example of an extended family. There are several different types of extended families:

1. A **joint family** consists of brothers and their nuclear families living together or of sisters and their nuclear families living together.
2. A **modified extended family** is several nuclear families living in their separate households but they maintain a sharing of a network of family belonging. Members of the modified extended family celebrate customs with one another and share a sense of belonging that is normally seen in an extended family.
3. A **composite family** is two or more nuclear families that share a common spouse; this is based on multiple husbands or wives. We shall discuss different types of marriage in the next section.
4. A **tribal family** exists with many families living together as a clan or tribe.

☞ Quick Glance

In preliterate society, each institution is distinct and separate.   T F

George Murdock identified the family as a cultural universal.   T F

The United States emphasizes the extended family.   T F

The family in "The Waltons" is an example of the joint family.   T F

◆ THINKING SOCIOLOGY

What would be the advantages of living in an extended family?

☞ Quick Glance

A joint family is one which smokes marijuana.   T F

Tribal families are an extended family.   T F

The family of orientation is the family we establish as adults.   T F

Your culture will have either a nuclear family or some form of extended family. Regardless of what type of family your culture favors, you and everyone else will be born into a family of orientation. If you marry and have children, you will be a member of a family of procreation.

1. The **family of orientation** is that family into which a person is born. In the family of orientation, we are considered the child.
2. The **family of procreation** is that family we establish when we leave the family of orientation. In this family, we are considered an adult.

WHAT IS MARRIAGE?

Marriage is a closely related concept to family, but not every culture has marriage in the sense that we do in the United States. **Marriage**, in general terms, is a legal or social contract usually between two or more people of the opposite sex. Marriage involves a public ceremony, ends when a spouse dies or is divorced, sex is expected and approved, procreation is expected and a set of norms determines the particular relation of parents to each other and to their children.

One culture which does not have marriage in the sense commonly accepted is the Nayar. Nayars live in India and, during adolescence, girls take several lovers. If she becomes pregnant, one or more of these lovers acknowledges paternity. The woman's relatives choose a man to be her husband for three days and he becomes responsible for the cost of delivering the baby. There are no other obligations to mom or the child. In fact, after the three days, the "husband" and "wife" may never see each other again. The wife's only further obligation is when the husband dies; she is expected to observe funeral rites. The mother's brother assumes the male responsibility in rearing the child; therefore, the child owes allegiance to the uncle rather than to the father. In turn, property and privileged status are transmit-

▲ AMERICAN CULTURE SUPPORTS MONOGAMY.
IMAGE COPYRIGHT ALEXANDRU VERINCIUC, 2008. USED UNDER LICENSE FROM SHUTTERSTOCK, INC.

ted not from father to son but from maternal uncle to nephew. Family life revolves about the brother-sister relationship. This is very different from what would be a "marriage" in our own culture.

The Nayars have a very different idea about marriage than do most cultures. In almost every culture there is a more formalized marriage system. In the United States, we practice monogamy. **Monogamy** allows for the marriage of one man and one woman. Monogamy, as a cultural norm, is preferred in only about 17% of the societies. But because there are about equal numbers of males and females at the time of marriage and because multiple spouses gets to be expensive, monogamy is very common even in societies which allow more than one spouse!

In societies like our own we get around having only one spouse by practicing what is called serial monogamy. **Serial monogamy** is the practice of having one spouse at a time, but having several spouses during a lifetime. Elizabeth Taylor has practiced serial monogamy; so far she has had nine husbands in her lifetime.

Polygamy is the form of marriage allowing for multiple spouses. In our culture, this is unlawful and is called **bigamy**. In other cultures, multiple spouses are preferred and accepted. There are several forms of polygamy:

1. **Polygyny** permits a male to have several wives. Polygyny is the most common form of polygamy. Even in cultures that practice polygyny, the common form of marriage may be monogamy. The Masaii of Kenya and Tanzania practice polygyny as do the Yanomamo of Brazil.
2. **Polyandry** allows a female to have multiple husbands. Polyandry is rare. Several examples include Todas in Southern India, Tibetans in India and several tribes in Africa. The usual pattern is for brothers or, less likely, fathers and sons to marry a single female.
3. **Cenogamy**, or group marriage, permits two or more men to legally mate with two or more women. This is an extremely rare marriage form. Where it is practiced, it is usually based on age mates. In a New Guinea group, for instance, all males born within a given period of time have duties and privileges in common that include the sharing of individual wives. In the United States, we have experimental groups such as communes attempting this type of relationship with very mixed results, usually that of failure. On the whole, group marriage does not work in the United States because of the problems of maintaining a monogamous relationship, let alone a group relationship, and we are not socialized to share spouses. Jealousy for members of the American culture definitely becomes a problem.

WHAT DETERMINES WHOM WE MARRY?

Whom we marry is governed by rules of endogamy and exogamy. **Endogamy** means that we must marry within a particular group. Some general rules of endogamy in our culture include marriage within a racial group and, many times, marriage within a religious or ethnic group. **Exogamy** means marriage outside a particular group. Many cultures, such as the Masaii, insist that the girl and boy must be from different clans. In most of the United States, we are not allowed to marry our first cousin or a brother or a sister. Not only is this a rule of exogamy, but it also follows what is called the **incest taboo**. All cultures have some group of people which to marry would be called incest. Some societies practice what is called parallel- or cross-cousin marriages; to a society practicing parallel-cousin marriage, my daughter marrying her father's sister's son would be incest, but marrying her mother's sister's son would not be incest! To us, both constitute first cousins and are unacceptable as marriage partners because of laws governing incest.

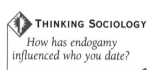

THINKING SOCIOLOGY
How has endogamy influenced who you date?

Not only does society specify rules of endogamy and exogamy, but different societies allow differing amounts of freedom in the choice of a mate. In some cultures, choice of a mate is not a decision made by young people. Marriage is considered an economic and political arrangement and is too important a decision for young people to make. The cultures provide for some method of selecting a spouse either through a prescribed marriage partner or go-between. Prince Charles, for example, was really very limited in his choice of mates; upper caste people of India still are very apt to arrange their children's marriages.

In many cultures, a dowry or a bride price must be paid before a marriage can take place. In cultures that practice a bride price, the groom or his family must pay a sum of goods or money to the bride's family or to the bride. This is not demeaning to the female but rather compensates her family for the loss of their daughter's services and children. When we were in Kenya, a Masaii elder offered 17 head of cattle for my daughter. A dowry is given by the female's family either to the female, to the spouse or to his family. The paying of a dowry was practiced in India and during the Middle Ages.

In our society we have a great deal of freedom in mate selection. Some of the factors that come into play when we choose a spouse are:

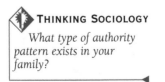
THINKING SOCIOLOGY

What factors contributed to your choice of dating partner or spouse?

1. *We tend to follow the rule of propinquity* because we tend to marry people who live near our family, go to school together or work together.
2. *We tend to be homogamous* in our marriages; this is particularly true for first marriages because we tend to marry someone of the same age, social class, race, religion, nationality, social attitudes, education, intelligence or previous marital status.
3. *We consciously or unconsciously try to match what we think we want in a spouse.* For example, my neighbor's girl wants to marry someone of her own religious faith; therefore, she has not had more than one or two dates with someone of a different faith.
4. *We want to marry someone to sustain us with the kind of emotional and psychological relationship we experienced or fantasized in childhood.* Parental influence has either a positive or negative effect on mate selection.
5. *Personality needs influence choice of mate.* We have a complementary need approach when, for example, a dominant and passive person marry. Personality needs can also be homogeneous when people are alike in personality characteristics, such as a very domineering man marrying a domineering woman.
6. *We say that we marry for romantic love (or lust).* Romantic love loosens ties with parents and encourages marriage.

Learning TIP
Use a day planner calendar to keep track of due dates for assignments, quizzes and exams.

🦅 *Quick Glance*

We tend to pick marriage partners with similar demographic characteristics.　　T　F

An engagement period with minimal conflict is a factor for a more successful marriage.　　T　F

The relationship with parents is not a factor for the success of a marriage.　　T　F

Romantic love encourages marriage.　　T　F

With this free choice of marriage partners, parents usually do not enter into the decision until the couple has already been dating seriously. Even though we have free choice of mate, most young people want parental approval of whom they marry.

Factors in addition to parental approval enhance the chances of a successful marriage. These factors include marriage in the ages between the mid to late 20s, agreement on religious beliefs, lengthy time of acquaintance and engagement, an engagement period which has minimal conflict, discussion of key issues such as money and religion before marriage, nonpregnant female, adequate sexual information from a competent source, healthy relationship with parents and significant others, good mental health and good self-esteem, education and similar amounts of education, common interests shared prior to marriage, similar gender role definitions, adequate income and share a definition of use and meaning of money.

▲ **AMERICANS TEND TO MARRY FOR LOVE.**
IMAGE COPYRIGHT YURI ARCURS, 2008. USED UNDER LICENSE FROM SHUTTERSTOCK, INC.

THINKING SOCIOLOGY

What type of authority pattern exists in your family?

WHAT AUTHORITY STRUCTURES EXIST WITHIN FAMILIES?

1. In a **patriarchy** structure, the father or his family is in control. This is the historic pattern in the United States.
2. In a **matriarchy** structure, the mother, the mother's mother or, usually, the mother's brother is in control. This authority system is found among the Hopi and Navaho Native Americans. This power system is generally found in horticultural societies.
3. In an **egalitarian** family, husband and wife share authority equally. This authority structure is found generally in nuclear families rather than extended families. In the egalitarian authority patterns, who makes the decision may be decided based on which spouse possesses knowledge in particular areas. Several variables control how egalitarian a family is: education of wife, labor force participation of wife and stage of life cycle.
4. A **matricentric or matrifocal family** is common in some cultures and is common among suburbs in our own culture. Mom has responsibility for the day-to-day decisions because dad works very long hours and is away from home a great deal. However, dad still maintains formal control.

Quick Glance

A patriarchy is when the father or his family has the authority.　T　F

The neolocal pattern of residence stresses that the bride and groom will live with his parents.　T　F

The neolocal pattern of residence is not found in the U.S.A.　T　F

In a matriarchal society, the mother is the most common person to make decisions.　T　F

Extended families are usually egalitarian.　T　F

Kinship is a state of being related.　T　F

Kinship ties may be based on adoption.　T　F

Bilineal descent places importance on the mother's family of orientation.　T　F

HOW IS FAMILY RESIDENCE DETERMINED?

For a newly created family unit, societal norms dictate where the couple will reside. In the United States, the preference is for a neolocal pattern of residence. The **neolocal** pattern of residence allows for the newly formed couple to set up their own separate household. In fact, we will go to extreme measures to ensure that we have our own home when we marry. However, in many other societies, the neolocal pattern of residence may not be the norm but rather be either patrilocal or a matrilocal. The **patrilocal pattern of residence** stresses that the bride and groom set up residence with the groom's family of orientation. Other societies practice the **matrilocal pattern of residence** which stresses that the bride and groom establish residence with the bride's family of orientation.

THINKING SOCIOLOGY
What descent pattern do we practice in the U.S.?

HOW ARE KINSHIP PATTERNS DETERMINED?

Kinship is a state of being related. Kinship is not necessarily determined biologically because kinship ties may be based on adoption.

1. **Bilateral or bilineal descent** means that both sides of the family are regarded as equally important. Both the mother's and father's family of orientation are important in determining kinship groups. In the United States, kinship is determined by bilateral descent.
2. **Patrilineal descent** patterns place importance on the father's family of orientation.
3. **Matrilineal descent** patterns place importance on the mother's family of orientation.

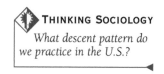

MARRIAGE IS THE RELATIONSHIP BETWEEN MAN AND WOMAN IN WHICH THE INDEPENDENCE IS EQUAL, THE DEPENDENCE MUTUAL, AND THE OBLIGATION RECIPROCAL.

L. K. ANSPACHER

WHAT ARE THE FUNCTIONS OF THE FAMILY?

The family as a major institution performs a number of functions for a society. Sociologist William Ogburn first studied and identified the functions of the family. These functions will now be discussed.

Sexual Regulation

There are several aspects of sexual regulation that we need to discuss:

1. *Incest is forbidden in all societies.* Incest is defined as sexual relationships between close relatives. Some societies forbid cousin marriage, but other societies recommend cross- or parallel-cousins marriages. All societies, except for a few exceptions, forbid sexual relationships between parent and child and brother and sister. The exceptions to this rule are several cases of marriages between royalty in the Incas, Egyptians and Hawaiians.

2. *Another aspect of sexual regulation is extramarital sex.* The very term "extramarital sex" is culture bound. Some societies permit sex outside the marriage bonds, but this is usually done with the permission of the spouse. A Masaii woman, for example, can have sex with someone in her husband's age group. In our culture, the ideal norm states that we should not engage in extramarital sex, but the real norm says that it does occur in about fifty percent of the marriages.

3. *Premarital sex is considered part of the institution of the family.* Some societies have a very liberal attitude towards premarital sex. For example, among both the traditional Hopi Indians and Samoans, there was a very free attitude towards sex before marriage. Other cultures, however, take the extreme view. Many Hispanic cultures and Moslem cultures sharply curtail their females activities prior to marriage to ensure that the female is a virgin when she marries. In the United States, we fall somewhere between the two extremes. The ideal culture is one of abstinence with no premarital sex for either the male or the female. The double standard states that premarital sex is all right for the male but not the female. This standard still exists in the United States. The third standard is permissiveness with affection. If we are in a bonded relationship, it is permissible to have coitus (sexual intercourse). The fourth standard is the recreational standard. This views premarital sex as a leisure time activity. All standards exist in the United States today. Over half of teenagers are engaging in premarital sex; but as sexually transmitted diseases (STDs) become more widely spread and as education levels go up, many teenagers and adults are showing more caution in their sexual relationships.

4. *Marital sex is an important aspect of marriage.* During Victorian days, sex was viewed as debilitating and to be avoided except for the procreation of children. We have shown a great deal of change since then. Now modern American couples are having sex more often and enjoying it with more creativity.

Reproduction

The family assures that there will be a constant supply of new members within a society. Reproduction can and does take place outside the context of the family. But in the United States, reproduction occurring outside of the family is defined as a social problem. If a girl finds that she is pregnant and not married, the common choices ensure that the child is not born or the child is placed

▲ REPRODUCTION IS ENCOURAGED IN THE FAMILY UNIT.

IMAGE COPYRIGHT SACHEEN METRANI, 2008. USED UNDER LICENSE FROM SHUTTERSTOCK, INC.

into an adopted family unit. If a girl chooses abortion, the child is not born outside of the family. If the girl puts the baby up for adoption or marries in order to provide a family, then the child is born into a family unit. The last option is to raise the child by herself. Many of these girls box themselves into a life of poverty because it is very difficult to complete an education and get a good job with the responsibilities of motherhood. The childbirth option within the family maximizes the chances that children will be well cared for by adults.

> OTHER THINGS MAY CHANGE US, BUT WE START AND END WITH FAMILY.
>
> ANTHONY BRANDT

Socialization

The family is given the primary responsibility for the socialization of the new members. As discussed in Chapter 4, the socialization process is shared with other agencies, but the family plays an important role in teaching the norms and values of the culture. Schools take over at a relatively young age in our culture, but the family unit is still very important. The family is particularly important in giving satisfaction and a sense of purpose.

Physical and Psychological Protection

The physical and psychological protection of family members has become a lengthy process in the latter part of the twentieth century in industrialized countries because of extended childhood and increasing importance of secondary groups such as the workplace. Within the family, individuals can make mistakes and learn from them in an atmosphere of protective security. The family is one of the few remaining places where complementary rather than competitive relationships can be fostered and enjoyed. Thus, the family provides a home base with stability that allows its members to develop naturally, in their own way, at their own pace. Children also provide protection against physical, psychological and social needs in old age.

THINKING SOCIOLOGY

Which function of the family do you feel is most important? Why?

Economic Protection

In our culture, this function has shifted from "making a living" to "earning wages." If we view the Amish family as a reflection of an American family during an earlier point in history, we shall see the family as a much more self-supporting unit. Now we earn money and buy what we need. (The reading for this chapter deals with the Amish family.)

Quick Glance

The family of procreation determines our life chances.	T F
Ideally, the family provides TLC.	T F
Ninety-five percent of Americans do not marry.	T F
Americans are a very romantic culture.	T F

Social Status

Our parents' positions in the stratification system determine where we start out in this hierarchy. The social status of the family of orientation may determine if we learn to play the piano, if we are provided preventive dental and health care and if we learn about our culture by going to Disney World and Washington D.C. We discussed "life chances" in Chapter 8.

Affection

The affectional function is extremely important and is the primary reason for the existence of the marital bond in the United States. The bond, however, is also important between parents and children and members of different generations such as grandmother and grandchild. Ideally, the family is the haven where we get lots of warm fuzzies or TLC (tender loving care). Due to our highly mobile society, in many cases, the person we have known the longest in our area of residence is our spouse or our parents. When married men were asked whom they consider to be their best friends, the majority responded, "my wife."

THINKING SOCIOLOGY

At what age did or do you intend to marry? Why?

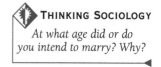

WHAT ARE THE TRENDS OF THE FAMILY IN THE UNITED STATES?

MEDIAN AGE AT FIRST MARRIAGE		
YEAR	MALE	FEMALE
1890	26.1	22.0
1900	25.9	21.9
1930	24.3	21.3
1950	22.8	20.3
1960	22.8	20.3
1970	23.2	20.8
1980	24.7	22.0
1990	26.1	23.9
2000	26.8	25.1
2003	27.1	25.3
U.S. BUREAU OF THE CENSUS		

Marrying Culture

We have a very high rate of marriage in our culture. Over 95% of all people will marry at least once during their lifetime. We are, however, delaying marriage in our culture. In fact, the age of marriage dropped since 1890 but is on the upswing again. In 1890, the average man married at 26 and the average woman married at 22. The ages steadily decreased until 1961 when the male married at 22.0 and the females married at 19.8. After this point, the average of marriage began to increase again. In 1992, the average age for the male at first marriage was 26 and for the female, the age at first marriage was 25.

There are several reasons why we are such a marrying culture:

1. *We are a very romantic culture*; many of our movies, songs and books have romantic themes; we even sell cars, shaving lotion and liquor based on romance.

2. *We have the notion that marriage is the answer to all our problems.* I have heard young people say they were having problems at home or at school, so they would get married! This is no solution; it only contributes to greater problems.

3. *There has been a reduction in economic risk.* We can charge almost indefinitely if we make the monthly payment on the credit card; we can buy a car and pay for it in four years. Women are also readily finding jobs and it is no longer the traditional family of the 1950s in which the man is supposed to support the family.

4. *We have earlier dating and going steady in our culture.* At five and six, we ask youngsters if they have a boyfriend or girlfriend; we plan dances for sixth grade graduation! Children as young as nine are now engaging in sexual relationships and having babies.

5. *Divorce has become much easier to obtain in our culture.* If there is no property or children, a divorce can cost under $100.

▲ AMERICANS TEND TO PREFER 1–3 CHILDREN.
IMAGE COPYRIGHT JURIAH MOSIN, 2008. USED UNDER LICENSE FROM SHUTTERSTOCK, INC.

Shrinking Family Size

The average household is shrinking in number of people. We have young couples choosing to remain child-free and more families opting for one child. Average size of the family has gone from 3.67 in 1960 to 3.26 in 2001. There are several reasons why we have smaller families:

1. *We have an aging population* and as the average age goes up, the birth rate goes down.

2. *We are waiting longer to have our first child*; there has been an increase in the span of time between marriage and birth of first child. In earlier times, the birth of the first child was expected soon after marriage. Now we say that we should establish ourselves as a couple or establish a career before starting our family. Many couples are now waiting until they are in their 30s or even early 40s before having their first child. With the age of starting later to be parents, there is less time to produce a large family.

3. *More people are using effective birth control.* The reason that we can plan family size so well is the wide availability and use of birth control. Sterilization has become the number one option for those families who feel that they have completed their family size.

4. *Our viewpoint about children has changed.* We now view children as an economic liability rather than as an asset. The cost of raising a child through age eighteen is a quarter to a half-million dollars. When we were an agrarian society, children helped with the workload; this is no longer true.

5. *More women are working outside of the home.* As women get involved in careers and jobs, they do not want to take up a great deal of their time with pregnancy and child care.

6. *Sexual behavior is now viewed as a recreational activity rather than for the purpose of procreation.*

🕮 **Quick Glance**

One of the trends of the American family is that we are having fewer children. T F

The definition of the American family has remained static. T F

The age of starting a family has remained constant among married couples. T F

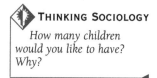

THINKING SOCIOLOGY

How many children would you like to have? Why?

HOUSEHOLD BY SIZE			
Year	Average Population per Household	Year	Average Population per Household
1930	4.11	1980	2.76
1940	3.67	1990	2.63
1950	3.37	2000	2.62
1960	3.35	2003	2.57
1970	3.14		

U.S. Census Bureau.

MEDIAN INCOME 2005	
MARRIED COUPLE FAMILIES	$65,906
MALE, NO WIFE	$41,111
FEMALE, NO HUSBAND	$27,244

U.S. CENSUS BUREAU, 2006

Changing Definition of What Constitutes a Family

The family in the United States has traditionally been defined as a husband, wife and their children living in one household with the dad being the economic provider and the mom providing the nurturing of the children. Today, this type of family is termed a **traditional family**. There are, however, several different types of families in the United States:

1. **single-person or one-person households**
   People living alone account for 21% of all American households. We are marrying later which frequently gives us time as a single-person household. The divorce rate has also increased the number of single-person households. Usually one or the other of the ex-spouses form a single-person household. In about 97% of the cases, it is the male. The increasing number of widows contributes to the number of single-person households.

2. **consensual family or cohabitation**
   An unmarried man and woman, perhaps with children, living together in one household is becoming increasingly prevalent. Unmarried cohabitants tend to be as personally committed to their partners as are engaged couples, but are less committed to the idea of marrying their partner. There is a tendency for cohabiting women to have higher commitment scores than their partners. There are at least three categories of people living together. The first is the traditional college-age people; these people say they live together as a trial

🕮 **Quick Glance**

Fewer people use birth control than ten years ago. T F

According to Wallerstein, parents usually get along after the divorce. T F

Children are viewed as an economic asset of modern parents. T F

Definition of what constitutes an American family has remained the same over the past 20 years. T F

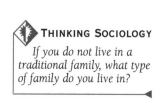

THINKING SOCIOLOGY

If you do not live in a traditional family, what type of family do you live in?

Quick Glance

Single person households account for 33% of families.   T F

Cohabitation is another name for binuclear family.   T F

A blended family is sometimes called a reconstructed family. T F

Dual career families are stress-free.   T F

Boomerang kids are children who have left the parental home and return once again to live.   T F

marriage but statistics indicate that those couples who live together before marriage are just as apt or more apt to get a divorce than couples who go through a traditional courtship. In second marriages, living together is more apt to predict marital success. Another category of people living together, rather than marrying, is senior citizens. They choose to live together rather than marry because of children's opinions and problems with inheritance and social security benefits.

3. **single-parented family**

This family is characterized by one parent living with one or more children. There are more singled-parented families because of divorce and females opting to keep babies born out of wedlock. Two out of five children born in the 1970s have lived in a single-parent home for at least part of their youth; 91% have lived with their mothers and 9% with their fathers. A small but growing trend is professional or older women who see their "biological clock" running down opting to have a child without a social father. The television show "Murphy Brown" took heat on this issue of an unmarried woman with a baby. These women generally have the resources to financially support a child.

THINKING SOCIOLOGY

Do you think you'll be part of a dual-career family? What would be the consequences for the functions of the family?

4. **blended, binuclear, step or reconstructed families**

This type of family consists of a husband and a wife with one or both partners having been married before, plus children from a previous marriage or marriages and children from those marriages. About 20% of all marriages are second or subsequent marriages involving either widowed or divorced persons. Blended families frequently experience problems with money (nonpayment of child support), sexual problems because of older children acting as chaperones and discipline problems with the other person's children.

5. **dual-career family**

There has been a change in attitude towards working women in our culture. The advantages of a dual-career family are more income and more to talk about. The difficulties include role overload, lack of adequate child care, job relocation and mutual vacation times.

I HAVE YET TO HEAR A MAN ASK FOR ADVICE ON HOW TO COMBINE MARRIAGE AND A CAREER.

GLORIA STEINEM

6. **post-rearing family**

As more of us live to be older and in good health, more of us enter what is called a **post-rearing family**. The family unit returns to a husband and a wife who have already reared their children. Two interesting phenomena have happened to many post-rearing families. **Boomerang kids** are children who have left the parental home and returned once again to live. This includes children who leave to go to college and return after receiving a degree. Some children also return home after a divorce or loss of a job. **Ping-pong kids** have a cycle of leaving and returning home. My daughter is a ping-pong kid. She attends college, but every vacation she is at home again and she lives at home during the summer months.

Quick Glance

Boomerang kids spend summer and Christmas vacation in the family of orientation.   T F

No-fault divorce is against the law.   T F

Family violence is rare in the U.S.A.   T F

7. **consensual unions**

These are unions which are outside the confines of strictly legal mating and include such practices as bonded homosexual relationships and common law

PERCENTAGE OF YOUNG ADULTS 18–24 LIVING AT HOME					
Year	Male	Female	Year	Male	Female
1960	52%	35%	2000	57%	47%
1970	54%	41%	2002	55%	46%
1980	54%	43%	2005	53%	46%
1990	58%	48%			

U.S. Census Bureau, Sept. 21, 2006.

CALL IT A CLAN, CALL IT A NETWORK, CALL IT A TRIBE, CALL IT A FAMILY. WHATEVER YOU CALL IT, WHOEVER YOU ARE, YOU NEED ONE.
JANE HOWARD

marriages (which are still allowed in several states). Although these types of relationships are still rare, this form is becoming more popular or at least more public, and many homosexual relationships between women result in stable long-lasting relationships. More male homosexual couples are beginning to form bonded couples. Some churches now perform a ceremony for homosexual marriages even though the ceremony is not recognized by the United States government.

8. **unmarried mothers**

Approximately 36 percent of all babies born in this country are to unwed mothers. The fastest increase of unmarried mothers is women in their 20s. It is common for these women to be cohabitating.

Ups and Downs of Divorce Rate

Since the early 1900s, the divorce rate has increased. The divorce rate increased because of the ease of getting divorced. Many states now have what is called a **no-fault divorce**. This type of divorce allows us to split two people without someone being a guilty party. We also "dissolve" marriages rather than having divorces. Society is more accepting of divorce than during the early part of this century. Now, however, the divorce rate has gone down. This has occurred because people would rather have a safe sex partner than no sex partner and people are getting married at a more mature age.

> **THINKING SOCIOLOGY**
> *Is there or has there ever been abusive behavior in your family? Why do you think abuse happens in families?*

Learning TIP
If you do not know a meaning of a word, look it up right away in the glossary or a dictionary. Write a brief definition in your book's margin.

WHAT ARE THE EFFECTS OF DIVORCE ON CHILDREN?

Judith Wallerstein in *Second Chances* studied 131 children over a period of 15 years within 60 families. Children were 2 to 18 years of age at the time their parents divorced. Wallerstein found the following effects of divorce on children:

1. Three out of five youngsters felt rejected by a least one of their parents.
2. Half of the children grew up in settings where the parents were warring with each other even after the divorce.
3. Two-thirds of the girls, many who had seemingly sailed through the crisis, suddenly became deeply anxious as young adults, unable to make lasting commitments and fearful of betrayal in intimate relationships.
4. Many of the boys, who were more overtly troubled in the post-divorce years, failed to develop a sense of independence, confidence or purpose. They drifted in and out of college and from job to job.

WHAT ARE THE STATIONS OF DIVORCE?

Anthropologist Paul Bohannan has identified six stations of divorce:

1. The emotional divorce starts with the mention of a divorce in the marriage. Emotions are a part of the divorce process whether the person wants the divorce or not.
2. The economic divorce calls for making decisions about what happens to the house and other property.
3. The legal station of the divorce involves beginning proceedings that will mean the end of the relationship through the legal justice system.
4. The community station for the divorce involves telling friends and relatives that the relationship is ending. There will be changes in friendships for each member of the dissolved relationship.
5. Coparental divorce includes making decisions regarding child custody, child support payments and visitation rights.
6. The psychic station of the divorce focuses on the people trying to regain autonomy. We have to shift our thinking from "we" to "me."

Quick Glance

The divorce rate continues to increase in the U.S.A.   T F

American society still condemns divorce just like in the 1880s.   T F

The only type of family abuse of interest is child abuse.   T F

The typical victim of elder abuse is a 75-year-old man.   T F

Learning TIP
Do not sacrifice your long term goals for short term goals. Think about where you want to be in 5 or 10 years and work for that goal.

Family Violence

Family violence has increased, or at least become more publicized. The types of family abuse include spouse abuse, child abuse and parent abuse. The very intimacy of the family contributes to the violence. Family members are intensely involved with one another. Intensity of family relationships tends to magnify the most trivial things such as a burned dinner or a whining child. Such minor offenses and small oversights often spark violent family fights. There are few outside constraints on violence. When a family quarrel threatens to become a fight, there are no bystanders to break it up, as there might be on the street or in some other public place. Police are reluctant to intercede in family quarrels, neighbors may know of child abuse, but resist getting involved. Victims may be too ashamed to report family violence. A small child may not know something is wrong or unusual when a parent holds his hand in a flame for punishment, parents are allowed and even encouraged to use physical force in the family. "Spare the rod, and spoil the child." Most people do not think of spanking as violence. Suppose a teacher hits a child across the face; this would constitute assault and battery in a court of law. Parenthood confers a license for hitting in our society. So, according to some, does marriage. In one survey, one out of four people agreed that it is sometimes justifiable for a husband to hit his wife. Battered wives often say and believe "I asked for it." Wife and husband abuse occur at about the same rates, but men are stronger and do more damage than do wives. Guns, however, are an equalizer and about 40–50% of all homicides occur within the family. Parent abuse is also called elder abuse or "granny bashing." The typical abused victim is a woman over 75 who is physically or mentally disabled in some way.

Increasing Dedication to Family Ideals

There has been an increasing dedication to family ideals. Nick Stinnett (1978) has identified six qualities that make families strong, functional support systems for its members:

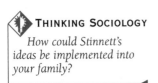

THINKING SOCIOLOGY

How could Stinnett's ideas be implemented into your family?

1. *Commitment is made by individual family members to promote each other's welfare. Value is placed by the individual members on the unity of the family.*

However, the commitment to the family is not to the extreme that individual members lose sight of their own individual selves. The commitment is a healthy relationship between members of the family.

2. *Appreciation is expressed and shown by members in a happy family.* The appreciation may be a "thank you," "I love you" or shown with signs of appreciation like a pat on the back, a hug, a kiss or a gift.

3. *Communication is open and encouraged.* Members enjoy being with one another and talking and listening to each other. The family is seen as a haven and members can talk within a safe environment where they are accepted as they are.

4. *Strong families spend time together.* Members of the family arrange their schedules to guarantee that they will be participating in spending time with each other. The importance for the family being together is seen by the individual members so individual efforts are made to gather together as a family. What the family does together is less important than the fact that they are together. My parents taught me to play "42" and they often would come to play with my husband and me when our children were small. Our oldest son loves the game and participate in "42 tournaments" at College Station, Texas. He and his wife now play "42" with us, as well as with his grandparents.

5. *Strong families are identified as having spiritual awareness.* They were not necessarily religious, but rather vice a feeling of awareness of a greater good or power in their lives. There is an emphasis on having values that may usually be associated with religion.

6. *Strong families are able to deal with family crises positively.* They are able to view stress or crises as an opportunity to grow, both as an individual, as well as a family.

Learning TIP
Take breaks about every hour when studying. Five or ten minutes is long enough!

MARRIAGE AND DIVORCE RATE					
Year	Marriage	Divorce	Year	Marriage	Divorce
1900	9.3%	0.7%	1980	10.6%	5.2%
1930	9.2%	1.6%	1990	9.8%	4.7%
1950	11.1%	2.6%	2000	8.5%	4.1%
1960	8.5%	2.2%	2004	7.4%	3.7%
1970	10.6%	3.5%	2005	7.5%	3.6%

U.S. Dept. of Health and Human Services, National Center for Health Statistics.

Quick Glance

Nick Stinnett identified two qualities of a happy family. T F

Communication in a happy family is closed and limited. T F

Expressing appreciation to one another is a characteristic of a happy family. T F

The structural functionalist theory looks at the exploitation of family members. T F

The conflict theory stresses the functions of the family. T F

The symbolic interactionist focuses on the communication with family members. T F

HOW DO THE THEORIES LOOK AT THE FAMILY?

When we discussed the functions of the family, we were analyzing the way the structural functionalist would view the family; this theoretical framework states that the family fulfills necessary functions for a society. The structural functionalist would also look at dysfunctions. For example, the nuclear family makes it very difficult for a family to care for children when the mother is sick, a parent dies or a family member is handicapped or seriously ill. Divorce destroys the functioning of a nuclear family; in an extended family, these factors are more easily handled.

The conflict perspective emphasizes family pain and conflict. This theory would, for example, look at the role of men's exploitation of women in family dynamics. Conflict theory analyzes the ways that economic forces determine family structure

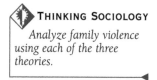

THINKING SOCIOLOGY

Analyze family violence using each of the three theories.

▲ VIOLENCE IN FAMILY INCREASES DIVORCE RATE.
IMAGE COPYRIGHT DUARD VAN DER WESTHUIZEN, 2008. USED UNDER LICENSE FROM SHUTTERSTOCK, INC.

and create problems. For example, the cost of raising children has contributed to a decrease in the birth rate. People in the middle and upper classes tend to socialize their children for independent thinking, while those in working class stress cooperation more. The problem of both parents working has created problems such as "latchkey kids" and high child care costs. Most families in industrial societies have a difficult time making ends meet financially, and marital disputes often center on money.

The symbolic interactionist focuses on the smaller units. When we discussed characteristics of successful families, what we looked for in a mate and how children adjusted to divorce, we were using the lens of the symbolic interactionists.

▼ CHAPTER SUMMARY

1. The institution of family has several characteristics: two or more members are united by blood, marriage or adoption; members typically live together; and members interact according to norms and roles established by the larger society.
2. The family takes on different forms in different cultures: nuclear or conjugal, extended or consanguine, joint, modified extended, composite and tribal. Most humans will belong to at least two forms of a family during their lifetime: family of orientation and family of procreation.
3. Marriage is a legal or social contract between two or more people of the opposite sex. The types of marriage may differ depending on the culture: monogamy or polygamy. Polygamy may be polygyny, polyandry or cenogamy.
4. Whom we marry is governed by rules of endogamy and exogamy.
5. The authority structures within a family depend on the larger society: patriarchy, matriarchy, equalitarian and matricentric are the four patterns.
6. The types of family residence that exist in the world are neolocal, patrilocal and matrilocal.
7. The types of kinship patterns that exist for the family are bilateral or bilineal, patrilineal and matrilineal.
8. The functions for the family are sexual regulation, reproduction, socialization, physical and psychological, economic protection, social status and affection.
9. There are several trends of the American culture: marrying culture, shrinking family size, changing definition of what constitutes a family, ups and downs of divorce rate, family violence, and increasing dedication to family ideals.
10. The structural functional theory looks at the necessary functions that the family fulfills, the conflict theory emphasizes the family pain and conflict, and the symbolic interactionist theory focuses on smaller units such as the interaction within a family.

▼ REFERENCES

Alder, J. 1994. "Kids Growing Up Scared." *Newsweek*, Jan. 10.
Aldous, J. and W. Dumon. 1990. "Family policy in the 1980's: Controversy and Consensus." *Journal of Marriage and the Family*, 52, 1136–1151.
Bohannan, Paul. 1970. *Divorce and After*. New York: Doubleday.

Car, J. 1988. *Crisis in Intimacy*. Pacific Grove, CA: Brooks/Cole.

Collins, R. and S. Coltrane. 1991. *Sociology of Marriage and the Family: Gender, Love and Property*. Chicago: Nelson-Hall.

Coontz, Stephanie. 1992. *The Way We Never Were*. New York: Basicbooks.

Davis, Kingsley. 1948. *Human Society*. New York: The Macmillan Co., 395–96.

Gertsel, N. 1987. "Divorce and Stigma." *Social Problems*, 34, 172–186.

Hertzler, J. O. 1961. *American Social Institutions*. Rockleigh, NJ: Allyn and Bacon, Inc., 232–38.

Murdock, George. 1945. "The Common Denominator of Cultures." In Ralph Linton (ed.) *The Science of Man in the World Crisis*. New York: Columbia University Press.

Murdock, George. 1940. *Social Structure*. New York: The Macmillan Co.

Ogburn, William. 1962. "The Changing Functions of the Family." In Robert F. Winch, Robert McGinnis and Herbert R. Barringer (eds.) *Selected Studies in Marriage and the Family*. New York: Holt, Rinehart and Winston, Inc., 158.

Stinnett, Nick, and John DeFrain. 1985. *Secrets of Strong Families*. Boston: Little, Brown.

Wallerstein, Judith and Sandra Blakeslee. 1989. *Second Chances*. New York: Ticknor & Fields.

Yorburg, Betty. 1993. *Family Relationships*. New York: St. Martin's Press, Inc.

READING

A LIVING HISTORY: THE OLD ORDER AMISH BY ADRIAN RAPP
AND LYNDA DODGEN*

Premarital pregnancy and divorce are virtually unheard of among the Old Order Amish because of their very strong family life. Many of the conditions that exist in modern America that contribute to a high divorce rate and a high premarital pregnancy rate do not exist among the Old Order Amish family. They lead a simple, ordered life with an emphasis on old-fashioned values and avoidance of worldly conveniences such as electrical kitchen appliances, computers, IPods and automobiles. Money has far less importance in their world than their understanding of how God would have them conduct their lives. The Old Order Amish family possesses a structure and way of life which echoes the family in the United States 200 years ago. Their communities are like ghosts from the past.

Twelve factors that have been demonstrated in sociological research to contribute to a stable family are to be discussed in this paper. The presence of these factors contributes to a low rate of divorce and premarital pregnancy rate among the Old Order Amish; the absence of these factors contributes to the high rate of divorce and premarital pregnancy in modern American society.

The first factor contributing to the very low rate of divorce among the Old Order Amish consists of the nonexistent grounds for divorce. Marriages are made under the very literal interpretation of the Bible which states that marriage is a lifetime commitment and divorce is not accepted or condoned. Marriage most definitely forms a lifetime commitment which is supported both by the community and by the church. The modern American marriage is no longer strongly entrenched as a religious vow not to be broken. Divorce has become a secular proceeding.

Secondly, the Old Order Amish has maintained many of the functions of the family which have been lost in the general American population. The family among the Old Order Amish is still a viable educational, religious, protectional, recreational and economic unit. In modern day America, education is conducted in public schools run by the government, while among the Old Order Amish, teachers, often Mennonites, conduct school in a one-room schoolhouse. Education reinforces family values. Religious services are conducted in the various homes of the members and the groups are kept small enough to be a primary group. Recreation occurs within the family and religious groups rather than through commercial recreation. Meals are eaten as a family unit and the evenings are spent as a family unit without television, radio and the many entertainments that take Americans out of the home. The Amish attend none of the cultural functions that other Americans may attend like the opera and theater. They do not dance, play cards or drink liquor. They have no pianos or other musical instruments. Nor do they read popular magazines or novels. They do not have a telephone. They do not celebrate most of our holidays such as Memorial Day, Labor Day and Washington's Birthday. Christmas and Easter are celebrated but the emphasis is religious rather than secular. Lack of automobiles also limits many of the activities the Amish might do. Much of the recreation centers around their religion. Socializing takes place before and after church services. On Sunday evenings the young people hold "sings." Certain religious holidays afford the chance to socialize as do weddings. Just plain visiting is also a favorite form of recreation. Church services are held every other week, and on alternate Sundays most families visit or are

Quick Glance

Money is very important to the Old Order Amish.　　T　F

The Old Order Amish have a high desertion rate.　　T　F

The Old Order Amish like television and automobiles.　　T　F

Quick Glance

Divorce rate is low among the Old Order Amish because marriage is a secular proceeding.　T　F

Among the Old Order Amish, recreation is centered in the family.　T　F

Among the Old Order Amish, recreation is religiously based.　　T　F

*Excerpted from a paper presented at the Southwestern Social Science Association, Houston, Texas on March 20–23, 1985. Updated 2007.

visited by relatives or friends. The Old Order Amish are also fond of family outings and picnics. From the amount of food consumed on these occasions, eating would have to be classified as a major recreational activity. Within their own homes they do some reading. They read the Bible, the Amish hymnal, the *Martyrs Mirror*, the story of early Anabaptist persecutions, and sometimes farm journals. Some Amish families subscribe to local newspapers. They occasionally play games, such as chess and checkers, and the youngsters engage in their own brand of athletics. Adult males chew tobacco and some districts permit smoking. Some men even occasionally "take a nip." Large numbers of Amish have no desire to lead any other kind of life. They accept the hard work and lack of leisure as the will of God. In modern day America one or both parents leave the home to go to work but among the Old Order Amish both men and women work near the home and supply many of the necessities of life within the family unit. In the functional sense, the Old Order Amish family is a remarkably strong unit. The modern American family has given up many of the functions to outside agencies which contribute to the high divorce rate.

Third, there is a strong sense of family by the people marrying. Not only do you marry a spouse, but you marry a family. Family structure among the Amish is an extended family. The extended families generally know one another and each family gives and offers much help to the newly married couple. The parents will always be ready to help out and advise the newlyweds so that the young people live satisfying lives. In modern America, marriage signals the reaching of adulthood and supposedly each couple should be a self-sustaining unit.

Fourth, the community commands great control over the activities of individuals. It has been proven sociologically that the most effective forms of social control are informal positive and negative sanctions. The most important means of control in the Amish community is the *Meidung*. This involves the presiding bishop placing a nonconforming member under the ban. This member then becomes *persona non grata* to all other Amishmen. No one, including his or her own family, can have anything to do with him or her. Even the spouse is forbidden to have normal marital relations with him or her. Moreover, any Amish person who does associate with the shunned member is placed under the ban. And since an Amishman normally associates only with other Amishmen, the *Meidung* isolates the member. This is at the very heart of social control among the Amish. Whether this ban is applied or not, the threat remains to control the activities of the Old Order Amish. It is so powerful a measure that it rarely has to be used. Another means of control is the *Ordnung*. Each congregation has its Ordnung, which is usually an unwritten body of rules that governs all aspects of daily life, including the way the farmer tills his field. This strict control of the people's lives contributes to a very low divorce rate and low premarital pregnancy rate. Secondary control is very prominent in modern American society. The police, the courts and other public officials have a much greater role in social control than it does in the Old Order Amish community.

Another factor of community control deals with the whole district rejoicing and anticipating the marriage. A new family unit is created and the perpetuation of the community is assured. Marriage is a crucial institution to the Old Order Amish and they go out of their way to emphasize this fact. The announcement is first made by publishing the banns at a church service, usually two weeks before the wedding takes place at the home of the bride. The ceremony itself is not elaborate but takes a long time. An enormous meal is held after the wedding which gives community support and a time for reinforcing group cohesiveness. Women throughout the district volunteer to get the meal and help serve. The groom moves into the house several days before the appointed date. His two witnesses, either brothers, cousins or best friends, usually selected in that order, arrive the day before the wedding. They give as much

The Old Order Amish marry the individual not the family.　T　F

Among the Old Order Amish the community has little influence over the individual.　T　F

Meidung means party time.　T　F

time as possible to helping prepare the tables. Two bridesmaids are also present; they may be sisters, cousins or friends. They, too, help with food preparation and kitchen chores. These helpers stay to help restore the home after the celebration. There is a great deal of community support for the wedding and ritual which is continued on after marriage. The marriage ceremony among the modern American couple is not a community effort but rather a family effort. The newly married couple then moves into their own quarters to begin life as a separate entity.

Fifth, roles among the Old Order Amish remain very traditional. Women remain in the home taking charge of kitchen and children. Women sew their clothes by hand and run small cottage-like industries making things like quilts (which can be sold to buy basic farm implements). The wife's duties also include cooking, cleaning, preparation of produce for market, preserving food and gardening. The extent to which a husband helps with household tasks is nominal. Women and adolescent girls frequently help with the harvest of crops, especially cornhusking. Men do the farming. Children are taught to follow in the parent's footsteps. The Old Order Amish believe that their children will grow up just as they did to become farmers and farmer's wives. Strict division of labor means that there is an interdependence of each spouse to provide for the needs of life and thus, is a source of stability for the family. This is no longer true in the modern American family in which both spouses work and share in household chores and child care.

Sixth, family organization has always been strictly monogamous and patriarchal. The Old Order Amish believe that the man is head of household and it is the wife's place to support her husband. (Man is the image and glory of God; but the woman is the glory of the man. 1 Cor. 11:7) A strong patriarchal family is associated with a low divorce rate. The modern American family is more equalitarian than the Old Order Amish family. Women have more rights and freedoms than does the Old Order Amish wife.

Seventh, there is no comfort orientation among the Amish as there is in modern America. The comfort-loving orientation of individuals in the United States and a refusal to tolerate discomfort and inconvenience has been suggested as one factor contributing to the high divorce rate. Among the Old Older Amish, their religion and life style are based on rigid, puritanical doctrines which demand that the people deny themselves all but the simplest pleasures and comforts. Automobiles and other technological advances are strictly prohibited. The Old Order Amish accept hardship and a lack of total happiness as the way life should be. This standard generally has not been acceptable to the modern American. It is generally believed that each person in the modern family should have happiness and contentment and, if these goals are not reached, divorce is an acceptable alternative so that satisfaction may be sought elsewhere.

Eighth, the standards of measuring success of marriage for the Old Order Amish is different than in the modern American family. The Old Order Amish measure the success of the marriage in terms of performance of traditional roles. In modern marriage, success is now measured in terms of personal satisfaction and happiness. Among the Old Order Amish, the boy looks for "poise" in his girl; he wants her to be accepted in her own group; she expects to find in him a good worker with a robust, not slender, figure which can give testimony in work, endurance and also ardor in his love. The young woman who is a good housekeeper, strong, healthy, considerate, alert, quick and eager makes a valued mate. These considerations exceed the attractions of a fair-skinned and quickly fading beauty. Amish youth place minimal importance on romantic love and physical attractiveness. They favor instead those traits which will make for a successful farm life; willingness to work, cheerfulness and reliability. Married Amish couples achieve happiness by the harmony of purpose

☞ *Quick Glance*

The wedding is a very short, simple affair among the Old Order Amish. T F

The Old Order Amish family is egalitarian. T F

The Old Order Amish form a matriarchal family. T F

rather than physical attraction. This gives their marriage a firm foundation lacking in the modern American family.

Ninth, the primary group provides for virtually all needs of the family. There is very little contact with secondary groups as in modern American society. Among the Old Order Amish, their whole life revolves around the family. The family may include four or five generations and contributes to the very conservative orientation of the Amish. Young people are not supposed to move so far away that they cannot see the smoke from the parents' chimney. Rarely do the Amish sell a farm out of the family. Moreover, the only time an Amish breadwinner will move from the area is when there is no more land available or when he has had a deep-seated rift with the bishop. In most cases, the Amish family system is perpetuated generation after generation with relatively little change. The church not only forbids change but should young couples get ideas, parents and other relatives are usually close enough to act as restraining influences. This strong family tie does not exist in the modern American family.

Another aspect of the primary group involves the fact that each individual congregation is kept small to maintain a primary group feeling which maximizes control over the individual. The functional unit is no larger than a group of people who can know one another by name, by shared ceremonial activity and by convention. The organization of the church increases community support. The Amish are organized into church districts and each district covers a certain geographical area and includes a certain number of families. Membership varies, depending on circumstances, but most districts average around two hundred members. When the figure exceeds this number, the district usually divides, a not infrequent occurrence due to the high birth rate. They do not have a church building but rather meet in individuals' homes. This is done on a rotating basis. Since 1564, all tunes of the 140 hymns they sang were passed down orally from generation to generation. Their hymnal has no musical notes, only words. Secondary groups are emphasized in modern-day life. Our place of worship, the organizations we belonged to and the work force are probably all secondary group membership in modern American society.

Tenth, parents still have a large influence in matching their children with a spouse. Strict obedience to parents is taught from a very early age. Marriage is endogamous. Amish parents forbid their young people to date the non-Amish. The only permissible dating is within the district or between districts that have full fellowship with one another. Endogamy among the Amish, therefore, does serve to limit the number of eligible mates. There is a strict belief in the gospel which includes a belief that the young should marry only their own spiritual kin. When the couple decides to get married, the young man is required to visit the deacon and make his intentions known. The deacon approaches the girl's father and requests formal permission for the marriage. Needless to say permission is usually granted. Mate selection is individually determined in modern American society and parental and religious support are not required. This contributes to a higher divorce rate among modern American couples.

Eleventh, there are large families among the Amish. The presence of children tends to hold a marriage together whether it is happy or not. Since the farm is an Amishman's daily concern, he usually has a large number of children to aid in the enterprise. Amish youngsters are generally exempt from school laws and child labor laws. Consequently, unlike the society at large, children are considered by their parents to be economic assets. Families with 10 to 12 children are not at all uncommon. The average number is around 7 or 8. Birth control in any form is not practiced. The lower family size may contribute to the rising divorce in modern America. In modern American families, families with many children have a lower divorce rate than families with none, one or two children.

Quick Glance

The overabundance of choice contributes to a higher divorce rate among people living in modern America.   T F

We define a successful marriage in modern America in terms of people performing traditional roles.   T F

Secondary groups play an important role in the lives of the Old Order Amish.   T F

Quick Glance

The Old Order Amish are organized geographically not in terms of population size.   T F

The center of the Old Order Amish is their beautiful church buildings.   T F

Old Order Amish practice exogamy.   T F

The family influence on partner selection contributes to low rate of divorce.   T F

Quick Glance

Small families have a lower divorce rate than large families.   T F

The Old Order Amish believe in extramarital sex.   T F

Premarital sex is a major problem among the Old Order Amish.   T F

Twelfth, there is no divorce or extramarital affairs among the Old Order Amish for couples to model their behavior. The Old Order Amish emphasizes conformity. Due to community pressure there are no premarital or extramarital affairs. Premarital sex is not a major problem among the Amish since it is associated with drinking, drugs, automobiles, contraception, motels and coeducational living all of which are taboo among the Amish. Occasionally an unmarried girl becomes pregnant, but it is rare. Illegitimacy and adultery are almost unheard of. Desertion is practically unknown, and no divorces have yet been reported. This is very unlike the modern American family with its rising rate of premarital pregnancy and extramarital affairs.

Bibliography and References

_____, "The Amish, the Automobile, and Social Interaction," *The Journal of Geography*, 71, January, 1972, pp. 52–57.

_____, *Amish Traditions*, Huntington, Pa.: Yoder Publishing Company, 1950.

Bachman, Calvin G., *The Old Order Amish of Lancaster County*, Pennsylvania, Lancaster, Pa.: The Pennsylvania German Society, reissued 1961.

Cromwell, Ronald, and Vicky Thomas, "Developing Resources for Family Potential: A Family Action Model," *The Family Coordinator*, January, 1976, pp. 19–20.

Hostetler, John, "The Amish Family," *Marriage and the Family*, in *World Readings, Fourth Edition*, edited by Ruth Shonie Cavan, 1974, New York: Thomas Y. Crowell Company, pp. 71–81.

Hostetler, John, *Amish Society: Third Edition*, Baltimore, Maryland: The Johns Hopkins University Press, 1980.

Kempler, Hyman, "Extended Kinship Ties and Some Modern Alternatives," *The Family Coordinator*, April, 1976, pp. 143–148.

Kephart, William M., "The Amish Family: Resistance to Change," in *The Family, Society, and the Individual*, Boston: Houghton Mifflin, 1972, pp. 191–212.

Klein, H. M. J., *History and Customs of the Amish People*, York, Pa.: Maple Press, 1946.

Kollmorgen, Walter M., *Culture of a Contemporary Community: The Old Order Amish of Lancaster County, Pennsylvania*, Washington, D.C.: U.S. Department of Agriculture, 1942.

Mook, Maurice A., "A Brief History of Former, Now Extinct, Amish Communities in Pennsylvania," *Western Pennsylvania Historical Magazine*, Spring-Summer, 1955, pp. 33–46.

Newswanger, Kliehl, and Christian Newswanger, *Amishland*, New York: Hastings House, 1954.

Redfield, Robert, "The Folk Society," *American Journal of Sociology*, January, 1947, 292–308.

Schreiber, William, *Our Amish Neighbors*, Chicago: University of Chicago Press, 1962.

THINKING SOCIOLOGY

How do you feel about each of the factors contributing to low divorce rate?

Which ones have you considered or will consider in your choice of a mate?

Which factors can we realistically adopt for modern America? Support your answer.

INDEX

A

"A Typology of Collectors and Collecting Behavior" (Dodgen and Rapp), 125–128

Acculturation
  as cultural assimilation, 178
  definition, 168

Achieved status, 90, 102, 106

Acting crowds, 110, 114

Adult socialization, 66, 76–77. *See also* Socialization

Adventist sect, 257

Affection, 297

Affective element (religious experience), 250, 254, 264

Age
  age-specific death rate, 188, 197–198
  demographic studies and, 196
  latent functions of education and, 275
  minorities and, 170
  of marriage, 298

Age of Enlightenment
  birth of sociology and, 6–7

Ageism
  definition, 168, 174, 183
  elderly abuse, 302
  in the elderly, 170
  voter participation and, 221

Agencies of socialization, 79–81
  definition, 66

Aggregate, 91

Agnostic, 250–251

Agrarian system, 230, 232, 243

Alienation, 90

All I Really Need to Know I Learned in Kindergarten, 274

Allport, Gordon, 171, 182

Altruistic suicide, 8

Amalgamation, 168

American Father of Sociology, 11–12

American Journal of Sociology, founding of, 12

Analysis. *See also* Scientific method; Theories
  macro/micro levels of, 12

Animatism, 254
  definition, 250

Animism, 254

Anomic suicide
  definition, 2
  Durkheim, Emile and, 8

Anomie
  definition, 2
  Durkheim, Emile and, 8

Anomie theory of deviance
  as structural functional theory, 181
  definition, 130

Anti-abortion movement, 117

Anti-bussing movement, 117

Anticipatory socialization
  definition, 66, 76
  role conflict/strain and, 104, 106

Antinatalist
  definition, 188
  policies, 203
  population and, 190

Asch, S. E., 141

Ascribed status, 90, 102, 106

Assimilation, 168, 178–179

"At Home in the Parliament of Whores" (O'Rourke), 225–228

Atheist, 250

Attitude, 168

Authoritarian government, 210, 213–214, 223

Authority, 210, 212–213

Avoidance as reaction of minority group, 180

B

Baby boomers and gentrification, 203

Becker, Howard S., 140

Behavior and minorities, 170

Berger, Peter L., 18–21

Bible, 253

Bigamy, 290

Bilateral/bilineal descent, 290, 295

Binuclear family, 290, 300. *See also* Families

Biological assimilation, 179

Biology. *See* Sociobiology

Birth/death rates. *See also* Demography
  demographic transition and, 193
  fertility and, 197–198
  population control and, 203
  top causes of death (U.S.), 199

Black Bourgeoisie, 181

Black liberation movement, 117

Black Muslim movement, 122

Blended family, 290, 300. *See also* Families

Blumer, Herbert, 114

Bogardus, Emory, 172–173

Bogardus Social Distance Scale, 172

Bohannan, Paul, 302

Bonding
  definition, 66
  socialization process and, 72

Boomerang kids, 290, 300

Buddhism. *See also* Religion
  beliefs and, 253–254
  religious trends and, 261

Bureaucracies. *See* Formal organizations

Burgess, Ernest, 200

Burnout, 230, 238, 243

C

Capital, 230–231

Capitalism
  definition, 230, 243
  industrial economic systems and, 233
  Protestantism and, 262

Caste system of stratification
  conflict theory and, 263
  definition, 149, 162

Casual crowds, 114
  definition, 110

Catholicism
  beliefs and, 255
  capitalism and, 262
  decline of, 260
  education and, 278
  formal organization of, 256

CBD (central business district), 188

Cenogamy (group) marriage, 290, 293. *See also* Marriage

Central Business District (CBD), 202

Certification function, 270

Challenge of Crime in a Free Society, The, 146

Chambliss, William J., 140

Change. *See also* Social change
  conflict theory and, 14
  future shock and, 46, 60

Charismatic authority, 210, 213

Childhood socialization, 77–79

Children and agencies of socialization, 79–81

Christianity. *See also* Religion
  beliefs and, 253, 255
  self-importance and, 251

Church of Jesus Christ Latter Day Saints, 257

City, 188, 199

Civil religion, 250, 258–259, 264

Civil Rights Movement, 121
Class consciousness
    definition, 148
    social class measurement and, 157
Class system of stratification, 162
Classical economic theory, 243
Closed system of stratification, 149
Cluster sample, 35
Coalition
    definition, 90
    group size and, 92
Cognitive characteristics and minorities, 170
Cohabitation. See Consensual family
Cohen, Albert, 138, 140
Coleman, James, 278
Collective behavior
    "A Typology of Collectors and
        Collecting Behavior" (Dodgen and
        Rapp), 125–128
    definition, 111, 123
    forms of, 112–117, 123
    future and, 123
    theories of, 120–123
Colonial democracy, 213
Colonial pattern and minority group
    emergence, 176
Columbia University, 12
Communism, 243
    as civil religion, 259
    definition, 230
    industrial economic systems and, 234
    John Birch Society and, 119
    Marx, Karl and, 11
Communities
    deviance and, 135
    "Living History, A: The Old Order
        Amish" (Rapp and Dodgen) and,
        306–310
    student volunteers and, 278
    support for education by, 277
Compartmentalization and role conflict/
    strain, 105
Competition, 90, 101, 106
Composite family, 290–291, 304. See also
    Families
Compositional theory of urban way of
    life, 201, 204
Compostitional theory, 188
Comte, Auguste, 7–8, 15
Concentric zone theory of urbanization,
    200, 204
Conflict
    definition, 90, 106
    social process and, 100–101
Conflict theory, 14–15
    and education, 281–282, 285
    and minority groups, 182
    and religion, 263, 264
    definition, 2, 143
    deviance and, 137–138

families and, 303–304
Keynesian economic theory as, 242
Marx, Karl and, 11
social stratification and, 154–155, 162
Conformist, 130
Conformity
    anomie theory of deviance and,
        136–137
    definition, 130
Confucianism
    beliefs and, 255
    religious trends and, 261
Conjugal family, 291, 304. See also
    Families
Consanguine family, 290–291, 304. See
    also Families
Consensual family, 290, 299, 300–301.
    See also Families
Conservative movement, 120
Conspicuous consumption. See also
    Consumption
    definition, 148
    status and, 151–152
    ZPG (zero population growth) and,
        190
Consumption, 236
    definition, 230
Contact hypothesis
    and minority groups, 182
    definition, 168
Contagion theory, 120
    definition, 110
Contagious magic, 252, 264
Content analysis
    advantages/disadvantages of, 32
    definition, 24
Conventional crowds, 110
Convergence theory, 110, 120–121
Conversionist sect, 257
Cooley, Charles Horton
    looking-glass self and, 73–74, 82
    on groups, 92–95
    symbolic interactionist theory and, 15
Cooperation
    definition, 90, 106
    social process and, 102
Cooptation of social movement, 119
Copyright and ethics, 37
Core of knowledge, 270, 278
Corporations
    as bureaucracies, 238
    economic trends and, 240–241
Cosmology, 250, 254
Countercultures, 46, 57–58. See also
    Jonestown, Guyana, South America
Craze, 110, 116
Credentialism, 270, 275
Criminal behavior. See also Deviance
    characteristics of, 133
    definition, 130, 142
    delinquent subcultures and, 138

determination of, 140
differential association theory of
    deviance and, 140
Cross-sectional study
    definition, 24
    time frames for research and, 33
Crowd, The: A Study of the Popular Mind,
    120
Crowds, 110, 113–114. See also Groups
Crude birth/death rates, 188, 197–198
Cult
    characteristics of, 259
    definition, 250, 264
    discussion, 257–258
    symbolic interactionist theory and,
        263–264
Cultural drift, 110, 117–118
Cultural lag, 46, 60
Cultural pluralism
    definition, 168
    majority treatment of minorities via,
        178
Cultural relativism, 46, 50
Cultural universal, 46
Culture. See also Majority group;
        Minority group
    assimilation of, 178
    characteristics of, 49–51
    definition, 46, 48–49, 60
    educational transmission of, 273
    society and, 47
Culture shock, 46, 60
Custom, 46

D

Dahrendorf, R., 15
Data
    definition, 24
    scientific method and, 33–35
Davis, Kingsley, 190
De facto segregation
    definition, 270
    education and, 279
    majority treatment of minorities via,
        177
De jure segregation
    definition, 270
    education and, 279
    majority treatment of minorities via,
        177
Death rates. See Birth/death rates
Debriefing, 24
DeFleur, Melvin, 173
Delinquent subcultures, 138
Democracy, 210, 214–216, 223
Democratic socialism, 230, 234
Demographic transition, 191–194, 203
Demographic transition theory, 188
Demography
    college enrollment (2004), 280
    definition, 188–189

demographic transition and, 191–194
factors of, 196–199
gentrification and, 203
marriage/divorce in U.S. and, 298
"Nations of the Western Community"
(Wattenberg and Zinsmeister),
205–207
religious trends and, 259
suburbanization and, 201–202
urban ecological processes, 202–203
voter participation and, 221
world's largest urban areas, 200
Denny, Reuel, 219
Denomination
as religious group structure, 264
characteristics of, 259
definition, 250
definition/discussion, 256
Dependency ratio, 188, 197
Dependent variables, 24, 27–28
Determinist theory of urban way of life,
201, 204
Deviance, 130
definition/discussion, 130
dysfunctions of, 142
functions of, 142
properties of, 142
Rich Get Richer and the Poor Get Prison,
The, 144–146
Dianetics, 261
Dictatorship, 210, 213
Differential association theory of
deviance, 130, 140, 143
Diffusion
cultural change and, 59
definition, 46, 61
Discovery
cultural change and, 58
definition, 46
Discrimination
definition, 168, 183
differences from prejudice, 171–174
Dissolution of social movement, 119
Divination, 252, 264
Divorce. See also Marriage
rate of, 301, 303
stages of, 302
structural functional theory and, 303
Doctrine of Predestination, 250, 262
Dodgen, Lynda
"A Typology of Collectors and
Collecting Behavior" (Dodgen and
Rapp), 125–128
"Living History, A: The Old Order
Amish" (Rapp and Dodgen),
306–310
"Not So SILI: Sociology Information
Literacy Infusion as the Focus of
Faculty and Librarian
Collaboration", 39–40
Doomsday Cult, 263
Dramaturgical approach, 66, 73, 76

Dual-career families, 14, 300
Durkheim, Emile
as a founding father of sociology, 8–9
on groups, 95
religion defined by, 251, 264
structural functional theory and, 15
Dyad, 90, 92, 105
Dysfunctional family, 291. See also
Families
Dysfunctions
definition, 2
structural functional theory and, 13,
303

E

Ecclesia
characteristics of, 259
definition/discussion, 250, 256, 264
Economic competition and emergence of
minority groups, 176
Economic determinism
definition, 2
Marx, Karl and, 10
Economics
authoritarian government and, 214
conflict theory of education and, 281
deviance and, 135
family function as protection of, 297
having children and, 299
higher education costs, 280
individual social mobility and, 161
industrial economic systems of,
232–234
latent functions of, 236–239, 243
manifest functions of, 235–237, 243
multiple nuclei theory of urbanization
and, 200
population control and, 190
postindustrial economic system of,
234
preindustrial systems of, 230–231
rates of assimilation and, 179
social inequality and wealth, 150–151
U.S. trends of, 239–242, 243
Economy, 230–231. See also Economics
Education
as agency of socialization, 81
as life chance, 153
college as secondary groups, 96
conflict theory and, 281–282, 285
definition, 270–271, 284
degrees conferred by level/gender, 176
effect of isolation of U.S. universities,
11
formalism and, 271
improvement suggestions for, 277–278
individual social mobility and, 162
informal structure of, 272–273
latent functions of, 275–277, 285
manifest functions of, 273–275
population control and, 190

rates of assimilation and, 179
social class measurement and,
156–157
status inconsistency and, 153
structural functional theory and, 281,
285
symbolic interactionist theory and,
283
trends in, 277–278, 285
voter participation and, 221
"What Your 1st Grader Needs To
Know" (Hirsch), 286–287
Educational achievement, 270, 273
Egalitarian, 295, 304
Egalitarian family, 290, 295
Egoistic suicide, 2
Electronic church, 261
Elitism, 210, 219–220, 223
Emergent-norm theory, 110, 121
Emigration
definition, 188, 196
sex ratio and, 204
Employment/income. See also Labor
as latent function of education,
275–277
deviance as source of, 134
economic trends and, 239–242
individual social mobility and, 161
meaningful work and, 237
social class measurement and,
156–159
social inequality and wealth, 150–151
social mobility and, 159–160
status inconsistency and, 154
teacher quality and, 277
unemployment/underemployment,
237, 243
"Work-and-Spend is a Middle-Class
Affliction" (Schor), 164–165
workplace as agency of socialization,
81
Endogamy, 290, 304
Environmental concerns and depletion of
world resources, 239
Equal rights for the handicapped
movement, 117
Escapism and role conflict/strain,
105–106
Essay on the Principle of Population as it
Affects the Future Improvement of
Society, An, 189
Ethicalism, 250, 254
Ethics
Humphreys, Laud and, 31
religious trends and, 260
research and, 37
Ethnic groups
definition, 168
minorities and, 170
U.S. trends of government and, 219
Ethnocentrism, 46, 50
Euthanasia, 194

Evolution (social v. biological), 9
Ex post facto study, 24, 33
Excitement stage of social movement, 118
Exclusion
  definition, 168
  majority treatment of minorities via, 177
Exogamy, 290, 293, 304
Expert power, 210, 212
Expressive crowds, 110, 114
Expressive movement, 120
Extended family. *See also* Families
  definition, 290–291, 304
  "Living History, A: The Old Order Amish" (Rapp and Dodgen) and, 306–310
Extrinsic factor, 230, 238

F

Face-work, 66, 76
Fads, 110, 115, 117
Families. *See also* Marriage
  academic standards and, 276–277
  authority structures of, 295, 304
  characteristics of, 291
  coalitions and, 92
  conflict theory and, 303–304
  definition, 290, 303–304
  determination of residence of, 295
  deviance and, 135
  functions of, 295–297, 304
  "Living History, A: The Old Order Amish" (Rapp and Dodgen) and, 306–310
  population control and, 190
  primary groups and, 93
  roles according to Marx, 11
  social processes in, 102
  social stratification and background of, 153
  structural functional theory and, 13, 303–304
  symbolic interactionist theory and, 16, 303–304
  types of, 291–292
  U.S. trends of, 298–303, 304
  violence in, 302
Family of orientation, 290, 292, 304
Family of procreation, 290, 292, 304
Family Planning Association of China, 190
Fascism as civil religion, 259
Fashions
  collective behavior and, 115–116
  definition, 110
  taste preferences, 153
Fatalistic suicide, 2, 8
Fecundity, 188, 197
Feminism, 184–185. *See also* Gender

Feral child, 66, 71
Fertility
  definition, 188, 204
  demographic studies and, 197
  "Nations of the Western Community (Wattenberg and Zinsmeister), 205–207
  rate of, 188, 197
  ration of, 188
Fischer, Claude, 201
Folkways, 46, 52
Force/coercion, 211–212
Formal organizations, 90, 96–99
Formal social control, 130, 141, 143
Formalism of educational system, 271–272, 284
Formalization of social movement, 119
Frazier, Franklin, 181
French Revolution, 120
Friedman, Milton, 242
Fulghum, Robert, 274
Functions
  definition, 2
  dysfunctions, 2, 13
  latent, 2, 13, 236–239, 243, 275–277, 285
  manifest, 2, 13, 235–237, 243, 251–253, 273–275, 283–284
  of families, 295–297, 304
Fundamentalists, 261. *See also* Religion
Future shock, 46, 60, 61

G

Gambling, 133
Gans, Herbert, 201
Gemeinschaft
  definition, 90, 106
  gesellschaft and, 96
Gender
  covert discrimination and, 171
  degrees conferred by level/gender, 176
  economic inequality and, 237
  "Introduction: Blame It on Feminism" (Faludi), 184–185
  labor trends and, 239–240
  legal protection and, 178
  "Living History, A: The Old Order Amish" (Rapp and Dodgen) and, 306–310
  minorities and, 170, 175
  symbolic interactionist theory in education and, 283
  voter participation and, 221
Generalized beliefs, 110, 122
Generalized others, 66, 75
Generational marker events, 72–73
Genocide
  definition, 168
  majority treatment of minorities via, 177

Gentrification
  as urban ecological process, 203
  definition, 188
Gesellschaft
  definition, 90, 106
  gemeinschaft and, 96
Glazer, Nathan, 219
Global concerns and economic trends, 241
Glorious One-Child Certificate, 190
Gnostic sect, 257
Goal displacement, 110, 119
Goffman, I., 15, 76
Government
  assessment theories of, 222–223
  "At Home in the Parliament of Whores" (O'Rourke), 225–228
  authority and, 213
  definition, 210–211, 223
  economic trends and, 240
  forms of, 213–216
  functions of, 216–217
  political socialization and voter participation, 221–222
  U.S. trends of, 217–219, 223
Great Depression
  as generational marker event, 73
  cooptation and, 119
Green Revolution, 195–196, 204
Greider, William, 217
Group involvement
  peers and children, 80–81
  socialization process and, 71–72
  sociological perspective and, 4–5
Group marriage. *See* Cenogamy (group) marriage
Groups. *See also* Social movements
  collective behavior and, 111
  definition, 91, 105
  ethnic, 170
  in-group and, 90, 95–96 99, 106, 107–108, 117
  out-group and, 90, 95–96, 99, 106, 107–108, 117
  pluralistic social movements and, 118
  primary/secondary, 92–95
  reference group, 99–100
  "Social Theory and Social Structure" (Merton), 107–108
  status and, 102
  summary diagram of, 106
Growth rates. *See* Population

H

Harlow, Harry, 71
Harris, Chauncey, 200
Harris, Marvin, 62–64, 69–70, 251
Harvard University, 12
Hawthorne effect, 24, 36
Hidden curriculum, 270

Hierarchy of role obligation, 105
Hinduism
  beliefs and, 255
  religious trends and, 261
Hirsch, Jr., E.D., 286–287
Horizontal mobility, 148, 159
Horticultural society, 232, 243
Horticultural system, 230
Hoyt, Homer, 200
Hubbard, Ron, 261
Humanism as civil religion, 259
Humphreys, Laud, 31
Hunters and gatherers, 230, 232, 243
Hypothesis, 24, 27

I

"I Lost My Daughters to a Cult" (Pickford
    and Safran), 265–268
Ideal culture, 46, 56–57, 61
Ideal type, 2, 10, 210
Ideology. See also Religion
  authoritarian government and, 213
  capitalism and, 233
  definition, 46
  social movements and, 117
  society and, 56
Illiterate America, 276
Illness and role conflict/strain, 104–105
Imitative magic, 252, 264
Immigration
  and demographic studies, 196
  and social mobility, 161
  definition, 188
  sex ratio and, 204
Impression management, 66, 76
In-group
  definition, 90, 106
  Japanese collective system and, 99
  out-group and, 95–96
  social movements and, 117
  "Social Theory and Social Structure"
    (Merton), 107–108
Incest taboo, 290, 293, 296
Income, 149. See also Economics;
    Employment/income
Independent variables of scientific
    method, 24, 27–28
Index crimes, 133
Individual behavior
  and social mobility, 162
  consumption and, 236
  democracies and, 215, 223
  effect on group behavior of, 5
  marker events and, 72–73
  meaningful work and, 243
  research difficulties and, 36–37
  self-importance via religion, 252
  "Sociology as an Individual Pastime"
    (Berger), 18–21
  stations of divorce and, 302–303

welfare/noneconomic functions and,
    235
  ZPG (zero population growth) and,
    191
Individual proprietorship, 230
Industrial economic systems. See
    Economics
Industrial Revolution
  demographic transition and, 192
  Protestant Reformation and, 262–263
Infant mortality rate
  definition, 188
  demographic studies and, 198
Inflation, 242
Influence, 210, 212. See also Power
Informal educational system, 284
Informal social control, 130, 141, 143
Informational power, 210, 212
Innovation, 46, 58, 61
Innovator, 130
Innovator response and anomie theory of
    deviance, 136–137
Inquiry into the Nature and Causes of the
    Wealth of Nations, 233
Institutionalization of social movement,
    119
Institutions, 46, 56, 61, 66. See also
    Organizations/institutions
Integration, 168, 179
Intergenerational mobility, 148, 159
Intrinsic factors, 238
Intrinsic proprietorship, 230
"Introduction: Blame It on Feminism"
    (Faludi), 184–185
Introversionist sect, 257
Invention, 46, 58
Islam (Mohammedanism). See also
    Religion
  beliefs and, 253, 255

J

Japan
  collective system of, 99
  educational funding in, 283
Jehovah's Witnesses, 257
John Birch Society, 119
Joint family, 290–291, 304
Jones, Jim. See Jonestown, Guyana,
    South America
Jonestown, Guyana, South America, 113,
    122, 257
Judaic Christian beliefs. See also Religion
  U.S. main religions and, 260
Judaism, 253, 255, 260. See also Religion

K

Keynes, John Maynard, 242
Keynesian economic theory, 242
Kinship, 290, 295, 304

Koran, 253
Kornhauser, William, 220
Kozol, Jonathan, 276
Ku Klux Klan, 119

L

Labeling theory of deviance
  tracking of students and, 283
Labor. See also Employment/income
  capitalism and, 233
  distribution of power and, 235
  economic inequality and, 237
  economic trends and, 239–242
  Japanese collective system and, 99
  societal characteristics and, 48
Laissez faire
  capitalism and, 233
  definition, 230
Land use. See Demography
Language
  conflict theory of education and, 282
  cultural assimilation and, 178
  definition, 46, 61
  ethnic groups and, 170
  looking-glass self and, 74
  society and, 55–56
LaPiere, Richard, 171
Latent dysfunction, 2
Latent functions, 2, 13
Laws, 46, 52–53
League of Women Voters movement, 117
LeBon, Gustave, 120
Legal protection
  definition, 168
  majority treatment of minorities via,
    178
Legitimacy, 210, 212
Leisure
  economic trends and, 240
  individual social mobility and, 162
  social stratification and, 153
Levine, Saul, 257
Levinson, Daniel, 82
Life chances
  definition, 148, 153
  prejudice/discrimination and, 175
Life expectancy, 188, 198
Life span, 188, 198
Linguistic relativity hypothesis, 46,
    55–56
Lipset, Seymour M., 222
Literacy, 273, 276. See also Education
"Living History, A: The Old Order
    Amish" (Rapp and Dodgen),
    306–310
Lofland, John, 263
Lonely Crowd, The, 219
Longitudinal study, 24, 33
Looking-glass self, 66, 73–74, 82

M

Macro level of analysis, 2, 12, 15
Magic, 250–251, 264
Mainstreaming (of students), 284
Majority group
  definition, 168, 182
  reaction of minority group to,
    180–181
  treatment of minority group by, 177–
    180, 183
Malinowski, Bronislaw, 251
Malthus, Thomas, 189, 203
Mana, 254
Manifest dysfunction, 2
Manifest functions, 13
Marginal adaptation as reaction of
  minority group, 180
Marker events, 66, 72–73
Market economy, 230, 233
Marriage
  as latent function of education, 275
  definition, 290, 304
  determination of participants in, 293–
    294, 304
  discussion, 292–293
  ethnic groups and, 170
  individual social mobility and, 162
  "Living History, A: The Old Order
    Amish" (Rapp and Dodgen) and,
    306–310
  population control and, 190
  U.S. trends of, 298–303
Marriage Encounter Movement, 117
Marx, Karl
  conflict theory and social stratification
    according to, 15
  early sociological thought and, 10–11
  religion and, 263
  socialism/communism and, 233–234
Mass hysteria, 110, 115, 117
Master status, 90, 102
Material culture, 46, 51, 61
Matriarchy, 290, 295, 304
Matricentric/matrifocal family, 290, 295,
  304. See also Families
Matrilineal descent, 290, 295
Matrilocal pattern of residence, 290, 295,
  304
Mead, George Herbert, 15, 74–75, 82,
  86–87
Meaning in life and religion, 253
Mechanical solidarity, 2, 9
Mechanization and social mobility, 161
Media
  academic standards and, 277
  effects of television, 81
  impact on education of, 285
  individual social mobility and, 162
  "Living History, A: The Old Order
    Amish" (Rapp and Dodgen) and,
    306–310

political behavior and, 222–223
prejudice/discrimination acquisition
  through, 174
soft-culture and, 234
Megalopolis, 188, 200
Meidung, 307
Mental differences and deviance, 133
Merton, Robert K.
  anomie theory of deviance and, 136–
    137, 140, 143
  as a founder of sociology, 12–13
  on in-/out-groups, 96
  on prejudice/discrimination, 174
  "Social Theory and Social Structure",
    107–108
  structural functional theory and, 15
Metroplitan Statistical Area (MSA), 188,
  200
Micro level of analysis, 2, 12, 15
Middle class
  conflict theory of education and, 281
  social stratification and, 157–160
  "Work-and-Spend is a Middle-Class
    Affliction" (Schor), 164–165
Migration
  as urban ecological process, 203
  definition, 188
  demographic studies and, 199
Migratory movement
  as social movement, 120
  definition, 110
  emergence of minority groups
    through, 176
Milgram, Stanley, obedience and, 141
Military junta, 213
Military protection. See also Government
  demographic studies and, 196
  ZPG (zero population growth) and,
    191
Mills, C. Wright, 6, 15, 219–220
Minority groups
  characteristics of, 182
  conflict theory and, 182
  contact hypothesis and, 182
  definition, 168, 182
  democracies and, 215
  economic inequality and, 237, 243
  emergence of, 176
  "Introduction: Blame It on Feminism"
    (Faludi), 184–185
  reaction to majority group by,
    180–181
  structural functional theory and, 181
  symbolic interactionist theory and,
    182
  treatment by majority group of, 180–
    181, 183
  types of, 169–170, 183
Mixed economy, 230, 233
Mobility. See Social mobility
Mobilization for action, 110, 122

Mobs, 110, 114, 117
Modal personality, 66
Modified extended family, 290–291, 304.
  See also Families
Mohammedanism. See Islam
  (Mohammedanism)
Monarchy, 210, 213
Monogamy, 290, 292, 304, 307
Monomorphic power, 219
Monopoly, 230, 233
Monotheism, 250, 253
Moon, Sun Mung, 261
Moore, Wilbert, 81
Morbidity
  definition, 188
  demographic studies and 2001 as
    generational marker event, 199
Mores, 46, 52–53
Mormons, 257
Mortality, 197–198. See also Birth/death
  rates
Mortality rate, 188
"Mother Cow" (Harris), 62–64
Mother Institution of Sociology
  (University of Chicago), 11
Movies/media. See Media
Multiculturalism
  definition, 270
  education and, 279
  U.S. sociology and, 11
Multiple nuclei of urbanization, 204
Multiple nuclei theory of urbanization,
  188, 200
Multiple-track system, 270–271
Murdock, George, 48, 291
Music and social mobility, 162

N

Naper, Sarah
  "Not So SILI: Sociology Information
    Literacy Infusion as the Focus of
    Faculty and Librarian
    Collaboration", 39–40
National Relations Act, 241
National Rifle Association (NRA), 120
"Nations of the Western Community"
  (Wattenberg and Zinsmeister),
  205–207
Nativism as reaction of minority group,
  181
Natural disasters and panic, 115
Nature versus nurture, 66, 69–70
Neo-Malthusians, 189–190, 203
Neolocal pattern of residence, 290, 295,
  304
Neutralization. See Deviance
New Age Movement, 261
No-fault divorce, 290, 301
Nonmaterial culture, 46, 51, 61
Nonobtrusive measures of scientific
  method, 24, 31

Nonparticipant observation of scientific method, 24, 30
Nonrandom samples, 34–35
Norms
  capitalism and, 233
  clarification through deviance, 134
  collective behavior and, 111–112
  definition, 46, 52
  reference groups and, 99
  roles and, 103
  values and, 52
"Not So SILI: Sociology Information Literacy Infusion as the Focus of Faculty and Librarian Collaboration", 39–40
Nuclear family, 290–291, 304. See also Families
Numbers in religion, 254

O

Obedience as social control, 141
Objective measure of social class, 156–157
Occupational socialization, 81
Ogburn, William, 295–297
Oligarchy, 210
One-person households, 299–300. See also Single-mother families
Open system of stratification, 149–150
Operational definition, 24, 28
Opinion research and scientifc method, 28
Oppression psychosis as reaction of minority group, 180
Organic solidarity, 2, 9
Organizations/institutions. See also Crowds
  as agencies of socialization, 81
  formal, 96–99
  Weber, Max and, 9–10
Organized crime, 133
Orgys, 110, 114, 117
O'Rourke, P.J., 211, 225–228
Out-group
  definition, 90, 106
  in-group and, 95–96
  Japanese collective system and, 99
  social movements and, 117
  "Social Theory and Social Structure" (Merton), 107–108
Overcompensation as reaction of minority group, 180–181
Overt aggression as reaction of minority group, 180

P

Palmer, Olia
  "Not So SILI: Sociology Information Literacy Infusion as the Focus of Faculty and Librarian Collaboration", 39–40

Panic, 110, 115, 117
Parochial schools. See Catholicism
Parsons, Talcott, 12, 13, 15
Participant observation and scientific method, 30–31
Partnership, 230
Passing reaction of minority group to majority group, 181
Pastoral system, 230, 232, 242–243
Patriarchy, 290, 295, 304, 307
Patrilineal descent, 290, 295
Patrilocal pattern of residence, 290, 295, 304
Patriotism as civil religion, 259
Peace movement, 117
Peer group pressure
  age group segregation in education and, 276
  as agency of socialization, 80–81
  "Work-and-Spend is a Middle-Class Affliction" (Schor), 165
People's Republic of China, 190, 214
Permanent war economy, 238
Peter principle, 90, 98
Physical differences and minorities, 170, 175
Physical traces/artifacts
  advantages/disadvantages of, 32–33
  definition, 24
Pickford, Kaylan, 265–268
Pietist sect, 257
Ping-pong kids, 290, 300
Planned experiment and scientific method, 24, 29–30
Pluralism, 210, 219–220, 223
Political alienation, 210, 222
Political annexation, emergence of minority groups through, 176
Political conventions as expressive crowds, 114
Political institution, 210–211
Political power and economics, 235
Political socialization, 210, 221–222
Polyandry, 290, 293, 304
Polygamy, 290, 293, 304
Polygyny, 290, 293, 304
Polytheism, 250, 253
Popular stage of social movement, 118
Population growth theory, 191–194
Population pyramid, 188, 196–197
Population. See also Demography
  data collection and, 34
  definition, 24, 188–189
  demographic studies and, 203
  demographic transition and, 188, 191–194, 203
  growth rates of, 191–194
  Malthus, Thomas and, 189–190
  "Nations of the Western Community" (Wattenberg and Zinsmeister), 205–207

rapid growth/overpopulation, 194–195
relocation, 168, 177
Post-rearing family, 290, 300. See also Families
Postindustrial economic system, 234, 243
Postindustrial society, 230
Poverty
  types of, 236, 243
Power
  absolute, 230
  "At Home in the Parliament of Whores" (O'Rourke), 225–228
  definition, 148
  definition/types, 211–212
  distribution of, 235
  elitism as, 219–220, 223
  individual social mobility and, 162
  pluralism as, 219–220, 223
  religion as sacred and, 251
  social stratification and, 152
  U.S. models of, 219–220
  U.S. trends of government and, 217–219
Power Elite, The, 219
Precipitating factors, 110, 122–123
Predestination, 262
Preindustrial society/economic systems, 230–231, 243
Prejudice
  definition, 168, 183
  differences from discrimination, 171–174
  religion and, 263
President's Commission on Law Enforcement and Administration of Justice, 146
Prestige. See Status
Primary deviance, 142
Primary deviation, 130, 132
Primary groups, 90, 92–95, 105
Primary industry, 230–231, 242
Principles of Sociology, 9
Privacy. See Ethics
Pro-bussing movement, 117, 123
Pro-choice movement, 117
Production, 230–231
Production/distribution of goods/services, 235, 242
Profane, 250–251
Professional criminal behavior, 133
Progress and birth of sociology, 6
Pronatalist, 188
Pronatalist policies, 203
Prostitution
  as criminal behavior, 133
  as deviant behavior, 133
Protection as family function, 297
Protestantism. See also Religion
  beliefs and, 255
  decline of, 260
Psychological assimilation, 179

Public opinion, 110, 116
Purposive sample and data collection,
    34–35

Q

Questionnaires, 28–29, 34–35
Quota sample, 34–35

R

Race, 168
Racial minority groups, 169–170
Racism, 168, 174, 183
Radical movement, 120
Random sample, 24, 34–35
Rapp, Adrian
    "A Typology of Collectors and
        Collecting Behavior" (Dodgen and
        Rapp), 125–128
    "Living History, A: The Old Order
        Amish" (Rapp and Dodgen),
        306–310
    "Not So SILI: Sociology Information
        Literacy Infusion as the Focus of
        Faculty and Librarian
        Collaboration", 39–40
Rational-legal authority, 210, 213, 223
Reactionary movement, 110, 119
Readings
    "A Typology of Collectors and
        Collecting Behavior" (Dodgen and
        Rapp), 125–128
    "At Home in the Parliament of
        Whores" (O'Rourke), 225–228
    "Coping With Losses" (Mead), 86–87
    "I Lost My Daughters to a Cult"
        (Pickford and Safran), 265–268
    "Introduction: Blame It on Feminism"
        (Faludi), 184–185
    "Living History, A: The Old Order
        Amish" (Rapp and Dodgen),
        306–310
    "Mother Cow" (Harris), 62–64
    "Not So SILI: Sociology Information
        Literacy Infusion as the Focus of
        Faculty and Librarian Collaboration"
        (Dodgen, Naper, Palmer and Rapp),
        39–40
    "Rich Get Richer and the Poor Get
        Prison, The" (Reiman), 144–146
    "Sociology as an Individual Pastime"
        (Berger), 18–21
    "Work-and-Spend is a Middle-Class
        Affliction" (Schor), 164–165
Real culture, 46, 56–57, 61
Rebel, 130
Rebel response, 137
Reciprocity, 230, 232
Reconstructed family, 290, 300. See also
    Families
Redistribution, 230

Reference groups, 90, 99–100, 106
Referent power, 210, 212
Reform movement, 110, 120
Regulations and U.S. trends of
    economics, 243
Reiman, Jeffrey, 140
Reisman, David, 219–220
Relative poverty, 230, 237
Religion
    beliefs/rituals and, 253–254
    birth of sociology and, 6–7
    Comte, Auguste and, 7–8
    conflict theory and, 262
    cultural assimilation and, 178
    definition, 250–251
    emergence of minority groups
        through, 176
    expressive movements and, 120
    fertility rates and, 197
    formal organization of, 256–257
    "I Lost My Daughters to a Cult"
        (Pickford and Safran) and, 265–268
    "Living History, A: The Old Order
        Amish" (Rapp and Dodgen) and,
        306–310
    manifest functions of, 251–253
    Marx, Karl and, 11
    minorities and, 170
    secular/civil, 258–259
    separation from schools, 280
    structural functional theory and, 13
    symbolic interactionist theory and,
        263–264
    three major theories view, 261–264
    trends in, 259–261
    U.S. trends of government and, 219
    Weber, Max and, 10
    ZPG (zero population growth) and,
        191
Religious beliefs, 250, 264
Religious experience (affective element),
    250, 254, 264
Religious objects, 250, 264
Religious rituals, 250, 254, 264
Repetitive magic, 252, 264
Reports/conclusions and scientific
    method, 35–36
Reproduction as family function, 296–
    297, 304
Reputational measure of social class, 157
Research. See also Scientific method
    designs, 24, 28–31, 38
    difficulties conducting, 36–37
    ethics and, 31, 37
    in the educational system, 275
    on learning processes, 280
Residence and social stratification, 152
Resocialization, 66, 79, 82
Retreatist, 130, 137
Revolutionary movement, 110, 120
Revolutionist sect, 257
Reward power, 210, 212

Rich Get Richer and the Poor Get Prison,
    The, 140, 144–146
Riots, 110, 114, 117
Rite of passage and role conflict/strain,
    104, 106
Ritualist, 130, 136–137
Rituals, 254, 257
Role, 90
Role complex (set), 90, 103
Role conflict, 90, 104–105, 106, 132
Role strain, 90, 104, 106
Role-taking, 66, 74–75, 82
Roles, 103–105
Rosenthal, Robert, 283
Rossides, Daniel, 158–159
Rumors, 110, 116
Rurban, 188, 202
Ryan, William, 150

S

Sabotage as covert discrimination, 171
Sacred
    definition, 250–251
    object characteristics, 255–256
Safran, Claire, 265–268
Saint Simon, Henri de, 7, 15
Sample, 24
Sample survey, 24, 28
Samuelson, Paul A.
    Keynesian economic theory and, 242
    on social inequality, 151
Sanctions
    definition, 46, 53–54, 61
    formal/informal social control and,
        141
    secondary groups and, 94
Sapir-Whorf hypothesis. See Linguistic
    relativity hypothesis
Scapegoating, 168, 171
Schismatic community breakdown, 130,
    138
Schwartz, Barry, 244–247
Science and Health, 253
Science. See also Scientific method
    definition, 25–26, 38
Scientific method
    birth of sociology and, 7
    conclusions/theories/reports of, 35–36
    data collection/analysis of, 33–35
    definition, 24, 38
    formulation of hypotheses of, 27–28
    literature survey of, 27
    problem identification of, 26–27
    research design/time frame of, 28–33
Scientology, 261
Secondary analysis and scientific method,
    31
Secondary assimilation. See Integration
Secondary deviation, 130, 132, 142
Secondary groups, 90, 92–95, 105
Secondary industry, 230–231, 242

Sect, 250, 256–257, 259, 264
Sector theory, 188
Sector theory of urbanization, 200, 204
Secular religion, 258–259
Secularization, 250, 260, 264
Segregation
    as urban ecological process, 204
    avoidance and, 180
    definition, 168
    education and, 279
    majority treatment of minorities via, 177
Self-concept, 66, 73, 81
Self-fulfilling prophecy
    definition, 168
    minorities and, 173
    tracking of students and, 283
Separatist movement, 110, 120
Serial monogamy, 290, 292
Sex ratio, 188, 196, 204
Sexism, 168, 174, 183
Sexual regulation as family function, 296, 304
Sexuality as societal characteristic, 47–48
Sheehy, Gail, 78
Shintoism, 261
Significant others, 66, 75
Simmel, Georg, 11, 15, 92
Single-mother families
    conflict theory and, 15
    definition of family and, 300
    social classes and, 159
    structural functional theory and, 15
Single-parented family, 290
Single-person households, 290, 299
Single-track system, 270–271, 284
Skepticism and birth of sociology, 7
Smelser, Neil J., 121–122
Smith, Adam, 233, 242
Snowball sample and data collection, 34
Social category, 91
Social change
    conflict theory and, 15
    cultural change and, 58
    definition, 46
    structural functional theory and, 12–13
Social class
    definition, 162
    measurement of, 156–157
    number in U. S., 158–159
    of stratification, 149–150
    system of, 148
Social control, 130, 141, 143
Social Darwinism. See Social evolutionism
Social distance, 168, 173
Social evolutionism, 9
Social exchange, 90, 102, 106
Social facts, 8
Social inequality, 148, 150–154
Social mobility

and individual behavior, 162
    definition, 148, 162
    discussion, 159–160
    factors affecting rates of, 160–161
    through open system of stratification, 149
Social movements
    characteristics of, 117–118
    definition, 110
    future and, 123
    stages of, 118–119
    types of, 123
Social problem, 130, 142, 143
Social process
    definition, 90, 106
    definition/discussion, 100–102
    summary diagram of, 106
Social sciences, 2
Social status as family function, 297
Social stratification
    basis of social inequality and, 151
    conflict theory and, 155–156
    definition, 149, 162
    importance of study of, 154
    society and, 156
    structural functional theory and, 155–156
    "Work-and-Spend is a Middle-Class Affliction" (Schor), 164–165
Social structure, 2–3
"Social Theory and Social Structure" (Merton), 107–108
Social unrest, 118
Socialism
    definition, 230
    industrial economic systems and, 233–234
    Marx, Karl and, 11
Socialization
    adult/child differences in, 77–79
    as family function, 297
    definition, 66, 82
    development of social skills through education, 274
    deviance from inadequate, 139
    functions of, 67–68
    political. See Government
    prejudice/discrimination acquisition through, 174
    processes of, 68–69
    resocialization and, 79
    social control and, 141
    summary diagram of, 85
    symbolic interactionist theory and, 243
    "The Self and the Organism" (Mead), 86–87
Society
    anomie theory of deviance and, 136–137
    characteristics of, 47–48

definition, 47, 61
    deviance and, 135
    government functions and, 216–217
    social control/cohesiveness and religion, 253
    social movements and, 117–118
    structural functional theory and, 13–14
Sociobiology, 66, 69–70
Sociological imagination, 2
Sociological perspective, 2, 4–6
Sociologists
    research difficulties and, 37
    "Sociology as an Individual Pastime" (Berger), 18–21
Sociology
    birth of, 6–7
    definition/discussion, 2–4
    founding fathers of, 7–11
    in United States, 11–12
    "Not So SILI: Sociology Information Literacy Infusion as the Focus of Faculty and Librarian Collaboration", 39–40
    "Sociology as an Individual Pastime" (Berger), 18–21
    "Sociology as an Individual Pastime" (Berger), 18–21
Soft culture, 230, 234
Spencer, Herbert, 9, 15
Spitz, Rene, 71–72
State, 210
State religion. See Ecclesia
Status
    as family function, 297
    definition, 90, 106, 148
    groups and, 102
    inconsistency of, 148, 154
    roles and, 103
    social stratification and, 151–152
Step family, 293, 300
Stereotypes
    definition, 168
    minorities and, 173
    social categories and, 175
Stinnett, Nick, 302–303
Strand, Erik, 251
Strata, 148
Stratification. See Social stratification
Structural assimilation, 178
Structural conductiveness, 110, 122
Structural functional theory
    and education, 281, 285
    and minority groups, 181
    and religion, 264
    classical economic theory as, 243
    definition, 2
    deviance and, 134–137
    discussion, 12–15
    families and, 303–304
    social stratification and, 155–156
Structural strain, 110, 122

Styles. *See* Fads; Fashions
Subcultural theory of urban way of life,
 188, 201, 204
Subcultures
  definition, 46, 57–58
  delinquent, 138
  in high school/college, 272–273
Subjective measure of social class, 157
Subjugation
  definition, 168
  majority treatment of minorities via,
  177
Substance abuse
  as criminal behavior, 133
  social problems and, 142
Suburbanization
  definition, 188
  definition/discussion, 201–202
  urban ecological processes and, 204
Suicide
  Jonestown, Guyana, South America
   and, 113
  types of, 2, 8
Sumner, William, 52, 95
Support via religion, 252
Sutherland, Edwin, 140
Symbolic interactionist theory
  and education, 285
  and minority groups, 182
  and religion, 263–264
  definition, 2, 143
  deviance and, 139
  discussion, 15–16
  families and, 303–304
  self-concept and, 74
Systematic sample, 35

T

Taboos
  as type of magic, 252, 264
  incest, 293, 296
Taste preferences and social stratification,
 153
Teacher expectancy, 270, 283
Tearoom Trade, 31
Television. *See* Media
Terrorism attack of Sept. 11, 73
Tertiary industry, 230–231, 242–243
"The Self and the Organism" (Mead),
 86–87
Theism, 250, 253
Theories
  conflict theory, 14–15
  definition, 24
  structural functional theory, 12–14, 15

summary diagram of, 15
symbolic interactionist theory, 15–16
Thomas, W. I., 15
Three major theories view, 261–264
  and religion
Time frames for research, 33
Tokenism as covert discrimination, 171
Tonnies, Ferdinand, 96
Total institutions, 66, 79
Totalitarian government, 213
Totalitarian state, 210
Tracking (of students), 270, 283–284
Traditional authority, 210, 212
Traditional family, 290, 299. *See also*
   Families
Triad, 90, 92, 105
Tribal family, 290–291, 304. *See also*
   Families
Tumin, Melvin, 156

U

Ullman, Edward, 200
Underground economy, 241–242
University of Chicago as Mother
   Institution of Sociology, 11–12
Urban ecological processes, 204
Urban growth theories, 201
Urban legends, 46, 56
Urbanization
  definition, 188
  urban growth theories, 200
  urban way of life theories, 201
  world's largest areas of, 200
  ZPG (zero population growth) and,
  191
Use-value, 230, 233

V

Value-added theory, 110, 121
Values
  collective behavior effect on, 112
  definition, 46, 54–55
  deviance and, 135
  peers and, 81
  structural functional theory and, 12
  taught in the education system, 277
Variables
  definition, 24
  formulation of hypotheses and, 27
  research difficulties and, 37
Verstehen, 2, 10
Vertical mobility, 148, 159
Victimless crime, 133
Voting. *See* Government

W

Wallerstein, Judith, 301
Ward, Lester, 11–12
Warner, Lloyd, 158, 162
Wattenberg, Ben, 205–207
Wealth
  definition, 148
  permanent war economy and, 238
  power and, 152
  social class measurement and, 156
  social stratification and, 150–151
Weber, Max
  as a founder of sociology, 9–10
  components of social stratification
   according to, 150–151
  on authority, 212–213
  on formal organizations, 98
  Protestantism and, 262
Welfare, 235
Western Electric Company, Hawthorne,
   Illinois, 36
Westie, Franklin, 173
"What To Do About Choice" (Schwartz),
   244–247
"What Your 1st Grader Needs To Know"
   (Hirsch), 286–287
White collar crime, 133
*Who Will Tell the People: The Betrayal of
   American Democracy*, 217
Wilson, Bryan, 257
Wilson, Edward O., 69
Wirth, Louis, 201
Withdrawl movement, 120
Women's liberation movement, 116
"Work-and-Spend is a Middle-Class
   Affliction" (Schor), 164–165
Working class, 157–160

Y

Young Republicans, 117

Z

Zinsmeister, Karl, 205–207
Zionism, 117
ZPG (zero population growth)
  as antinatalist policy, 190–191
  attainment of, 203
  definition, 188